Victimizing Vulnerable Groups

Recent Titles in

PRAEGER SERIES IN CRIMINOLOGY AND CRIME CONTROL POLICY

The Sociology of Shoplifting: Boosters and Snitches Today
Lloyd W. Klemke

American Skinheads: The Criminology and Control of Hate Crime
Mark S. Hamm

State Crime, the Media, and the Invasion of Panama
Christina Jacqueline Johns and P. Ward Johnson

Varieties of Criminology
Gregg Barak, editor

A History of Federal Crime Control Initiatives, 1960–1993
Nancy E. Marion

Rethinking White-Collar Crime
Tony G. Poveda

Criminal Justice in England and the United States
J. David Hirschel and William Wakefield

The Psychopathology of Serial Murder: A Theory of Violence
Stephen J. Giannangelo

Chaos, Criminology, and Social Justice: The New Orderly (Dis)Order
Dragan Milovanovic, editor

War Stories: An Oral History of Life Behind Bars
Susann Walens

Asphalt Justice: A Critique of the Criminal Justice System in America
John Raymond Cook

Critical Criminology at the Edge
Dragan Milovanovic

VICTIMIZING VULNERABLE GROUPS

images of uniquely high-risk crime targets

edited by

CHARISSE TIA MARIA COSTON

foreword by FREDA ADLER

PRAEGER SERIES IN CRIMINOLOGY AND CRIME CONTROL POLICY

Westport, Connecticut
London

Library of Congress Cataloging-in-Publication Data

Victimizing vulnerable groups : images of uniquely high-risk crime targets / edited by Charisse Tia Maria Coston ; foreword by Freda Adler.

p. cm. — (Praeger series in criminology and crime control policy, ISSN 1060-3212)

Includes bibliographical references and index.

ISBN 0-275-96614-3 (alk. paper)

1. Victims of crimes—Government policy. 2. People with social disabilities—Crimes against. 3. Minorities—Crimes against. 4. Aged—Crimes against. 5. Women—Crimes against. 6. Abused children. 7. Animal welfare. I. Title: High-risk crime targets. II. Coston, Charisse Tia Maria, 1958– III. Series.

HV6250.25.V523 2004

362.88—dc22 2003068983

British Library Cataloguing in Publication Data is available.

Library of Congress Catalog Card Number: 2003068983
ISBN: 0-275-96614-3
ISSN: 1060-3212

First published in 2004

Praeger Publishers, 88 Post Road West, Westport, CT 06881
An imprint of Greenwood Publishing Group, Inc.
www.praeger.com

Printed in the United States of America

The paper used in this book complies with the Permanent Paper Standard issued by the National Information Standards Organization (Z39.48-1984).

10 9 8 7 6 5 4 3 2 1

■ ■ ■

copyright acknowledgments

The following publishers are gratefully acknowledged for granting permission to reprint material in the chapters indicated:

Chapter 1: Human Sciences Press.

Chapter 11: *Journal of Crime and Justice*, volume 21, number 1, pages 53–70. Copyright © Anderson Publishing Company.

Chapter 15: Reprinted by permission of Waveland Press, Inc. from Charles B. Fields and Richter H. Moore, Jr., *Comparative Criminal Justice: Traditional and Nontraditional Systems of Law and Control* (Prospect Heights, IL: Waveland Press, Inc., 1996). All rights reserved.

Chapter 20: "Victimization of Women: A Theoretical Perspective on Dowry Deaths," from *I R Victimology*, volume 3, number 4, pages 297–308. Reprinted by permission of A. B. Academic Publishers.

"That all men are equal is a proposition which, at ordinary times, no sane individual had ever given his assent."

—**ALDOUS HUXLEY** (1894–1963)

contents

foreword

Crime victims are not an equal opportunity lot. King Hammurabi of Mesopotamia realized that when he provided special protection of merchants being robbed while traveling through his realm (circa 1750 B.C.) The focus of victim identification and protection changed vastly over the next almost four millennia. Foreign merchants were no longer all that vulnerable. Other victims took their place, and their variety increased over time: children, women, the elderly, ethnic minorities, those of nonmainstream sexual orientation, and the poorest, the homeless, those in the sex trade, and the unemployed or unemployable, and others yet to emerge.

It took researchers almost four thousand years to identify all the population groups that, over time, have become likely crime victims. And it took criminologists decades to determine why and how such population groups are being victimized, how such victimizations can be decreased or avoided altogether, and how best to provide remedial services to those victims. Hans von Hentig, in his seminal work, *The Criminal and His Victim* (1948), has provided us with the theoretical basis for victimization, indeed, for *victimology*. Unhappily, in the almost six decades since then, no scholar has put the research-derived information about special victims into book form. Dr. Coston has seen the need. She devoted herself to the task, as evidenced by her own several chapters in this book. Moreover, she scoured the research literature on special victims, selected the major contributions, and brought them all together in this unique volume. Well done, Charisse! The profession owes you a great debt of gratitude.

Freda Adler
Professor II, Rutgers University
Past President, American Society of Criminology

acknowledgments

God has blessed me deeply, and I am grateful for the direction, inner peace, and spirituality He has afforded me. Special thanks, thus far in life, go to my mother, Pearl Willabeatrice McNear, and my father, Ernest Coston, without whom this book and my success thus far in life, would not have been possible. May they both rest in peace.

I wish to extend my gratitude to the following individuals without whose kind support this book would not have been possible: my mentors—chair of the Department of Criminal Justice at the University of North Carolina at Charlotte Dr. Bruce Arrigo, who has given me much needed motivation, inspiration, and direction, and Drs. Freda Adler and Coramae Ritchey-Mann have been my role models and mentors for over 20 years—and of course my editor Heather Staines and all the terrific people at Praeger Publishers.

Special thanks also go to the following individuals who assisted with the copyediting of this book: Catherine Church, Jamila McClendon, Amit Patel, Velda Pruner, Brooke Sims, Sahara Taybron, and Ashely Wilson.

introduction

Victimization varies across the population. Some people are more victim-prone than others. This collection of essays is about especially vulnerable, high-risk targets for criminal victimization. Discussions about notions of unique vulnerability, victimization experiences, and matters relating to social policy form the foci of this book. This work provides initial bases for examining and comparing the experiences of especially high-risk groups. It is expected that these discussions will result in the pondering of more queries—at least we will be able to make suggestions and outline strategies for addressing the unique needs of the varied populations addressed in this book.

Multidisadvantaged groups, the subject of part 1, are often stigmatized and represent some of the fringes in our society. In chapter 1, Coston and Finckenauer describe the forces that lead to a lifestyle, and the lifestyle itself, of living on the street as a homeless woman. One of the lifestyle characteristics encountered by this group is that they are constantly confronted by the threat of tormentors and other villains. They live on the streets with no visible means of support and no permanent residences. Their personal troubles have become public spectacles. Coston, in chapter 2, examines homeless females' victimization experiences and the worries that these women confront every day. Criminal victimization, while not a primary worry, is something that has become a concern for homeless women. Those without money for bare necessities are often marginalized and often do not get the requisite medication needed to remedy physical ills. Bing, in chapter 5, discusses the unique plight of being black, poor, and reliant on public health care in a system that has been traditionally viewed as insensitive to mainstream segments of minorities in society, particularly the poor. The oldest of the old, according to Hanrahan and Gibbs in chapter 7, are a stigmatized group. Being urban, black, elderly, and female poses peculiar issues for reformers in a society that as been defined as being hostile towards its ever-growing population of the elderly. In chapter 6, Blowers discusses how the elderly are abused in domestic situations: they are often socially excluded, stolen from, physically battered, and otherwise taken advantage of by those who are relatives. African-American grandmothers who are caring for their children's offspring while they are incarcerated have a host of personal and situation concerns that these caretakers face daily: Ruiz, Zhu, and Crowther examine this group in chapter 3. The children of these caretakers are vastly in need of empowerment. Not only are they black, but often are poor, drug-addicted, arrested more often than their wealthier or nonminority counterparts, and struggle every day to lead lives of value while employing strategies aimed at avoiding social and economic exclusion. In chapter 4, Pettiway theorizes the "otherness" related to AIDS in the black community; he highlights strategies aimed against further stigmatization by using empathy and understanding. Mexican immigrants in the United States are often exploited as laborers due to their economic deprivation and differentness while struggling to speak and understand a language that is not the primary one for them. These experiences are explored by Jenks and Jenks in chapter 8.

Part 2 offers a collection of articles about those who may have in some way distinctly contributed to their predicament and thus their own downfall—the undeserving vulnerable. In chapter 9, Rector and Wonders discuss the plight of being poor, black, female, pregnant, and addicted to crack cocaine. These women are often stigmatized and criminalized further by a criminal-justice system that does not penalize anyone else for the plight of drug addiction. Those who are in power have socially constructed and enforce such laws and as a consequence exclusively punish these women. In chapter 10, Brennan discusses the plight of juveniles who have been convicted of crimes and are serving time with adult criminals. Their victimization experiences and unique vulnerabilities, along with suggested policy, are outlined. Coston and Ross describe in chapter 11 the worries of female streetwalkers and note that worrying about criminal victimization does not dominate over their struggles for other survival modes. In chapter 12, Fishman identifies a subgroup of inmates with AIDS and examines the strategies that it uses to gain respect within jail and prison settings.

Part 3 represents chapters covering populations that are complex and outlines methods for remedying these dilemmas: the uniquely, uniquely vulnerable. Some of these strategies focus on distinct cultural characteristics such as disabilities and may involve a restructuring of these societies along class lines. Foreign students studying in the United States, according to Coston (in chapter 13), have a unique set of circumstances when compared to students who are U.S. citizens. She describes these peculiarities and examines criminal-victimization experiences, coping strategies, and foreign students' fear of crime. In chapter 14, Bates and

Ardovini-Brooker and Coston and Helal (in chapter 15) discuss the cultures in underdeveloped countries and how (in some cases) these countries are modernizing in the wake of rapid development, while simultaneously maintaining relatively stable and/or low crime rates. In chapter 16, Protz describes what it is like for a person to be victimized and targeted for expulsion by their own culture—in this case, during the red scare of the 1950s in the United Sates. Berry (chapter 17) discusses a truly oppressed population: nonhuman animals. In so doing, she further links their powerless, otherness, and strategies of exclusion relating to their predicament along with the similarities of the historic troubles of women and minorities. In chapter 18, Petersen delves into the marginalized population of Native Americans and highlights their economic and social obstacles while also highlighting their culture, which has been historically treated as a "disability." Robyn, in chapter 19, discusses the plight of a particular group of Native Americans—the Potawatomi, emphasizing how it has been discredited, stereotyped, and marginalized by insensitive nonminorities throughout its history. Natarajan (chapter 20) presents research describing the occurrence of domestic violence, including dowry deaths suffered by some women in eastern India. In chapter 21, Berry has painstakingly gathered data resulting in ground-breaking revelations on the topic of the sexual battery (both verbal and physical) of airline personnel by government-placed airport screeners in the aftermath of the terrorist attack that toppled the World Trade Center towers in New York City.

Part 4 examines those groups that are differentially vulnerable. In chapter 23, Patel describes the vulnerabilities and victimization experiences associated with children who lack social representation—those who are exploited in carnivals, freak shows, and circuses. Pepinsky, in chapter 24, notes the vulnerabilities of victims of childhood violence, and in chapter 25 Dudley provides a glimpse into the world of antiabortion stalkers—which is becoming an epidemic in the United States. Abortion providers and their clientele are targets of these fanatical individuals and groups who justify their actions as stemming from the demands of higher powers.

All of the above contributors describe the unique vulnerabilities of their high-risk groups, discuss the nature of their victimization experiences, and suggest various remedies that are needed in terms of social, legal, and practical policy initiatives. Additionally, they offer both short- and long-term strategies for rectifying the inequalities that are often associated with the marginalized and stigmatized in a hostile world whose aim should be to empower and strengthen the masses.

PART ONE

Multipli-Disadvantaged Groups

CHAPTER ONE

Fear of Crime among Vulnerable Populations

homeless women

Charisse T. M. Coston
James O. Finckenauer

Homeless women are not like most of us. They are a part of those "other" people about which American society has become increasingly aware in recent years—the homeless (Rossi 1989; Wright 1989). These women wander around the streets. They are often dirty and unkempt. They have no particular means of support. They have no permanent residences. They often carry their belongings (perhaps all they own in life) in shopping carts and shopping bags—hence the name "bag ladies." They generally live in public spaces—often open and exposed public places.

Estimates by the Manhattan Bowery Corporation and other similar bodies are that there are approximately 60,000 homeless people on the streets of New York City, and women make up about 15,000 to 20,000 of this population. These estimates are the best information we have since the homeless usually maintain no means of self-enumeration, such as telephone listings. They are not listed in census reports (although the 1990 census made the first nationwide attempt to enumerate the homeless) or on the rosters of unemployment offices.

The type of women we interviewed offer a number of reasons to explain why they are homeless. The forces that may lead to a lifestyle of living on the streets seem to be extremely varied. The most prevalent societal explanation is the massive deinstitutionalization of mental patients that has occurred over the last 20 years, and this certainly *does* seem to be one important explanation. But the women themselves also mention such things as the reduced availability of decent, low-cost housing; the lack of safe, available shelters; the withdrawal of family support; unemployment; and divorce (Coston 1989). In fact, no one event or crisis fully explains why a woman chooses to live on the streets. It appears rather that the process of resorting to a life of living on the streets is a gradual one rather than an abrupt occurrence (Baxter & Hopper 1981; Coston 1989; Martin 1982). It further appears that many of the women have made a considered decision (although it would not be their preference, all other things being equal) to live on the streets.

Mentally troubled women are an exception to this rational-choice rule. They frequently end up on the streets as the result of not having adequate care to bridge the gap between being released from a mental hospital (being *deinstitutionalized*) and being reintegrated into society. Because of their irrationality, such women were not included in the sample interviewed here.

Given the circumstances of conditions on the streets, how do homeless women adapt to it? The precarious street life obviously results in a number of daily survival concerns. Strategies for locating food and shelter, warding off threats from potential tormentors, medical care, cleanliness, and loneliness are just a few of the persistent daily survival problems faced by homeless women. An extensive communications network, revolving around these concerns, appears to exist among them (Coston 1989). Any one of them who learns from another or from passersby of places to go for eating, sleeping, or for meeting other needs immediately passes on this information to others, who hence do the same. Yet this sharing of information is not usually followed by any effort on the sharer's part to join others in exploiting the newly discovered resources. This suggests that while homeless women may involve themselves in a kind of group information sharing, they tend to act alone as far as their own individual survival is concerned. This is evidence of the sort of self-imposed isolation that is attendant to being a homeless woman. One of the daily concerns faced by these women is one shared by many other urban dwellers, but in their case it is escalated by their greater exposure to risk. That concern is their fear of crime.

FEAR OF CRIME

A principal survival concern that is not directly addressed in the limited research literature on homeless women is their fear of crime, although they have been shown to be often victimized by crime. The most frequent type of victimization reported by Coston (1989) was what she calls "combination victimization." Eighty percent of the women in her study reported suffering two or more types of crimes in one victimization incident. These types of combination victimizations generally involved rape, robbery, assault, and theft.

Hundreds of studies have been conducted on the fear of crime, with most focusing on the factors associated with this fear—the correlates. Those variables shown to contribute to the general public's fear of victimization of course may also contribute to homeless women's fear of crime. Thus they must be considered as a starting point for possible inclusion in any explanatory model. The data on homeless women in this chapter will be compared with that of prior studies involving groups and subgroups from the general population. The principal factors previously identified are listed below.

Age

The level of the fear of crime has been shown to be greater among the aged (Biderman 1967; Ennis 1967; Reiss 1967; Conklin 1975; Clemente & Kleiman 1976; Yin 1980; Innes 1982; Baker et al. 1983). Past studies indicate that older persons perceive themselves as being highly vulnerable to physical and property victimization; they suffer feelings of powerlessness and restrict their lives so as not to become victimized (Sundeen & Mathieu 1976; Riger, LeBailley, & Gordon 1983). Since homeless women vary considerably in age, we can look at what effect age has upon their level of fear. We also look at their lifestyle restrictions that may be used as protective measures.

Socioeconomic Status

Prior research has found that education and income are negatively correlated with the fear of crime (Clemente & Kleiman 1976; Baker et al. 1983). This is so in part because persons who have attained higher levels of education usually have higher incomes and are financially more able to move out of high crime areas and/or to install or employ security measures. With respect to income, some homeless women *do* receive money via general delivery at the post office from friends and family members. This money comes from various sources—personal donations, trust funds, social or supplemental social security, welfare checks, and food stamps (Baxter & Hopper 1981; Coston 1989). Contrary to results from studies of the general population, however, it is possible that the homeless women who report having an income source will be more fearful of crime because they have to carry their money around. In this case, greater financial resources increase vulnerability rather than decrease it.

Health

Studies show that people with perceptions of good health are less fearful of crime (Sundeen & Mathieu 1976). Will this also be true among a population whose general level of health is poorer than the norm? Will homeless women who perceive themselves to be in poorer health relative to their peers feel even more vulnerable to victimization? Will they also be more fearful? Two factors that are more specifically, but not exclusively, concerned with the homeless are:

Exposure to Risk. Studies of homeless women indicate that the length of time spent living on the streets can vary from one day to over 20 years (Baxter & Hopper 1981). It would seem that the longer a woman lives on the street—the longer the exposure to risk—the greater would be the likelihood of victimization. Do homeless women who have lived on the streets for a longer time in fact have more fear of criminal victimization?

Social Support. Over half of the homeless females interviewed by Coston (1989) were not from New York. Most of these women came to New York City from the South, searching for the opportunity that they had heard existed there. It would appear that women who come into the city from elsewhere are even less likely to have any kind of family support. This led us to question whether those homeless women not originally from New York City, and without support from family or friends, would feel more vulnerable to victimization and more fearful of crime.

VICTIMIZATION AND VULNERABILITY

A number of past studies reveal that prior victimization is a good predictor of the fear of crime (Reynolds, Jones, & Lawton 1976; Lawton & Yaffee 1980), while other results indicate that self-perceived vulnerability to victimization, and certain personal characteristics, may mediate both the effects of past victimization and the fear of crime (Hindelang, Gottfredson, & Garofalo 1978; Bishop & Klecka 1978; Linquist & Duke 1982; Miethe & Lee 1984).

Miethe and Lee divided the fear of crime into two types: fear of violent personal crime and fear of property loss. They found that the two types of fear were strongly related to each other, but that they had different predictors. The type of past victimization has also been divided into two types—direct and indirect. *Direct victimization* experience refers to personal victimization; *indirect victimization* refers to victimization of other people, whether or not they are known to the respondent. The latter is also known as *vicarious victimization.* Direct victims have been found to be more fearful of crime than people who have only heard about the victimization experience of someone else (Miethe & Lee 1984). These findings led us to ask what would be the relation between past victimization experiences (direct and indirect) and the fear of crime among homeless women.

One of the most curious and intriguing of the issues that comes out of the fear of crime literature is that of the interaction of victimization, vulnerability, and fear. The existing research suggests that self-perceived vulnerability is a strong element in explaining the fear of crime in the general population (Yin 1980; Miethe & Lee 1984). The latter, for example, found that an individual's estimation of the probability of being victimized was a stronger predictor of fear of crime than either direct or indirect victimization. Warr and Stafford (1983) and Warr (1985) argued that fear is a function of both perceived risk and perceived seriousness of harm. Fear, they said, increases as the likelihood of victimization is seen to increase. In particular, the heightened fear of women and the elderly is felt to result from their perceptions of their special social and physical vulnerabilities.

But perceptions of vulnerability seem to have a complex relationship to feelings of fear. Stanko (1987), who has also considered this issue, says that despite the reported low level of risk of victimization (as determined by actual victimizations), women constitute the group most fearful of crime. She believes that this fear is linked to their feelings of powerlessness. "Women's assessments of risk include their perception of risk linked with their perceptions of physical competence and the degree of . . . [their attachment to their communities]" (Stanko 1987, 128). Thus it seems that vulnerability is not only a question of the probability of something terrible happening to you, but is also a function of your ability to deal with that terrible happening. Stanko compares the contrasting perceptions of men and women in this regard:

> [W]hile men of all ages appear to be at greater risk of criminal victimization than women, on the whole they report feeling safer than women. "Young males are at risk," states Maxfield, "but their lower fear may be the product of either reckless disregard for their own well-being . . ., or a self-assured confidence that neighborhood streets hold no dangers for them." (Stanko 1987, 125)

On the one hand, women who are at relatively lower risk of victimization are more fearful of victimization; on the other, men who are at greater risk are less fearful. Does this mean that each group is irrational, but in a different way? Does it mean that each is engaging in a form of cognitive dissonance? Possibly. Or does it also mean that vulnerability is only partially the result of perceptions of the actual risks of victimization, and that it relates to fear through a complicated interaction with what are variously called "coping, managing, or normalizing strategies"? We will consider all of these possibilities in the context of a group of women who we assume are at much higher relative risk of victimization.

As previously indicated, the likelihood of a homeless female being victimized is high. Will homeless women who have been victimized report higher estimates of vulnerability to victimization than those who have not been victimized? Does this indicate greater fear? What about the effects of vicarious victimization? Personal characteristics and past victimization experiences have been found to influence the sense of vulnerability to victimization. There is evidence to support the causal link that increased feelings of vulnerability lead to heightened fear, which results in the use of precautionary behaviors (Riger, LeBailley, & Gordon 1983; Miethe & Lee 1984; Warr 1985). These actions, in turn, can lessen the level of fear of crime. This model has been used to explain the high fear but low victimization finding among the elderly and females (Riger, LeBailley, & Gordon

1983). Following this logic, we can ask whether those homeless women who use precautionary behaviors (avoiding dangerous situations and carrying weapons) are less fearful than their counterparts who do not employ such security measures? We cannot determine the causal ordering of these events because of the cross-sectional nature of our data. We can, however, look at their relationships. Are those homeless women who use neither or only one of two possible types of precautionary measures—namely, carrying weapons and avoiding dangerous situations—more fearful of crime than those who employ both? Is the latter a form of managing their fear?

A number of variables thus appear to influence the fear of crime. The intent of this chapter is to examine some of these influences with respect to homeless women. Specifically, we look at age, race, whether or not homeless women were originally from New York City, length of time spent living on the streets, education, income, self-perceived health condition, direct and indirect (vicarious victimization) past victimization experiences, self-perceived vulnerability to victimization, and two types of precautionary behaviors (avoiding dangerous places and carrying weapons). Both fear of physical harm and fear of property loss are considered as elements of the fear of crime. Fear of crime here is conceptualized as the degree of worry about the possibility of being victimized, rather than as an immediate response to an actual criminal event.

METHODS

Because the actual number of homeless women is unknown, equal probability sampling is impossible. We used instead an availability sample in which we sought to ensure a degree of heterogeneity. This was done by choosing women at three different homeless shelters ($N = 150$) and, in addition, by interviewing women in bus and train stations and on the streets as well ($N = 50$). The three shelters are in the main homeless territory between 30th and 52nd Streets on the east and west sides of Manhattan. We do not claim that our sample is representative of all homeless women in New York City. In particular, those women who displayed obvious signs of mental illness or who could not be understood were excluded from the sample. Further, those who might avoid these public locations are also not represented.

The data for this chapter are both observational and self-reported. The first author conducted separate interviews with each of the 200 women and also noted any information that could be discerned simply by observation. The interviews were conducted between June and December of 1987. In addition to the demographic characteristics of age, race, income, education, self-perceived health condition, length of time spent living on the streets, and city of origin, we elicited information about the numbers and nature of past direct and indirect victimization experiences.

Self-perceived vulnerability was operationally defined by responses to a scale measuring the likelihood of occurrences. Respondents were asked to indicate, on a seven-point scale, the "likelihood" of any of five crimes happening to them. They were also asked about their avoidance of dangerous situations and what they did to manage risks in the face of possible danger.

Fear admittedly has different dimensions. Here we define fear as the "degree of worry." The fear of crime variable was divided into items representing worry about property loss and worry about personal victimization. Responses were again captured using a seven-point ordinal scale that asked respondents about their degree of "worry" concerning any of five crimes. The crimes in both scales (i.e., vulnerability and fear) were murder, rape, robbery, assault, and theft.

RESULTS

The average reported age among these homeless women was 50. Table 1.1 shows the demographic characteristics of the sample. As can be seen in this table, about half of the sample was white and about half was black. Five percent of the sample was composed of Hispanics and Asians. Two-thirds of the sample reported that they were originally from New York City. Of the one-third who were not, most were from Southeastern states. Only 4 percent of the sample reported origins outside of the United States: Poland, France, Germany, and Haiti.

The subjects reported having been on the streets about one to two years, with a range from two months to ten years. Sixty-eight percent of the homeless women interviewed reported no income source. Of those who had some income, most relied upon supplemental social security income. Other income sources included welfare, food stamps, and money given to them. The average reported educational level was the twelfth grade. Most homeless women had graduated from high school (61 percent), and about half of those had at least some college.

Table 1.2 shows self-perceptions of physical health. It appeared that many of the homeless women, when asked, had inflated what seemed to the observer to be poor health conditions into fair-to-good health conditions. They have possibly redefined the meaning of poor health so that it is congruent with life on the streets. If so, this could have bearing on the issue of coping strategies.

Table 1.3 reports the nature and extent of past victimization experiences of homeless women, both before and while living on the streets. Over half of the homeless women reported being victimized while living on the streets. The number of past victimizations reported ranged from one to four. The type of victimization that occurred most often was a combination victimization: multiple victimizations occurring in combination in the same

Table 1.1
Demographic Characteristics of the Sample (*N* = 200)

Characteristic	*Percent*	*N*
RACE		
black	46	92
white	49	98
other	5	10
PLACE OF ORIGIN		
New York City	67	134
Northeast	6.5	13
Southeast	11	22
Midwest	6.5	13
Northwest	2	4
Southwest	3.5	7
outside U.S.	3.5	7
INCOME SOURCE		
no income source	68	136
prime source:		
Social Security	17	34
welfare and food stamps	10	20
monies received from a friend, relative, or passerby	5	10
EDUCATION		
less than high school degree	39	78
high school graduate	61	122
those who have had:		
some educational/vocational training	46.5	93
some college	30	59
college degree (or more)	11.5	23

Characteristic	*M*	*MD*	*S*	*Range*
AGE	51	50	13	57
LENGTH ON STREETS (months)	22	12	28.2	294

incident. The most common form of combination victimization was robbery and assault, although rape, assault, and theft were also reported. Likewise, over half of those interviewed reported being victimized before living on the streets. Reports of having something stolen from them predominated. Rape, robbery, assault, and burglary were also reported.

While most homeless women had heard of other homeless people being victimized, vicarious victimization was not a significant variable in

Table 1.2

Self-Reported Perceptions of Health

Characteristic	*Percent*	*N*
OVERALL HEALTH		
excellent	9.5	19
good	39.5	79
average	31	62
fair	15	30
poor	5	10
FREQUENCY OF PHYSICAL ILLNESS		
never	12	24
rarely	36.5	73
sometimes	41	82
frequently	10.5	21
TYPE OF MEDICATION CURRENTLY TAKING[1]		
no medication	3	6
for blood pressure	67	134
tranquilizers	7.5	15
epilepsy	11	22
insulin	2.5	5
methadone	1.5	3
virus medication	2	4
for heart condition	3	6
asthma	2.5	5
VISUAL INDICATORS OF HEALTH CONDITION[2]		
swollen, ulcerated feet and/or legs	65.5	131
other (e.g., broken limbs, psoriasis)	3.5	7
no visual indicators	34.5	62

Notes: [1]Of those who reported taking medication, only one type was mentioned.
[2]Based on observations by the author.

explaining their fear of crime. The existing communications network that exists among these vagrants is relied upon as a daily means of survival. It seems that reports of victimization on the streets are followed by forewarnings about what areas of the city are safe or unsafe, and these thus reduce the fear of victimization. Homeless women, although eager to give and rely upon the information necessary for street survival, surprisingly do not join one another in exploiting these resources.

Our respondents, on average, believe that they are likely to be victimized while living on the streets ($X = 5$). When these homeless women were asked how much they worry about victimization, however, the average response was that they were unworried ($X = 3$). In other words, while

Table 1.3
Victimization Experiences of Homeless Women

Characteristic	WHILE LIVING ON STREET N	WHILE LIVING ON STREET Percent	BEFORE LIVING ON STREET N	BEFORE LIVING ON STREET Percent
EXTENT OF PREVIOUS VICTIMIZATION[1]				
never	47	94	116	58
once	53	106	84	42
twice	25	26	25	30
three times	18	19	16	19
four times	11	12	9	11
TYPE OF PREVIOUS VICTIMIZATION				
rape	6	12	7	3.5
robbery	14	28	39	19
assault	11	22	46	23
theft	47	93	43	22
burglary	—	—	6	3
combination victimization[2]	57	112[3]	21[4]	10
VICARIOUS VICTIMIZATION (only hearing about victimization experiences of other homeless people)	84	167	—	—

Notes: [1]No homeless woman mentioned more than four victimization experiences while on or before living on the streets. [2]Combination victimization is when two or more types of crimes occur in one incident. [3]Includes 24 cases of rape and assault, 64 cases of robbery and assault, 21 cases of rape, robbery, and assault, one case of burglary, rape, and assault, and two cases of burglary, robbery, and assault. [4]Includes seven cases of rape and assault, nine cases of robbery and assault, three cases of burglary, robbery, and assault, and two cases of burglary, rape, and assault.

homeless women believe that victimization is likely, their fear of such victimization is relatively low. This is the high vulnerability/low fear paradox to which we referred earlier. We will come back to it shortly.

Most homeless women reported avoiding certain places where there is a high risk of victimization (see table 1.4). Areas avoided due to the threat of possible victimization included places where drugs are bought, sold, or used, unfamiliar places, abandoned buildings, areas where prostitutes hang out, overcrowded places, deserted areas, and parks. Likewise, most homeless women reported carrying some kind of weapon. The type of weapon carried most often was some form of chemical such as lye, ammonia, rubbing alcohol, or hair-spray; other types included knives, scissors, cloth bags with rocks in them, lead pipes, and even guns. In some instances, subjects said that their faith in God or training in karate was their weapon.

An important question raised in our literature review sought to exam-

Table 1.4
Homeless Women's Use of Precautionary Behaviors

Characteristic	*Percent*	*N*
AVOIDED PLACES DUE TO VICTIMIZATION RISK	82	162
PLACES AVOIDED[1]		
where drugs are bought, sold, or used	38	76
sleeping out-of-doors	9	18
abandoned buildings	9	18
where prostitutes hang out	8.5	17
overcrowded places	8	16
unfamiliar places	6.5	13
deserted places	4	8
parks	2.5	5
WEAPONS CARRIED DUE TO VICTIMIZATION RISK	69	137
TYPES OF WEAPONS CARRIED		
chemicals	15	30
knife	13.5	27
scissors	10	20
prayers/faith in God	9	18
cloth bag with rocks	6	12
lead pipe	5	10
long fingernails	4.5	9
gun	3	6
karate	3	6

Note: [1]A few homeless women mentioned more than one type of place avoided.

ine the trivariate relationship among (1) carrying weapons, (2) avoiding places, (3) fear of crime, and (4) self-perceived vulnerability. Table 1.5 shows the results of this examination, which indicate that those homeless women who do not carry weapons nor avoid places are more fearful of crime and have heightened self-perceptions of vulnerability than those who engage in both precautionary activities.

Chi-square and probit regression analyses were used to assess the effects of the various correlates on the fear of crime. The items that comprised the vulnerability scale were highly intercorrelated (A = .88). As a result, these items were collapsed to give a mean self-perceived vulnerability score for each homeless woman. These mean scores were then dichotomized at the median so as to classify subjects into low- and high-vulnerability categories. The reliability coefficient of items in the fear-of-crime scale indicated that these items were highly intercorrelated as well

Table 1.5

Fear of Crime, Self-Perceived Vulnerability, and Homeless Women's Use of Precautionary Behaviors

USE OF PRECAUTIONARY BEHAVIORS	*does not carry a weapon*		*carries a weapon*	
	does not avoid places	avoids places	avoids places	does not avoid places
FEAR OF CRIME[1]				
low	8	20	68	14
high	14	21	53	2
SELF-PERCEIVED VULNERABILITY[2]				
low	5	13	21	7
high	17	28	100	9

Notes: [1]x^2 = 10.62; at 3df; p = .05; Cramer's V = .23. [2]x^2 = 7.82; at 3df; p = .05; Cramer's V = .20.

(A = .95). Items in that scale were thus collapsed to give each respondent an average fear score, and then dichotomized at the median into low and high fear. Dichotomizing the dependent variables (fear of crime and self-perceived vulnerability) at the median was because both were ordinal-level variables. In order to be able to use probit regression analysis, the dependent variable must be dichotomous. There was no difference between property crime and personal crime in either the perception of vulnerability or the respective fear, as is evidenced by the high intercorrelation of items that comprised these two scales. This finding is contrary to that of Miethe and Lee (1984), who demonstrated that there was a difference between these two in their study involving the general population.

The statistical results and raw scores are shown in tables 1.6 and 1.7.

Table 1.6

Chi-Squared Results of Explanatory Factors Associated with Homeless Women's Fear of Crime

	FEAR OF CRIME				
	Low	*High*	*X^2*	*Ø*	*P*
NUMBER OF TIMES VICTIMIZED ON STREETS					
low	48	44	7.7	.20	.05
high	42	66			
SELF-PERCEIVED HEALTH CONDITION					
low	57	41	6.4	.18	.05
high	40	62			

Table 1.6 (continued)

	FEAR OF CRIME				
	Low	*High*	X^2	*Ø*	*P*
PAST VICTIMIZATION EXPERIENCES WHILE LIVING ON THE STREETS					
no	54	38	6.3	.18	.05
yes	43	65			
LENGTH OF TIME ON STREET					
low	58	43	5.8	.18	.05
high	39	60			
CARRYING WEAPONS					
no	23	40	4.6	–.16	.05
yes	74	63			
SELF-PERCEIVED VULNERABILITY					
low	58	45	4.5	.16	.05
high	39	58			
PAST VICTIMIZATION EXPERIENCES BEFORE LIVING ON THE STREETS					
no	65	54	3.8	.14	.05
yes	32	49			
INCOME SOURCE					
no	43	35	.00	.99	NS
yes	33	31			
RACE					
nonwhite	58	44	.29	.03	NS
white	52	46			
AGE					
young	62	43	1.4	.08	NS
old	48	47			
ORIGINALLY FROM NEW YORK CITY					
no	40	26	1.2	.07	NS
yes	70	64			
AVOID PLACES					
no	22	16	.15	.02	NS
yes	88	74			
VICARIOUS VICTIMIZATION					
no	18	15	.03	.00	NS
yes	92	75			
HIGHEST EDUCATIONAL LEVEL COMPLETED					
low	43	35	.00	.00	NS
high	67	55			

Table 1.6 indicates that self-perceived vulnerability, past victimization experiences, carrying weapons, the number of past victimization experiences, self-perceived health conditions, and length of time spent living on the streets are all significantly associated with homeless women's fear of crime. All of these relationships are positive, with the exception of carrying weapons. Unfortunately, our cross-sectional data do not permit examining the chronological relation between fear and carrying weapons. We do not know, therefore, whether initially highly fearful subjects became less fearful after adopting a weapon.

There is a low positive association between self-perceived vulnerability and fear of crime (.16). This result suggests that these two concepts are largely separate, even though some overlap exists between them. The probits of having fear-of-crime and self-perceived vulnerability scores equal to or greater than the median is indicated by the equation:

$$[\text{Probit} = (p/p - 1) + 5)];$$

Probit (worry) = 5.53 + .39 vul + .50 length + –.88 carry + .45 health + .49 times/sts. + .42 pve/sts. + .46 pve/be.sts.

Probit (vul) = 10.01 + .70 (pve/be.sts.) + .50 (pve/sts.) + .47 (times sts.) + .23 (times/be.sts.) + .32 (vicarious victimization) + .33 (income) + .29 (health).

Each of the independent variables has been scored as a dichotomy, with 1 equaling a score above the median, and 0 equaling a score below the median. The ratio of each of the coefficients to its standard error was greater than 1.96; thus each is significant beyond the .05 level. One can conclude that this overall probit regression equation is as able to predict bag ladies' fear of crime as if the sample had been generated in a random fashion. A comparison of the *z*-scores within the probit regression analysis indicates that the effects of the relationships of the variables are real; significant relationships in the probit equation were isolated to rule out any misleading inferences based upon the equation. It should also be noted that the data did not present a problem of multicollinearity. Age, race, whether these women had an income source, education, whether these women were from New York City, their avoidance behaviors, and their vicarious or indirect victimization experience were not significantly correlated with their fear of crime in either the chi-square or probit analysis. The results with regard to age, income, and education are contrary to those from studies of the general population. Statistical results of all independent variables and the fear of crime can be seen in table 1.6.

Table 1.7 shows that past victimization experiences both before and while living on the streets, along with the number of times victimization experiences occurred on the streets and before living on the streets, vicarious victimization, whether these women had an income source, and self-

Table 1.7

Chi-Squared Results of Explanatory Factors Associated with Homeless Women's Self-Perceptions of Vulnerability

	SELF-PERCEIVED VULNERABILITY				
	Low	*High*	X^2	*Ø*	*P*
NUMBER OF TIMES VICTIMIZED BEFORE LIVING ON STREETS					
low	41	5	11.2	.23	.005
high	104	50			
NUMBER OF TIMES VICTIMIZED WHILE ON THE STREETS					
low	37	85	9.4	.21	.005
high	9	69			
PAST VICTIMIZATION EXPERIENCES WHILE LIVING ON THE STREETS					
no	30	62	8.8	.21	.005
yes	16	92			
VICARIOUS VICTIMIZATION					
no	14	19	8.4	.20	.005
yes	32	135			
PAST VICTIMIZATION EXPERIENCES BEFORE LIVING ON THE STREETS					
no	35	84	6.8	.18	.010
yes	11	70			
INCOME SOURCE					
no	37	99	4.2	.14	.05
yes	9	55			
SELF-PERCEIVED HEALTH CONDITION					
low	28	70	3.4	.12	.10
high	18	84			
AVOID PLACES					
no	12	26	1.9	.09	NS
yes	34	128			
CARRYING WEAPONS					
no	18	45	1.60	.08	NS
yes	28	109			
LENGTH OF TIME ON STREETS					
low	27	74	1.60	.08	NS
high	19	80			
AGE					
young	27	78	.91	.06	NS
old	19	76			

continued

Table 1.7 (continued)

	SELF-PERCEIVED VULNERABILITY				
	Low	*High*	X^2	*Ø*	*P*
HIGHEST GRADE COMPLETED					
low	16	30	.44	.04	NS
high	62	92			
ORIGINALLY FROM NEW YORK CITY					
no	14	52	.17	.02	NS
yes	32	102			
RACE					
nonwhite	24	78	.03	.01	NS
white	22	26			

perceived health conditions were all positively correlated with homeless women's self-perceived vulnerability. The insignificant correlations with self-perceived vulnerability are also listed in table 1.7.

Discussion

Our findings are supported by both the statistical results and journal notes made during the interviewing process. There is empirical evidence from this study that supports the notion that self-perceived vulnerability to victimization (an individual's estimation of the likelihood of victimization) and the fear of crime (the extent to which a person worries about the occurrence of victimization) are two separate concepts. Homeless women, on the average, consider the possibility of their victimization while living on the streets to be likely. When they were asked how much they worry about victimization, however, their responses suggest that they are generally *not* worried. This result leaves us with a finding of high vulnerability paired with low fear of crime.

There are several bases upon which we rely for reaching the finding of the seeming paradoxical relationship of low fear of crime with high self-perceived vulnerability. First, the mean self-perceived vulnerability score was five, whereas the mean fear score was three. Second, the correlation between vulnerability and fear, albeit positive, is small (.16). Third, journal notes made during the interviews offer many responses that lend support for this notion. For example, "anything can happen out here, but if I were that fearful I wouldn't have chosen to do this"; "I know that my chances are high. I can't walk around terrified. I do something about my fear. I stay away from 42nd Street"; and "sure . . . anything is possible, but if I was that afraid I'd go back home." Finally, in a subsequent study using identical measures of both vulnerability and fear (Coston 1991), the correlation between self-perceived vulnerability and fear of crime among a small sample of homeless women in New York City was found to be negative (–.06).[1] We believe that this latter finding in particular reinforces our conclusion about the suggested paradox.

When asked about the probability (the odds) of experiencing victimization, it appears that a careful assessment of prior victimization experience and considerations about living a life on the streets results in very rational responses about this possibility. Fear, on the other hand, is more emotional than rational (Crow 1971, 104). Emotions are dynamic and often stimulate "behavior that makes the person less rational as the emotion takes possession of him" (Crow 1971, 105). This aroused-fear state also prepares the body for physical activity and can either stimulate a person's total action system and enhance the quality of life, or can restrict behavior to a point where he or she is unable to function with full effectiveness (Kaplan 1965, 159). The more familiar a person is with their surroundings and the more prepared a person is in the face of danger, the less fearful they will be. According to Sluckin (1979), people who face their fears and do something constructive about them are most likely to make an adequate response to their stress.

We can apply this idea of "rational" fear to the homeless women's fear of crime. Their street existence is precarious. Subjectively, homeless women perceive that the likelihood of experiencing victimization is high. Objectively also, one can see the vulnerability to victimization in their lifestyle. Logically then, it would seem that the anticipation of harm based upon the potential for dangerous events should evoke fear in homeless women. But the use of protective behaviors (avoiding certain places and carrying weapons) is one way they appear to reduce their fear. Other research indicates that this successful preparedness *does* reduce the perceived likelihood of a potentially harmful outcome, thus reducing the fear (Kaplan 1965; Sluckin 1979). Statements from the homeless women in our study further support this notion of a rational fear followed by a coping process: "I couldn't live out here if I didn't do something about the fear, ya know?" (westside cluster). About her use of precautionary behaviors, another bag lady said: "I stay away from 42nd Street. That's where all the vermin is. I carry lye with me in case there's a problem" (First Moravian Church). These women seem to seek to achieve a balance among thinking (self-perceived vulnerability to victimization risk), feeling (fear of crime), and doing (avoiding places and carrying weapons).

Is the lower-than-expected fear of our subjects the result of the "reckless disregard" or "self-assured confidence" reportedly characteristic of young men? Or is it something else? We believe the latter, that it is something else. As suggested above, one possible explanation for the low fear and the seeming paradox is the use of coping strategies. Another is the idea of cognitive dissonance (Stanko 1987, 126). What have been variously referred to as "coping strategies" (Gordon & Riger 1989), "precautionary strategies" (Stanko 1987), and "normalizing behavior" (Hanrahan 1990) provide a means for a vulnerable person to avoid victimization. Defense mechanisms or mechanisms of adjustment such as cognitive dissonance, on the other hand, enable a vulnerable person to regulate his or her feelings so that the fear he or she experiences is at a manageable level.

Let us consider both of these possibilities. The first type involves a behavioral response. The elderly women in senior citizen centers in Newark, New Jersey, who were studied by Hanrahan are good examples of this type. These women coped with the perceived threats in their lives "by making accommodations and using available resources to reduce risk and enhance their sense of safety" (Hanrahan 1990, 132). Most of the women were not actively suffering from a gnawing sense of fear, but most had changed their routines and activities in order to ensure that "their level of fear stays manageable." "Fear, the emotion," according to Hanrahan, "is experienced rarely." This was because "[m]ost of the women have all but eliminated the situations in which they are likely to experience fear. They have learned and practice various accommodations to crime" (Hanrahan 1990, 105). These women normalized the situation; they accepted fear of crime as a part of life's situation, and in effect normalized that fear. They were like Gordon and Riger's "Invincibles" who accept crime as a normal part of everyday life. "The 'Invincibles' don't admit to a great deal of fear, perhaps because to do so would make the stress unbearable. Nevertheless, they engage in many precautionary behaviors and in other ways indicate that crime and avoidance of victimization are important factors shaping their lives" (Gordon & Riger 1989, 116). Our subjects also manage their fear by being routinely cautious and on guard.

Another or additional way of interpreting our results is through the concept of defense mechanisms that are psychological rather than behavioral. Looked at in this light, such mechanisms may "alter or mask the individual's perception of a threat by reconstructing his attitudes and feelings so that he senses little or no fear" (Kaplan 1965, 224). Kaplan refers to this type of defense mechanism as "rationalization." Rationalization might enable bag ladies to justify, excuse, or explain away their fear. This would enable them to continue living on the streets. They, in effect, make peace with themselves. We found evidence that this happens with our subjects. One lady summed up her low fear level by saying, "You can't live like this and be too fearful. Sure anything is possible, but if I was that afraid I'd go back home" (Port Authority Bus Terminal).

We agree with Kaplan that people try to avoid being fearful. Fear, after all, is undesirable; it interferes with our comfort or plans. Fear can be dealt with by coping and managing, as we and others have shown. But it can also be dealt with by denying and repressing. Perhaps these homeless women repress much of their fear in order to maintain better emotional health? The reports of low fear levels expressed by homeless women could at least in part be the result of their own self-deception.

Festinger (1957) refers to the rationalization process as "cognitive dissonance," a process that involves two related concepts. If the two concepts of vulnerability and fear are related, then this relationship must be either consonant or dissonant. As previously shown, there is some small overlap between the two. If, says Festinger, when considering a pair of concepts "either one does follow from the other, then the relationship between them is consonant" (Festinger 1957, 12). On the other hand, a dissonant relationship exists between two concepts if, "for one reason or another, they do not fit together." The relationship between vulnerability and fear of crime in homeless women could be considered an instance of a dissonant relationship. High self-perceived vulnerability to victimization risk does not result in high fear of crime for them.

Based upon the theory of cognitive dissonance, homeless women would not be expected to be able to live their lives in a constant high state of fear. Thus, in addition to altering their physical states (coping by precautionary behaviors), they might also alter their mental states in order to adjust to living within the constraints of that fear. One way this can be done is to rationalize away the intensity of the fear. Since the reality of the streets cannot be drastically changed, it is the fear itself that must be.

In situations where many persons who associate with one another suffer from identical dissonance, it is easier to reduce dissonance by obtaining social support (Festinger 1964). Homeless women, although isolates, *do* rely on a communications network. One woman who summed up her feelings about this network said, "We look out for one another . . . we'll tell them where to go" (westside cluster). Some homeless women attributed their low fear to strong beliefs: of God, the police, or in fate. Other homeless women said that there were simply other things to worry about besides fear.

The women also indicated that they had chosen this lifestyle from among other alternatives. For better or worse, it is a lifestyle that has to be gotten used to. Fear of victimization is just one of its disadvantages. Several women implied that if living on the streets was not a viable alternative (even considering the victimization risk), then they would not have chosen it.

CONCLUSIONS

The results of our research have several implications. This study is the first of its kind to analyze the role of fear within an especially vulnerable population. It thus opens the way for other studies involving similarly vulnerable groups; it also widens the scope of the study of the fear of crime. We believe that this preliminary step in explaining the phenomenon has merit. We can question the variables correlated with the fear of crime from general population studies that were tested in this research and were found to be insignificant. We have also refined and sharpened the focus of the concept of "fear of crime."

There are many suggestions for future research. It is important, for example, to assess homeless women's fear of crime in relation to their other fears and concerns. It would also be valuable to assess the nature of victimization and the fear of crime among homeless men, and then to compare those results with homeless-female results.

With the exception of a study conducted by Wiltz (1982) that focused on the fear of crime among elderly blacks, we are unaware of any other studies of particularly vulnerable groups. It might be argued that Hanrahan's elderly women also qualify. In any event, we suggest that more studies of the fear of crime among especially vulnerable populations are needed.

The lifestyle of the homeless woman raises many questions. This research has attempted only to examine her fear of crime. We recognize that this is only one of the dynamics of a precarious street existence. More research that looks at the characteristics of this subculture, and at adaptation strategies and barriers to survival, needs to be done. It might be that once a clearer understanding of all the dynamics of life on the streets for homeless women and others is gained, society would then be in a better position to try to solve these problems.

NOTE

1. Worries about crime—self-perceived vulnerability:

	Low	*High*	*Total*
Low	5	2	7
High	34	9	43
Total	39	11	50

Fisher's Exact Test = 48.68; at 1df; $p < .05$; phi = –.06.

REFERENCES

Baker, Mary A., Barbara C. Nienstedt, Ronald Everett, and Richard McCleary. (1983). "The impact of a crime wave: Perceptions, fear, and confidence in the police." *Law and Society Review 17*:319–23.

Baxter, Ellen, and Kim Hopper (1981). *Private lives/public spaces.* New York: Community Service Society.

Biderman, Albert. (1967). *A report on a pilot study in the District of Columbia on victimization and attitudes towards law enforcement.* Washington, DC: U.S. Government Printing Office.

Bishop, George, and William Klecka. (1978). "Victimization and fear of crime." *Social Problems 26*:343–58.

Clemente, Frank, and Michael Kleiman. (1976). "Fear of crime among the aged." *Gerontologist 16*:207–10.

Conklin, John E. (1975). "Dimension of community response to the crime problem." *Social Problems 18*:373–84.

Coston, Charisse. (1989). "The original designer label: Prototypes of New York City's shopping-bag ladies." *Deviant Behavior 10*:157–72.

———. (1991). "Worries about crime: Rank-ordering survival concerns among urban transient females." Paper presented at the annual meeting of the American Society of Criminology, November.

Crow, Lester. (1971). *Human development and learning.* New York: American Book Company.

Ennis, Phillip H. (1967). *Criminal victimization in the United States: A report of a national survey.* Washington, DC: U.S. Government Printing Office.

Festinger, Leon. (1957). *A Theory of cognitive dissonance.* Stanford, CA: Stanford University Press.

———. (1964). *Conflict, decisions and dissonance.* Stanford, CA: Stanford University Press.

Gordon, Margaret T., and Stephanie Riger. (1989). *The female fear.* New York: Free Press.

Hanrahan, Kathleen J. (1990). *Exploring fear of crime among elderly urban females.* Unpublished doctoral dissertation, Rutgers University, Newark.

Hindelang, Michael, Michael Gottfredson, and James Garofalo. (1978). *Victims of personal crime: An empirical foundation for a theory of personal victimization.* Cambridge, MA: Ballinger Publishing Company.

Innes, Christopher. (1982). *Coping with the fear of crime.* Unpublished doctoral dissertation, University of Michigan.

Kaplan, George. (1965). *Foundations of human behavior.* New York: Harper & Row.

LaGrange, Randy L., and Kenneth F. Ferraro. (1989). "Assessing age and gender differences in perceived risk and fear of crime." *Criminology 27*:697–719.

Lawton, Michael, and Stephen Yaffee. (1980). "Victimization and fear of crime in elderly public housing tenants." *Journal of Gerontology 35*:768–79.

Lee, Gary. (1982). "Sex differences in fear of crime among older people." *Research on Aging 4*:284–98.

Linquist, John, and Janice Duke. (1982). "The elderly victim at risk: Explaining the fear–victimization paradox." *Criminology 20*:115–26.

Martin, Marsha. (1982). *Strategies of adaptation: Coping strategies of the urban transient females.* Unpublished doctoral dissertation, University of Michigan.

Miethe, Terrance, and Gary Lee. (1984). "Fear of crime among older people: An assessment of the predictive power of crime-related factors." *Sociological Quarterly 16*:397–414.

Reiss, Albert. (1967). "Studies in crime and law enforcement in major metropolitan areas." President's Commission on Law Enforcement and Administration of Justice. Washington, DC: U.S. Government Printing Office.

Reynolds, Mark, Mary Jones, and Marie Lawton. (1976). "Fear of crime among the elderly." *Social Forces 56*:857–69.

Riger, Stephaine, Margaret Gordon, and Robert LeBailley. (1982). "Coping with urban crime women's use of precautionary behaviors." *American Journal of Community Psychology.*

Riger, Stephaine, Robert LeBailley, and Margaret Gordon. (1983). "Community ties and urbanites's fear of crime: An ecological investigation." *American Journal of Community Psychology 8*:225–30.

Rossi, Peter H. (1989). *Down and out in America: The origins of the homeless.* Chicago: University of Chicago Press.

Skogan, Wesley, and Michael Maxfield. (1984). *Coping with crime.* Beverly Hills, CA: Sage Publications.

Sluckin, William. (1979). *Fear in animals and man.* New York: Van Nostrand Reinhold.

Stanko, Elizabeth A. (1987). "Typical violence, normal precaution: Men, women and interpersonal violence in England, Wales, Scotland and the USA," in *Women, violence and social control,* ed. Jalna Hanmer and Mary Maynard. Atlantic Highlands, NJ: Humanities Press International.

Sundeen, Richard, and James Mathieu. (1976). "The fear of crime and its consequences among elderly in three urban communities." *Gerontologist 16*:211–17.

Warr, Mark. (1984). "Fear of victimization: Why are women and the elderly more afraid?" *Social Science Quarterly 65*:681–702.

———. (1985). "Fear of rape among urban women." *Social Problems 32*:238–50.

Warr, Mark, and Mark Stafford. (1983). "Fear of victimization: A look at the proximate causes." *Social Forces 61*:1033–43.

Wiltz, Charles. (1982). "The fear of crime, criminal victimization and elderly blacks." *Phylon 4*:283–94.

Wright, James D. (1989). *Address unknown: The homeless in America.* New York: de Gruyter.

Yin, Peter. (1980). "Fear of crime among the elderly: Some issues and suggestions." *Social Problems 27*:492–504.

CHAPTER TWO

Worries about Crime

rank-ordering survival concerns among urban transient females

CHARISSE T. M. COSTON

NUMEROUS STUDIES HAVE FOCUSED on the correlates of the fear of crime (Skogan & Klecka 1977; Hindelang, Gottfredson, & Garofalo 1978; Skogan & Maxfield 1981; Stafford & Galle 1984; Miethe 1984). The preponderance of evidence shows that the elderly, females, minorities, and urban residents are most fearful of crime. In recent years, research on the fear of crime has advanced beyond a simple search for correlates. Some scholars are now looking at the relative priority of the fear of crime in relation to other concerns. Although Yin (1982) found the elderly to be fearful of crime, he also found that they were *more* fearful of having a lack of money and poor health. The focus of this study is on a particularly vulnerable population—urban transient females in New York City—and its worries about becoming the victim of a crime. The goal of this study is to explore the seeming paradox between homeless female's high rates of self-perceived vulnerability and low rates of worries about crime. If homeless women *deprioritize* worries about crime in this study, then Maslow's (1954) hierarchy of human needs theory may explain this occurrence.

Urban transient females are also referred to as "homeless females" in this chapter. This group has been defined as adult females who live on the streets with no visible means of support and no permanent residences. They live out of shopping carts and/or shopping bags. This class of indigent female wanderers represents a truly vulnerable population.

Urban transient females are a subculture representing one of the lowest socioeconomic groups within the United States (Baxter & Hopper 1981), and thus they confront many challenges while living on the streets.

Physiological survival concerns include strategies for finding food, clothing, shelter, medical care, and resources for hygiene (Coston 1982). Baxter and Hopper (1981, 58) summed up the lifestyle frustrations of this especially vulnerable group by stating:

> They are unlike the general public in terms of their lifestyle. They have no place to go. They live on the streets, wandering from darkened doorways to empty park benches. They rummage through garbage cans for food and clothing. They must constantly ward off the threats of thieves and other tormentors.

Today, the personal lives of homeless females are public issues and a matter of public concern. The study of the worries about crime in a subpopulation from among the lowest socioeconomic class of people in the United States is an initial step towards understanding worries about crime in the general population. The results of this study provide the basis for more detailed and rigorous comparative studies of socioeconomic classes regarding worries about crime, and they also establish a foundation for more involved studies that explore worries about crime within especially vulnerable and deviant subcultures. These findings provide the groundwork for more extensive work that, hopefully, will lead to the development of policy concerning the homeless.

Homeless women are an extremely complex group of individuals and a number of researchers (Baxter & Hopper 1981; Martin 1982; Coston 1989; Rossi 1989; Wright 1989; Barak & Bohm 1989; Barak 1992) have sought to remove some of the mystery surrounding them, especially since their personal troubles have turned into public issues. Through tape-recorded interviews and interactions with researchers, homeless women have expressed an array of reasons for living on the streets and describe a plethora of coping strategies utilized for daily street survival (Coston 1982; Rossi 1989; Wright 1989). In every instance, the transition from a socially accepted lifestyle to life on the street was a gradual process, rather than an abrupt occurrence for homeless females. One interesting result contained in Coston's (1982) research that further stimulated the focus of her subsequent research was that 95 percent of the homeless females that she had interviewed had been victimized while living on the streets. In 1989, Coston examined the nature and extent of their criminal victimization, self-perceived vulnerability, use of precautionary behaviors, and worries about crime (Coston 1989).

Researchers have criticized past fear-of-crime studies because the indicators of fear used in these are really indicators of worry, anxiety, vulnerability, or concern about crime (Gibbs 1986; Hanrahan 1991). These contemporary researchers have separated "fear" from "anxiety," "worry," and "concern" about crime, stating that all of these concepts are different (Gibbs 1986; Hanrahan 1991). This chapter focuses on *worries* about crime. While most studies of the fear of crime had focused on the correlates of the fear of crime and vulnerability among groups and subgroups within mainstream segments of the United States—that is, females and the elderly—Coston's (1988) research was the first to focus on the correlates of victimization within a particularly vulnerable subculture of urban transient females and introduce "worry" as the major concept involved. One of the most compelling findings in Coston's research was that while over half of the 200 urban transient females interviewed had been victimized and felt that the likelihood of future victimizations was high, when asked how much they worried about the possibility of victimization, urban transient women replied that they were "somewhat unworried" (Coston 1988). Thus, the data revealed a seemingly paradoxical relationship between high vulnerability and low worries about crime, even though there was a low positive correlation between these two concepts.

Past research involving AIDS patients and other highly vulnerable populations, such as prostitutes and male ghetto residents, also has indicated paradoxical relationships between self-perceived vulnerability and fear (Skogan & Klecka 1977; Yin 1982). The present study, therefore, examined the paradoxical relationship between vulnerability and the worries about crime by placing that paradox within the larger context of urban transient females' struggles to survive on the streets of New York City. The research question was: What is the relative importance of worries about victimization in relation to other survival concerns of urban transient females?

Urban transient females are a growing challenge to American public policy-makers. Little is known about homeless women. Their precise number is not known. Since homeless women maintain no means of self-enumeration and are not on unemployment rosters and were not, until recently, listed in census reports and hence on unemployment rosters, researchers can only estimate their number and distribution by gender and age (Schwann 1983, 1988, 1992; U.S. Census 1990). However, from these estimates, Schwann (1988) reports that New York City has the highest concentration of homeless females in the United States, and their numbers are increasing. Schwann (1988) estimated that there were approximately 45,000 homeless people on New York City's streets in 1988, or higher than the earlier estimate of 36,000 in 1983. Schwann (1992) estimates that women represent about 14,000 of the overall homeless population in New York City.

Maslow (1954) is best known for his theoretical work, the "human growth" or "fulfillment model" based upon man's needs. He conceptualized human needs in a hierarchy (see figure 2.1). These needs are specifically ordered so that one level of need-satisfaction must be met before a progression to the satisfaction of a higher need, although 100 percent satisfaction is not required for a need to no longer be dominant. The first need level, *physiological*, is the desire to satisfy hunger, physical rest, and thirst. The second need level, *safety*, is the desire for protection against deprivation, threats, and danger. The third need level, *social*, is the need to give and receive love and friendship. The fourth need level, *ego*, is the

NEED FOR SELF-ACTUALIZATION
(to be fully what one can be)

NEED FOR SELF-ESTEEM
(self-respect, adequacy, mastery, competence)

NEED FOR BELONGINGNESS AND LOVE
(affection, intimacy, need to have roots in family or peer group)

NEED FOR SAFETY
(avoidance of pain, anxiety, desire for security)

PHYSIOLOGICAL NEEDS
(deficits like hunger, thirst, fatigue)

Figure 2.1 Maslow's hierarchy of needs.

desire for achievement and self-confidence. And the fifth need, *self-actualization*, is realizing one's own potential. Coston's (1993) finding of a seeming paradox between self-perceived vulnerability and worries about crime might be explained by examining homeless female's worries. Perhaps worries about physiological needs, expressed by homeless women, overshadow their worries about becoming the victim of a crime.

METHODS

This research utilized availability and judgmental sampling techniques (Higginbotham & Cox 1979; Babbie 1992). These approaches were generated from Coston's (1989) experience with field and survey techniques during prior research within the homeless female population in Manhattan (Coston 1982, 1989, 1993).

Several strategies utilizing survey research were involved: (1) asking homeless women to list their five biggest worries; (2) then asking them to rank-order their five biggest worries, from most important to least important; and (3) asking homeless females about the likelihood of future victimization and the extent to which they worry about becoming a victim of crime. Background and personal information were also obtained. These measures of vulnerability to and worry about crime were initially used in interviews in 1988 by Coston and refined in this present study to determine if the paradoxical relationship between vulnerability and worry exists for homeless women. To ensure the rapport and easiness of respondents within their own environment, the interviews took place in the streets and in two shelters, open 24 hours a day, that homeless females frequent for meeting their daily survival needs (e.g., bathing, sleeping, eating, medical care). These research sites are located in the main homeless territory between 30th and 52nd Streets on the east and west sides of the borough of Manhattan in New York City as circumscribed by Baxter and Hopper (1981). Each homeless woman was paid a nominal sum for her participation in the study.

To comply with concerns regarding the protection of human research subjects, no names or other identifying information were recorded that could be used to trace these women. Interviews were tape-recorded in order to allow uninterrupted time for probing their responses. Homeless women who displayed obvious signs of mental incoherence were excluded. There were sufficient numbers of homeless women who were rational and willing and able to relate what was going on in their lives in a meaningful fashion. All data were aggregated.

RESULTS

As seen in table 2.1, which includes the characteristics of the sample, the average reported age of a homeless woman was 57 years. Coston's 1982 study of homeless women revealed the average age to be 50, and in her 1989 study, the average age was 53. According to the U.S. Census Bureau's statistics (1980, 1990), the average age of a female in the general population in 1970 was 28; in 1982 it was 32; and in 1988 it was 35. It appears that the population of homeless women, while 20 years older than the average for the general population of women, is becoming older at the same rate as females in the general population. This could be due to a decreasing birthrate and increasing longevity. The median length of time spent living on the streets for homeless women in this study was 24 months, with a range from two months to ten years.

Table 2.1 reveals that over half of the sample was black (58 percent), and somewhat less than half was white (42 percent). Also, three-fourths of the sample (72 percent) had been victimized while living on the streets. Thirty-six homeless women who were interviewed had been victimized. Twenty-eight percent of them had experienced at least four victimizations. About half (50 percent) of the homeless women in the study reported that they were victims of combination-victimizations—that is, two or more types of victimization in one incident. The most frequent type of combination-victimization was robbery and assault (n = 20 cases). However, incidents of rape, robbery, and assault (n = 3 cases) and rape and assault (n = 2 cases) were also reported. This finding of combination-victimization is consistent with previous research findings of this subculture (Coston, 1982, 1989). Vicarious victimization experiences—that is, only hearing about the victimization experiences of other homeless women—was evident in 88 percent of this subculture of female wanderers.

Through the use of a Likert-type scale in which responses ranged from

Table 2.1
Selected Characteristics of the Sample

Characteristic	*Percent*	*N*
RACE		
black	58	29
white	42	21
VICTIMIZATION WHILE LIVING ON THE STREETS		
no	28	14
yes	72	36
EXTENT OR PREVIOUS VICTIMIZATION		
once	12	6
twice	14	7
three times	18	9
four times	28	14
TYPE OF PREVIOUS VICTIMIZATION[1]		
rape	6	3
robbery	24	12
assault	10	5
theft	10	5
combination victimization[1]	50[2]	25
VICARIOUS VICTIMIZATION		
no	12	6
yes	88	44
EXTENT OF WORRY ABOUT CRIME		
low	74	37
high	26	13
EXTENT OF SELF-PERCEIVED VULNERABILITY		
low	18	9
high	82	41

Notes: [1]Victimization experiences are counted only once. Combination victimization is when two or more types of crimes occur in one incident. [2]Includes 20 cases of robbery and assault; three cases of rape, robbery, and assault; and two cases of rape and assault.

one (not worried) to seven (extremely worried), these women were asked about the extent to which they worry about becoming the victim of a crime. These findings were also consistent with Coston's (1988) in which homeless women indicated their worry about five types of crime possibly happening to them. These items were also highly intercorrelated in the present study (a = .95) and consequently were collapsed into a median

Table 2.2

Worries about Crime Based upon Self-Perceived Vulnerability

	SELF-PERCEIVED WORRIES ABOUT CRIME VULNERABILITY		
	Low	*High*	*Total*
LOW	5	2	7
HIGH	34	9	43
TOTAL	39	11	50

Notes: Fisher's Exact Test = 48.68; at ldf; p = <.05; phi = –.06.

worry score for each homeless woman, yielding an average worry score of three out of seven. Similarly, each homeless woman was given an average self-perceived vulnerability score, because the five items that asked homeless women to estimate the likelihood of becoming the victim of particular types of crime were highly intercorrelated (a = .88). This finding was consistent with Coston's (1988) earlier work in this area. The median estimate of self-perceptions of vulnerability to victimization risk (which ranged from one—not likely, to seven—extremely likely) in the current study was 6.5 or "extremely likely." This finding was higher than the result indicated in Coston's (1988) previous study, which averaged 5.0 (somewhat likely). The relationship between self-perceived vulnerability and worry about crime in this study lends support for a paradoxical finding: although there is some overlap between these two concepts (phi = –.06), they are essentially separate (see table 2.2). The average "vulnerability to victimization risk" and "worried about crime" scores were then dichotomized at the median for low and high self-perceived vulnerability to victimization risk and worry about crime (see table 2.2).

Table 2.3 reveals 12 worries cited by the urban transient females studied. Fifty percent of the 50 homeless women intensively interviewed ranked worrying about the lack of money as their primary concern. Worrying about being in poor physical health and the lack of proper nutrition were the next most frequently mentioned—the second (36 percent) and third (32 percent)—survival worries, respectively. Just over one-fourth of the sample (26 percent) reported that their fourth worry was their family's well-being, while three-fourths of the sample ranked getting mugged fifth. For a ranking of the top five worries in relation to all 12 worries, see table 2.3. Only 2 percent of the sample reported worries about getting mugged as a primary concern. Worries about crime are less severe for the urban transient female, even though she reports the odds of criminal victimization to be extremely likely.

Table 2.3

Worries of Urban Transient Females

	WORRY FREQUENCY OF RANKINGS				
	1	*2*	*3*	*4*	*5*
FAMILY'S WELL-BEING	9(18)	3(6)	2(4)	13(26)	—
GETTING ENOUGH SLEEP	—	3(6)	1(2)	1(2)	3(6)
GETTING MUGGED	1(2)	1(2)	4(8)	3(6)	38(76)
LACK OF MONEY	25(50)	14(28)	6(12)	3(6)	—
LONELINESS	1(2)	2(4)	—	4(8)	—
LOSS OF PSYCHOLOGICAL HEALTH	1(2)	1(2)	—	2(4)	—
POOR PHYSICAL HEALTH	8(16)	18(36)	8(16)	9(18)	4(8)
PROPER NUTRITION	—	1(2)	16(32)	3(6)	—
SOURCES FOR EATING	1(2)	2(4)	3(6)	4(8)	—
SOURCES FOR MEDICAL CARE	—	1(2)	2(4)	2(4)	3(6)
SOURCES FOR SLEEPING	4(8)	4(8)	3(6)	1(2)	—
THEFT	—	—	5(10)	5(10)	2(4)
TOTAL NUMBER IN EACH CATEGORY	50	50	50	50	50

Note: Raw numbers represent frequencies; percentages are in parentheses.

DISCUSSION AND CONCLUSIONS

These findings support the paradoxical relationship between high self-perceptions of vulnerability and correspondingly low levels of worries about crime among homeless women. The urban transient female has deprioritized worries about crime in her life. Instead, the perilous and precarious life of living on the streets has forced the urban transient female to focus on fulfilling her primary needs such as proper nutrition and health concerns.

The results of the rank-ordering of homeless females' worries is applied to Maslow's (1954) hierarchy of needs theory in figure 2.2. Urban transient females indicated that the lack of money, poor health, the lack of proper nutrition, and their family's well-being superseded worries about getting mugged. Their first three needs appear to coincide with Maslow's first need level, since they focus on physiological concerns. Similarly, their family's well-being, the fourth worry, seems to fall into the category of safety. According to notes taken during the interviewing sessions, this is apparently because a number of them rely on their families for the finan-

SELF-FULFILLMENT

Self-Actualization
Esthetic Needs

AFFECTIVE NEEDS

Achievement/Prestige
Approval/Recognition
Belongingness/Love
Acceptance/Affection

PHYSICAL NEEDS

Safety and Security (family well-being)
Freedom from Fear (worry about victimization)
Good Health (poor health)
Financial Stability (lack of money)
Food and Drink (lack of proper nutrition)
Shelter (very homeless)

Figure 2.2 Maslow's hierarchy of needs applied to homeless women.

cial support that enables them to buy food and provide medical self-care. Because they have a need for acceptance, belonging, and love, social needs are also closely tied to family considerations. Homeless females rely on one another for meeting daily survival needs, but no camaraderie appears to exist beyond that point (Coston 1989). Their fifth-ranked worry, getting mugged, is not as important to them, because their first four needs are primarily physiological. Although worrying about getting mugged is clearly a safety need, it seems to have little connection to their most basic survival need of satisfying physiological necessities.

This study of urban transient females lends support for looking beyond a simple search for correlates of anxieties, worries, concerns, and/or fears about crime. When we look for correlates of people's anxieties, fears, worries, and/or concerns about crime, rather than looking at these phenomena in relation to other concerns, we may erroneously conclude that the concern in a person's life has a higher priority than it actually has. As a result of this research, we, as academicians and policy-makers, will be in a better position to examine the salience of the fear of, or anxieties and worries and/or concerns about, crime in the lives of the general population as well as within and between especially vulnerable subpopulations before searching for correlates of this phenomenon.

REFERENCES

Babbie, Earl. (1992). *The practice of social research*, 6th ed. Belmont, CA: Wadsworth.

Barak, Gregg. (1992). *Gimmie shelter: A social history of homelessness in contemporary America*. New York: Praeger.

Barak, Gregg, and Robert Bohm. (1989). "The crimes of the homeless or the crime of homelessness?: On the dialectics of criminalization, decriminalization, and victimization." *Contemporary Crises 13*:275–88.

Baxter, Kim, and Ellen Hopper. (1981). *Private lives/public spaces*. New York: Community Service Society.

Coston, Charisse. (1982). *The original designer label: Prototypes of New York City's shopping bag-ladies*. Unpublished Master's thesis, Rutgers University, Newark.

———. (1989). "The original designer label: Prototypes of New York City's shopping-bag ladies." *Deviant Behavior: A Multidisciplinary Journal 10*:157–72.

———. (1993). "Fear of crime among New York City's population of urban transient females." *Journal of Social Distress 2*:1.

Gibbs, John. (1986). "Fear of crime: A concept in need of clarification." Paper presented at the annual meeting of the American Society of Criminology.

Hanrahan, Kathleen J. (1990). *Exploring fear of crime among elderly urban females*. Unpublished doctoral dissertation, Rutgers University, Newark.

Higginbotham, John, and Kevin Cox. (1979). *Focus group interviews: A reader*. Chicago: American Marketing Association.

Hindelang, Michael, Michael Gottfredson, and James Garofalo. (1978). *Victims of personal crime: An empirical foundation for a theory of personal victimization*. Cambridge, MA: Ballinger Publishing Company.

Martin, Marsha. (1982). *Strategies of adaptation: Coping strategies of the urban transient female*. Unpublished doctoral dissertation, Columbia University.

Maslow, Abraham. (1954). *Motivation and personality*. New York: Harper & Row.

Miethe, Terrence. (1984). "Fear of crime among older people: A reassessment of the predictive power of crime-related factors." *Sociological Quarterly 16*:397–414.

Rossi, Peter. (1989). *Down and out in America: Origins of the homeless*. Chicago: University of Chicago Press.

Schwann, Kevin. (1983). *Shopping-bag ladies: Homeless women. A report to the Fund for the City of New York*. New York: Manhattan Bowery Corporation.

———. (1988). *Shopping-bag ladies: Homeless women. A report to the Fund for the City of New York*. New York: Manhattan Bowery Corporation.

———. (1992). *Shopping-bag ladies: Homeless women. A report to the Fund for the City of New York*. New York: Manhattan Bowery Corporation.

Skogan, Wesley, and James Klecka. (1977). *The fear of crime*. Washington, DC: American Political Science Association.

Skogan, Wesley, and Michael Maxfield. (1981). *Coping with crime: Individual and neighborhood reactions*. Beverly Hills, CA: Sage Publications.

Stafford, Mark, and Omar Galle. (1984). "Victimization rates, exposure to risk and the fear of crime." *Criminology 22*:173–85.

U.S. Census Bureau. (1980). *Summary characteristics of social economic and housing*. Washington, DC: U.S. Government Printing Office.

———. (1990). *Characteristics of the population.* Washington, DC: U.S. Government Printing Office.

Wright, James. (1989). *Address unknown: The homeless in America.* New York: de Gruyter.

Yin, Peter. (1982). "Fear of crime as a problem for the elderly." *Social Problems 30*: 240–45.

CHAPTER THREE

Personal and Situational Characteristics of Custodial African-American Grandmothers

DOROTHY S. RUIZ
CAROLYN WEI ZHU
MARTHA R. CROWTHER

CHANGING DEMOGRAPHIC AND SOCIOECONOMIC trends have drastically influenced the structure of African-American families (Billingsley 1992). The early 1990s brought about increased research, policy, and program attention to the number of grandchildren living in grandparent-maintained households. However, census data document a beginning trend as early as the 1970s. According to the Census reports (1992), the number of children under age 18 living in grandparent-maintained households increased from 2.2 million in 1970, to 2.3 million in 1980, to 3.3 million in 1992. In 1970, slightly more than 3 percent of all children under age 18 were living in a home maintained by a grandparent. This number had increased to almost 5 percent by 1992. Recent research and census data show that this trend has continued. In 1997, for example, 3.9 million children lived in a home maintained by a grandparent, constituting 5.5 percent of all children less than 18 years old (Bryson & Casper 1999).

In addition to these general trends, significant increases have occurred in the number of children living with grandparents where only one or no biological parent is present. Between 1970 and 1992, the greatest increase was among grandchildren living with grandparents with only one parent present (Bryson & Casper 1999). However, between 1992 and 1997, the greatest increase has occurred among grandchildren living with grandparents only, with no biological parent present. Szinovacz (1998) found that

26 percent of African American and approximately 23 percent of Hispanic children lived in households with grandparents, in comparison to 11 percent for whites. She concluded that more than 25 percent of African-American grandmothers and 13 percent white grandmothers are custodial grandmothers at some time during their lives. African Americans were more likely to be grandparent caregivers than other races; however, very little empirical research has explored their experiences. A general conclusion in demographic studies (Fuller-Thomson, Minkler, & Driver 1997; Szinovacz 1998) is that custodial caregiving among grandmothers is prevalent in the population and involves long-term commitment.

Grandmothers often assume care of their grandchildren as a result of family crises such as drug use among parents, unemployment, teenage pregnancy, divorce, abuse and neglect, abandonment, and death of a parent (Billingsley 1992; Burton 1992; Minkler, Roe, & Price 1992). They also assume care of their grandchildren because of some of the more recent societal problems such as acquired immunodeficiency syndrome (AIDS), (Honey 1998; Lesar, Berber, & Simmel 1995–96; LeBlanc, London, & Aneshensel 1997) and incarceration of the parents of the grandchildren (Barnhill 1996; Dressel & Barnhill 1994).

However, in spite of the growing interest among researchers, policymakers, and practitioners, currently there is very little empirical research on the demographic, social, and health factors influencing caregiving among African-American grandmothers raising their grandchildren. This chapter provides information regarding social, demographic, and health characteristics of intergenerational families comprised of African-American grandmothers who are raising their grandchildren.

BACKGROUND

African-American Grandmothers: Raising a Second Generation

In African-American families, it not uncommon for grandparents to assume responsibility for a grandchild, great-grandchild, niece, or nephew when a parent is no longer able or willing to care for his or her child. The high proportion of African-American children living with grandparents—grandmothers in particular—reflects a continuing pattern of co-residence and shared caregiving in African-American families (Roe, Minkler, & Barnwell 1994; Stack 1974; Wilson 1986). Over the past two decades, the crack-cocaine epidemic, AIDS, and the incarceration of the grandchildren's parents have contributed to the dramatic increase in the prevalence of surrogate parenting by African-American grandmothers. It is this unprecedented proliferation of grandmothers who are caring for large numbers of grandchildren that has received the nation's attention.

Many of these grandmothers are elderly and encounter a number of challenges, including their failing health or the need to provide support to the absent parent of the grandchild. Other challenges might include lack of support, need for or lack of respite care, affordable housing, access to good medical care, psychological issues, as well as other family problems that put a strain on her ability to care for the grandchildren (Burton & De-Vries 1993; Kelley 1993; Minkler & Roe 1993, 1996). Some grandparents may not have financial resources to take care of their grandchildren and must return to work or use their savings to support them; others are simply not comfortable in the role of grandparent, particularly young grandmothers who experience role conflict between work and caregiving (Burton & DeVries 1993). The above challenges are intensified by the conditions of some grandmothers who dwell in communities infested with crime, poverty, disorganization, and the sale and use of crack-cocaine.

African-American Grandmothers: Caring for Grandchildren Affected by the Crack-Cocaine Epidemic

The crack-cocaine epidemic has serious consequences for African-American families and communities (Seamon 1992). A number of studies have cited the consequences of the crack-cocaine epidemic on African-American grandmothers who are caring for their grandchildren (Burton 1992; Minkler, Roe, & Robertson-Beckley 1994; Roe, Minkler, & Barnwell 1994; Seamon 1992). Substance abuse is the most common reason for the increase in the number of children living with grandparents (Minkler, Roe, & Robertson-Beckley 1994), although not much is known about how this problem affects the well-being of the grandchildren and the grandmother-caregiver. Caring for grandchildren in the midst of the drug epidemic may result in emotional problems and hardships for the grandmother as well as for grandchildren whose parents are actively involved with drugs.

In a 1992 Congressional Hearing on "Grandparents as Parents: Raising a Second Generation," Dr. Evelyn Davis, director of Developmental Pediatrics at Harlem Hospital Center, reported findings from a study of 175 African-American children under six years old who were prenatally exposed to crack-cocaine and other drugs. She testified that approximately 40 percent of all children referred to her were cared for by grandparents. In her statement, she emphasized the problems grandparents faced in trying to care for their drug-exposed grandchildren with unique behavioral and developmental problems. Davis found that the grandchild suffered from a number of abnormalities resulting from the mother's drug use. Among these were premature births (36 percent), language delay (90 percent), fine motor delay (63 percent), gross motor delay (37 percent), delay in social skills (50 percent), hyperactivity (39 percent), neurological problems requiring treatment (30 percent), retardation and autism (8 percent), cerebral palsy (8 percent), and sleep problems (50 percent). A majority of the children had problems with impulsive behavior and the inability to learn from past mistakes.

New problems for African-American grandmothers present challenging role responsibilities. In their study of surrogate parenting, Burton and DeVries (1993) reported that African-American grandparents, for the most part, view their role as necessary for the survival of the family. This role assumption reflects the strengths of grandmothers and the resiliency and adaptability of African-American families (Billingsley 1992). It is common in African-American families for grandmothers to routinely place the needs of their family above their own. Satisfying the needs of the family is synonymous with satisfying their own needs. In fact, the needs of the family are intricately attached to their own identity. The strength and survival of African-American families are dependent on the commitment and unselfish acts of grandmothers.

Although grandmothers love their grandchildren and are committed to caring for them, their grandparental roles may not always be gratifying (Burton & DeVries 1993). Some grandmothers expressed dismay because there were so many things they had to deal with in providing care for their grandchildren. Concerns involved the permanence of child-care, school, social, and physical activities. Other problems included multiple child-care responsibilities resulting in stress, job-related conflicts for grandmothers who were working, and limited time for themselves (Burton & DeVries 1993).

Consequences of Custodial Parenting among African-American Grandmothers

The health and social problems associated with custodial caregiving among African-American grandmothers have resulted in considerable stress (Burton 1992; Davis 1992; Minkler, Roe, & Robertson-Beckley 1994). Burton (1992), in her study of grandmothers caring for children affected by the crack-cocaine epidemic, found that 86 percent of the sample felt depressed or anxious most of the time. Similarly, Davis (1992) found that grandmothers reported feeling overwhelmed by the many clinic visits required by their disabled grandchildren. Retarded or autistic children are often involved in special programs requiring the weekly involvement of the primary caregiver. Because of their involvement with the grandchildren, grandmothers often neglect their own social, emotional, and physical needs (Davis 1992). Minkler, Roe, and Robertson-Beckley (1994) found that many women reported decreased contact with family and friends and a decline in marital satisfaction.

The importance of African-American grandmothers in black families is unquestioned (Billingsley 1992; Frazier 1939; Hill 1971, 1997; Ladner & Gourdine 1984); however, the contemporary roles and challenges present serious consequences, if not a threat, to the strong tradition of African-American families. African-American families have traditionally been described as extended family networks with a lot of cooperation and support. However, Burton (1992) found that African-American grandmothers are not receiving consistent and reliable support from family members. Minkler and Roe (1993), on the other hand, found that African-American grandmothers had a rich social network of family members and friends. To the contrary, however, they also found social isolation among the younger grandmothers who were experiencing role conflict caused by employment and childcare (Minkler & Roe 1993). Other psychological responses included feelings of guilt and shame because of the drug use of their children. Raising grandchildren with special needs (Davis 1992; Brown & Monye 1995; Burton 1992; Minkler & Roe 1993), as well as caring for adolescents (Kee 1997) who have their own unique set of needs, all present social, health, and psychological problems for African-American grandmothers.

In their exploratory study of the physical and emotional health of African-American grandmothers, Minkler, Roe, and Price (1992), using a self-rated measure, found that 44 percent of the respondents were in pain at the time of the interview: 49 percent had back pain; and 25 percent had heart trouble and other physical symptoms. Slightly over one-third reported a worsening of already-existing poor health. Fifty-four percent of the sample reported being in good or excellent physical health, and almost 50 percent stated that their health never interfered with their caregiving roles. A number of other health problems such as depression, insomnia, hypertension, back and stomach pain, and other problems associated with the physical and emotional demands of child care have been reported (Minkler & Roe 1996). Although the number of health problems reported by African-American grandmothers is high, it may still be under-reported, since they tend to minimize the severity of the health problems in an effort to show that they are capable of taking care of their grandchildren. Changes in social behaviors such as an increase in cigarette smoking and alcohol use by the grandmothers are also associated with the demands of caring for grandchildren (Burton 1992; Minkler & Roe 1996: Minkler, Roe, & Price 1992).

The unprecedented proliferation of grandmothers who are caring for large numbers of grandchildren has gotten the nation's attention. However, in spite of the growing interest among researchers, policy-makers, and practitioners, currently there is very little empirical research on the demographic, social, and health factors influencing caregiving among custodial African-American grandmothers. And, with the increase in AIDS, crack-cocaine use, and the incarceration of the parents of the grandchildren, custodial grandmothers face escalating financial and social burdens. In an effort to shed light on the challenges that African-American grandmothers face, this chapter will provide a descriptive analysis of selected social, demographic, and health variables among grandmothers who are primary caregivers in intergenerational households, by using a sample of grandmothers obtained from the Piedmont region of North Carolina.

METHODS

Sample

A cross-sectional design was used to examine the demographic characteristics, health, and psychological well-being among African-American grandmothers who have primary responsibility for raising their grandchildren. The study population consisted of 99 African-American custodial grandmothers who resided in the Triangle and Piedmont areas of North Carolina. Grandmothers who were eligible for the study were required to meet the following criteria: (1) had been the primary caregiver for one or more child under the age of 18; (2) were noninstitutionalized; (3) resided in the Triangle and Piedmont areas of North Carolina; and (4) viewed herself as being in a grandparenting relationship with the grandchild.

Data Collection

Five North Carolina counties were involved in the study; these included Durham, Guilford, Mecklenburg, Orange, and Wade. A number of organizations and persons provided assistance in identifying grandmothers who met the study criteria. The North Carolina Division on Aging, Durham County Social Services, Durham County Housing Authority, Orange County Housing Authority, senior centers, support groups, churches, community nurses, mental health centers, family social workers in public schools, and juvenile-detention facilities were among the agencies involved. Representatives from these agencies were asked to identify grandmothers within their domain who were custodial caregivers for at least one grandchild. The study also used word-of-mouth recruitment through local African-American churches, cultural community organizations, and grandparent participants. After a list of grandmothers had been identified, those who expressed an interest in the study were prescreened to determine their eligibility for inclusion. Once the inclusion criteria were satisfied, appointments were made by the first author to meet with the grandparent at a location convenient to the subject. Most of the interviews (n = 90) took place in subjects' homes, with the exception of a few (n = 9) who were interviewed at support-group meetings or other locations designated by the respondent.

The data-collection instrument was pretested by using a focus group of ten grandmother-caregivers to eliminate any difficult questions and make the protocol more understandable and relevant to this sample. All interviews were conducted by the (principal-investigator) first author between August 1999 and November 2000. Most interviews took from two-to-three hours each to complete. However, it was not unusual for an interview to take as long as four or five hours, depending on the openness and personality of the grandmother. This was the only opportunity for many grandmothers to discuss their experiences and vent their difficulties and frustrations. In approximately 20 percent of the cases, where an interview became too extensive, a follow-up meeting was scheduled or completed over the telephone. These were instances where the grandchild may have returned from school and needed the attention of the grandmother, or the grandchild's parent may have entered the home and hence the grandmother did not wish to discuss her child-care burdens in her/his presence. Because of the demanding work schedules of some grandmothers, telephone interviews were necessary.

Measures

The Institutional Review Board of Duke University Medical Center approved all instruments used in this study. The instrument consisted of approximately 350 questions comprised of primarily quantitative information, and approximately 30 questions consisted of qualitative information. The major issues discussed in the questionnaire included the following 11 components: demographic characteristics, household composition, economic resources, family competing demands, reasons for providing care, church and social support, value orientation and family relationships, physical health and chronic conditions, life satisfaction, depression, and stress symptoms. Only demographic and social characteristics, reasons for caregiving, physical health status, and psychological health are included in this analysis.

Demographic and Social Characteristics. The demographic characteristics include age, income, education, marital status, sources of income, religiosity, and household composition. Reasons for providing care is a listing of 16 reasons, and each respondent was asked to check only those that were relevant to their situation. Besides caring for grandchildren and great-grandchildren, grandmothers may also have competing family demands, which might require caring for a sick husband, ailing parents, or some other family member. Grandmothers were asked to respond to questions pertaining to their caregiving responsibilities, their thoughts and feelings regarding caregiving, and their value system regarding the role of caregiving in families. Additionally, relationship questions were asked related to the quality of the relationship between the child and grandmother, the child and the biological father, the child and the biological mother, and the grandmother and the son or daughter of the child/children. Religious participation consisted of a set of questions about church participation and involvement. These included church membership, frequency of church attendance, and frequency of participation in church service and related church activities. They were asked about the extent to which their spiritual beliefs helped in providing care for their grandchildren.

Physical Health. This measure consisted of a list of physical health conditions that the respondent might have (Brown & Monye 1995). The conditions included arthritis, cancer, stroke, diabetes, problems breathing, high blood pressure, circulation problems, heart problems, glaucoma, and kidney disease.

Psychological Health. Psychological health was measured by a modification of the Center for Epidemiological Studies Depression Scale (CES-D) (Radloff 1977). There were no changes in the content of the questions. All questions from the CES-D were included in their original version. However, the response categories were combined into a yes/no format for reporting the presence or absence of a symptom during the week preceding the interview. The revised instrument has been tested extensively by Duke University investigators (Blazer, Burchett, Service, & George 1991) to determine its comparability to the original CES-D Scale. Their results indicate that the modified instrument was virtually identical to the original one. Previous studies have shown that a score of 16 on the original scale represents clinically significant depressive symptom (Radloff 1977). Blazer and colleagues (1991) showed that a score of nine or greater on the revised scale was equivalent to the score of greater than or equal to 16 on the original scale. Accordingly, we use a dichotomous variable with a score of nine or greater to indicate the presence of depressive symptoms in the sample.

Results

Table 3.1 shows the social and demographic characteristics of the 99 grandmothers included in this study. The grandmothers ranged in age from 38 to 88, with an average age of 58. Sixty-five percent of the sample were 45 to 64 years old; 20 percent were considered elderly, ranging in age from 65 to 74; and 6 percent were among the oldest-old (75 and older). The average years of schooling was 11.5. Thirty-six percent were high school graduates, and 38 percent were high school dropouts. Twenty-five percent received some college education. Almost three-quarters of grandmothers (74 percent) were unmarried and heads of household. Twenty-six percent of the grandmothers in this sample were married and lived with their spouses. Just over half of the grandmothers (51 percent) were retired. Many grandparents had full-time and/or part-time employment. Twenty-nine percent were employed full-time, and 9 percent were employed part-time. The remaining 9 percent who reported that they were neither employed nor retired were grandmothers who had never been in the paid workforce.

There is considerable variation in the grandmothers' income levels. The average family income in this sample of grandmothers was $21,100, with a median income of $17,500 (1998 dollars). Eleven percent had incomes below $5,000; 22 percent had incomes between $5,001–10,000; 24 percent between $10,001–20,000; 15 percent between $20,001–30,000; 11 percent between $30,001–40,000; and 16 percent greater than $40,000. The higher incomes were associated with married grandmothers, or grandmother-maintained households consisting of employed adult children. Grandmothers received their income from a number of sources: 54 per-

Table 3.1

Sociodemographic Characteristics of African-American Caregiving Grandmothers (*N* = 99)

Variables	*Mean (s.d.)*
Age	**57.6 (10.1)**
Younger than 45 (%)	8.1
45–54 (%)	35.4
55–64 (%)	30.3
65–74 (%)	20.2
75 or older (%)	6.1
Years of schooling completed	**11.5 (2.6)**
Less than high school (%)	38.4
High school graduate (%)	36.4
Some college (%)	21.2
College graduate (%)	4.0
Marital status (%)	
Married	26.3
Divorced/separated	40.4
Widowed	22.2
Never married	11.1
Years lived in current home	**14.5 (11.2)**
Employment status (%)	
Retired	51.5
Full-time	29.3
Part-time	9.1
Not employed	9.1
Other	3.0
Family income (in 1998$)	
Income ('000$)	21.1 (16.0)
Median income ('000$)	17.5
Less than $5,000 (%)	11.1
$5,001–$10,000 (%)	22.2
$10,001–$15,000 (%)	15.2
$15,001–$20,000 (%)	9.1
$20,001–$30,000 (%)	15.2
$30,001–$40,000 (%)	11.1
Greater than $40,000 (%)	16.2
Sources of income (%)	
Wages and salaries	53.5
Social Security (excluding SSI)	43.4
Welfare payments/Work First	38.4
Retirement pension	23.2
Disability payments	15.2
SSI	13.1
Assistance from family members or other sources	6.1
Wealth	
Own home (%)	56.6
Own any other real estate (%)	16.2

Table 3.1 (continued)

Variables	*Mean (s.d.)*
Religion (%)	
Baptist	55.6
Methodist	11.1
Other religion	25.3
No religion	8.1

cent received their incomes from wages and salaries; 43 percent from social security; 38 percent from welfare payments; 23 percent from retirement pensions; 15 percent from disability payments; and 13 percent from Supplemental Social Security Income. Six percent of their income came from relatives or other sources. Nearly 57 percent owned their own homes, and 16 percent reported owning other real estate property. A majority of the home-owners lived in rural North Carolina, primarily in mobile-home dwellings.

Religion is very important to the custodial grandparents in the sample. More than 50 percent of the sample were Baptist (56 percent); 11 percent were Methodist; and 25 percent reported other religious affiliations including Catholic, Lutheran, Muslim, Pentecostal, Presbyterian, and Holiness. Only a small number of grandmothers in the sample (8 percent) were not church members. However, regardless of their lack of church membership, all grandmothers said that their spiritual beliefs were very important in providing care to their grandchildren. Typical responses were: "Prayer keeps me going," "Without God, I don't know what I would do," "My belief in God helps me to discipline better," or "My spiritual beliefs give me more patience."

Table 3.2 shows a variety of reasons for caregiving among African-American grandmothers. Grandmothers often reported multiple reasons for providing care to their grandchildren. The primary reason was abuse of drugs and alcohol (45 percent) by the parents of the grandchildren. This is also the paramount reason reported in the literature (Burton 1992; Minkler & Roe 1993; Minkler, Roe, & Price 1992; Roe, Minkler, & Barnwell 1994). The next most-often reported reason for grandchild care was parents' neglecting the grandchild's needs, consisting of 38 percent of the sample. Other reasons included the need to work (23 percent); teenage pregnancy (18 percent); parent has emotional or mental problems (17 percent); incarceration (12 percent); and parent deceased (10 percent) among the parents of the grandchildren.

A combined 16 percent reported taking care of their grandchildren because of the parents' divorce, needing a break, AIDS, physical disability, mental and sexual abuse of the child, and school. Almost one-third (30 percent) of the sample reported taking care of their grandchildren for rea-

Table 3.2

Reasons for Providing Care for Grandchildren Reported by African-American Caregiving Grandmothers (N = 99)

Grandchild's parent	*Percentage*
Abused alcohol and drugs	45.5
Neglected child's needs	38.4
Needed to work	23.3
Teenager	18.2
Had emotional/mental problems	17.2
Incarcerated	12.1
Deceased	10.1
Divorced	4.1
Needed a break	3.0
Has AIDS	3.0
Physically disabled	2.0
Mentally abused child	2.0
In school	1.0
Sexually abused child	1.0
Other reasons	30.3

sons other than those listed on the questionnaire. Reasons in this category consisted of financial-related problems, such as the mother of the child not being able to afford a place to live. It should be noted that these reported reasons are not mutually exclusive experiences.

Table 3.3 reports the physical and psychological health of the grandmothers in this sample. Grandmothers had a number of chronic illnesses that could interfere with child-care responsibilities. More than 15 percent of the grandmothers reported having seven of the ten chronic conditions inquired in the survey: almost 62 percent of the sample suffered from hypertension; 44 percent had arthritis; 25 percent had problems breathing; 25 percent had diabetes; 22 percent had circulation problems; 17 percent had heart problems; and 17 percent had glaucoma. Among grandmothers who reported having a chronic condition, we also asked whether the condition interfered with daily life and child-care responsibilities. Many grandmothers who had arthritis, breathing problems, circulation problems, and kidney problems reported that the condition interfered with their daily activities. Thirty-two percent of the grandmothers who reported having arthritis said that it interfered with their daily lives; 28 percent of those who had breathing problems; 36 percent of those with circulation problems; and 28 percent of those reporting kidney disease. Cancer (8

Table 3.3

Physical and Psychological Health of African-American Caregiving Grandmothers (*N* = 99)

Variables	*Mean (s.d.)*	*Condition interferes with daily life*[1]
Physical conditions (%)		
high blood pressure	61.6	6.4
arthritis	44.4	31.8
problems with breathing	25.3	28.0
diabetes	25.3	16.0
circulation problems	22.2	36.4
heart problems	17.2	23.5
glaucoma	17.2	11.8
cancer	8.1	12.5
stroke	8.1	25.0
kidney disease	7.1	28.6
Psychological health		
CES-D score (range 0–20)	4.5 (5.0)	—
depressed[2] (%)	19.2	—

Notes: [1]Among those who report having the condition only. [2]"Depressed" is defined to be having a CES-D score of nine or higher.

percent), stroke (8 percent), and kidney disease (7 percent) were less often reported to have interfered with the grandmothers' daily activities. We measured the grandmothers' psychological health using a modified CES-D Scale. The scores ranged from 0 to 20; the average score of this sample was 4.5. Nineteen percent of the sample scored in the range for depressive symptomatology.

Discussion

The primary purpose of this chapter was to provide a sociodemographic and health profile of custodial African-American grandmothers. There is a greater prevalence of grandmother-headed households in African-American families (Szinovacz 1998). We found that 74 percent were unmarried and heads of households. The grandmothers ranged in age from 38 to 88, with a mean age of 58. The average family income was $21,100. Thirty-three percent had incomes below $10,000. The primary reason for providing care, consistent with existing literature and census reports, was abuse of drugs and alcohol by the parents of the grandchildren. The grandmothers in the sample had a number of chronic physical-health conditions that often interfered with child-care responsibilities.

Conditions such as arthritis, breathing problems, circulation problems, and kidney problems all interfered with activities of daily living. More than 15 percent of the grandmothers reported having seven of the ten chronic conditions listed in the study. In spite of the observed stress, only 19 percent of the grandmothers scored in the range for depressive symptomatology as measured by a modified CES-D Scale. It is very likely that a stress or anxiety measure could be more appropriate.

The grandparenting role presents a number of problems for grandmother caregivers. These include not having enough money to obtain the things they needed, not having enough time for themselves, not being able to attend church, lost friendships, the need for after-school and summer programs, poor health, inability to discipline properly, inability to negotiate school problems, lack of cooperation and support from parents, lack of parental involvement in the child's life, and social abuse from the grandparents' children.

In cases where grandparents are elderly, this problem, along with many others, become much more serious for the grandchild as well as the grandparent caregiver. Twenty-six percent of the grandparents in our study were age 65 and older. Grandmothers love their grandchildren and feel that they are providing the best care; however, more research is needed to determine the quality of care concerning different issues of caregiving. Although grandparental care seems to be the next best thing to parents, more attention needs to be given to the impact of grandparental caregiving with respect to parenting skills on the grandchild's development. The vast majority of the children were born to single mothers. Most children did not know their father or had little or no contact with him, and most had little or no relationship with their mother. In cases where there was a relationship with the mother, it was often inconsistent and strained. More research is needed that addresses the complex social interactions among children, grandparents, and parents, and how these might affect the long-term success of children who are in the care of grandparents.

All but a few grandmothers in this sample stated that they felt overwhelmed by the responsibility. Burton (1992) found that grandparents frequently requested respite care for parenting. However, out of guilt that they might have failed as parents, and out of fear that child-protective services might remove the children from their care, African-American grandmothers are often reluctant to seek opportunities for a break. In comparison to younger grandmothers, older African-American grandmothers report feeling less overwhelmed by responsibility and their attitudes about caregiving were generally more approving. Older African-American women place caregiving at the forefront of their existence. Caregiving helps older African-American women define who they are and their worth in society. The sacrifices they make for their children and grandchildren are central to their belief system concerning their roles as women and their devotion to children, which is shaped by their West

African heritage. Older women's beliefs about family, and the extended family network, have a strong influence on their attitudes about caregiving roles. Although the support of the extended family has a long history in Black-American culture, it can no longer shield grandmothers from the burdens and stresses of caregiving brought on by the crack-cocaine epidemic, AIDS, and the incarceration of young African-American mothers and fathers. Being once the norm in African-American families, changes in family structure and the impact of societal problems have contributed to the erosion of extended family support.

The head-of-household status of the grandmother increases her role responsibilities within the family unit. She is not only the "guardian of the generations" (as described by E. Franklin Frazier [1939]), she describes herself in the present study as caretaker, nurturer, role model, setter of family values, maid, spiritual teacher, advisor, leader, source of wisdom, one who keeps the family together, financial provider, social and emotional supporter, mother, father, and everything to everyone. In spite of her age, frailty, or financial status, the custodial African-American grandmother is typically depended upon by all members within the family unit, as well as by grown children not living in the home. African-American grandmothers not only provide social, emotional, and financial support to their children, they also serve as enablers for them, which encourages dependency. For example, one frail 78-year-old grandmother does the laundry for a grown, healthy daughter using washtubs. Aware that her mother did not have laundry facilities, the daughter did not seem to be concerned about how the job got done. Another elderly grandmother cared for three teenage boys while her son lived in the home and provided no financial support and no child-care assistance. Grandparents were routinely taken advantage of by their grown children. However, in spite of the overwhelming responsibility, African-American grandmothers take pride in their role as caregivers.

Researchers must focus on the needs of unmarried custodial grandmothers. There is little empirical research on the impact of raising grandchildren on African-American grandmothers. In spite of the increasing numbers of grandparental caregivers in the population, not much is known about the broad social and demographic characteristics of African-American grandmothers. Longitudinal studies are needed to get a closer look at the long-term effects of caregiving on African-American grandmothers.

The circumstances under which grandparents assume care of their grandchildren have not been well-researched. We believe that research on this issue would broaden our understanding of the transition from parental care to grandparental care. In addition to the process of how children came to the care of grandparents, more information is needed concerning how informed are African-American grandmothers in providing care at different stages of the grandchild's social and emotional development. Although many similarities exist among African-American and white custodial grandmother caregivers, many differences are present (Fuller-Thomson, Minkler, & Driver 1997; Szinovacz 1998). The meaning of caregiving across different racial and ethnic groups suggests different needs for research and program development.

To date, much of the research on custodial African-American grandparenting has focused on the impact of the crack-cocaine epidemic. While this is a serious issue and should not be neglected, the impact of incarcerations of young mothers and the AIDS epidemic must also be considered in research efforts. The issues surrounding imprisonment, such as the initial separation and later reunion with the mother, visitations, and transportation, all affect the grandparental caregiver. However, how these factors affect grandmothers has not been fully explored. All three issues, as well as many others discussed in this chapter, are having devastating and long-term consequences on African-American communities nationwide.

Several limitations must be taken into account concerning this sample of custodial grandmother caregivers. This sample included only grandmothers who were mobile and generally healthy, with only a few debilitating problems. We do not know what differences there might be among custodial caregivers who are less mobile and who have more severe health conditions. The sample does not represent a broad range of income, education, and occupational differences. However, in spite of these limitations, there are specific characteristics in this sample that have similarities to national data (Bryson & Casper 1999; Fuller-Thomson, Minkler, & Driver 1997; Szinovacz 1998). We hope this chapter has given a more distinct picture of the characteristics and plight of African-American grandmothers who are primary caregivers in intergenerational households. Perhaps we can refocus our attention on the need to support families maintained by grandmothers by assisting them in developing strong family units. Policies that support intergenerational families must be an ongoing agenda in the twenty-first century.

ACKNOWLEDGMENTS

This research was supported by the Duke University Center for the Study of Aging and Human Development and the National Institutes of Health, National Institute on Aging, Physiology in Aging Grant #2T32AG00029. I would like to thank Dr. Linda K. George, my mentor, for her support, advice, and assistance. My deepest appreciation is extended to the grandparent caregivers who agreed to share their time and caregiving experiences.

REFERENCES

Barnhill, S. (1996). "Three generations at risk: The imprisoned women, their children, and the grandmother caregiver." *Generations 20*, no.1:39.

Billingsley, A. (1992). *Climbing Jacobs's ladder: The enduring legacy of African American families*. New York: Simon & Schuster.

Blazer, D., B. Burchett, C. Service, and L. George. (1991). "The association of age and depression among the elderly: An epidemiologic exploration." *Journal of Gerontology 46*, no. 6:M210–15.

Brown, D. R., and D. B. Monye. (1995). *Midlife and older African Americans as intergenerational caregivers of school-aged children*. AARP Andrus Foundation Final Report. Research Information Center, Washington, DC.

Bryson, K., and L. Casper. (1999). *Co-resident grandparents and grandchildren*. U.S. Census Bureau, Current Population Reports, Special Studies, Washington, DC, pp. 23–198.

Burton, L. M. (1992). "Black grandparents rearing children of drug-addicted parents: Stressors, outcomes, and social service needs." *Gerontologist 32*, no. 6: 744–51.

Burton, L. M., and C. DeVries. (1993). "Challenges and rewards: African-American grandparents as surrogate parents," in *Families and Aging*, ed. L. Burton. Amityville, NY: Baywood Publishing.

Davis, E. (1992). "Grandparents as parents: Raising a second generation." Special Congressional Committee on Aging, serial no. 102-24.

Dressel, P., and S. Barnhill. (1994). "Reframing gerontological thought and practice: The case of grandmothers with daughters in prison." *Gerontologist 34*: 685–90.

Frazier, E. F. (1939). *The Negro family in the United States*. Chicago: University of Chicago Press.

Fuller-Thomson, E., M. Minkler, and D. Driver. (1997). "A profile of grandparents raising grandchildren in the United States." *Gerontologist 37*:406–11.

Hill, R. (1971). *The strengths of black families*. New York: Emerson-Hall.

———. (1997). *The strengths of the African-American family: Twenty-five years later*. Washington, DC: R and C Publishing.

Honey, E. (1998). "AIDS and the inner city: Critical issues." *Social Casework: The Journal of Contemporary Social Work* (June):365–70.

Kee, D. M. (1997). *Grandparents as caregivers of adolescent grandchildren*. M.A. thesis, California State University, Long Beach.

Kelley, S. J. (1993). "Caregiver stress in grandparents raising grandchildren." *Image: Journal of Nursing Scholarship 25*, no. 4:331–37.

Ladner, J., and R. Gourdine. (1984). "Intergenerational teenage motherhood: Some preliminary findings." *A Scholarly Journal of Black Women 1*, no. 2:22–24.

LeBlanc, A., A. London, and C. Aneshensel. (1997). "The physical costs of AIDS caregiving." *Social Science and Medicine 45*, no. 6:915–23.

Lesar, S., M. Berber, and M. Simmel. (1995–96). "HIV infection in children: Family stress, social support and adaptation." *Exceptional Children 62*, no. 3:224–36.

Minkler, M., and K. Roe. (1993). *Grandmothers as caregivers: Raising children of the crack-cocaine epidemic*. Newbury Park, CA: Sage Publications.

———. (1996). "Grandparents as surrogate parents." *Generations 20*:34–38.

Minkler, M., K. Roe, and M. Price. (1992). "The physical and emotional health of grandmothers raising grandchildren in the crack-cocaine epidemic." *Gerontologist 32*:752–60.

Minkler, M., K. Roe, and R. Robertson-Beckley. (1994). "Raising grandchildren from crack-cocaine households: Effects on family and friendship ties of African American women." *American Journal of Orthopsychiatry 64*:20–29.

Radloff, L. S. (1977). "CES-D scale: A self-report depression scale for research in a general population." *Applied Psychological Measurement 3*:385–401.

Roe, K., M. Minkler, and R. Barnwell. (1994). "The assumption of caregiving: Grandmothers raising the children of the crack-cocaine epidemic." *Qualitative Health Research 4*, no. 3:281–303.

Seamon, F. (1992). "Intergenerational issues related to the crack-cocaine problem." *Family and Community Health 15*, no. 3:111–19.

Stack, C. B. (1974). *All our kin: Strategies for survival in a black community.* New York: Harper & Row.

Szinovacz, M. E. (1998). "Grandparents today: A demographic profile." *Gerontologist 38*, no. 1:37–52.

U.S. Bureau of the Census. (March 1992). *1990 census of the population, marital status and living arrangements.* Current Population Reports, Population Characteristics, no. 461. Washington, DC: U.S. Government Printing Office, p. 20.

Wilson, M. N. (1986). "The black extended family: An analytical consideration." *Developmental Psychology 22*:246–58.

CHAPTER FOUR

Race and Crime

vulnerability at the margins

LEON E. PETTIWAY

THE DEMARCATION OF MARGINALITY is never static or fixed on the space-time continuum. It shifts with the dawning of enlightenment, and reveals that what was, can no longer be viewed as the margins because the center, our point of reference, has shifted. From our disciplinary critical gaze we construct the margins of human achievement and development, and from this reality we find those individuals who are the most vulnerable. For some agents who construct reality, those at the margins are the individuals most susceptible to injury; they are the most unprotected from danger, attack, and criticism. In a cursory manner, this chapter explores vulnerability in terms of the disciplinary power exerted by criminology. Vulnerability is assessed in light of the inner and outer parameters that affect the formation of the self and the thoughts and dreams that go unrealized. In the end, thoughts *do* matter.

With respect to race and its impact on the question of justice, the discipline has not been silent. Countless studies relate to the overrepresentation of African Americans in the criminal-justice system. So much so that many scholars would agree with Walker, Spohn, and Delone (2000, 1) who assert that an early everyday problem related to criminal-justice issues involves matters of race and ethnicity. The reasons are obvious: Half of the prisoners in the United States (49.4 percent in 1996) are African American, despite the fact that African Americans constitute only 12 percent of the population. . . . About 40 percent of the people currently on death row and 53 percent of all the people executed since 1930 are African Americans (Walker, Spohn, & Delone 2000, 1). Therefore, the discussion of race and crime has always turned on the notion of the disproportionate representation of African Americans, but what has never been addressed in any systematic fashion is "white crime" and "white criminality."

Since white Americans are said to be privileged, empowered by virtue of their race and the status it affords, white criminality would appear to be even more problematic and would appear as fertile ground for criminologists. Why do white Americans commit so much crime? While their numbers do not represent a disproportionate representation, the amount of crime committed by whites, given their majority status, has a profound impact on the quality of life in America. Why is it that criminologists have not ventured into the field of white studies? For criminology, race has come to mean "nonwhite."

Overwhelmingly, mainstream American culture and the intellectual critique of that culture has been articulated by white writers who have positioned themselves as dispassionate researchers of the lives and fortunes of black Americans. However, white writers writing about whiteness are extremely rare, and those who do are primarily concerned with what it means to be human, standing in for how racial identity influences the lives of white folks. In contrast, African-American writers may be viewed as offering insights into the world of minorities; however, their explanation is viewed as being subjective.

In our discussions of the disproportionate representation of African Americans, the statistics suggest that there might be a disparity in terms of justice, but within this discussion, the seemingly more important question is whether discrimination exists in the criminal-justice system. Mann (1998) and Wilbanks (1987) are cited as two titans with respect to this question. Wilbanks forcefully assails the mythical existence of systematic racism in the criminal-justice system, while Mann assaults the system with a minority perspective that emphasizes the differential treatment of minority people by the criminal-justice system. Consequently, the search for this disparity and attempts to clarify the nature and manner of discrimination continue.

While these questions and the research generated in response to them may be the fodder for the intellectual gristmill, what has been produced is rather pointless and banal. A system that is concerned primarily with the idea of justice can produce nothing other than disparities, because the notion of justice, by its very nature, centers itself in injustice. Ultimately, it is the desire for justice that spawns injustice, or a response to injustice that spawns attempts to garner justice; therefore, the notion of injustice arises dependently upon, and is therefore "inherently" embedded in, any construction of justice. Consequently, in this dualistic frame, we have relegated our investigations to the dichotomous distinctions of presence versus absences, yes versus no, or at best some statement of presence as a contingent phenomenon. As such, it is pointless to center our discussions of race and the criminal-justice system on the question of whether such disparities exist. The more relevant questions *might* be inquiries related to where, how, and under what condition these disparities exist. Therefore, the question of "when" is loaded with possibilities.

The notion of "when" points to the totality of circumstances and conditions favoring and producing a particular outcome. This notion also denotes unique opportunities to grasp at or be attracted to the existence of some phenomena or outcome. It also designates the permanence or momentariness of any given situation or phenomena, and it hints at the simultaneousness and cooperation necessary to produce other occurrences. Moreover, it shows the interdependence and interrelatedness of everything involved in a situation or phenomenon. It becomes apparent that those factors that are present and effective in the creation of any phenomena are by their nature either supported by other conditions or are supported in accordance to their intrinsic nature. It can be said that any outcome is so entirely dependent upon the innumerable conditions that produced it that in no way can or would the conditions retain their individuality and hence must be seen as having no individuality of their own.

The notion of "systematic discrimination" implies the occurrence of discrimination at all stages of the criminal-justice system and suggests that discrimination, in its spatiotemporal patterns, is ubiquitous in the decision to arrest, to prosecute, and to sentence African American offenders. In this formulation, race gains its primacy as the producer of discriminatory outcomes. Alternative renderings attempt to explain discrimination in terms of the manner in which it occurs institutionally, contextually, or individually, but certainly not in a systematic context. Again, we are confronted with a dualistic presentation of reality that centers on difference and separateness rather than wholeness.

African American may be said to be vulnerable because of the manner in which criminologists have viewed race. The central problem is the conceptualization of race and the primacy this concept has gained. One *might* consider whether any concept truly exists. Is "race" a truly existent thing, and can its nature be determined from its own side (not merely something assumed by virtue or having a name applied to it) or from something that is distinct from anything else? That is, is race independent of imputation?

In order to fully understand the conceptualization of race within the discipline, it might be more constructive to investigate the ways in which we instinctively grasp at race as a concept that is supposedly established by its very nature. As it is currently constructed, race is viewed as being distinct in itself: it is not the outcome of other conditions but is believed to be a self-contained phenomenon. We instinctively grasp at the notion of race when certain conditions or circumstances arise. Great hostility arises when we are "assaulted," and we feel an emotional response that propels us to protect some notion of the self. This only reinforces the accusation leveled as an "assault." Therefore, the internal conceptualization of race rises vividly from the center of our hearts and becomes an indication of the manner in which race is central in our consciousness. As such, it becomes important to determine the manner in which race has been envisioned by criminologists.

It is clear that sometimes race is imputed on the body and sometimes it is imputed on the mind. Therefore, the body and mind become the bases of imputing the person, and the body and mind appear to merge into one board set. It is this self-evident expression of race that appears to be something more than an idea imputed onto this set. Race appears to be something that is self-contained, a distinct unit on its own.

Over the collection of its parts and their contents arises the self-evident, all-embracing thing covered by the word "race." The same is true when we talk of a scholar; the basis of imputation is merely the set of the scholar's mind and body, but something self-evident and independent presents itself to us. Therefore, when we recognize only the parts and make use of different arguments of logic, we are relying upon secondhand mental images and everything will be mere words because race does not present itself on it own accord—it merely reactivates our thoughts of race as an object of analysis. As such, one only arrives at some theoretical form of the concept, and race becomes a mixture of the appearance of conventional truth and true existence. As such, African Americans are vulnerable to this form of disciplinary construction and the historical and intellectual traditions that produced it.

A presumption emerges that the world of our thoughts about race, for example, is identical with the world of experience. This delusion is perhaps the main source of our erroneous conception of the world. While it is true that the world we experience includes the world of our thoughts, the opposite is *not* true. In thinking about the reality of race, we do something that is comparable to what a painter does in depicting three-dimensional objects or spaces by rendering them on two-dimensional surfaces. In painting the objects in this way, the painter must renounce certain qualities belonging to the higher dimension and introduce a new order of value, proportion, and optical illusion or foreshortening. Such alterations are only valid from the standpoint of the painting's artificial unity created from the point of view of the artist. Therefore, what has been ascribed to race as a consequence of the laws of logic has resulted in sacrificing the qualities of the higher dimension and generating a perspective formed from what can only be said to be an arbitrary viewpoint or perspective. Consequently, race and the so-called importance of race can only be seen from one side at a time and in the proportion or all the foreshortening associated with the relative position of the articulated viewpoint. So just as the artist deliberately transfers the impression from one dimension to another and has no intention to imitate or reproduce an objective reality but only to express his reaction in front of the object, those who "think" about race, for the most part, have fallen prey to the illusion of having grasped the reality of race and race-membership within their thoughts.

This has been achieved because they have accepted the foreshortening perspective of their one-sided logic as a universal truism.

This is not to say that the use of logic in thinking about race is not justified or necessary, but it *is* to say that such a perspective is important only as a medium of expression, not as a criterion of reality. Formulations derived from the laws of logic should be regarded as only the "means towards understanding the dimensions of consciousness of various mental natures that communicate the various impressions and experiences of different planes or levels that are combined into some organic whole as represented by the thinker."

The value judgments surrounding race also detract us from the reality of race. These value judgments are addictive in quality, but as they become less so our ill-will decreases, because the intensity of our addictions has lessened. Ill-will and addiction to value judgments are related and enhance each other. If one is addicted to "whiteness," for example, one will continue to attempt to possess it, and one shall try to hinder those who lack "whiteness" from sharing what is so strongly coveted by scheming and doing whatever is necessary in order to hold onto "whiteness." In effect, this is the aggrandizement of a sense of self that has its roots in possessiveness and is coupled with ill-will towards others that make for an inseparable union. Consequently, those who speak of the importance of race are in fact deeply a part of their observations with respect to it. A researcher who has experienced anything is part of that experience; a thought is a part of the thing thought of, and we are forced to analyze it from the viewpoint of experience, not from theoretical postulation and deductive verification.

Since all repeated experiences are essentially only analogous occurrences of the first experience, an experience occurs only once. Therefore, a thing or material substance is a series of events that are interpreted as a "thing," and have no more substantiality than any other series of events that we might arbitrarily single out. As such, our discussions are mere figures of speech and are, to some extend, as untrue as the statement that the sun "rises" or "sets."

Some whites have fallen prey to their created conviction that there is something "special" about whiteness, and have been so successful that they have convinced those with other hues of the "truth" and "reality" of their position. While there have been references to white as a "color" of purity, cleanliness, beauty, and sacredness, it has also been the "color" of aging, fear, cold, death, bones, emptiness, and ghosts. However, there is little evidence that whites thought of themselves as symbols of death or viewed themselves as ghostlike characters. In fact, beginning in the fifteenth century, whiteness was a puzzlement (Malcomson 2000), because Europeans began to confront darker-skinned people that caused some to marvel at both their own whiteness and at the diversity of human life.

However, in the early years, race was attributed to other people and not to whites, but the attitude of whites toward nonwhites created the necessary juxtaposition to make them white.

Whiteness developed as a response to blackness, but Malcomson (2000) conveys a general reluctant on the part of white colonial Americans to embrace the codification of whiteness. However, there was solidarity surrounding the desire to distance oneself from blackness, which is reflected in David Hume's opinion written in 1753 that "I am apt to suspect the negroes, and in general all the other species of men (for there are four or five different kinds) to be naturally inferior to whites. There never was a civilized nation of any other complexion than white, nor even any individual eminent either in action or speculation." In a fundamental sense, being white meant not being black, and the quality of whiteness manifested itself in the cultural thinking associated with ancestry and sex. Therefore, it was the absence and exclusion of qualities that manifested the desired effect, but the adoption of American universalism would also mean the extinction of American whiteness.

INNER AND OUTER PARAMETERS OF VULNERABILITY

While the direction of the relationship between drugs and crime is unclear, the connection existing between them has been firmly established. As a consequence of the so-called war on drugs, those who participate in these subcultural worlds are seen as shadowy figures, occupying a landscape that is portrayed as dangerous and hostile. In this construction, these environments and those who reside within them are objects of fear within the general field of anxiety that encompasses much of America.

Social scientists have generally concentrated on the dysfunctional aspects of these subcultures by taking the functional concepts and themes associated with day-to-day life and successfully twisting them (by careful scientific analysis) into the dysfunctional aspects of subcultural life, which are then viewed as endemic or unique to that subcultural world. The overarching backdrop of these research efforts is a desire to document the pain and terror experienced by the most vulnerable and marginalized segments of America society.

The social realities of the marginalized are vulnerable to the conclusions reached by those who view their lives as self-destructive largely because they participate in drug selling or other forms of illegal activity that produce particular personal and societal pressures. As such, it is believed that their lives must be understood within the contextualized history of racial hostility and the structural economic dislocation they experience. Therefore, the wealthy industrialized state is largely responsible for human suffering. This assertion is interesting, given the manner in which liberal structuralist present the nature of suffering and the ways in which they refuse to link any formulation of agency to structualism or even the presentation of culture as a structural phenomenon (see West 2001). As presented by most criminologists and social scientists, suffering appears only in its negative connotation. Therefore, urban ethnographies of vulnerable and marginalized populations stress the gun-and-knife-wielding intimidaters, focus on the knock-down-drag-out fights between observational units, emphasize the emotional scars associated with physical and psychological battering, present data on the increase in child abuse, and document the poisoning of fetuses with drugs and alcohol over the past generations. For the most part, this is the nature of the criminological and social-scientific depiction of misery.

The existence of these conditions is deplorable; however, a more reflexive investigation of suffering might be more insightful. When researchers construct suffering in this manner, they only view the surface of these so-called maladies. Such a view suggests that human suffering would diminish, if not altogether disappear, if the structures that produced these conditions would simply vanish. However, a concern with the alleviation of suffering necessitates a clear and undeluded assessment of the truth and nature of suffering. The truth of suffering cannot be understood or appreciated solely in adhering to the traditional manner in which failed socialization has been presented in the discourses of most social-scientific inquiry. It would, however, be extremely illuminating to investigate the manner in which failed socialization has been given primacy in the construction of human suffering, particularly in marginalized urban communities.

The truth is that human suffering is pervasive, human suffering results from change, and human suffering is misery. If the researcher's interest in vulnerable populations centers primarily on the issues of injustice and oppression associated with the troubles of vulnerable populations by explaining these troubles in light of structures, they misrepresent the social realities facing these populations as well as those who are not members of those populations. Essentially, such a construction can only mean an extreme attachment to the importance of structure as a fundamental element of human success and achievement. It is, in effect, the a priori acceptance of the primacy of structure in social inquiry, and, moreover, it is within the context of this acceptance that proponents fail to understand that suffering also results from the pleasures one experiences. When one retreats from the coldness of winter to find the warmth of a fire but withdraws from that which initially brought relief in order to seek coolness, one has experienced suffering. The pleasure of air conditioning that dispels the ravaging heat on a sultry summer day turns to the chill of suffering that comes with too much coolness. The pleasure that comes in the realized joy of a higher income collapses in the realized suffering that arises under the weight of greater responsibility. The failure to realize that being raised, nurtured, and socialized by structures that do not represent the dysfunctional aspects associated with marginalized life but *do* produce nonetheless individuals who are self-cherishing and absorbed is therefore as self-destructive and "violent" to the social order as any member of any marginalized group. The generalized failure is this: the inability to see that what is viewed as endemic in the marginalized is merely a reflection of the general unhealthiness of the society—unhealthiness in that very part that is believed to be "healthy and functional."

In the end, this is a failure of perception and perspective. The "outsider," as the agent of disciplinary discourse, has been privileged by the socialization afforded to him by the structures that he now assails; however, that privilege is false. It is false because a reliance on structure produces the belief that those external to his "*circumscribed field of analysis*" are not victims of suffering, and it reinforces a reliance on structure as a primary explanation for the social ill witnessed by these agents of disciplinary discourse. As a consequence, it is impossible for some agents *not* to perceive the marginalized as navigating the agents' mentally produced maze—a maze they believe is outside their frame of reference, understanding, construction, and navigation because they reside in a different terrain, one where there is no suffering from the structure found in privilege. Any other construction would destroy their sense of "outsiderness" and the sense of privilege it affords. From this perspective, the notion of "outsider" is both a reality and illusion, but they are realities that are ultimately based on a desire for separateness and uniqueness.

With respect to explaining crime participation and commitment, the desire for separateness and uniqueness creates the belief that something unique occurs in the lives of marginalized people and in the settings they occupy that is different from the experiences and worldviews of the nonmarginalized. For example, to have "juice," according to Bourgois (1996), is be respected on the street through the extreme use of ruthlessness and cruelty as instruments of violence and intimidation. Therefore, researchers who attempt to explain the horrors of urban life assert that "*respect and the search for respect*," as well as adherence to mainstream values embodied in the protestant work-ethic, illuminate their explanations of the social world of the streetwise and the code that sustains them (Anderson 1990, 1999).

Anderson (1999) argues that "decent families" are almost always concerned with hope for the future, if not for themselves then for their children. They are viewed as being more accepting of mainstream values than "street families." Therefore, decent families are more likely to ally themselves with traditional social institutions; they value hard work and self-reliance; they view their difficult situations as tests from God and derive support from faith within their loving church community. In decent families, the "man of the house," according to Anderson, heads his household with such authority that the woman is his partner and the children are his subjects. He is the breadwinner, and any man who is unable financially to support his family invites disrespect from his partner. In decent families, the male has complete control and makes a striking picture in public:

> I witnessed such a display one Saturday afternoon at the Gallery, an indoor shopping mall with a primarily black, Hispanic, and working- to middle-class white clientele. Rasheed Taylor, his wife, Iisha, and their children, Rhonda, Jimmy, and Malika, wandered about the crowded food court looking for a place to sit down to eat. . . . Mr. Taylor . . . summoned his family, and they walked forward promptly and in an orderly way to take their seats. The three children sat on one side and the parents on the other. Mr. Taylor took food requests and with a stern look in his eye told the children to stay seated until he and his wife returned with the food. The children nodded attentively. After the adults left, the children seemed to relax, talking more freely and playing with one another. When the parents returned, the kids straightened up again, received their food, and began to eat, displaying quiet and gracious manners all the while. It was very clear to everybody looking on that Mr. Taylor was in charge of this family, with everyone showing him utter deference and respect. (Anderson 1999, 39)

Ultimately, it appears that Anderson reads this scene as "good or desirable" because it reinforces and confirms his particular self-concept and the conceptualizations he embraces in the sociological discourse. To maintain a consistent "position" with respect to "the marginalized," disciplines must factor-out large amounts of experience and data that would call our consistencies into question. In so doing, Anderson represses Mr. Taylor's negative qualities. On the other hand, in order to speak of the horrors, violence, and all the troubles associated with the code of the streets embraced by the street families, Anderson must repress their positive qualities. Therefore, what seems curious in Anderson's assessment of Mr. Taylor and his family and the manner in which he controls and demands respect is the absence of any consideration of the feminist critique with respect to paternalism.

Any attempt to "search for respect," beyond the internalized struggle for self-realization, produces problems that results in domination and oppression. The continued perpetuation of the belief that respect is a dance between external forces, locked in a battle for dominance, diverts the attention and discussion from what is truly important and meaningful. One may argue that anyone who seeks self-respect from others indicates an emptiness that speaks to their own lack of wholesomeness. Therefore, searching for respect, whether by members of decent or street families, indicates a diminished capacity to realize one's social and psychological health, and the search for respect in objects and things external to the self suggests an over identification with the self or a kind of self-cherishing. It suggests that the individual can only love himself in and through some external object and points to a serious handicap that cannot be called "healthy." Anderson has described unhealthy states in both types of families by adhering to the tendency of researchers in this area to rely upon some notion of external respect as a causal agent.

Assessments of the observed differences between decent and street families may be better served by centering our discussing on individual motivations and whether the individual's or the system's intended consequences are directed towards wholeness and health and not directed towards supporting a structural configuration that may be unhealthy in its current formulation. As discussed by Anderson and others, a search for respect, and the negative consequences associated with this search, are not unique to marginal populations and do not adequately explain the drives and behaviors of so-called marginalized populations. They do, however, make marginalized populations particularly vulnerable to so-called social agents of change by impacting the individual's self-formation. While researchers (e.g., Bourgois 1996; Anderson 1999) continue to express concern that their ethnographies will be misconstrued by those who dismiss the arguments of structuralism for the arguments of agency, researchers continue to build a criminology that is largely unreflexive (see Bourdieu 1977).

REFERENCES

Anderson, Elijah. (1990). *Streetwise: Race, class, and change in an urban community*. Chicago: University of Chicago Press.

———. (1999). *Code of the street: Decency, violence, and the amoral life of the inner city*. New York: Norton.

Bourdieu, Pierre. (1977). *Outline of a theory of practice*. Cambridge: Cambridge University Press.

Bourgois, Philippe. (1996). *In search of respect: Selling crack in El Barrio*. Cambridge: Cambridge University Press.

Malcomson, Scott L. (2000). *One drop of blood: The American misadventure of race*. New York: Farrar Straus Giroux.

Mann, Coramae R. (1998). *Unequal justice: A question of color*. Bloomington: Indiana University Press.

Walker, Samuel, Cassia Spohn, and Miriam DeLone. (2000). *The color of justice: Race, ethnicity, and crime in America*. Belmont, CA: Wadsworth Thomson Learning.

West, Cornel. (2001). *Race matters*. Boston: Beacon Press.

Wilbanks, William. (1987). *The myth of a racist criminal-justice system*. Monterey, CA: Brooks/Cole.

CHAPTER FIVE

The Persecution and Ill-Treatment of African Americans in the Health-Care System in the United States

ROBERT L. BING III

In the United States, most individuals enjoy a higher standard of living than in any other country in the world. U.S. citizens have access to those things that improve the quality of life—adequate housing, food, automobiles, entertainment, education, and health care. Of these areas already identified, health care has become an area of major concern. Sufficient health care, for example, increases quality of life and minimizes long-term medical costs, resulting from inadequate preventive health care. In 2002, Better Nutrition *reports "the United States spends more money per capita than any other country in the world, almost $10,000 for every man, woman, and child." Despite this, the United States ranks seventeenth in the world for health of its citizens.*

—***Better Nutrition*** **(2002)**

COMPOUNDING THE ISSUE of general health care is the fact that certain populations in the United States (e.g., blacks, Hispanics, and the economically disadvantaged) have lower levels of accessibility to health care when compared to their white counterparts. Disturbingly, blacks also suffer from inferior and substandard quality health care, an issue that represents the theme of this chapter. The research consistently shows evidence of disparate treatment of blacks with regard to health care, which suggests that they are victimized by the U.S. health-care system.

ISSUES IN THE EMPIRICAL LITERATURE

A review of the literature reveals much disparity in the treatment of blacks and whites generally. Disparity between blacks and whites exists in all areas of the health-care system: treatment and prevention of illness/disease, use and delivery of health-care services, and health indicators such as mortality and hospitalization rates. The health-care system in America is, at best, apathetic, and, at worst, unconcerned about the health or wellness of blacks in this country. Because preventive measures may often be withheld, blacks frequently receive more surgeries for illnesses that if diagnosed and treated would have resulted in fewer intrusive surgeries (McBean & Gornick 1994).

In contrast, when compared to whites, blacks have a higher incidence of certain types of cancers, including prostate, lung, and colon. Shavers and Brown (2002) reviewed 87 studies of cancer treatment and survival; they found that whites consistently received more aggressive therapy (e.g., surgery) than other groups for lung, prostrate, and colorectal cancers. Similarly, whites received less aggressive therapy (e.g., breast-conserving therapy instead of mastectomy) when its benefits were well-established (Shavers & Brown 2002).

In a study by researchers at the University of California, San Francisco (2001), data revealed disparate use of a highly effective clot-reducing drug used to alleviate the effects of strokes. In fact, only 1.1 percent of blacks received the drug compared to 5.3 percent of whites. After adjusting for age, gender, insurance status, and severity of stroke, racial disparity persisted in all areas of the United States except the Southeast. Another study, conducted on Medicare recipients, attempted to assess racial disparities in quality of care. Researchers found that blacks were less likely to receive beta-blocker medication after suffering heart attacks, eye examinations for those with diabetes, and breast-cancer screening (Schneider, Zaslavsky, & Epstein 2002). Concomitantly, these same investigators specifically identified blacks as being less likely than whites to receive follow-up care for mental illnesses.

In an effort to discover unequal treatment, McBean and Gornick (1994) hypothesized that treatment rates should be similar to disease-prevalence rates. The researchers examined treatment rates among Medicare recipients (a system presumed to guarantee equal access) and found "the prevalence of diabetes among black persons 65 years of age or over is 88 percent greater than among white persons, much lower than the 262 percent greater amputation rate among black [Medicare] beneficiaries in 1992." Simply put, blacks get diabetes almost twice as often as whites, but they suffer amputation of their limbs at nearly four times the rate for white patients.

Meanwhile, Mayberry, Mili, and Ofili (2000) conducted an extensive review of health-related literature; they focused on research published since the secretary of the Department of Health and Human Services released his report revealing disparate treatment of minorities in health care in 1985. Areas in the report include heart disease, stroke, cancer, diabetes, HIV/AIDS, prenatal care, immunization, and mental health; the evidence shows disparate treatment and lower levels of access to health-care services concerning blacks. What is significant about this finding is that in the instance of universally accessible health-care systems, such as the VA system, Medicare, and Medicaid, racial disparities were found, leading the authors to conclude that equal access does not result in equality of treatment (Mayberry, Mili, & Ofili 2000).

Reluctance to Seek Treatment

Young, urban black males face unique barriers to health care though they may well be among those most in need of it. This group suffers disproportionately from violence, sexually transmitted diseases, and HIV infection. Rich (2001) reports that social pressures (i.e., the need to appear "tough") contribute to the reluctance of black males to seek medical attention. There are surely many other reasons for which we can attribute or assign unequal treatment for blacks in American society. Beyond male stupidity and toughness, some of the reluctance may be traced to the treatment of black men in Tuskegee, Alabama in 1932. In one of the most unethical experiments ever to occur in this country (designed to document the course of untreated syphilis), hundreds of afflicted black men were permitted to suffer the disease's debilitating effects—sores, hair loss, weight loss, body pain, paralysis, blindness, dementia, and death. When an effective treatment became available, it was purposefully withheld in the name of science. Arguably, one effect of the Tuskegee experiment continues to be increased levels of suspicion among African Americans, resulting in a representative sample who, simply put, do not trust medical doctors (Lillie-Blanton, Brodie, Rowland, Altman, & McIntosh 2000).

Relatedly, Reiman (2001) reports that black men, in comparison to their white counterparts, receive fewer referrals and tests to diagnose abnormal conditions. In fact, Reiman makes the point that when the referrals were made, it was often too late. These observations point toward the low valuation of life for minority-group members, especially black males. Another inference to be made here is that black males in the year 2002 continue to be treated as guinea pigs, much like their predecessors in Tuskegee. In another interpretation, blacks may be victimized by benign or gross neglect by members of the medical profession. In this case, physicians arguably do not care about the diagnosis or progression of the disease. Why? In part, because there may be few consequences and too numerous financial incentives not to recommend follow-up treatment. In another possible scenario, there may be biases among some in the health-care profession directed toward poor people and visible minorities. This bias probably transcends all income groups, but profoundly impacts black men.

The possible reasons for unequal access to health care and treatment by medics are numerous and may interact in complex ways. Fiscella et al. (2000), for example, cite many ways in which socioeconomic status can affect health care: affordability, transportation, education, literacy, health beliefs, child care, and provider bias. Since blacks make up a large proportion of the lower socioeconomic strata in this country, it stands to reason that they will be among those most adversely affected by these factors. In addition to socioeconomic status, other recurrent themes in the literature are quality of care, trust in providers of health care, and racial discrimination. In a study of a black community, Miller, Seib, and Dennie (2001) found three areas of major concern: people in the community reported an inability to afford health insurance; problems with quality of care, such as long wait times leading to frustration; and a lack of trust in the provider based on the belief that "managed-care plans create financial incentives to underserve patients." On the other hand, Randall (1993) cites unintentional, institutional racial discrimination as the underlying cause of the disparity experienced by blacks. Taken together, the reasons for disparate treatment of black males by primary health-care professionals range from historical indifference to a general insensitivity to the medical needs and interest of minorities (see, for example, Randall [1993]).

VICTIMIZATION

> *If African Americans are sicker as a result of disparate treatment in the health-care system, then they are victims of unequal access to health care. Without decent health, it becomes nearly impossible for African Americans to gain the other attributes (money, education, contacts, know-how) necessary to gain access to the American economic system. Therefore, when African Americans are sick and poor, they are just as enslaved as if the law made them so.*
>
> **—Randall (1993, 129)**

Inequalities between blacks and whites are pervasive throughout the American health-care system. Virtually all areas are affected and the disparities are well-documented. However, the reported findings are not the problem; rather, they are descriptions of symptoms of a larger ill—namely, the victimization of blacks by the health-care system. Blacks, very clearly, do not have the same experiences as their white counterparts; in fact, their experiences with the health-care system are radically different from those of whites. Many black men and women have a different perception of the health-care system: one of distrust and suspicion. Such views are often responsible for a decision not to seek health care. The point to be made here is that in either scenario, there is activity or inactivity that results in the victimization of blacks and people of color.

Access to health care is limited for blacks in many ways. Blacks are often of lower socioeconomic status and may not be able to afford adequate insurance, doctor visits, medications, or transportation to health-care service providers. Compounding the matter, many cannot afford to take time off from work to keep medical appointments, and many cannot afford to pay for extra child care while they visit a doctor. Certainly, some of the more costly treatments are out of reach for poor blacks. By contrast or comparison, there is literature (cf. Reiman [2001]) revealing that the victimization of blacks transcends economic status. Restated, when researchers controlled for the income status of black patients, the medical response continued to be characterized by malfeasance and racial indifference.

Regardless of economic status, experts estimate that blacks actually receive only three-fourths of the amount of care provided to whites (Watson 2001). And while there may be difficulty assigning this victimization to racial bias, the research reveals that blacks may feel more comfortable with a black physician than with a white one. Understandably then, blacks tend to be somewhat mistrustful of the health-care system. The specter of the Tuskegee Syphilis Study continues to haunt many black Americans who cannot trust a system that so blatantly experimented on poor black males during the early 1930s and continued for nearly 40 years. It is conceivable that blacks today fear that they may become contemporary victims of medical doctors engaged in experimentation (Rich 2001; King 1992; Dula 1997). In short, blacks have very legitimate concerns that they may not be treated fairly by the health-care system, a fact that is supported by current research (Lillie-Blanton, Brodie, Rowland, Altman, & McIntosh 2000). Some may refuse necessary surgeries based on suspicion of the physicians' motives such as financial incentives, population control, and genocide, such as in the Tuskegee Syphilis Study (Galavotti & Richter 2000).

One of the most insidious ways in which the health-care system has victimized blacks is in the criminalization of prenatal drug use. The American criminal-justice system uses the health-care system to target black mothers for prosecution. The law requires government-funded hospitals to report positive toxicology results to law-enforcement agencies. Since many consumers of public hospital services are poor black mothers, this group is most adversely affected (Roberts 1997). Instead of receiving treatment, which would allow the family unit to survive, black drug-addicted mothers are sentenced to prison and their children are placed in the homes of extended family members or they become another statistic in the already-overburdened social-services system. Some argue that the public health would be better served by redefining drug abuse as a medical problem rather than a criminal one (Carter 2002).

Suggested Policy Initiatives

Solutions are difficult to identify partly because the issue of racial disparity in the health-care system is not a "hot button" issue for most Americans. Lillie-Blanton and colleagues (2000) found that more than half of whites do not believe that race affects health care in any way. And some studies are hamstrung because some medical forms may not include race, making it difficult to determine the true extent of the pervasiveness of the disparate treatment between white and black Americans. It remains to be seen if the surgeon general's ambitious project (Healthy People 2010) will achieve its goal of eliminating such disparity. Certainly, some benefits will stem from increased public awareness. Researchers recommend expanded insurance (Randall 1993), monitoring doctors' referrals and highlighting differential treatment, which usually results in the doctor altering his/ her practice (Page 1995), and improved documentation of treatment based upon race (Fiscella, Franks, Gold, & Clancy 2000; McBean & Gornick 1994).

Education and information may be one way in which to address the issues and concerns that appear in this chapter. It is hoped, for example, that more information and more research appearing in medical and nonmedical journals will result in a heightened sense of awareness and public embarrassment. Other strategies pertain to improved data-collection as a means of tracking racial disparity and monitoring doctors referrals; subsequently, publishing these disparities may be the only way to increase awareness—with an informed public asking questions about the apparent unequal treatment of minorities. It seems that proactive measures merit discussion as well. One such measure would be to increase efforts to get more black students in medical schools. It has already been demonstrated by the U.S. Department of Health and Human Services (1985) that minority physicians fill critical needs of access to care in low-income inner-city and rural areas. The point here is that access to health care may result from more minority physicians—who can bring a special sensitivity and genuine concern about the health-care needs of black patients. Next, treating the substance-abuse problem in the black community as a public health problem is another proactive initiative that would minimize society's reliance upon traditional criminal-justice responses (cf. Roberts 1997) such as arrests and "brick and mortar." This is surely one way to reduce the victimization of blacks by the health-care and criminal-justice systems.

The health-care system is replete with inequities; the literature shows that even when blacks have equal access, their treatments are at variance with their white counterparts. When race and income interact, the findings suggest that race is more predictive than income among black patients. It is believed that a major part of the problem today may be the increased reliance upon HMOs—where physicians make decisions based upon unwritten economic incentives. New research should address the extent to which physicians "write off" the health-care needs of minority patients (unlike their white counterparts) in pursuit of economic incentives for nonreferrals by the HMO.

Acknowledgment

The author wishes to thank Rhonda Cupp, a graduate research assistant at the University of Texas at Arlington. This project could not have been completed without her assistance.

References

Better Nutrition. (2002 July): 64, 21.

Carter, C. (2002). "Perinatal care for women who are addicted: Implications for empowerment." *Health and Social Work 27*:166–75.

Dula, A. (1997). "Bearing the brunt of the new regulations: Minority populations (and poor people may end up being most of the subjects on experimentation) (In case of emergency: no need for consent)." *Hastings Center Report 27*:11–12.

Fiscella, K., P. Franks, M. R. Gold, and C. Clancy. (2000). "Inequality in quality: Addressing socioeconomic, racial, and ethnic disparities in health care." *Journal of the American Medical Association 283*:257–99.

Galavotti, C., and D. L. Richter. (2000). "Talking about hysterectomy: The experiences of women from four cultural groups." *Journal of Women's Health and Gender-Based Medicine 9*:63–67.

King, P. A. (1992). "The dangers of difference. (Twenty years after: The legacy of the Tuskegee Syphilis Study)." *Hastings Center Report 22*:35–38.

Lillie-Blanton, M., M. Brodie, D. Rowland, D. Altman, and M. McIntosh. (2000). "Race, ethnicity, and the health-care system: Public perceptions and experiences." *Medical Care Research and Review 57*:218–35.

Mayberry, R. M., F. Mili, and E. Ofili. (2000). "Racial and ethnic differences in access to medical care." *Medical Care Research and Review 57*:108–45.

McBean, A. M., and M. Gornick. (1994). "Differences by race in the rates of procedures performed in hospitals for Medicare beneficiaries (health care needs of vulnerable populations)." *Health Care Financing Review 15*:77–90.

Miller, S. T., H. M. Seib, and S. P. Dennie. (2001). "African-American perspectives on health care: The voice of the community." *Journal of Ambulatory Care Management 24*:37–44.

Page, L. (1995). "HCFA study: Race, income factors in access to care (health-care financing administration)." *American Medical News 38*:10–11.

Randall, V. R. (1993). "Racist health care: Reforming an unjust health-care system to meet the needs of African Americans." *Health Matrix: Journal of Law Medicine 3*:127–94.

Reiman, J. (2001). *The rich get richer and the poor get prison: Ideology, class and injustice.* Boston: Allyn & Bacon.

Rich, J. A. (2001). "Primary care for young African Americans." *Journal of American College Health 49*:183–86.

Roberts, D. (1997). *Killing the black body.* New York: Pantheon Books.

Schneider, E. C., A. M. Zaslavsky, and A. M. Epstein. (2002). "Racial disparities in the quality of care for enrollees in Medicare managed care." *Journal of the American Medical Association 287*:1288–94.

Shavers, V. L., and M. L. Brown. (2002). "Racial and ethnic minorities may receive less appropriate cancer treatment." *Journal of the National Cancer Institute 94*:334–57.

Watson, S. D. (2001). "Race, ethnicity and quality of care: Inequalities and incentives." *American Journal of Law and Medicine 27*:203–5.

CHAPTER SIX

Exploiting the Aged in Familial Settings

Anita Neuberger Blowers

A SIGNIFICANT AMOUNT OF RESEARCH has been conducted on ways to reduce abuse against women and children, but very little research has been done on the domestic abuse of elderly persons (Davis & Medina-Ariza 2001). Unlike other forms of family violence, elder abuse has only recently begun to attract scholarly attention. Whereas the 1960s was the decade in which concern spread about child abuse, and the 1970s was the decade in which attention was placed on spouse abuse, attention on elder abuse did not widely surface until the 1980s (Payne & Gainey 2002). Although interest in the area of elder abuse has begun to develop, knowledge about it is analogous to the extent of knowledge about child abuse 20 years ago. In fact, federal definitions of elder abuse, neglect, and exploitation only appeared for the first time in the 1987 Amendments to the Older Americans Act. These definitions were provided only as guidelines for identifying the problems and not for enforcement purposes. Currently, state laws define elder abuse, but state definitions vary considerably from one jurisdiction to another in terms of what constitutes the abuse, neglect, or exploitation of the elderly.

While there is no true agreement on the prevalence of elder abuse, it is clear that elder abuse in domestic settings—namely, in a person's own home, apartment, or other noninstitutional living arrangement—is a serious problem, affecting hundreds of thousands of elderly people across the country (National Center on Elder Abuse 1999a). According to the National Elder Abuse Incidence Study (NEAIS), the best national estimate is that a total of 444,924 elderly persons age 60 and over experienced abuse and/or neglect in domestic settings in 1996. When elderly persons who experienced self-neglect are added, the number increases to approximately 555,000 in 1996 (National Center on Elder Abuse 1998). Yet these figures only begin to estimate the extent of the problem. The NEAIS research is ground-breaking because it provides, for the first time, national incidence estimates of elder abuse. Its findings confirm that officially reported cases of abuse are only the "tip of the iceberg," or a partial measure of a larger, unidentified problem. This study shows that only 16 percent of the estimated cases were reported and substantiated by adult protective service (APS) agencies. The NEAIS has found that there were over five times as many new incidents of elder abuse and neglect previously unidentified and unreported as those that were reported to and substantiated by APS agencies.

The extent of elder abuse is one that will continue to intensify. Estimates from the National Center on Elder Abuse reveal an increase of 150 percent in reported cases of elder abuse nationwide since 1986 (National Center on Elder Abuse 1999b), and the number of victimizations will continue to rise as the older population increases.

THE OLDER POPULATION

The number of elderly persons living in the United States has increased dramatically. In 2000, the older population—persons 65 years and older—numbered 35 million and represented 12.4 percent of the U.S. population, about one in every eight Americans. Since 1900, the percentage of Americans 65 years and older has more than tripled (4.1 percent in 1900 to 12.4 percent in 2000). The older population itself is getting older. In 2000, the 65–74 years age group (18.4 million) was eight times larger than in 1900, but the 75–84 group (12.4 million) was 16 times larger, and the 85 years and older group (4.2 million) was 34 times larger. Additionally, there were 50,545 persons age 100 or over represented in 2002 (.02 percent of the population). This represents a 35 percent increase since 1990.

The older population will continue to grow significantly in the future. By 2030, there will be about 70 million older persons, more than twice their numbers in 2000. People 65 years and older will make up 20 percent of the population by 2030. Minority populations are projected to represent 35.4 percent of the elderly population in 2030, up from 16.4 percent in 2000 (Administration on Aging 2001).

DEFINING ELDER ABUSE

The debate about what constitutes abuse is probably more pronounced in the area of elder abuse than in other subfields of abuse (Barnett, Miller-Perrin, & Perrin 1997). There is enormous disparity in the definitions offered by researchers, policy-makers, and law-makers. One of the difficulties lies in defining *who* is considered to be elderly. Definitional problems persist because there is no agreement on the age requirement of what constitutes "elderly." Some determine the threshold being at age 65 and older, while others may use the age of 60 years. Further, gerontologists have long acknowledged that it may be misleading and inappropriate to rely on biological age as the sole indicator of what is meant to be an elder. There is tremendous variation in the behavioral and cognitive abilities of individuals regardless of age. Thus, functional age may not always be consistent with chronological age.

Determining *abuse* may also be elusive. Although there is a general consensus that physical violence constitutes abuse, there is far more controversy concerning terms like psychological and emotional abuse, mistreatment, and neglect. One difficulty is that there are no clear norms or moral rules about who is responsible for elder care (Philipson 1993). For example, there is no legal requirement that adult children are obligated to help an elder parent in need. "There are no agreed-upon moral or legal standards concerning the responsibility for elders, thus it is difficult to know who should be held accountable for their care or neglect" (Barnett, Miller-Perrin, & Perrin 1997, 255). Similarly, determining the intentionality of the abuse may be complex. This is particularly true in cases where the abuser is elderly. For example, suppose a situation involves an elderly couple in which the wife is heavily dependent on her spouse to be the primary caretaker. The husband may himself suffer from dementia or other problems that render him less able to care for a dependent elder. In this situation, behaviors that appear to be apparent neglect or abuse may not be intentional, but may simply result from limitations or incompetence on the part of the caretaker (Barnett, Miller-Perrin, & Perrin 1997). The first issue is what legal responsibility does the spouse have to provide adequate care, and second, to what extent should they be liable if they are not able to effectively carry out this responsibility?

Another issue is whether self-neglect should be included in definitions of elder abuse. While there is general consensus that neglect situations need to be considered when one is examining elder abuse, there is less agreement as to whether self-neglect should be included. While some researchers exclude self-neglect, others include it as an important category. Determining the appropriate parameters for defining cases of self-neglect can be complicated due to the conceptual ambiguity surrounding this type of abuse (Moody 2002; Barnett, Miller-Perrin, & Perrin 1997). As Moody (2002, 114) states: "[T]his ambiguity and the contradictions that surround the problem of self-neglect among elderly persons result in decisions regarding intervention that may become mired in a morass of ethical dilemmas." Who is to say that behavior that is perceived by some as foolish or harmful is actually a form of self-neglect? If an elder chooses to live in an unsatisfactory living environment or chooses to voluntarily give all their money to someone who appears to be taking advantage of their vulnerabilities, at what point would these acts constitute cases of self-neglect? The line between foolish and neglectful behavior is left open to interpretation. The issue involves balancing the desire to protect a vulnerable individual against the person's right to self-determination (Moody 2002). At what point do the needs to protect outweigh an individual's decision about how they choose to live their life?

The problems in defining elder abuse is indicative in the fact that at least 33 different types of elder abuse have been considered since the concept was first introduced (Jones 1994). The National Center on Elder Abuse divides elder abuse into the following categories: physical abuse, sexual abuse, financial abuse, emotional or psychological abuse, and neglect and violation of rights. The difficulty is that there is little consistency in the precise definitions used by researchers and policy-makers. More recent attempts at defining elder abuse encourage integrated definitions encompassing numerous professional specialties. For example, Harpold (1994) solicited opinions from 63 professionals in law, medicine, psychology, public health, and social work. The final taxonomy consisted of four forms of elder mistreatment (physical, social, psychological, financial). Several years later, Payne, Berg, and Byars (1999, 81) surveyed police chiefs, nursing home professionals, and students enrolled in criminal justice and sociology courses. Payne, Berg, and Byars (1999) offer a broad definition of elder abuse: "Any criminal, physical, or emotional harm or unethical taking advantage of an elderly person." In essence, the lack of a concrete definition has made it virtually impossible to establish a clear understanding of the extent and nature of elder-abuse incidents.

WHY ARE ELDERS AN ESPECIALLY VULNERABLE POPULATION?

Elderly individuals represent a particularly vulnerable segment of society. One of the biggest problems is that most of the abuse is hidden. Reports of domestic elder abuse are often met with disbelief. People just do not think it happens. Overall, elder abuse is even more difficult to detect than child abuse, since the social isolation of some elderly persons may increase both the risk of maltreatment itself and the difficulty of identifying that maltreatment. Further, elder abuse carries with it enormous stigma. Elders do not like to talk about it because they feel ashamed, embarrassed, and humiliated. Thus, they often deny the abuse and are less likely to report cases of mistreatment.

Elderly persons who are unable to care for themselves and/or are mentally confused and depressed are especially vulnerable to abuse and neglect. Approximately a quarter of elders live alone, and many others interact primarily with family members and see very few outsiders (National Center on Elder Abuse 1998). The physical and sensory impairments that accompany old age increase an older adult's vulnerability to abuse. Nationwide, approximately 15 percent of older people are depressed at any one time; 10

percent suffer from some form of dementia; and approximately 14 percent have difficulties with one or more activities of daily living. While rates of depression remain fairly stable across the adult life-span, physical and mental frailties increase, especially among those over the age of 85 (National Center on Elder Abuse 1998). Because of these impairments, elderly individuals may be less aware of their surroundings and less able to detect impending danger; they may have slower reaction times; may lack the physical ability to defend themselves; may be less likely to identify an offender; may be less capable of properly reading and understanding contracts and other written agreements; and are more likely to have predictable daily routines. All of these factors result in increasing the vulnerability of older persons.

Furthermore, the age, health, and sometimes limited resources of elderly persons may make it more difficult for them to recover from their abuse. The physical condition of the elderly may make them more vulnerable to injuries. For example, "older victims suffer internal injuries more than others and are more likely to lose consciousness or suffer cuts and bruises" (Powell 1981, 35). Thus, a relatively minor injury can cause serious, permanent damage. Also, limited incomes mean that a loss of a small amount of money may have much more significant impact on an elderly person. Consider the example of an elderly woman whose apartment was burglarized. Her Social Security check was too small to both pay her living expenses and to repair the broken lock. "I've either got to stop eating for the next two weeks or live in constant fear" (Bard & Dangrey 1979). Also, older victims are psychologically less likely to cope effectively with their victimizations.

Another issue is that society has not established clear norms or moral rules about who carries the responsibility for elder care (Philipson 1993). This ambiguity places elders in an especially vulnerable position by which they are easily forgotten and often neglected. Because there are no agreed-upon moral or legal standards concerning the responsibility for elders, it is difficult to know who should be held accountable for their care or neglect.

Crime Statistics

Most studies and polls on the concerns of older people reveal that the fear of crime ranks as one of their biggest worries. However, crime statistics consistently indicate that older citizens are less likely to be victims of crime than younger ones. According to data from the National Crime Victimization Survey (Klaus 2000), persons age 65 or older had lower victimization rates than any other age groups for all types of violent and property crimes. For violent crimes in particular, the elderly experienced much lower rates than other age groups. Each year from 1992 through 1997, there were five violent crimes per 1,000 U.S. residents 65 years old or older, less than a tenth the rate of 56 crimes per 1,000 of those age 12 through 64.

Relatives, intimates, and other persons well-known to the victim committed about one-fifth of the violence against persons age 65 and older. About two-thirds of these cases occurred while the victim was at home. Further, older victims of murder were two times more likely than younger victims to have been killed by relatives or intimates (Klaus 2000). In general, compared with crime incidents involving other age groups, most crimes against the elderly were more likely to occur in or near their homes and to occur in daylight hours. Differences in lifestyle may account in part for when and where crimes against the elderly occurred. About 22 percent of elderly victims of violence reported that they never went out at night for entertainment, shopping, or other activities, compared to about 3 percent of victims under age 50 (Klaus 2000).

While the pattern that elderly persons experience lower rates of fatal and nonfatal violence is stable, a recent study of violent victimizations from 1976 to 2000 reported by the Uniform Crime Reporting Program and the National Crime Victimization Survey (Klaus & Rennison 2002) shows differences among the relative rates experienced among older adults. For example, a comparison of nonfatal violent victimizations from 1991 through 2000 indicates that the 50 to 64 years age group was the only category that experienced an increase in the victimization rates. Whereas the four age groups that span between individuals age 12 and 49 all indicated substantial declines in percent changes (anywhere from 39–50 percent), the 50 to 64 years age group reported an *increase* of 13 percent. Furthermore, individuals in the age 65 and older group reported the slightest decline of all age groups (14 percent).

Not only are the elderly victimized less often, but a greater percentage of victimizations against the elderly, compared to those against younger persons, were property crimes. Of all victimizations from 1992 to 1997, 92 percent of those reported by a person age 65 or older were property crimes, versus 72 percent of those reported by a person under the age of 65. The only crime category that affected the elderly at about the same rate as most others in the population was personal theft, which includes purse-snatching and pickpocketing (Klaus 2000).

DYNAMICS OF ELDER ABUSE

Elder abuse, like other types of domestic violence, is extremely complex. Research on elder abuse has revealed few consistent differences between victims and nonvictims (Barnett, Miller-Perrin, & Perrin 1997). Generally, a combination of psychological, social, and economic factors, along with the mental and physical conditions of the victim and perpetrator, contributes to the occurrence of elder mistreatment (National Center on Elder Abuse 1999a). Neglect is the most common form of elder abuse in domestic settings. Excluding cases involving self-neglect, 55 percent of the cases that were substantiated in 1996 involved neglect. Physical abuse accounted for 14.6 percent, and financial or material exploitation represented 12.3 percent of the substantiated reports (National Center on Elder Abuse 1999a). Emotional abuse accounts for approximately 7.7 percent of the abuse cases, and sexual abuse contributes 3 percent of the cases.

Victim Characteristics

According to the National Center on Elder Abuse (1999a, b), the majority of elder-abuse victims are female, although the gender gap appears to be narrowing. In 1990, 68.3 percent of all reports involved female victims. In 1996, the incidence was 67.3 percent. Data from the National Elder Abuse Incidence Study (1998) reports that the greatest disparity between men and women was in the category of financial abuse, in which 92 percent of the victims were women. While research finds some gender differences, one must be cautious in interpreting these findings. It is possible that some of the gender discrepancy may be due to the fact that the elderly population is disproportionately female. Another reason for the gender difference is that women tend to sustain more serious abuse, and more serious cases of abuse are more likely to be reported to Adult Protective Services (Barnett 1997).

The majority of domestic elder abuse victims are white (66.4 percent), while 18.7 percent were black. Hispanic elders accounted for 10.4 percent of the elder abuse victims. The median age for elder abuse victims was 77.9 years old. The proportions of Native Americans and Asian American/Pacific Islander were each less than 1 percent.

Offender Characteristics

According to the NEAIS (1998), the majority of perpetrators are male (52.5 percent) and most are younger than 60 years of age. Approximately two-thirds (65.8 percent) of the perpetrators of elder abuse were persons who were 59 years old and younger, while approximately 25 percent of the perpetrators were persons who were 70 and older. In addition, slightly less than 10 percent of the perpetrators were between the ages of 60 and 69. The ages of the perpetrators of domestic elder abuse reveal an interesting relationship. The majority of perpetrators are in the youngest age groups; however, there is a relatively large proportion of perpetrators in the oldest age group. In terms of race/ethnicity, approximately three-fourths (77.4 percent) of elder-abuse perpetrators in the substantiated cases in 1996 were white, and somewhat less than one-fifth (17.9 percent) were black. Only small percentages of persons from other racial/ethnic groups were represented among the perpetrators of elder maltreatment (National Center on Elder Abuse 1998).

The vast majority of elder-abuse cases involve perpetrators who are family members, typically serving in a caretaker role. In the NEAIS, the abusers were family members in 90 percent of the cases. Adult children are the most frequent abusers of the elderly (47.3 percent). Spouses represented the second largest group of perpetrators, comprising 19.3 percent. In addition, other relatives were the third most frequent category of perpetrators (8.8 percent), with grandchildren following closely (8.6 percent). This is contrary to the image that elder abuse is caused primarily by paid caregivers and/or strangers.

When the victim–offender relationship is examined by type of abuse, it is apparent that adult children are the most likely perpetrators of all types of maltreatment. Among children-perpetrators, most studies found that sons are more likely to be abusive than daughters (Brandl & Cook-Daniels 2002). While abusive adult children are seen in higher percentages by adult protective services, some research suggests that incidences of spouse/partner abuse may also be occurring at significantly higher rates than reported (Brandl & Cook-Daniels 2002).

THEORETICAL EXPLANATIONS OF ELDER ABUSE

Many explanations about elder abuse have been offered but few theories have been fully developed and adequately tested. Part of the difficulty is that there is so much variance among different forms of elder abuse that it is virtually impossible to derive one theory to explain the phenomena. In fact, it is likely that different types of elder abuse are caused by different factors (Payne & Gainey 2002). When dealing with domestic elder abuse, three explanations are most commonly offered: situational stress, psychopathological problems of abusers, and intergenerational violence.

Situational Stress

One common explanation focuses attention on caregiver stress. This is often referred to as "situational stress." This perspective holds that well-intentioned caregivers are so overwhelmed by the burden of caring for dependent elders that they end up harming the elder. In other words, the stress associated with caregiving produces abusive behavior. This perspective has recently been receiving considerable attention due to the growth of the "sandwich generation"—adult children who are raising young children while simultaneously being responsible for the care of their elderly parents. This is particularly stressful in instances where families designate one sibling who lives near the aging parent as caretaker. Instead of the responsibility being shared among family members, one sibling often carries the burden (Barnett, Miller-Perrin, & Perrin 1997). Although stress may explain some instance of elder abuse, it is only believed to explain a small percentage of cases. A recent review of 13 articles published between 1998 and 2000 found only two studies indicating a possible correlation between stress of caregiving and abuse (Brandl & Cook-Daniels 2002). In fact, there is probably greater support that it may actually be the *abuser's* dependence on the elder that contributes to the abuse (Payne & Gainey 2002; Barnett, Miller-Perrin, & Perrin 1997).

Psychopathological Problems of Abusers

Particularly in the case of adult children, abusers often are dependent on their victims for financial assistance, housing, and other forms of support. Many of these abusers suffer from their own troubles such as substance-abuse problems, arrest records, poor employment histories, mental illness, social isolation, and inadequate coping skills (Barnett, Miller-Perrin, & Perrin 1997). This perspective holds that elder abusers who suffer from their own personal problems and dysfunctions are often dependent upon their elderly parent. "The adult dependent child feels powerless because of societal expectation that individuals become independent members of society when they get to a certain place in the life course. When they fail to meet societal expectations . . . feelings of powerlessness may ensue, and violence is used as a strategy to regain a sense of control" (Payne & Gainey 2002, 157). There is some support in the research that shows that adult children who are financially dependent upon their elderly parent and those with personal problems are more likely to be abusive (Brandl & Cook-Daniels 2002; Payne & Gainey 2002; Barnett, Miller-Perrin, & Perrin 1997).

Intergenerational Violence

This theory, often referred to as the "cycle of violence," suggests that domestic violence is a learned behavior transmitted from one generation to the next. This explanation suggests that violent actions experienced or witnessed early in life increase the likelihood that one thus exposed will become violent later in life. Thus, adults who were abused as a child may be likely to exhibit abusive behavior either because they have not been taught more effective coping skills, or because they retaliate against the violence their parents used against them. Although a great deal of research suggests that child abuse is a predictor of future violence, the link between child abuse and elder abuse has not been clearly established.

Recommendations for Future Research and Policy

The problem of elder abuse is increasingly receiving attention from governmental agencies, yet our society has only begun to adequately address the phenomenon. Clearly, much more research is needed. The scholarly knowledge of the area is still in its infancy. We do not yet have a clear understanding of the nature and extent of the problem and without this, it is impossible to identify effective prevention and treatment strategies. Future research must acknowledge that elder abuse entails a very complex social problem that must be examined from an interdisciplinary perspective. It is necessary that social scientists from various disciplines come together to provide an integrated approach to studying the victimization of elderly persons (Payne 2000). Ambiguities in defining *who* elders are and *what* constitutes abuse must be clarified in order for policymakers to develop more consistent laws and reporting practices.

Just as our research endeavors need to require the use of interdisciplinary approaches, policy approaches need to rely on more coordinated strategies. It is essential that communities encourage collaboration and linkages among the various legal, social-service, and medical agencies that work with elderly populations. For example, collaboration between social-service and law-enforcement agencies is a growing trend. Some jurisdictions have organized specialized collaborative teams. This approach, often referred to as SALT (Seniors and Lawmen Together), creates teams that include police officers and a number of representatives from community agencies (area agencies on aging, adult-protective services, public health department, and so on) to work jointly together in responding to cases of elder abuse.

Policy initiatives must recognize the uniqueness of elderly crime victims. Older victims have different experiences and needs and these must be recognized. For example, most elderly victims of spouse abuse do not find the integrated assistance they require. Domestic-violence shelters are not designed to help older victims, who often have different needs than younger victims. Shelters for abused elders are rare and most will not serve an elder who needs more than minimal assistance. General elder-abuse interventions are not particularly useful because they tend to focus on situations involving children-perpetrators. Consequently, older spouse-abuse victims do not usually receive proper interventions.

Lastly, it is imperative that we devote greater funding to the problem of elder abuse. In the United States today, the federal government spends $153.5 million on programs addressing elder abuse, neglect, and exploitation. This is in sharp contrast to the funding allocations for combating violence against women ($520 million) and on child-abuse ($6.7 billion) prevention efforts (U.S. Senate Special Committee on Aging 2002). Currently, the U.S. Senate is considering the adoption of legislation that would provide a major advancement in the federal government's response to combating elder abuse. The Elder Abuse Act is designed to create a national focus on elder abuse to increase detection, prevention, prosecution, and victim assistance. The bill would establish a dual office of Elder Justice and Health and Human Services to coordinate disparate federal, state, and local elder-abuse prevention efforts, while also establishing new programs to assist victims and provide grants for education and training. If this legislation is passed, it will provide the impetus that has long been needed in recognizing elder abuse as a complex social problem.

REFERENCES

Administration on Aging. (2001). *A profile of older Americans.* Washington, DC: U.S. Department of Health and Human Services.

Bard, M., and D. Dangrey. (1979). *The crime victims.* New York: Basic Books.

Barnett, Ola W., Cindy L. Miller-Perrin, and Robin D. Perrin. (1997). *Family violence across the lifespan: An introduction.* Belmont, CA: Sage Publications.

Brandl, Bonnie, and Loree Cook-Daniels. (2002). *Domestic abuse in later life.* National Center on Elder Abuse. Available at <http://www.elderabusecenter.org/research/index.html>.

Cantrell, Betsy. (1994). "Triad: Reducing criminal victimization of the elderly." *FBI Law Enforcement Bulletin*:19–23.

Davis, Robert C., and Juanjo Medina-Ariza. (2001). *Results from an elder-abuse prevention experiment in New York City.* Washington, DC: National Institute of Justice.

Forsyth, Craig J., and Robert Grambling. (1988). "Elderly crime: Fact and artifact," in *Older offenders: Perspectives in criminology and criminal justice,* ed. B. McCarthy and R. Langworthy. New York: Praeger.

Gurnack, Anne M., and Richard G. Zevitz. (1993). "Components of variation in elderly crime victims' perception of neighborhood safety: The role of specialized police services for seniors in Milwaukee, Wisconsin." *Police Studies 16,* no. 1: 20–27.

Harpold, Joseph A. (1994). "The FBI and the elderly." *FBI Law Enforcement Bulletin 62,* no. 2:10–11.

Jones, J. S. (1994). "Elder abuse and neglect: Responding to a national problem." *Annals of Emergency Medicine 23*:845–48.

Klaus, Patsy. (2000). *Crimes against persons age 65 or older, 1992–97.* Washington, DC: U.S. Department of Justice.

Klaus, Patsy, and Callie Marie Rennison. (2002). *Age patterns in violent victimization, 1976–2000.* Washington, DC: U.S. Department of Justice.

Moody, Harry R. (2002). *Aging: Concepts and controversies,* 4th ed. Thousand Oaks, CA: Pine Forge Press.

National Center on Elder Abuse. (1998). *The national elder abuse incidence study: Final report.* Available at <http//:www.aoa.gov/abuse/report/default.htm>.

———. (1999a). *Trends in elder abuse in domestic settings.* Elder Abuse Information Series No. 1. Available at <http//:www.elderabusecenter.org/basic/fact2.pdf>.

———. (1999b). *Trends in elder abuse in domestic settings.* Elder Abuse Information Series No. 2. Available at <http//:www.elderabusecenter.org/basic/fact2.pdf>.

Payne, Brian K. (2000). *Crime and elder abuse: An integrated perspective.* Springfield, IL: Charles C. Thomas.

Payne, Brian K., Bruce Berg, and K. Byars. (1999). "A qualitative examination of the similarities and differences of elder abuse definitions among four groups." *Journal of Elder Abuse and Neglect 10*:63–85.

Payne, Brian K., and Randy R. Gainey. (2002). *Family violence and criminal justice: A life-course approach.* Cincinnati: Anderson Publishing.

Philipson, C. (1993). "Abuse of older people: Sociological perspectives," in *Mistreatment of elderly people*, ed. P. Decalmer and F. Gendenning (pp. 88–101). Newbury Park, CA: Sage Publications.

Powell, D. E. (1981). "The crimes against the elderly." *Journal of Gerontological Social Work 3*:27–39.

Reulbach, D. M., and J. Tewsbury. (1994). "Collaboration between adult protective services and law enforcement: The Massachusetts model. *Journal of Elder Abuse and Neglect 6*:9–21.

Rykert, Wilbur L. (1994). "Law-enforcement gerontology." *FBI Law Enforcement Bulletin 62*:5–9.

Stiegel, L. (1995). *Recommended guidelines for state courts' handling cases involving elder abuse.* Washington, DC: American Bar Association.

———. (1996). "What can courts do about elder abuse?" *Judges Journal 35*, no. 1: 38–47.

U.S. Senate Special Committee on Aging. (2002). "Breaux, Hatch introduce first-ever elder justice bill." Available at <http//:aging.senate.gov/whatsnew/107th/091302.html>.

CHAPTER SEVEN

Fear of Crime

its meaning in the lives of elderly women

KATE HANRAHAN
JOHN J. GIBBS

CRIME AND OUR RESPONSES to it have a significant impact on our daily lives. For some people, the impact of crime and fear of crime is quite far reaching. Extensive research suggests strongly that women, the elderly, minorities, and those living in urban areas are the people most likely to live with fear of crime. The purpose of this chapter is to describe what we learned about fear of crime and its impact on daily life from talking with people who share these characteristics. That is, we interviewed elderly African-American and Caucasian women living in a large city. Our objective was to look at the world through the eyes of our respondents and to get a sense of where fear of crime fits in their everyday lives.

The women's descriptions of their daily lives provided us not only with information on their subjective experience of fear of crime in the context of their lives, but also led us to reflect on how we go about conducting research on fear of crime and how we interpret the results of our research. At a very basic level, we learned that straightforward questions about fear of crime, and probably about most other life experiences, do not generate results that have straightforward interpretations. You have to know quite a bit about how people experience their lives on a daily basis before you can understand their answers to seemingly simple questions.

We begin this chapter with an overview of a portion of the voluminous academic literature on fear of crime, and then a discussion of how fear of crime has been conceptualized and measured in the academic and professional literature. The second half of the chapter describes what our sample of older women living in Newark, New Jersey had to say about fear of crime and the complicated role it plays in their lives.

FEAR-OF-CRIME RESEARCH

Fear of crime has been studied fairly continuously in the United States since the early 1970s. Most observers point to the climbing crime rates of the 1960s as the origin of widespread fear of crime among the general population. Others note that fear of crime emerged at the same time as civil rights and Vietnam-era social unrest. Regardless of the impetus for its emergence as a social issue, fear of crime quickly became a political issue; that is, one that has lent itself to manipulation by politicians of both stripes (but more notoriously by Republican and conservative elected officials). As noted by Warr (2000), "[I]f nothing else, the eagerness of political figures to capitalize on public fear of crime is testimony to its central place in modern life" (p. 480). Moreover, in the rapidly growing fields of criminal justice and criminology and related disciplines, fear of crime remains a central measure of "quality of life" and thus occupies a broader role in academic research than might be immediately apparent.

This convergence of factors has meant steady interest in fear of crime among scholars, elected officials, and the general public. It has also resulted in numerous well-funded and carefully executed studies of the fear of crime in the United States and elsewhere (perhaps most notably in Great Britain). In the United States, the fear of crime is regularly assessed by the National Crime Victimization Survey, by polls conducted routinely by Gallup and NORC (the National Opinion Research Center), and by numerous individual researchers.

The general conclusions of these studies can be summarized as follows: the fear of crime is fairly widespread among the general public (although levels have been declining); it is highest among those with personal characteristics that suggest vulnerability (e.g., the elderly, women, minorities, and those living in urban areas); and it is only indirectly related to actual victimization or to risk of victimization as measured by official victimization data (*Sourcebook of Criminal Justice Statistics* 2001). In fact, the literature contains many discussions of the latter "victimization paradox": the apparent disjuncture between the levels of fear among the people identified as most fearful—that is, elderly women—and what official data indicate about the actual rate of victimization for this group. We will return to this paradox below. Here, we need to point out that this conventional wisdom about the fear of crime has been questioned in a variety of ways.

Criticisms of Fear-of-Crime Research

As noted, there is a long tradition of study of the public's fear of crime. Running parallel to it is an equally lengthy tradition of scholarship about *how* we measure fear of crime—that is, how we "count noses" to determine, first, the general level of fear in the population, and then to identify the characteristics of the fearful. Criticism of our methods, of course, calls to question what we actually know about the fear of crime, including the thumbnail sketch provided above. The central challenges to the study of the fear of crime can be collapsed into three interrelated categories:

Definition of the Fear of Crime. First, there is a lack of conceptual agreement about the fear of crime. One of the most fundamental questions raised about fear-of-crime research is this: What *is* "fear of crime"? Given its relatively lengthy and well-researched history, it may be surprising that there is still debate among researchers about the exact meaning of "fear of crime" (see, for example, Ferraro and LaGrange [1987] and Warr [2000]). Upon even modest self-inquiry, however, this seemingly straightforward concept shows its complexity, and the literature is filled with efforts to define its nature.

The terms of the debate are many: Is fear of crime an emotion or a worry (Garofalo 1981)? A concern or caution (Furstenburg 1971)? Is it a feeling, a perception, or a cognition—or is it anxiety (Warr 2000)? Is the fear "formless" or "concrete" (Joseph 1997), rational or irrational? Or is the fear of crime merely the assessment of risk of victimization for self (Warr 1984) or others? The latter has been called "altruistic" or "referred" fear of crime (see, for example, Gilchrist, Bannister, Ditton, and Ferrell [1998]). Should we avoid any perceptual measure and focus instead on behaviors taken in response to the fear of crime (Sacco & Nakhaie 2001)? Should we study safety, not fear (Gibbs & Hanrahan 1993)? Should the fear of crime be studied only at the level of the individual who is afraid, or also at the neighborhood or community level (Warr 2000)?

In short, there are a variety of ways in which we can approach and understand "fear of crime," and most have been used in one study or another. There has been some consistency in measurement, of course. According to Walklate (2001), most large-scale professional surveys conceptualize the fear of crime as an individual perception of risk of crime or of personal safety. This slight consistency has not settled this issue, nor has the measurement itself gone unchallenged.

Measurement of the Fear of Crime. The second line of questioning involves methodological decisions in the measurement of the fear of crime. In particular, critics have questioned the tendency to rely on single-item measures of the fear of crime, such as the common survey item, "Is there any area near where you live—that is, within a mile—where you would be afraid to walk alone at night?" or its principal alternate, "How safe do you feel or would you feel walking alone in your neighborhood at night?" (Meithe & Lee 1984; Ferraro & LaGrange 1987; *Sourcebook of Criminal Justice Statistics* 2001; Warr 2000). Further, the measures themselves have been widely criticized for vagueness and for the hypothetical nature of the activity (Ferraro & LaGrange 1987; Garofalo 1979; Yin 1980). During the 1990s, researchers responded by developing more comprehensive measures. The National Crime Victimization Survey, for example, now includes many more fear-of-crime measures than did its predecessor (National Crime Victimization Survey 1997). But improved questionnaire items alone do not solve the problem.

In addition to shortcomings of the measures themselves, many researchers have criticized the nearly exclusive use of quantitative survey methods to measure something as ephemeral as "fear" or, more fundamentally, to tally incidents of the fear of crime versus the lived experience of the fear of crime. As noted by Walklate (2001), surveys merely count the incidents of victimization: "[B]ut these incidents are still measured as incidents. They are countable as isolated events which people experience, and identify and can talk about. They cannot tap the routinized, daily threat to personal security which characterizes so many women's lives" (p. 88). We will return to this point in our discussion.

The Context of the Fear of Crime. Finally, a third set of issues, related both to measurement and conceptualization of the fear of crime, concerns the tendency to study fear of crime in isolation from other concerns and experiences. Several researchers have argued that the fear of crime needs to be understood in the context of other life worries or fears (Yin 1980, 1982; Stein, Linn, & Slater 1984; Hanrahan 1990; Gibbs & Hanrahan 1993). There is evidence that measuring the fear of crime in a vacuum, separate from the other concerns of daily life, distorts its importance relative to those other concerns (Yin 1982).

Concern about the context of the fear of crime has led some commentators to question the meaning of the personal characteristics of age, gender, and race and their relation to the fear of crime. Pain (2001) notes that (1) each of these categories contains within it so much variation as to render the category almost meaningless (for example, that the elderly are no more a homogeneous group than are the middle-aged); and (2) these particular categories have in common their location at the margins of social life—that is, women, the old, and members of minority groups occupy "subordinate social, economic, and political status" (p. 900) that may contribute to being fearful:

> [I]t is inappropriate to deal with race, gender, age, and other social identities simply as descriptive categories in analysis of the fear of crime. Rather, in each case, fear of crime (and the crimes feared) are often *structured* by age, race, and gender. . . . When gender, age, and race are viewed as social *relations*, which are based upon unequal distributions of power, they begin to explain who is most affected by fear, and where. (Pain 2001, 910 [emphasis in original])

Victimization Paradox. The "victimization paradox" mentioned above provides a good example of the issues being raised about how we study the fear of crime. The victimization paradox refers to the fairly consistent survey finding that the most fearful group in the general population—elderly women—are the least likely to be victimized, at least as measured by official victimization surveys. Several responses to this characterization have been made: among the most telling are the observations that much of the crime to which women and the elderly are exposed is domestic crime and thus very unlikely to be counted in conventional crime surveys. With respect to women, some scholars note that women are routinely subjected to harassment on the street (Stanko 1987) and this type of incivility may understandably lead to feeling unsafe. This argument has been extended to the elderly (see, for example, Pain [1995] and Gilchrist, Bannister, Ditton, and Ferrell [1998]), to members of minority groups, and to gays and lesbians (Nelson & Griffiths 2001). Interviews conducted with elderly respondents by Pain (1997), for example, revealed that many of her older respondents noted that they were not well-treated by younger people, particularly teenagers: "[I]nterviewees reported incidents of harassment targeted at elderly men and women by children or teenagers in local shops, on the streets, or on public transport" (p. 121; see also Walklate [2001] and Gilchrist, Bannister, Ditton, and Ferrell [1998]). Pain (1995) has also argued that researchers have not taken into account the potential cumulative impact of "experiences of violence and abusive behavior" (p. 545) over the course of the life of elderly respondents.

Concerns about the conceptualization and measurement of the fear of crime and its correlates have led many to urge that we approach understanding fear of crime from the perspective of those who live with it. In the words of Pain (1997), the "missing discourse in work on crime and elderly people is the perceptions of elderly people themselves" (p. 119). That is, if we want to understand the meaning of the fear of crime among the general public or any segment of it, we need to talk to those who are experiencing that fear and to understand where and how the fear of crime fits in their everyday lives. That was the focus of the study described below.

STUDY SITE AND METHODS

This study combined focus-group interviews and qualitative personal interviews with elderly (65 and older) female residents of a Northeastern city. The interviews were conducted in Newark, New Jersey, a city long associated with high crime rates. Respondents were selected from among the female participants at three of the 22 senior citizen centers operated by the city of Newark. At each site, a group interview with between eight and ten members of the center and intensive personal interviews with 16 to 20 other center participants were conducted. All told, three focus groups and 57 personal interviews were conducted.

The women interviewed ranged in age from 65 to 85, with an average age of just over 74 years old. About one-third of the respondents were white; the majority (63 percent) was African American. Most were long-term residents of the city and lived alone in rented apartments. In short, given their personal characteristics, the women interviewed were the most likely to experience fear of crime, according to fear-of-crime research: they were elderly, female, living in an urban setting notorious for its crime problem, and most were members of a minority group.

FINDINGS

Our goal was to understand the fear of crime from the perspective of the women we interviewed. In particular, we wanted to know: (1) the nature of the experience (how is fear of crime experienced, what is its impact on daily life?); (2) the extent of the fear of crime among the respondents and its salience, compared to other concerns; and (3) how respondents cope with the fear of crime.

Nature of the Fear of Crime

Most of the women interviewed had difficulty describing or articulating their fears about crime. It was obvious from their responses that the fear of crime had a significant impact on their lives, yet the women we interviewed were hard-pressed to recount a particular incident when they were afraid of crime. For example, when asked to recall an incident when she was afraid, most respondents could not do so. As one of the women we interviewed replied: "I don't know of any special incidents, you know. I think it's just general, not anything special. Just have crime on my mind. . . . I don't say fear [of crime] but you have to be cautious. . . . Daytime, I'm not as afraid but not 100 percent. . . . You say, 'Let's try to be careful.'" Another respondent tried to explain that we were asking her to do something that really could not be done: "It's no describable feeling [fear]. Some things you don't describe, you just have a natural instinct for a lot of things. And you don't describe it. First of all, you never had to, so you never thought of it in that way."

In light of the earlier discussion of the lack of agreement about conceptualizing the fear of crime, one central goal of the project was to determine whether the response to crime was *fear* (the emotion) or *worry* (a more cognitive activity). Certainly, the women understood the difference between fear and worry; however, they did not see the relevance. Dealing with crime is all of one piece in their lives. Most do not experience fear—the emotion—in relation to crime; or if they do, it is a rare event. This is because they structure their lives to avoid provoking fear, and they do so, at this point, with little explicit attention to the accommodation. Crime has shaped the lives of our respondents to such an extent that respondents no longer notice its impact. For example, the following respondent has just been asked if there is anything in her neighborhood that makes her feel unsafe: "No, I wouldn't say it the way you bring it out. It doesn't strike me as that. It's just that I get in the habit. I didn't bother going out anymore. And there was nothing to go out for, because everybody else seemed to stay home. They are all out during the day and that's it." Pain (1997) conducted a study similar to the one described here and her conclusions are similar in this respect. We describe the fear of crime as permeating the lives of our respondents. Pain (1997) says that the fear of crime had become the backdrop of her respondents' lives. It is an apt description of the women we interviewed.

Extent of the Fear of Crime

The conventional wisdom about the fear of crime is that it is most common among those with personal characteristics that suggest vulnerability: namely, being older, female, minority, and living in urban areas. The impact of these characteristics is believed to be linear and additive (Skogan & Maxfield 1981). Thus, the odds were that the women we interviewed would be very afraid of crime. And, in addition to the level of fear, we were interested in the salience of the fear of crime for the respondents. We wanted to know how that fear stacked up against other cares and concerns.

The conventional wisdom regarding elderly women and the fear of crime has been questioned (Yin 1980, 1982; LaGrange & Ferraro 1989; McCoy, Wooldredge, Cullen, Dubeck, & Browning 1996; Pain 1995; Hanrahan 1993). Yin (1982), for example, argued early on that the high levels of fear recorded by survey researchers were to some extent an artifact of measurement. The nature of the fear of crime as described above obviously makes its measurement challenging. Accordingly, we used a number of measures of the fear of crime. Many were unstructured; for example, we asked the women to describe a typical day in their lives, from the time they woke up in the morning until they went to bed at night. We then coded spontaneous mentions of crime or the fear of crime. We also asked directly about the fear of crime, of course; for example, all respondents were asked the common survey item: "Is there anywhere near where you live—that is, within a mile—where you would be afraid to walk alone at night?"

The women we interviewed varied in the extent and salience of their fear of crime. Most indicated some fear of crime:

- The primary characteristics of the fear of crime as described by our sample include the following:
  - mugging or purse-snatching was the crime most feared. About 80 percent of the respondents said they feared having their money or purse taken forcibly while on the street.
  - the appearance of young people, particularly young men, was most likely to elicit fear. Over half the respondents mentioned seeing youths as a reason for their fear of crime.
  - fear was more evident outside the home than within the home (note that most women we interviewed lived alone).
  - fear of crime was far more prevalent after dark.

- Compared to other central concerns (health or support, for example), the fear of crime was less important for practically all respondents. It was mentioned spontaneously by a total of four of the 57 respondents, and was the primary concern for only two of them.
- Unstructured measures of fear resulted in far fewer mentions of the fear of crime. For example, when asked to list the most pressing problems or concerns they face, only 10 percent of the respondents mentioned crime or fear of crime. In contrast, when respondents were given a list of common concerns, just over 60 percent selected the fear of crime as a concern.
- One critical exception to the pattern with respect to unstructured measures of the fear of crime involves descriptions of daily activities. The majority of women we interviewed spontaneously mentioned crime and fear of crime as in some way shaping their daily round of activities. Fully 58 percent of the women reported changing their daytime activities in response to crime, and 76 percent reported an impact on nighttime activities.
- In response to the standard fear-of-crime survey questions, over 90 percent (93.5 percent) of the women agreed that there was an area within a mile of their homes where they would be afraid to walk alone at night, and 80 percent would feel either "very afraid" or "afraid" walking alone in their neighborhoods at night.
- Most of the women did not recognize restrictions on their activities or precautions taken as related to the fear of crime. As seen above, these consequences of the fear of crime are now normalized.

As noted earlier, elderly women are no more a homogeneous group than are middle-aged women or elderly men. Not everyone is fearful. Some respondents reported that their life experiences had given them the ability to keep the fear of crime in perspective. This is not an automatic benefit of living to a certain age; instead, it is a hard-won acceptance of the nature of life and the risks of living. As one woman stated: "Well, I tell you, I learn to live with life now. I learn not to worry about things that I won't accomplish. If it comes my way, all right. If it doesn't, all right. I learn to live according to how I can live. Don't worry about these things that I can't do no more." A similar finding was reported in a study of older men and women living in the northeast of England. Pain (1997) reports that for some, "[L]ife experiences [have] the effect of contextualizing crime and reducing the fear it provokes" (p. 125).

Coping with the Fear of Crime

By and large, the women we interviewed rarely experienced fear, yet its influence is apparent in the accounts of how they spend their time and how they lead their lives. Their stories are much more about coping with the fear of crime than about experiencing the emotion. These women do not live with fear; instead, they live with precautions.

Two broad strategies for coping with the fear of crime were evident in the interviews. The first, and the most common, is to normalize the fear of crime and restrict activities in ways that virtually preclude victimization. The second strategy has to do with religion or personal philosophy: some women reported their belief in a personal god who cares for and protects them.

Normalizing the Fear of Crime. Virtually all the women we interviewed had so integrated safety measures and precautions within their daily lives that they found it hard to respond to questions about the fear of crime. Nevertheless, their interviews are filled with evidence of restricted behavior and caution. Some idea of the scope of their restrictions emerges from the interviews. First, virtually all activity takes place during the day:

> There's nothing I need to go out there for . . . because I arrange it that way, you know. It would have to be some emergency, which I can't think of what the emergency would be for me to go, but mean you get where you live where you arrange so you won't be going out at night. . . . I just don't have any need to go for nothing. Anything I need can wait.

And, many restrict their activities still further, to specific hours during the day: "But then I go [to the bank] at a time when I think nobody's around, like in the morning. I won't go at noontime when the kids are out of school or anything. Best to go about 10:00, 9:30 in the morning. After that you're in trouble. The kids are out of school." Others simply eliminate activities:

> When I was a member of the choir, I used to go to choir rehearsal. But, a lot of things when I say "used to do," I don't do anymore now because of the risk you take when you go out at night. And all of those rehearsals were at night. A lot of things that I would probably do, I don't do, because I just don't feel safe out in the streets.

Throughout the interviews, the women reported, both directly and indirectly, a pervasive sense of caution as they go about routine activities. Thus, the impact of crime on the lives of these women is not incident-specific. Crime and fear of it are more a subcontext of their lives. Asking respondents to tell us about the incident during the past six months by which they were made most afraid yielded answers like the following:

> I don't know of any special incidents, you know. I think it's just general, not anything special. Just have crime on my mind . . . out there at night. But I don't know of anything special. . . . I don't do much walking around. But am I afraid then? I think it's always some, I don't say fear, but you [have to be] cautious. [T]hat's not fear, I guess, to be cautious. . . . There's not as much—daytime I'm not as afraid but not 100 percent [safe], you still [feel] a little fear there, you say "let's try to be careful."

We asked respondents what kinds of precautions they took regularly, either at home or on the street. In many cases, these precautions had become too routine to recall. Most respondents could think of only one or two things; many could think of nothing. The average number of precautions reported was less than one. When read a list of activities, the women reported about eight protective activities on average. The most common were things such as locking windows and doors, using a peephole to see who is at the door, and similar precautions. Considered as a whole, the measures include both avoidance and self-protection (Gordon & Riger 1989)—but avoidance behaviors clearly carry the day.

Finally, a small group of women denied that they were fearful, yet regularly engaged in rituals of protection. For example (*I* = interviewer, *R* = respondent),

> *I:* . . . what about times when you`re worried about your safety?
>
> *R:* I don't worry about it.
>
> *I:* But you take a lot of precautions.
>
> *R:* But I just take precautions. That's why I don't worry about it. I just take precautions. When the lady that lives two floors up—she told me some of the things that she does to her door at night. So I do that. Get into bed and sleep like a top.
>
> *I:* What does she do?
>
> *R:* Well, the chain. I fixed it so that a person can't cut it with a razor—I mean, a saw. I fold it this-a-way, and fold it up at the bottom. And then I take a string and tie it around this way, and like this . . .
>
> *I:* The door and the lock?
>
> *R:* And I put a chair [behind the door]. Because if you push that chair, I can hear you.

Faith in God. Several of the respondents, particularly the African-American respondents, reported either formal religion or belief in a personal god as protecting them from crime and fear of crime: "I haven't thought about being afraid. . . . I don't live in fear. Because if I lived in fear, I'd be in bad shape. . . . I believe there is somebody watching over me and that I don't have to be afraid. That's Jesus."

CONCLUSION

The picture of the fear of crime that emerges from listening to accounts of the daily lives of these respondents is that their fear of crime is diffuse, hard to recognize and articulate, and has become under most circumstances an accepted fact of life. Basically, fear of crime limits or constrains activities (often dramatically), requires vigilance that is nearly second nature under some circumstances, and, above all, it has been normalized. The fear of crime is largely unemotional for these women. Real fear—the emotion—is likely to be experienced only if the restrictions and precautions should fail for some reason.

Given this picture, what can we say about the fear of crime? Substantively, it seems clear that the behaviors reported by our respondents reduce not only the chance of victimization, but also the quality of life. Other researchers have commented on the risk-reduction approach and its impact on the lives of those who respond in this way. Walklate (2001), for example, quotes Kinsey as noting that "the picture that has emerged is one of people of the inner city—especially women—living under curfew" (p. 82). The women we interviewed are far more constrained than the notion of curfew can suggest: nearly all activities are circumscribed by the need for safety.

It seems to us that reduction in the quality of life is an insidious form of victimization, perhaps as crippling to the individual and the collective lives of senior citizens as any other form of nonlethal victimization. Avoidance behaviors adopted by whole categories of citizens function to exclude those groups from social life (Pain 2001). This aspect of the fear of crime deserves further study: What are the consequences at both individual and social levels for the exclusion of groups of citizens? Warr (2000) also recommends study of "the large-scale social consequences of fear" (p. 481).

From a measurement perspective, it seem clear that the fear of crime as it is experienced in the lives of this group of women does not lend itself very well to measurement by quantitative survey. And if the measurement objective is to tap or capture the fear of crime as it is experienced in everyday life, then focusing on emotion is not the best way to go about it. The evidence suggests that these elderly women rarely experience the emotion of the fear of crime. Instead, they cope with the perceived threats in their lives by making accommodations and using available resources to reduce risk and enhance their sense of safety. What we need is a way to measure this broader experience of concern with personal safety, rather than a narrower concern about the fear of crime.

The idea that we may be better served by taking a broader view of the fear of crime is hardly original. Stanko (1987), for example, suggests looking at "safekeeping" or the "dynamic process of negotiating danger and the potential of violence in everyday life" (p. 12). In Stanko's view, "[f]ear of crime, framed as an aberrant part of civilized life, may not be a useful concept to us at all. Many women, and some men, express fear about personal safety as part of the normal, typical experience of contemporary living" (p. 12).

The measures we use should be capable of locating the fear of crime or need for safety within the broader context of the individual's problems, needs, and concerns. The approach should rely more on coping—that is, on the interaction between the individual and environment. Borrowing again from Stanko (1987), "personal safety is an ongoing day-to-day accomplishment" (p. 2). The measure should seek to capture that transaction.

We have argued elsewhere that the fear of crime is best studied through a transactional framework (Gibbs & Hanrahan 1993). Again, we are not alone: several investigators have commented that the fear of crime should be examined from a person–environment transaction perspective (Baumer 1978; Taylor & Hale 1986; Ward, LaGory, & Sherman 1986). For example, Taylor and Hale (1986) conclude after testing models of the fear of crime that

> the performance of sociodemographic predictors should not obscure the consistent role played by residents' perceptions of local conditions and by involvement in locale. These factors reflect person–environment transactions and inform us about the congruence, or lack of congruence, between the resident and his or her immediate environment. (p. 188)

We believe a measure of the fear of crime that locates the problem in the environment as well as within the individual will be more accurate, and more productive. Studying the interaction of person and environment will provide the context of the fear of crime. We will then better understand the meaning of the fear of crime in the lives of those who experience it, and perhaps a better understanding of how to reduce its impact.

REFERENCES

Baumer, T. L. (1978). "Research on fear of crime in the United States." *Victimology 3*(3–4):254–64.

Ferraro, K. F., and R. LaGrange. (1987). "The measurement of fear of crime." *Sociological Inquiry 57*(1):70–101.

Furstenburg, F. F. (1971). "Public reaction to crime in the street." *American Scholar 40*:601–10.

Garofalo, J. (1979). "Victimization and the fear of crime." *Journal of Research in Crime and Delinquency 16*(1):80–97.

———. (1981). "The fear of crime: Causes and consequences." *Journal of Criminal Law and Criminology 72*(2):839–57.

Gibbs, J. J., and K. J. Hanrahan. (1993). "Safety supply and demand: An alternative to fear of crime." *Justice Quarterly 10*:369–94.

Gilchrist, E., J. Bannister, J. Ditton, and S. Ferrell. (1998). "Women and the fear of crime: Challenging the accepted stereotype." *British Journal of Criminology 38*(2):283–98.

Gordon, M. T., and S. Riger. (1989). *The female fear*. New York: Free Press.

Hanrahan, K. (1990). *Fear of crime among elderly urban females*. Unpublished doctoral dissertation, Rutgers University, Newark.

———. (1993). "Fear of crime among elderly urban women," in *It's a crime: Women and justice*, ed. R. Muraskin and T. Alleman. Englewood Cliffs, NJ: Prentice Hall.

Joseph, Janice. (1997). "Fear of crime among Black elderly." *Journal of Black Studies 27*(5):698–718.

LaGrange, R. L., and K. F. Ferraro. (1989). "Assessing age and gender differences in perceived risk and fear of crime." *Criminology 27*(4):697–717.

McCoy, H. V., J. J. Wooldredge, F. T. Cullen, P. J. Dubeck, and S. Browning. (1996). "Lifestyles of the old and not so fearful: Life situation and older persons' fear of crime." *Journal of Criminal Justice 24*(3):191–205.

Meithe, T., and G. Lee. (1984). "Fear of crime among older people: A reassessment of the predictive power of crime related factors." *Sociological Quarterly 25*: 397–415.

National Crime Victimization Survey. (1997). *Criminal victimization in the United States, 1994*. U.S. Department of Justice, Bureau of Justice Statistics. Available at: <www.ojp.usdoj.gov/bjs/>.

Nelson, A. L., and C. Griffiths. (2001). "Perceptions of risk amongst minority groups: Causes and consequences." *Crime Prevention and Community Safety: An International Journal 3*(1):55–65.

Pain, R. H. (1995). "Elderly women and fear of violent crime: The least likely victims? A reconsideration of the extent and nature of risk." *British Journal of Criminology 35*(4):545–98.

———. (1997). "'Old Age' and ageism in urban research: The case of fear of crime." *International Journal of Urban and Regional Research 21*(1):117–28.

———. (2001). "Gender, race, age and fear in the city." *Urban Studies 38*(5–6): 899–913.

Sacco, V. F., and M. R. Nakhaie. (2001). "Coping with crime: An examination of elderly and non-elderly adaptations." *International Journal of Crime and Psychiatry 24*:305–23.

Skogan, W., and M. Maxfield. (1981). *Coping with crime: Individual and neighborhood reactions*. Beverly Hills, CA: Sage Publications.

Sourcebook of Criminal Justice Statistics. (2001). Available at: <www.Albany.edu/sourcebook>.

Stanko, E. A. (1987, July). "Fear of crime and concepts of personal safety." Paper presented at the British Criminology Conference.

Stein, S., M. Linn, and E. Slater. (1984). "Future concerns and recent life events of elderly community residents." *Journal of the American Geriatrics Society 32* (6):431–34.

Taylor, R. B., and M. Hale. (1986). "Testing alternative models of fear of crime." *Journal of Criminal Law and Criminology 77*:151–89.

Walklate, S. (2001). *Gender, crime and criminal justice*. Cullompton, Devon, UK: Willam Publishing.

Ward, R. A., M. LaGory, and S. R. Sherman. (1986). "Fear of crime among the elderly as person/environment interaction." *Journal of Clinical Psychology 41* (4):517–20.

Warr, M. (1984). "Fear of victimization: Why are women and the elderly more afraid?" *Social Science Quarterly 65*:681–702.

———. (2000). "Fear of crime in the United States: Avenues for research and policy," in *Measurement and analysis of crime and justice*, vol. 4. Washington, DC: U.S. Government Printing Office.

Yin, P. P. (1980). "Fear of crime among the elderly: Some issues and suggestions." *Social Problems 27*(4):492–504.

———. (1982). "Fear of crime as a problem for the elderly." *Social Problems 30*(2): 240–45.

CHAPTER EIGHT

Where Are You Now, Cesar Chavez?

the unique vulnerabilities and victimization experiences of Mexican immigrants in the United States

DAVID A. JENKS
CATHERINE A. JENKS

CESAR CHAVEZ LEARNED OF INJUSTICE early in his life. While still a young boy, he watched as his father agreed to clear 80 acres of land in exchange for another 40 acres that adjoined his small adobe home in Yuma, Arizona. After completing the work, the deal was not honored and his family was left with nothing. As history has proven, Cesar acted on his lessons and formed the National Farm Workers Association in 1962, which was later renamed the United Farm Workers. His lifelong struggle for fair-and-equal treatment of farm workers, which precipitated a larger movement in California for Hispanic equality in all venues, seems to have diminished in recent years, even as the Hispanic population continues to increase (U.S. Bureau of the Census 2000).

Hispanics represent the fastest-growing minority group in the United States, of which the largest proportion (66 percent) is Mexican (U.S. Bureau of the Census 2000). Thirty-eight percent of the Hispanic population in the United States are immigrants (RAND 2001). In California, non-Hispanic whites are in the minority (U.S. Bureau of the Census 2000). The Washington, D.C.–based Center for Immigration Studies reports that the number of Mexican immigrants in the United States increased from 800,000 in 1970 to nearly eight million in 2000. The U.S. Census Bureau projects that

Hispanics will comprise 43 percent of the entire state population in California by the year 2025. According to the 2000 census, the population of Mexicans is the least skilled and educated. They have the largest concentration of unskilled workers and dependent children. The Mexican population has long struggled to be freed from the grasp of poverty; unfortunately, there remains work to be done. This chapter will briefly outline the nature of victimization among Mexicans, focusing the majority of attention on those who live in the state of California. The cultural differences of this population, among other things, makes it uniquely vulnerable. A section outlining the current state of victimization of farm workers will be provided. This will be followed by a section outlining some of the economic crimes being perpetrated on many Mexicans outside the agriculture industry. Direction on how these problems are being addressed, along with the current strategies utilized, will be discussed.

VULNERABILITIES

Hispanic immigrants in California, who are largely from Mexico, have numerous social vulnerabilities that increase their risk of victimization. Many sectors of the government in Mexico are corrupt. Thus, Mexican immigrants have an inherent distrust of government agencies and police when they arrive in the United States. They are fearful of police retaliation and are therefore less likely to report abuse, injustices, and crime by both police and other sources. Inherent in the assumption of equal treatment of all individuals under the law, all persons are supposed to be able to trust those systems that are in place to deal with injustices. Immigrants to this country, and especially those from countries like Mexico, however, fear the very systems that are supposed to protect them. In addition, language and cultural differences contribute to their unique vulnerability.

Both undocumented and documented Mexican immigrant workers suffer similar victimizations and unique ones as well. Understandably, undocumented citizens are the most vulnerable to abuse and are at higher risk for all types of violence. Undocumented citizens are unfamiliar with many of the laws that are in place to protect them and often live in constant fear of deportation. For example, police agencies in California are prohibited from threatening deportation when questioning a suspect and are limited in their ability to contact Immigration and Naturalization services. These changes were put into place to help reduce the fear felt by many illegal immigrants when considering calling the police. In practice, however, many police officers still refer to deportation as an option if illegal immigrants do not cooperate with investigations.

Discrimination against Mexicans in general is commonplace and affected by illegal immigration. There is a common stereotype among the populace that most Mexicans in the United States are here illegally. Competition among minorities only exacerbates the problem. In Los Angeles, there is tension among various other minority groups and Mexicans over moving into the South-Central area of the city. Typically, South-Central Los Angeles had been occupied predominantly by blacks (U.S. Bureau of the Census 1990). By 1992, it was 55 percent Hispanic, the vast majority of whom were from Mexican decent. Minority groups in this area, including a new but growing number of Koreans, are competing for the same entry-level jobs and low-cost housing.

New laws since September 11, 2001 make Mexican immigrants even more vulnerable. They are more afraid to report victimization, just when police were turning the other cheek with regard to their status in the United States and were becoming more attuned to their victimization experiences. With an ever-increasing emphasis on immigrants and their link to threats against national security, immigrants are once again becoming wary of turning to the police for help.

Public policy can have a tremendous effect on the status of immigrants. For example, in the case of Central and Eastern Europe, a large majority of the Roma population, which is among the most widely discriminated against group in the region, was excluded from citizenship by new rules for citizenship implemented by each state as it became independent of the Soviet Union. Without citizenship, the Roma population could not vote, own certain property, or receive state assistance for a variety of problems. Similarities in the United States can clearly be seen, as a large number of immigrants in this country do not have the right to vote, and thus do not have one of the basic rights of representation guaranteed in our constitution.

Other problems regarding public policy have also been reported. Bibler-Coutin (2001) reported that the procedures in place to deal with illegal immigrants were so vague that in many cases, persons who sought asylum in the United States were denied solely because they had no documentation of prejudice in their home country. Considering this lack of documentation and the inability to obtain it in many Third World countries clearly puts those attempting to flee persecution at even greater risk than those in other parts of the world, where nongovernmental organizations have long documented abuses.

VICTIMIZATION

A high proportion of Hispanic immigrants find work in entry-level and agricultural jobs, restaurants, and retail stores:

> Demographically, Hispanics are less educated and less skilled, and tend to work in sectors of the economy [that are] harder-hit during recessions, such as manufacturing and retail. They are less likely to have health insurance and more apt to be ineligible for unemployment insurance, in part because they often seek part-time work. (Bibler-Coutin 2001)

They take jobs that U.S. workers consider to be too menial, tedious, dangerous, or physically demanding.

Hispanics have a long history of being victims in the workplace, especially in California as migrant farmworkers. They have suffered and continue to suffer from sexual abuse, often involving bosses and co-workers. They also suffer in the area of compensation. Mexicans were often not paid minimum wages or for overtime, and in some cases migrant workers were paid with bad checks. Many immigrants were often required to perform tasks not in the job description, especially cleaning duties. Some have been subjected to being fired if they cannot produce specific legal documents, even though they possess other documents that prove a legal right to work in the United States.

U.S. labor law protects all workers except day-laborers, regardless of immigration status. Unfortunately, even many protected migrant workers are not knowledgeable about the law and therefore are vulnerable to exploitation. Undocumented workers, however, are not entitled to back pay according to the most recent ruling of the U.S. Supreme Court in *Hoffman Plastic Compounds vs. NRLB* (01-1595). This 5–4 decision makes it easier for employers to discriminate against undocumented workers. U.S. employers who fire undocumented workers do not have to pay back wages, because the court has ruled that such practice is not compatible with U.S. immigration policy.

Many groups believe that *all* workers' rights should be protected, and have taken steps to ensure that workers are informed of their rights. The *Houston Chronicle* reports that "[i]n an unprecedented move, the Mexican Consulate joined with several U.S. government agencies and nonprofit civil rights advocacy groups to encourage Mexican immigrants to come forward and report violations of wage and hour laws and discrimination" (Bibler-Coutin 2001). Notices on billboards in Spanish throughout cities, donated by Clear Channel Communications, advertised a telephone number for workers to call for information about their rights.

Agriculture is the second most-dangerous occupation in the United States, after mining. While children under the age of 18 are prohibited from mining, in the agriculture industry, children as young as 12 are allowed to be employed under the Fair Labor Standards Act (FLSA). In addition, the FLSA does not provide the basic protections afforded children in all other occupations. For example, in any other occupation, children may not work more than three hours a day while school is in session; they must be given overtime pay; and they are prohibited from working in hazardous areas until they are 18 years of age. In stark contrast to these protections, children working in agriculture put in 12-hour days regardless of whether school is in session, receive no overtime pay, and can work in hazardous areas at age 16. Human Rights Watch (2000) reported:

> The Fair Labor Standards Act claims to prohibit "oppressive child labor." Yet the FLSA permits oppressive child labor in agriculture to continue. The FLSA's bias against farmworker children amounts to de facto race-based discrimination: an estimated 85 percent of migrant and seasonal farmworkers nationwide are racial minorities; in some regions, including Arizona, approximately 99 percent of farmworkers are [from Latin American countries]. In addition to raising serious concerns under the Equal Protection clause of the U.S. Constitution, this discrimination may violate numerous provisions of international law.
>
> It is discrimination in legal protection—de jure discrimination against farmworker children as opposed to other working children, with a doubly discriminatory effect against Latino children—that leads directly to deprivation of other rights, most notably the right to education and the right to health and safety. By allowing agricultural employers to work children for unlimited hours, United States law severely undermines their opportunity to participate fully in universal education. Longer hours worked also increase the risk to children of pesticide exposure, repetitive-motion disabilities, fatigue and injuries, and depression and substance abuse.

The victimization of farmworkers, especially those under age 18, has clearly continued—many years after the fight by Cesar Chavez to end these practices. In addition to the failure in federal law, many states offer even less protection. They offer no protections for workers of any age and do not require health coverage, even though several commentators have noted that numerous health problems arise from the pesticides commonly used in the fields (Human Rights Watch 2000). As with any population, there is also the possibility of fraudulent claims being made. In the Hispanic community, however, there are particular issues that lead to unique vulnerabilities. As with violent crimes and the reluctance to report them, fraudulent claims or scams in these communities have used these weaknesses to obtain thousands of dollars from individuals and families.

One of the most common types of fraud in California has revolved around *notarios* (notaries public). *Notarios* claim to be attorneys and inform victims that they can obtain U.S. government work permits for new illegal immigrants. They then inform the victims that in order to gain a work permit they must file for asylum in the United States, and in order to do so, they must pay a large portion of the fees up front. After obtaining the false fees, the *notario* then fails to appear at the hearing. Victims in these cases were attempting to obtain legitimate green cards through what they thought were legitimate sources. Another similar case involves other individuals claiming to be immigration experts who falsely promise to help expedite the paperwork through Immigration and Naturalization services. The immigrants often pay large sums of cash—typically more than a thousand dollars—and end up without papers and the possibility of facing deportation. Predators, who already know that many victims will not report the crime due to fear of other deportations in the family, reduce even further their chances of being caught by having their victims deported to their homelands.

Another type of fraud deals with the promise of housing that is inherently liked with the "American Dream." Fraudulent realtors prey on immigrants through ads promising affordable housing with little credit. These perpetrators have no lawyer present at the closing, and in some cases no interpreters. Loan documents are fabricated, inflating the family's gross annual income and assets, and properties are sold to them at incredibly overvalued prices. Although anyone could become a potential victim of this type of scam, recent predators have specifically targeted the Hispanic community. Often in these cases, the family purchases the house but is unable to make the mortgage payments. It subsequently ends up in foreclosure and possibly driven into bankruptcy, further increasing the probability of becoming a victim of even more crime. Another inherent harm to the community in general is that housing fraud artificially inflates property values, which in turn increases problems with taxation and therefore may price low-income individuals out of the market.

Mexican immigrants are also prime targets for robbery. Those who are in the United States illegally carry cash on their person because they cannot obtain bank accounts and because of fears that it will be stolen if it is left at their residences, which are most often shared with several peers. While the U.S. Bureau of Justice Statistics (2001) reported that Hispanics' violent-crime victimization dropped during the period 1993 through 2000, the rate at which they were victimized (5.7) was more than 200 percent higher than the victimization rate (2.4) for Caucasians. Some have accredited this phenomenon to the lack of trust in financial institutions found in many Mexican communities. This was noted in a recent press release in Austin, Texas, which, like California, has a large Mexican immigrant population (City of Austin, Texas 2001):

> Hispanics are increasingly targeted for robberies. According to police crime statistics, 47 percent of Austin's robbery victims in 2000 were Hispanic. Robbery was also the motive in four Austin murder cases involving newly arrived, Spanish-speaking immigrants during the same year. In an effort to address this troubling trend, police, civic, and business groups have banded together to find solutions to one of the key factors in the crimes—carrying large amounts of cash.

Predators, who often come from similar backgrounds, know the tendency for immigrants to carry large sums of cash on their person. This, in addition to the fact that after being victimized many people are afraid to go to the police, increases the likelihood of continued victimization. Some steps, however, are being made to help reduce this disturbing trend in Texas and California (City of Austin, Texas 2001):

> The Austin Police Department is partnering with the Texas Secretary of State, Mexican Consulate, Greater Austin Hispanic Chamber of Commerce, and Wells Fargo in Austin to help potential robbery victims protect themselves by securing their funds in financial institutions. The project is called *Banca Facil*—Easy Banking.
>
> In November 2000, Austin Police Chief Stan Knee directed the launch of an outreach program to alert the community about the increase in robberies of Hispanics. The program consisted of a series of news conferences and an appeal to Hispanics to report crimes against them. Posters, bumper-stickers, and radio public-service announcements were distributed in both English and Spanish.
>
> Investigators for the Austin Police Department determined that a prime motive for the violence could be curbed by convincing potential victims—many of whom have never deposited funds in banks—to secure their funds in financial institutions.

Wells Fargo pioneered the acceptance of identification cards issued by the Mexican government and distributed through the Mexican consulates in the United States. The cards contain the holder's birth date, place of birth, U.S. address, and encoded information to prevent fraudulent duplication. The use and acceptance of the cards by U.S. financial institutions helps workers transfer money to family members in Mexico more easily and safely. Moreover, the ability of immigrant workers to establish bank accounts may prove to reduce their risk of victimization. As the number of banks for Mexicans, owned by Mexicans, increases, this type of victimization will also decrease.

Extremely vulnerable populations are defined as such due to the multiplicative nature of variables that enhance the probability of their victimization. In the case of Hispanics, the group is a minority, has a large proportion of its population working hourly jobs with little-to-no benefits, faces a language barrier, and contains a large percentage of people who are in the country illegally. While any of these conditions increases the likelihood of victimization, the combination illustrates the ample opportunities presented to potential offenders. If anything, we should be surprised that the amount of victimization within the Hispanic community is not higher.

There is, however, a number of groups fighting to combat these problems. As discussed above, city, state, and local governments in conjunction with community leaders, police agencies, and other community groups have begun the process of empowering the Hispanic populace. These attempts have included everything from reading programs to self-defense courses and have been widely accepted in many areas of California. As the number of immigrants crossing the U.S. border continues to rise, even more effort has to be undertaken in this regard.

Cesar Chavez died peacefully in his sleep in 1993. President Clinton later described him as having "possessed a deep personal understanding of the plight of migrant workers, and he labored all his years to lift their lives." Clearly, his work helped lift the Hispanic culture in California and throughout the country from the depths of poverty. Nonetheless, the victimization of Hispanics continues and is one of the major issues facing the culture today. While it is unlikely that we will approach the success of Cesar Chavez, he is certainly a man who can be emulated in his struggle and dedication.

References

Bibler-Coutin, S. (2001). "Questionable transactions as grounds for legalization: Immigration, illegality and law." *Crime, Law and Social Change 37*:19–36.

City of Austin, Texas. (2001). *Police, business, civic groups partner to promote safety of immigrants*. Public Information Office, 974-5017.

Human Rights Watch. (2000, June). *Fingers to the bone: United States' failure to protect child farmworkers*. Human Rights Watch.

RAND. (2001). *America becoming: The growing complexity of America's racial mosaic*. Policy brief.

U.S. Bureau of the Census. (1990). *United States Census 1990*. U.S. Department of Commerce.

———. (2000). *United States Census 2000*. U.S. Department of Commerce.

U.S. Bureau of Justice Statistics. (2001). *Rate of violent crime victimization among hispanics drops more than 50 percent in last seven years*. U.S. Department of Justice, Office of Justice Programs.

PART TWO

The Undeserving Vulnerable

CHAPTER NINE

Intersecting Identities and Pregnant Drug-Users

victimization and vulnerabilities to criminalization

PAULA K. RECTOR
NANCY A. WONDERS

PREGNANT DRUG-USERS CONSTITUTE an under-researched but particularly vulnerable population within the United States. Of course, some pregnant drug-users are more vulnerable than others. Differential enforcement patterns have ensured that people of color, especially black women and women who are poor, are more likely to be identified and prosecuted for drug use during pregnancy. But it is also true that an increasing number of women from all backgrounds are being prosecuted for their pregnancy behaviors (South Carolina Advocates for Pregnant Women 2001).

In this chapter, we draw on the existing criminalization of pregnancy literature to highlight the way in which identities matter for understanding who is criminalized for drug use during pregnancy. In particular, we analyze the way that race, class, and gender and their intersections shape reactions to pregnant drug-users. We argue that identity increases the vulnerability of some pregnant drug-users to certain kinds of harm, but also to state intervention. Our goal is to add to the literature on the criminalization of pregnancy, raising awareness regarding the inequalities that surround some pregnant drug-users and heighten their vulnerability.

To accomplish this goal, we review the existing literature that has considered the impact of race, gender, and class on the criminalization of pregnant drug-users. We explore the link between the criminalization of pregnant drug-users and race by analyzing how images of crack mothers and black mothers shape social perceptions about culpability and harm. We also explore the way that gender relations shape patterns of drug use in this country. Additionally, we analyze the way that social class position, particularly poverty, affects access to social services and reporting procedures in hospitals, increasing the vulnerability of poor women to social control for drug use during pregnancy. Finally, we briefly note some of the policy conclusions that can be drawn from our analysis and offer some concluding thoughts about ways to reduce the vulnerability of pregnant drug-users.

RACE

As many others have noted, identities *matter* in shaping opportunities and experiences (Minow 1990, 1997; Wonders 2000). Both historically and contemporarily, racial classifications have been one significant strategy for creating differences between groups of people (Ferrante & Brown 1998). Such classifications have also served as a strategy for social control and exclusion of certain groups (Criminal Justice Collective 2000; Reasons, Conley, & Debro 2002; Silliman & Bhattacharjee 2002). Evidence of this is present in both perceptions of and responses to crack cocaine-users.

According to Humphries (1998), amid the ever-increasing presence of the war on drugs during the 1980s, Americans learned about crack mothers. For example, on October 24, 1988, NBC News aired a story about Tracy Watson, a pregnant black woman. She was shown smoking crack in her New York apartment. Tracy admitted that she knew smoking crack was bad for her baby and that it could cause a premature birth. She also disclosed that she spent around a hundred dollars a day on crack (Humphries 1998). This would not be the last time America would hear about crack mothers and their babies. Throughout the next decade, stories of crack mothers continued to air on the evening news as well as images of "crack babies." What became clear over time was that the identities of those using crack mattered and shaped how society responded. According to the existing literature, the view that crack mothers were inner-city, poor women of color, combined with the war on drugs and its punitive policies, directed the criminalization of pregnancy (Humphries 1998).

Equally interesting is the subject of black motherhood in relation to the criminalization of pregnancy. Roberts (1997) argues, quite convincingly, that efforts to criminalize pregnancy have been targeted against black women to punish them for having babies. Roberts (1997) maintains that, historically, black motherhood has been devalued, and that this continues to be true with the criminalization of pregnancy: "The blatant racial impact of the prosecutions can be overlooked only because it results from an institutionalized system that selects black women for prosecution and from a deeply embedded mythology about black mothers" (Roberts 1997, 940). Roberts (1997, 942) states that "for centuries, a popular mythology has degraded black women and portrayed them as less deserving of motherhood." Roberts (1997) also maintains that criminalization diverts attention from other serious social ills in society, and black mothers become the scapegoats for the black community's problems. Roberts (1997, 943) argues that punishing black women takes away "any guilt the nation might feel at the plight of an underclass" and, we would add, our historic legacy of prejudice and discrimination against African Americans.

Race has played a significant role in defining perceptions of pregnant drug-users as well as the response to pregnant drug-users, even though drug-usage rates are similar among racial groups (Donzinger 1996; Cole 1999). Although research on drug-usage rates for pregnant women are problematic because many of the statistics are gathered through hospital reports, (which, as we will demonstrate, do not necessarily reflect actual rates of drug usage), it is reasonable to assume that drug-usage rates among pregnant women would be consistent with usage rates prior to pregnancy. Thus, at this time there is no evidence to suggest that black pregnant women use drugs during pregnancy more than white women. Crack mothers have been portrayed as black women, which has played upon historic prejudices and fueled punitive responses toward pregnant drug-users. It appears that black women are especially susceptible to legal efforts to have their pregnancies criminalized. In the next section, we examine the role of gender in criminalizing pregnancies.

Gender

Society fosters idealized perceptions of how men and women should behave according to ascribed gender roles. As many others have evidenced, those who fail to live up to "gendered" standards are often subject to social exclusion, prejudice, and discrimination (Levit 1999). In this section, we explore the literature that argues that gendered notions of proper motherhood are, in part, responsible for punitive policies against pregnant drug-users (Paltrow 1990). Additionally, we investigate the way that gendered victimization, both prior to and during pregnancy, often shapes women's drug-use and increases their vulnerability to harm and state intervention.

The fact that so many women become involved in drugs is itself a telling story of power relations in our country, and of women's vulnerability. It appears that many women who use drugs have a long history of abuse, especially from men. Significantly, 80 to 90 percent of women addicts have been victims of rape or incest (Paltrow 1990; Szalavitz 1999). As one woman who heads a treatment facility notes, "this is the first place that many of our woman have been where they can't get high" (Paltrow 1990, 43). Szalavitz (1999, 45) states that "female addicts are demonized by our drug laws—and drugs are blamed for their problems when, in fact, they are simply one way they've found to cope with painful, horrifying, heartbreaking lives." Because of this, women are vulnerable to law enforcement and judicial scrutiny in ways that men are not.

Although it is only women who face scrutiny from the justice system for the impact of their behaviors on the unborn, it is important to note that often women's drug use is related to their victimization experiences at the hands of men. Men's behavior poses risks to both pregnant women and their fetuses, although this is rarely addressed by the justice system. It is estimated that 4 to 8 percent of pregnant women are battered, and a recent study found that only 17 percent of patients at a prenatal clinic had *not* been abused (Gutavsson & MacEachron 1997 [emphasis added]). This particular clinic was used primarily by poor women. One poignant story illustrates this double standard of justice well: A woman in Laramie, Wyoming went to a police station to file a claim against her husband for battering. Rather than receiving support from the police, she ended up being arrested for child abuse when she admitted that she had been drinking (Paltrow 1990). The existing literature maintains that justice officials are more concerned with criminalizing and controlling women than in protecting them. Mariner and Glantz (1990) argue that it is easier to blame women who use drugs during pregnancy than to recognize other possible problems women face.

To demonstrate how gender matters in shaping the criminalization of pregnant drug-users, it is useful to explore some common, though stereotypical, perceptions about women who use drugs. Women who use drugs are viewed as selfish, wanting to please only themselves, rather than making family members or others their primary priority (Szalavitz 1999). "Female addicts are seen as doubly deviant" because of their behavior and this is why "our response to addicted women tends to be more punitive than our admittedly harsh treatment of male addicts" (Szalavitz 1999, 43). The existing literature illustrates that women who do not live up to societal expectations of motherhood and femininity face harsher treatment by the justice system than either other, more conventional women, or men (Belknap 2001). Importantly, only women are viewed as responsible for a fetus, and only women are expected to sacrifice for a fetus. If women fail to do this, blame is placed solely upon their shoulders because of their failures. "No other group of Americans are expected to sacrifice their individual autonomy, privacy, or even health, to enhance the viability of another person, much less a developing fetus" (Gustavsson & MacEachron 1997, 674).

Policies to criminalize pregnant drug-users also mirror gendered notions of motherhood. For example, Mariner and Glantz (1990) maintain that a person cannot be accused of a crime when the crime has not been defined; yet this absence of definitional clarity is common in the criminalization of pregnant drug-users. No state has clearly determined via the law the degree of health that a woman has a duty to produce. Many things can affect the outcome of the health of the fetus or newborn. Actions such as flying, walking on ice, using fetal monitors, and environmental risks can all contribute to the well-being of a fetus, yet little state effort has been put into regulating these potential harms.

While we do not deny that maternal drug use *may* contribute to fetal problems, it is also true that paternal drug use can have negative effects on fetal development and morbidity. Research has evidenced that men who abuse drugs have an elevated risk of infertility and chromosomal damage, and that drug use can have detrimental effects on the morphology of sperm (Gustavsson & MacEachron 1997). Despite this, men are not targeted for criminalization when there are problems with a fetus or newborn—the blame is based solely on women. Policies to criminalize pregnant drug-users solidify the idea that women are solely responsible for the outcome of a fetus: "No woman can provide the perfect womb, criminal prosecutions come dangerously close to turning pregnancy itself into a crime" (Paltrow 1990, 43).

Despite the fact that research has documented a correlation between violence against women and drug abuse, and despite what is known regarding the risks that paternal drug use pose to fetuses, only women are held responsible for the demise of a fetus or newborn. Pregnant drug-users are cast as being horrible mothers who are singularly responsible for their failure to live up to idealized notions of motherhood. In this way, women are made uniquely accountable for the ways that drug use and other harms affect fetal development. In the following section, we explore how class biases affect pregnant drug-users.

Class

Just as race and gender identities matter in shaping who is criminalized for pregnancy, so to does social class. Beckett (1995, 601) states that "all of the women who have been prosecuted for drug and alcohol abuse while pregnant have been poor, and almost all have been minorities while drug use is evenly distributed by social class." In this section, we explore several reasons why poverty is so closely tied to the criminalization of pregnancy. In particular, we discuss how cuts in social services have affected poor pregnant women, and how class biases influence the identification and prosecution of pregnant drug-users.

The war on crime and drugs is expensive, and the money to enforce drug laws has to come from somewhere. This "somewhere" has turned out to be the money that was previously used for social services (Danner 1998). This has led to a steady and further decline in the quality of life for the lower class, but especially for poor pregnant women. Significantly, because of the lack of public funding for abortion, poor women do not have the same rights over their reproductive choices as middle class and wealthy women (Humphries 1998). Lack of general and preventative health care for the poor is also extensive. Part of the reason for this is the fact that "Reaganomics brought substantial reductions in federal funding for health care, including maternal health programs" (Siegal 1990, 171). This has had profound effects on poor pregnant women. Siegal states that "prenatal care and delivery services have diminished at the same time that drug addiction has worsened" (1990, 171). She cites a study in Los Angeles that found that some patients at public clinics had to wait 19 weeks for an appointment to receive prenatal care; in San Diego, clinics turned away 1,254 pregnant women during a three-month period because they had inadequate resources to care for the women. This shortage of health-care services heightens the vulnerability of many groups, but particularly poor, pregnant drug-users.

Class status and cuts in social services affect who is criminalized for pregnancy behaviors primarily because of the different reporting procedures for public and private hospitals. Because their choices are limited by financial constraints, poor women tend to rely on less expensive public hospitals for health-care and maternity services. Many public hospitals are mandated to report the drug use of pregnant women; therefore, poor women who use these hospitals get tested much more often than women in private hospitals (Humphries 1998). Beckett (1995, 601) notes that "even private hospitals that are mandated to report drug use often do not." Additionally, doctors and other health-care workers in private hospitals may see their patients as more like themselves and may, therefore, be unwilling to report them to the authorities.

Furthermore, the criteria used by many hospitals and health-care workers for deciding who to drug test are discriminatory. One of the main criteria that doctors and nurses use is the lack of prenatal care; but not surprisingly, "[p]oor women are more likely to delay prenatal care" (Humphries 1998, 50). Health-care services, including prenatal care, can be very difficult for poor minority women to obtain, and Medicaid benefits for prenatal care often do not begin until after 19 weeks of pregnancy (Siegal 1990).

Unfortunately, since these mandatory reporting policies in hospitals have been established and enforced, a new and equally serious problem has emerged that further heightens the vulnerability of pregnant drug-users. Today, many pregnant drug-users are not going to clinics and hospitals to receive prenatal care at all because they are afraid of being arrested. Because of these circumstances, when it comes time to deliver, many of these women (primarily poor black women) are even more susceptible to drug testing. In addition, upon arrest for a pregnancy and drug-related charge, poor women lack the resources necessary to respond to a criminal prosecution. Poor women do not have the same options in the justice system as middle-class or wealthy people (Belknap 2001).

Thus, class identity and conditions of poverty strongly influence who is identified as a pregnant drug-user. Health-care workers have discretion as to whether or not to obtain a forensic sample to be used as evidence against some pregnant drug-users. And, as we have noted, failure to receive prenatal care, though clearly shaped by the lack of affordable health care in the United States, is seen as a personal failure and red flag warranting state intervention. Public hospitals are used primarily by poor and minority women, making them more vulnerable to drug testing. The criteria used to identify pregnant drug-users reflect class biases, as does the powerful discretion of health-care workers to decide which women to drug test. In the following section, we examine how race, gender, and class intersections shape the disproportionate criminalization of poor black women for drug use during pregnancy.

Identity Intersections

Pregnant drug-users are never just black or poor or female; they occupy many identities at once. These intersecting identities affect pregnant drug-users and their criminalization. As Roberts (1991, 1432) states: "Poor black women bear the brunt of prosecutors' punitive approach, not because they are more likely to be guilty of fetal abuse, but because they are black and poor." She goes on to add that "poor women who are disproportionately black that are more likely to be in close contact with government agencies" (Roberts 1991, 1432). These government agencies include public hospitals, welfare agencies, and probation officers. In the case of pregnant drug-users, public hospitals ensure that testing is almost exclusively directed at poor black women and that wealthy white women are not targeted (Roberts 1991; Siegal 1990). This is an important consideration, because even though drug-usage rates are similar, black pregnant women are reported as being drug-users at ten times the rate of white pregnant women (Logan 1999).

Some of the attitudes toward pregnant drug-users exhibited by health-care workers, law-enforcement officials, and others can be linked to the long history of "child-saving" in this country. Kasinsky (1994) argues that the new child-savers are middle-class people: they are legislators, attorneys, doctors, and social workers who cooperate together to impose their raced, classed, and gendered values. In their professional roles, they decide if women are living up to normative views of motherhood—not only after a child is born, but even during pregnancy. The state's attempt to regulate and control pregnancy has the greatest impact on poor women of color (Kasinsky 1994). "As it is more difficult for them to meet the ideal middle-class standard of what a woman or mother should be, society is more likely to punish them for making reproductive decisions that do not meet this ideal" (Kasinsky 1994, 119).

Roberts (1991, 1443–44) frames the dilemma faced by poor women of color as a question. She asks: "Why is it that under Medicaid, 'sterilization is the only publicly funded birth-control method readily available to poor women of color' while information regarding 'access to other contraceptive techniques and abortion' is not available?" As in the Progressive Era, it appears that many policies are in place to ensure that poor minority women have as little reproductive freedom as possible. Why is it that out of all the possible kinds of maternal conduct to focus on, those who have the power to criminalize pregnant women have focused on crack use (Roberts 1991)? It seems as though poor black women, who are more likely to use crack, are easy targets for this new era of child-savers.

We believe that intersections of race, gender, and class are important considerations for understanding who is criminalized for their pregnancy behaviors. Utilizing existing criminalization of pregnancy literature, it is evident that identity intersections are influential in shaping punitive responses toward pregnant drug-users. Holding women solely responsible for fetuses, racialized notions of drug use, and women's inability and fear to obtain prenatal care, in combination, ensure that poor black women will be more vulnerable to efforts to control their behavior during pregnancy.

POLICY CONSIDERATIONS: THE CONSEQUENCES OF CRIMINALIZING PREGNANT DRUG-USERS

Policies to criminalize pregnant drug-users are actually doing more harm than good to women and fetuses. There are several negative consequences that have developed as a direct outcome of punitive responses to pregnant drug-users. We have already documented the racist, sexist, and gendered nature of these policies. We have also discussed how some pregnant drug-users are no longer going to clinics or doctors to receive prenatal care because they are afraid of being arrested. This is why so many medical associations are against policies to criminalize pregnant women (National Advocates for Pregnant Women 2001).

There are other ways that women and fetuses have been adversely affected by the policies to criminalize women. First, it appears that there have been cases where women have obtained abortions to avoid prosecution or imprisonment for using drugs while being pregnant (Paltrow 1990; Szalavitz 1999). It is ironic that abortion may be the only way some women can avoid prosecution or imprisonment. Second, many women have been subject to "protective incarceration," with more concern given to the fetus than the woman herself. Some convicted women have been jailed until they give birth, because the court has reasoned that jail will protect the fetus from further drug abuse (Gustavsson & MacEachron 1997). Yet, ironically, little prenatal care, if any, is provided in jail, nor are jails drug-free. Also, miscarriage rates for women in jails and prisons are very high. It is also clear that such protective incarcerations are gendered, raced, and classed since affluent people can free themselves on bail, and white middle-class people and men are not targeted for enforcement in the first place.

Those creating policy need to recognize that sending individual people to prison is not an effective solution. Instead of focusing on individual women, legislators and policy-makers need to address the issues that lead to drug use, especially violence against women, poverty, and racism. Drug use is a consequence of inequality (Humphries 1998). Until the causes of drug use are taken seriously, women will continue to turn to drugs to deal with their troubled lives.

Additionally, serious consideration needs to be given to drug treatment that addresses women's specific needs. A few token treatment centers that are geared toward women will not fill the need. Treatment centers for women must be capable of providing a family environment, since many drug-using women have children. In addition, drug-treatment centers need to provide counseling and treatment regarding domestic violence and prior abuse, since these are factors related to drug abuse. In fact, increased drug treatment for men is also important, given current research that addresses the effects of drug use on sperm morphology.

Until society truly values the lives of women, including poor women and women of color, punitive responses toward pregnant drug-users will continue. Yet policies that criminalize pregnancy only increase the vulnerability and victimization of pregnant drug-users. They also foster race, class, and gender divides that ought to be intolerable within a democratic society. Hopefully, those who are against these policies and are supportive of the rights of all women will continue to educate others about the many negative effects of these policies. It is our hope that this chapter will increase awareness about the unique vulnerabilities that pregnant drug-users face, and that it will help to promote the social justice that all people deserve.

References

Beckett, Katherine. (1995). "Fetal rights and 'crack moms': Pregnant women in the war on drugs." *Contemporary Drug Problems 22*(4):587–612.

Belknap, Joanne. (2001). *The invisible woman: Gender, crime and justice.* Belmont, CA: Wadsworth.

Cole, David. (1999). *No equal justice: Race and class in the American criminal justice system.* New York: New Press.

Criminal Justice Collective of Northern Arizona University. (2000). *Investigating difference: Human and cultural relations in criminal justice.* Boston: Allyn & Bacon.

Danner, Mona J. E. (1998). "Three strikes and it's women who are out: The hidden consequences for women of criminal justice policy reforms," in *Crime control and women: Feminist implications for criminal justice policy*, ed. Susan L. Miller (pp. 1–14). London: Sage.

Donzinger, Steven R. (1996). *The real war on crime.* New York: HarperPerennial.

Ferrante, J., and P. Brown. (1998). *The social construction of race in the United States.* New York: Longman.

Gustavsson, Nora S., and Ann E. MacEachron. (1997). "Criminalizing women's behavior." *Journal of Drug Issues 27*(3):673–88.

Humphries, Drew. (1998). "Crack mothers at 6." *Violence Against Women 4*(1):45–62.

Kasinsky, Renee. (1994). "Child neglect and 'unfit' mothers: Child savers in the Progressive Era and today." *Women and Criminal Justice 6*(1):97–121.

Levit, Nancy. (1999). *The gender line: Men, women and the law.* New York: New York University Press.

Logan, Enid. (1997). "The wrong race, committing crime, doing drugs, and maladjusted for motherhood: The nation's fury over crack babies." *Social Justice 26*(1):115–40.

Mariner, Wendy K., and Leonard H. Glantz. (1990). "Pregnancy, drugs, and the perils of prosecution." *Criminal Justice Ethics 9*(1):30–41.

Minow, Martha. (1990). *Making all the difference: Inclusion, exclusion, and American law.* Ithaca, NY: Cornell University Press.

———. (1997). *Not only for myself: Identity, politics, and the law.* New York: New Press.

National Advocates for Pregnant Women. (2001). Available at: <http://www.advocatesforpregnantwomen.org>.

Paltrow, Lynn M. (1990). "When becoming pregnant is a crime." *Criminal Justice Ethics 9*(1):41–48.

Reasons, Charles E., Darlene J. Conley, and Julius Debro. (2002). *Race, class, gender, and justice in the United States: A text reader.* Boston: Allyn & Bacon.

Roberts, Dorothy E. (1991). "Punishing drug addicts who have babies: Women of color, equality, and the right of privacy." *Harvard Law Review 104*(7):1419–81.

———. (1997). "Unshackling black motherhood." *Michigan Law Review 94*(4): 938–65.

Siegal, Loren. (1990). "The criminalization of pregnant and child-bearing drug-users." *Drug Law Report 2*(15):169–76.

Silliman, Jael, and Anannya Bhattacharjee. (2002). *Policing the national body: Race, gender and criminalization.* Cambridge, MA: South End Press.

South Carolina Advocates for Pregnant Women. 2001. Website: <http://www.scapw.org>.

Szalavitz, Maia. (1999). "War on drugs, war on women." *On the Issues 8*(1):42–47.

Wonders, Nancy. (2000). "Conceptualizing difference," in *Investigating difference: Human and cultural relations in criminal justice*, ed. Criminal Justice Collective of Northern Arizona University (pp. 11–26). Boston: Allyn & Bacon.

CHAPTER TEN

Disregarding Harm

an examination of the vulnerabilities of youth incarcerated in adult correctional facilities

PAULINE K. BRENNAN

CURRENTLY, IN A NUMBER OF STATES across the country, youth are incarcerated in adult jails and prisons, an interesting reality considering that, for most of the twentieth century, justice and corrections officials avowed the value of separately confining juveniles. Those who believe juvenile offenders should be treated no differently from adults see little wrong with abandoning the policy of separate housing. What is missed from the "old-enough-to-do-the-crime, old-enough-to-do-the-time" equation, however, is a failure to consider that young offenders are not equally equipped to survive the harshness of life behind bars. More specifically, youthful offenders are mentally and physically at a disadvantage. Consequently, because they are perceived as weak, they are likely to be targeted for victimization. In this chapter, I focus on this high-risk group and why they are especially vulnerable to attack and suicide when housed in adult correctional facilities.

This chapter begins with a brief historical overview of policies pertaining to the confinement of youth in adult facilities. This is followed by a discussion of guidelines related to the age at which juvenile offenders may be prosecuted in the adult system, since these are the juveniles who may end up serving time with adults. Data are then provided on the number of juveniles held in adult facilities, along with variations in housing policies by state, so that the reader may understand the extent to which persons under 18 years old are affected. Following that discussion, the risks of victimization and suicide for juveniles held in adult prisons and jails are highlighted. The chapter concludes with suggestions for changes in correctional policy.

HISTORICAL OVERVIEW

Prior to 1899, juveniles were treated no differently from adults—they were confined in the same jails and prisons. The many problems with housing young offenders with adults were noted by Progressive Era reformers, including the vulnerability of youth so placed. Moreover, the "child-savers," as they came to be known, believed that children who were confined with adults were likely to return to society as hardened criminals, because the impressionable youth learned from older and more experienced offenders. In short, the reformers argued that juveniles were different from adults and, consequently, deserved to be protected from the harshness of the adult criminal-justice system.

With these arguments at its base, the first juvenile court was established in Cook County, Illinois, in 1899, where children under the age of 18 were adjudicated and sentenced. The court was separate and different from the one(s) that processed adult offenders. And, when sentenced to periods of incarceration, juvenile offenders were sent to training schools and centers, apart from adult offenders, where they received treatment.

Ideas about how youth should be processed and punished have altered in recent years, mainly due to a shift in punishment ideology—from *rehabilitation* (i.e., treatment) to *crime control* (i.e., deterrence, retribution, and incapacitation). The rehabilitation–deterrence debate ignited during the 1970s, sparked by the publication of Robert Martinson's (1974) assessment about the effectiveness of prison rehabilitation (see also Gendreau & Ross 1983–84; Palmer 1983; Wilson 1980). Although Martinson never concluded that *all* treatment strategies were ineffective, many critics of the then-current system used his general conclusion that very little seemed to work as a reason to "get tough" on crime. This was done primarily by increasing the severity of punishment (e.g., via mandatory sentencing, guidelines-based sentencing, and reinstatement of capital punishment in many jurisdictions). Juvenile offenders were not spared.

Criticisms of an ineffective juvenile-justice system, especially with regard to rehabilitation, were coupled by increases in rates of juvenile crime. "Beginning in the late 1980s, communities across the nation began to experience dramatically increased rates of juvenile crime. . . . Rates of serious crime committed by juveniles remain well above historical levels" (Austin, Johnson, & Gregoriou 2000, ix; see also Redding 1999a, b; Snyder 1998; Parent, Dunworth, McDonald, & Rhodes 1997). Fear of youth crime, coupled with crime-control ideology, lead to harsher responses to juvenile offenders.

To illustrate that point, the main sponsor of the Violent Crime Control and Law Enforcement Act of 1995, Bill McCollum (R-Florida), stated that serious juvenile offenders "should be thrown in jail, the key should be thrown away, and there should be little or no effort to rehabilitate them" (cited in Merlo, Benekos, and Cook [1997, 2]; see also Redding [1999a, 2; 1999b, 92]). To ensure that youthful offenders are "thrown away" for longer periods of time, legislators have passed laws that allow a greater number of juveniles to be tried and sentenced as adults, and to later be incarcerated in adult facilities (Podkopacz & Feld 2001, 998; Austin, Johnson, & Gregoriou 2000, ix; Carter 1997, 2; Parent, Dunworth, McDonald, & Rhodes 1997, 1; Ziedenberg & Schiraldi 1997, 1). Unfortunately, as shall be shown, housing youth with adults has many deleterious consequences.

Adult Criminal-Court Jurisdiction of Juvenile Offenders

It is important for one to be aware of the laws that allow a child or adolescent to be tried as an adult, since they "often become the basis for a juvenile to be housed in a jail, if charged and awaiting court disposition, or in a prison, if the juvenile has been convicted and sentenced" (Austin, Johnson, & Gregoriou 2000, 27). A number of state legislatures have lowered the general age of adult court jurisdiction and altered their state transfer laws. With regard to transfer, states have lowered the age of requirement, expanded the list of transferable crimes, and/or changed the process for conducting transfer hearings (e.g., no longer requiring the judge to consider amenability to treatment before transfer) (Redding 1999a, b; Parent, Dunworth, McDonald, & Rhodes 1997, 1; Torbert et al. 1996; Sickmund 1994).

In a recent Bureau of Justice Assistance (BJA) report, Austin and his colleagues (2000, 3) noted that the age of adult court jurisdiction has been lowered to 16 years old in seven states (Georgia, Illinois, Louisiana, Massachusetts, Michigan, South Carolina, and Texas), and three states (Connecticut, New York, and North Carolina) have lowered it to 15 years old. This means, of course, that in these states, youth who commit crimes at age 16 years (or older) are automatically tried and, if convicted, sentenced as adults.

The other, more popular method of lowering the age at which juveniles may be tried as adults is by transferring young offenders to adult court. Through the mechanism of transfer, a juvenile may be tried as an adult in all 50 states (Snyder & Sickmund 1995; see also Redding 1999a, 3). There are essentially three transfer mechanisms: judicial waivers, prosecutorial direct-file provisions, and legislative mandatory or automatic transfers (Strom 2000, 2; see also Redding 1999a, b). As the first type may imply, juvenile court judges are authorized to waive jurisdiction and transfer juveniles to adult court. In 46 states and the District of Columbia, juvenile court judges are allowed to do this at "their discretion" (Strom 2000, 2). Fewer states allow prosecutors to make the decision; as of 1997, 15 states allowed the prosecutor to decide whether to file the case in either juvenile or criminal court (Strom 2000, 2).

With regard to mandatory transfer, certain offenders under 18 years old are automatically excluded from juvenile court jurisdiction; typically, juveniles above a certain age who commit certain offenses are transferred. The offenses are often violent felonies, such as murder, robbery, rape, kidnapping, and aggravated assault (Redding 1999a, b). In most states, for serious crimes against persons, minimum ages for transfer range from 13 to 16 years old (Parent, Dunworth, McDonald, & Rhodes 1997, 2). It is also likely that a juvenile who commits a crime with a firearm will be transferred. For example, children 13 years and older who commit violent crimes with a firearm on federal property are permitted to be prosecuted as adults (Redding 1999a, 1; 1999b, 92). Serious drug offenses committed by juveniles are also likely to require transfer (Redding 1999a, 3).

Across the country, the range of juvenile offenders eligible for transfer is increasing (Austin, Johnson, & Gregoriou 2000, 3; Howell 1997, 109; Parent, Dunworth, McDonald, & Rhodes 1997, 1; Sickmund, Snyder, & Poe-Yamagata 1997; Torbert et al., 1996). Missouri, for example, recently lowered the age of transfer to 12 years old for juveniles charged with any felony, including a property offense (Austin, Johnson, & Gregoriou 2000, 3). Indeed, contrary to what one might expect, waiver provisions are often applied to nonviolent offenders: "despite policymakers' focus on violent juvenile crime, only 34 percent of the transferred cases in 1992 involved crimes against persons. Property crimes accounted for 45 percent, drug crimes 12 percent, and public-order offenses 9 percent" (Parent, Dunworth, McDonald, & Rhodes 1997, 2). More recent figures paint a similar picture. The majority of delinquency cases waived to adult court, in 1996, were also for property, drug, and public-order offenses. At the same time, however, Austin and colleagues (2000, 3) also observed that a slightly higher number of the waived cases were for crimes against persons. In short, although the most frequent offenses currently related to the use of waivers involve person offenses, most juvenile offenders are waived for other crimes.

Given changes in transfer policies, it is not surprising that the number of juvenile offenders transferred to adult courts has increased greatly over time. From 1985 to 1994, judicial transfers increased by 71 percent (Sickmund, Snyder, & Poe-Yamagata 1997). According to Parent and his colleagues (1997, 2), transfers of juveniles, from 1988 to 1992, doubled for persons accused of crimes against persons (from 2,000 to 4,000) and for juveniles charged with drug offenses and public-order offenses (from 1,200 to about 2,400).

Youth Confinement in Adult Facilities

Due to changes in policy related to the age at which a juvenile may be tried as an adult, the number of offenders under 18 years old held in adult jails and prisons has increased substantially over time. It is necessary for one to have a sense of the number so held in order to better understand the issue of youth confinement in adult facilities. As of mid-year 2001, 3,147 youth were incarcerated in state and federal prisons, representing less than 1 percent of the total prison population (Beck, Karberg, & Harrison 2002, 6). A larger number of juveniles is held in jail. Figures for 1999 (the most recent data available) indicated that approximately 9,500 youth were housed in local jails (Mlyniec 2001, 3).

Consistent with a "get tough" stance on juvenile crime, from 1993 to 1995, the number of juveniles who were tried or awaiting trial as adults in jail nearly doubled (from 3,300 to 6,018) (Howell 1997, 85). In terms of prison admissions, the number of juvenile offenders admitted more than doubled between 1985 and 1997 (from 3,400 to 7,400) (Austin, Johnson, & Gregoriou 2000, 5; Strom 2000, 1). Obviously, over time, the likelihood of incarceration has increased for juveniles. "Between 1985 and 1997, the likelihood of incarceration relative to arrests increased for persons under age 18. In 1997, an estimated 33 persons under age 18 were admitted to state prison for violent offenses for every 1,000 arrests, up from 18 per 1,000 violent arrests in 1985" (Strom 2000, 5). Thus, it is not surprising that about 22 percent of correctional systems surveyed in 1998 were planning to expand their juvenile-offender capacity (Austin, Johnson, & Gregoriou 2000, 41).

While the number of juveniles incarcerated in adult facilities has increased over time, one should be aware that admissions vary greatly from state to state. In a recent Bureau of Justice Statistics bulletin, statistics indicated that ten states accounted for the vast majority (68 percent) of prison admissions for persons under 18 years old (Beck, Karberg, & Harrison 2002, 6). The states with the most juveniles in prison included Florida, Connecticut, New York, North Carolina, and Texas (Beck, Karberg, & Harrison 2002, 6).

Policies pertaining to housing youthful offenders with adults also vary from state to state. However, the most common practice is to allow juveniles to be incarcerated in adult prisons and jails, with no differentiation between housing units (Abramsky 2001, 16–18; Austin, Johnson, & Gregoriou 2000, 43; Strom 2000, 1; Levinson & Greene 1999, 61; Carter 1997, 2; Parent, Dunworth, McDonald, & Rhodes 1997, 2). According to Austin and colleagues (2000, 43; see also McLean 1986, 13): "This finding is perhaps not surprising when viewed in the context of the rationale for moving youth to adult correctional facilities—the increasing severity of their crimes, the failure of rehabilitation, and the difficulty experienced in managing their behavior." Although most states do not provide different housing for adults and juveniles, one should be aware that two states prohibit the incarceration of children under the age of 16 in adult facilities (i.e., California and North Dakota), and six states require separate housing for those under age 18 (i.e., Arizona, Kentucky, Hawaii, Montana, Tennessee, and West Virginia) (Abramsky 2001, 16–18; Strom 2000, 10; Torbert et al. 1996). In other states, a policy of graduated incarceration is utilized (Strom 2000, 10; Torbert et al. 1996). Under this policy, youthful offenders begin their sentences in a juvenile facility and later transfer to an adult facility when they reach a certain age, usually 18 years old (Strom 2000, 10; Torbert et al. 1996). Eight other states utilize a policy of segregated incarceration, where "certain underage offenders" are assigned to specific facilities based on age and programming needs (Strom 2000, 10; Torbert et al. 1996). For example, "in Florida, persons under age 18 convicted in criminal court can be sentenced to the youthful-offender program that separates 14–18 from ages 19–24" (Strom 2000, 10).

It may appear that a number of states have taken care to separate juveniles from adults. However, Austin and colleagues (2000, 36–37) provide the following caution: "The presence of separate housing for youthful offenders does not mean that all youthful offenders were housed in these separate facilities. States with large youthful-offender populations, by necessity, often housed youthful offenders with the adult population when their housing capacity was exceeded." Thus, even in states with policies of separate housing, juveniles are likely to end up in housing units shared by adults.

THE CONSEQUENCES OF INCARCERATING JUVENILES WITH ADULTS

Juveniles housed in adult facilities are at a much greater risk of harm than juveniles incarcerated in juvenile facilities. They are more likely to be victimized, including sexually assaulted, when housed with adults (Abramsky 2001, 17; Austin, Johnson, & Gregoriou 2000, 8; Redding 1999a, 9; Reitman 1998, 7; Carter 1997, 2; Howell 1997, 105; Roush & Dunlap 1997, 12; Ziedenberg & Schiraldi 1997, 3; Forst, Fagan, & Vivona 1989; McLean 1986, 13). They are also, perhaps consequently, more likely to attempt and complete suicide.

Before providing the reader with a glimpse of victimization and suicide for youth confined in adult facilities, it is necessary to acknowledge the limitations of statistical data in these areas. The existence of the "inmate code" should make one skeptical of reports of victimization. As part of the code, male inmates are encouraged to fight (i.e., in order to prove their manhood), mind their own business, and not report incidents to the administration (for a brief discussion of life behind prison walls and the inmate code, see Clear and Cole [2003, 268–85]). Of course, this results in an underreporting of victimization incidents. Prison officials are also likely to underreport incidents of victimization and suicide, "because they are administratively embarrassing to the prison system, and could be used as evidence for lawsuits" (Ziedenberg & Schiraldi 1997, 1, 2). This may explain why some states lump suicide deaths under the category of "unspecified cause," and why others list rape with the more generic category of "inmate assaults" (Ziedenberg & Schiraldi 1997, 1, 2). Thus, the statistics provided in the sections that follow should be viewed as conservative at best.

Sexual Assault

The following news accounts provide a glimpse of the harsh realities of prison and jail life for young offenders:

> On November 13, 1995, he was sentenced to an adult prison in Brazoria County, Texas. Two weeks later he wrote his father that he had been raped by another prisoner. "I was examined by Dr. Davis and he found two tears inside my rectum—butt. I will be taking an HIV test in a few days, because there are about 2,200 inmates here, half are HIV positive." (Lewis 1997, A17)

> In Ohio, a judge placed a 15-year-old runaway girl in an adult jail to teach her a lesson. Her jailer raped her on her fourth night there." (Mlyniec 2001, 6; see also Ziedenberg & Schiraldi 1997, 1)

How common are such experiences? To date, only one study has compared the victimization experiences of youths confined in juvenile versus adult correctional facilities. Specifically, Forst, Fagan, and Vivona (1989) interviewed nontransferred youths, who were subsequently incarcerated in juvenile training schools, and juveniles who were transferred to criminal court, who were later imprisoned. The training school sample consisted of 59 chronic juvenile offenders who were interviewed upon release. The matched (i.e., for offense type and history) juvenile prison sample, in contrast, was interviewed while incarcerated; it consisted of 81 offenders. Both groups were adjudicated or tried for violent offenses between 1981 and 1984.

Forst and his colleagues (1989) found that five times as many youth held in adult prisons answer "yes" to the question, "Has anyone attempted to sexually attack or rape you?" than those held in juvenile institutions. Close to 10 percent of the juveniles who were housed in adult prisons reported that they had been the victim of a sexual attack or rape attempt. In comparison, closer to 1 percent reported the same in the juvenile institution.

Results gleaned from surveys administered in other countries support these findings, although they suggest that the extent of sexual-assault victimization for young offenders in adult institutions may be higher than initially thought. A survey of 183 Australian inmates aged 18 to 25, who were housed in New South Wales Prison, showed that one-quarter reported being raped or sexually assaulted (Heilpern [1995], as cited in Ziedenberg and Schiraldi [1997, 3]). In addition, more than half said they lived in fear of experiencing that type of victimization (Heilpern [1995], as cited in Ziedenberg and Schiraldi [1997, 3]).

In a Canadian survey, reports of sexual victimization were also high (Cooley [1993], as cited in Ziedenberg and Schiraldi [1997, 3]). Of the 117 inmates surveyed, 65 incidents of sexual assault were reported. In summarizing some of Cooley's (1993) other findings, Ziedenberg and Schiraldi (1997, 3) noted: "The odds of victimization were eight times higher for a 20-year-old prisoner than the oldest inmates in the system. 'Compared to nonvictims,' the study reports, 'victims tended to be younger, housed in higher security settings, and in the early part of their prison term.'"

Why is sexual assault of young offenders so common in adult facilities? Jeffrey Fagan, of Columbia University's School of Public Health, provides the following possible explanation: "Because they are physically diminutive, they [juveniles] are subject to attack. . . . They will become someone's 'girlfriend' very, very fast" (as cited in Ziedenberg and Schiraldi [1997, 3]). Whatever the reason, there is evidence to suggest that juvenile offenders are very likely to become the victims of sexual assault in adult facilities.

Other Victimization

In addition to assessing the likelihood of youth rape in prisons, Forst and his colleagues (1989) also discovered that 47 percent of the juvenile prisoners (versus 37 percent of the juveniles in training schools) suffered violent victimization, including violence at the hands of staff. The juveniles placed with adults were twice as likely to report being "beaten up" by staff (see also Reitman 1998, 7; Roush & Dunlap 1997, 21). Juveniles in adult prisons were also 50 percent more likely to report being attacked by a weapon (Forst, Fagan, & Vivona 1989).

The fear of victimization in adult prisons is illustrated by Reitman's (1998) account of one juvenile prisoner's experience. Paul Ludlow, a 17 year old incarcerated in an adult prison in Texas, told Reitman how he avoided (and feared) being assaulted:

> By keeping to himself but not acting afraid, he's avoided getting "checked," or hassled by other inmates. Since coming to prison, he's learned "the game": to be able to watch TV while watching everyone else; listen to 50 conversations while phoning in on eight. Paul has learned to read lips and hand movements, talk to other inmates by holding a mirror through the bars of his cell, and use the mirror to see who might be coming down his cell row. "It's about about survival," he says. (Reitman 1998, 6)

There is evidence that the "game of survival" is more life-threatening in adult than in juvenile institutions, since the injuries suffered there are more serious than those suffered in juvenile facilities. To illuminate that point, using data from the *Corrections Yearbook*, an annual survey of the state of America's prisons compiled by the Criminal Justice Institute (CJI), Ziedenberg and Schiraldi (1997, 2) noted that "inmates are seven times more likely to be referred for medical attention due to an inmate assault in an adult prison in Connecticut than in one of the state's juvenile institutions." Death may also be a possibility, as the following account demonstrates: "Seventeen-year-old Chris Peterson went to an adult jail in Boise, Ohio, for failure to pay his traffic fines. He was tortured for three days and then murdered by the adult prisoners in his cell" (Mlyniec 2001, 6). One must wonder what the effect of living in an environment plagued by violence would have on the likelihood of youth suicide.

Suicide

Ziedenberg and Schiraldi (1997, 1) provide the following examples of youth suicide in adult jails: "In Kentucky, 30 minutes after a 15-year-old is put in a jail cell following an argument with his mother, the youth hangs himself." "In one year, four children being held in Kentucky jails 'for offenses ranging from disorderly conduct, to nonoffenses, like running away from home' committed suicide." A review of the literature indicates that the situation in Kentucky is not unique, and the issue of youth suicide in adult facilities is a harsh reality. The most recent American and most comprehensive study on youth suicide in adult institutions and youth facilities was published in 1980 (Flaherty 1980), which explains why it is so heavily cited by researchers who study the effects of incarcerating youths with adults (see, for example, Mlyniec 2001, 6; Austin, Johnson, & Gregoriou 2000, 8; Reitman 1998, 7; Howell 1997, 36; Ziedenberg & Schiraldi 1997). Flaherty (1980), whose research was funded by the Office of Juvenile Justice and Delinquency Prevention (OJJDP), obtained data on the number of suicides in a thousand jails and juvenile detention centers. He found the suicide rate for juveniles held in jails to be five times higher than that for youth in the general population, and eight times greater than that for adolescents detained in juvenile facilities.

More recent data on prison suicides, based on a British study, supports the findings reported by Flaherty. According to Ziedenberg and Schirladi (1997, 2), an organization called the Prison Reform Trust analyzed data collected by Her Majesty's Prison Service. The Trust researchers found that "while people aged 15 to 21 made up only 13 percent of the prison population, they comprised 22 percent of all suicide deaths" (Ziedenberg & Schiraldi 1997, 2). Thus, the likelihood of suicide was higher among younger inmates.

Why is the likelihood of suicide higher for young inmates incarcerated with older adults? Redding (1999a, 9) and others (see, for example, Parent, Dunworth, McDonald, & Rhodes 1997, 2) attribute the higher suicide rate to the stressful living conditions that young inmates must endure—greater physical and sexual abuse by older inmates. And, unfortunately, security for those younger than age 18 appears to be a special concern only in facilities that separate this population from adult inmates (Levinson & Greene 1999, 61).

As a possible solution to victimization, youth may intentionally violate institutional rules so that they may be placed in segregated confinement. In fact, Levinson and Greene (1999, 61) noted that juveniles tended to have more disciplinary incidents than their adult counterparts and had a higher rate of segregation commitments. Unfortunately, isolated confinement may add to their likelihood of suicide. Parent and his colleagues succinctly summarize this possibility: "Young inmates who cannot survive such a situation have little choice but to enter protective custody, which is usually a separate, secure housing unit in which they spend a great deal of time in isolation—a setting that is especially conducive to suicidal behavior" (Parent, Dunworth, McDonald, & Rhodes 1997, 5). One reason why isolation may be especially likely to result in suicidal behavior among juveniles in adult prisons is because of a lack of adequate psychological care, as suggested by Forst and his colleagues (1989). Specifically, they found that treatment services in juvenile facilities (as opposed to adult facilities) were rated higher in three areas—medical care, counseling, and family relations. It may also be true that youth who are detained in adult facilities are likely to be mentally ill or suffer from severe emotional disturbances; isolated confinement would aggravate their conditions (for similar arguments, see Mylniec [2001, 4, 6] and Austin, Johnson, and Gregoriou [2000, 16]).

When young offenders are housed with adults or placed in segregated confinement, it may not be practical or possible to develop specialized programming or counseling that addresses their unique needs and problems, because they make up such a small percentage of the total incarcerated population (Parent, Dunworth, McDonald, & Rhodes 1997, 5). Indeed, there is little evidence that state correctional administrators make efforts to customize programs for youthful offenders housed with adults or offer specialized training for staff in how to deal with younger inmates (Austin, Johnson, & Gregoriou 2000; Strom 2000; Levinson & Greene 1999).

SUMMARY AND POLICY RECOMMENDATIONS

In 1899, a separate justice system was created to handle juvenile offenders, because Progressive reformers believed that children had to be protected from the harshness of the criminal-justice system, especially from being housed in adult facilities where they would be vulnerable to victimization and corrupting influences. It is distressing that Americans, a hundred years later, have come to disregard the harm juvenile offenders are likely to suffer when placed in adult jails and prisons. Politicians, driven in part by public sentiment, continue to push for harsher handling of children who commit crime. This is evident in policies that continue to expanded the range of young offenders who may be prosecuted in adult court. It would appear that, in this "get tough" era, we are far from returning to a system that treats those under the age of 18 differently from adults.

In light of this reality, one may wonder what may be done to protect the young who end up serving time in adult institutions. First, juvenile offenders should be confined separately from adults. It is alarming that the majority of states have little problem with the idea of integrating juveniles into a population comprised of significantly older inmates. Administrators must come to realize the problems with such a policy. Second, specialized programming, including adequate psychological counseling, must be provided for juvenile inmates. In particular, a psychiatrist or psychologist should be readily available for youth confined in isolation, since their likelihood of suicide is intensified. Third, correctional staff, especially the officers who maintain the most contact with the inmates, must be trained in how to effectively handle the younger inmates. It is disturbing that correctional officers have been found to be more likely to assault juveniles held in adult prisons than those incarcerated in training schools. Correctional administrators should examine that issue more closely and take appropriate action. By implementing policies that acknowledge that juveniles are different from adults, even when they are confined in the same place, Americans may start to regard the harm that juveniles suffer when incarcerated with adults.

Acknowledgments

Special thanks go out to Ms. Yoshiko Takahasi, graduate assistant in the Department of Criminal Justice at the University of North Carolina at Charlotte, for her invaluable assistance in acquiring many of the references used in this chapter. Ms. Frada Mozenter, Social Science Reference Librarian and Electronic Search Services Coordinator at the Atkins Library, University of North Carolina at Charlotte, provided invaluable, and much appreciated, assistance at well. I am also grateful for the efficient services provided by the university's interlibrary-loan specialists.

References

Abramsky, Sasha. (2001). "Hard time kids: Handing down adult prison sentences to juvenile criminals isn't solving their problems—or ours." *American Prospect 12*(15):16–21.

Austin, James, Kelly Dedel Johnson, and Maria Gregoriou. (2000). *Juveniles in adult prisons and jails: A national assessment.* Washington, DC: U.S. Department of Justice, Office of Justice Programs, Bureau of Justice Assistance.

Beck, Allen J., Jennifer C. Karberg, and Paige M. Harrison. (2002). *Prison and jail inmates at midyear 2001.* Washington, DC: U.S. Department of Justice, Office of Justice Programs, Bureau of Justice Statistics.

Carter, Beth. (1997). "Youth violence update: Federal juvenile legislation misses the mark." *Juvenile Justice Digest 27*(13):1–6.

Clear, Todd R., and George F. Cole. (2003). *American corrections*, 6th ed. Belmont, CA: Wadsworth Publishing.

Flaherty, M. (1980). *An assessment of the incidence of youth suicide in adult jails, lock-ups, and juvenile detention centers.* Champaign, IL: Community Research Forum.

Forst, Martin, Jeffrey Fagan, and T. Scott Vivona. (1989). "Youth in prisons and state training schools: Perceptions and consequences of the treatment–custody dichotomy." *Juvenile and Family Court Journal 40*(1):1–14.

Gendreau, Paul, and Robert R. Ross. (1983–84). "Correctional treatment: Some recommendations for effective intervention." *Juvenile and Family Court Journal 34*(winter):31–39.

Howell, James C. (1997). *Juvenile justice and youth violence.* Thousand Oaks, CA: Sage Publications.

Levinson, Robert B., and John J. Greene III. (1999). "New 'boys' on the block: A study of prison inmates under the age of 18." *Corrections Today 61*(1):60–63.

Lewis, Anthony. (1997). "Suffer the children." *New York Times 146*(N):A17.

Martinson, Robert. (1974). "What works? Questions and answers about prison reform." *Public Interest 35*(spring):22–54.

McLean, Gordon. (1986). "Adult prison is no place for a kid." *Christianity Today 30*(December 12):13.

Merlo, Alida V., Peter J. Benekos, and W. J. Cook. (1997). "'Getting tough' with youth: Legislative waiver as crime control." *Juvenile and Family Court Journal 48*(3):1–15.

Mlyniec, Wallace J. (2001). "The hidden evil of children living in jail." *Children's Legal Rights Journal 21*(1):2–11.

Palmer, Ted. (1983). "The 'effectiveness' issue today: An overview." *Federal Probation 47*(2):3–10.

Parent, Dale, Terrence Dunworth, Douglas McDonald, and William Rhodes. (1997). *Key legislative issues in criminal justice: Transferring serious juvenile offenders to adult courts.* Washington, DC: U.S. Department of Justice, Office of Justice Programs, National Institute of Justice.

Podkopacz, Marcy R., and Barry C. Feld. (2001). "The back-door to prison: Waiver reform, 'blended sentencing,' and the law of unintended consequences." *Journal of Criminal Law and Criminology 91*(4):997–1071.

Redding, Richard E. (1999a). "Juvenile offenders in criminal court and adult prison: Legal, psychological, and behavioral outcomes." *Juvenile and Family Court Journal 50*(1):1–20.

———. (1999b). "Examining legal issues: Juvenile offenders in criminal court and adult prison." *Corrections Today 61*(2):92–95, 120–24.

Reitman, Janet. (1998). "Tough justice: Adult prison sentences for teenagers." *Scholastic Update 131*(5):4–7.

Roush, David W., and Earl L. Dunlap. (1997). "Juveniles in adult prisons: A very bad idea." *Corrections Today 59*(3):21.

Sickmund, Melissa. (1994). *How juveniles get to criminal court.* Washington, DC: U.S. Department of Justice, Office of Justice Programs, Office of Juvenile Justice and Delinquency Prevention.

Sickmund, Melissa, Howard N. Snyder, and Eileen Poe-Yamagata. (1997). *Juvenile offenders and victims: 1997 update on violence.* Washington, DC: U.S. Department of Justice, Office of Justice Programs, Office of Juvenile Justice and Delinquency Prevention.

Snyder, Howard N. (1998). *Juvenile arrests in 1997.* Washington, DC: U.S. Department of Justice, Office of Justice Programs, Office of Juvenile Justice and Delinquency Prevention.

Snyder, Howard N., and Melissa Sickmund. (1995). *Juvenile offenders and victims: A national report.* Washington, DC: U.S. Department of Justice, Office of Justice Programs, Office of Juvenile Justice and Delinquency Prevention.

Strom, Kevin J. (2000). *Profile of state prisoners under age 18, 1985–1997.* Washington, DC: U.S. Department of Justice, Office of Justice Programs, Bureau of Justice Statistics.

Torbert, Patricia, Richard Gamble, Hunter Hurst IV, Imogene Montgomery, Linda Szymanski, and Douglas Thomas. (1996). *State responses to serious and violent juvenile crime.* Washington, DC: U.S. Department of Justice, Office of Justice Programs, Office of Juvenile Justice and Delinquency Prevention.

Wilson, James Q. (1980). "'What works?' revisited: New findings on criminal rehabilitation." *Public Interest 61* (fall):3–7.

Ziedenberg, Jason, and Vincent Schiraldi. (1997). *The risks juveniles face when they are incarcerated with adults.* San Francisco: Justice Policy Institute. Available at: <http://www.cjcj.org/jpi/risks.html>.

CHAPTER ELEVEN

Prostitutes as Prey

empirical support for the lifestyle/exposure model as an explanation of personal victimization and worries about crime

CHARISSE T. M. COSTON
LEE E. ROSS

GIVEN THE VERY NATURE of their profession, prostitutes (or street-walkers) appear to be high-risk targets for criminal victimization. The professional goals of these women involve selling sexual services for money to strangers. These customers have been procured from public spaces, defining a lifestyle, characteristic objectively associated with personal risk. In this chapter, we explore and describe the lifestyle, criminal-victimization experiences, unique vulnerabilities, and worries of this little-studied subgroup within society. Although other studies have focused on fear and victimization among mainstream segments of the general population (females, the poor, urban residents, and the elderly, to name a few), this chapter attempts to give the academician, policy-maker, law-enforcement community, and the popular audience a view of what it is like working as a female street-walker, making her living in public spaces. This study utilizes the lifestyle model of victimization developed by Hindelang, Gottfredson, and Garofalo (1978), which is offered as a theoretical background for the victimization of this subculture.

BACKGROUND

Hindelang and colleagues' (1978) theoretical lifestyle model of victimization focuses on demographic characteristics, and a number of conditions exist prior to personal victimization that drives the probability of certain criminal events. Role expectations, structural constraints, adaptations, lifestyle associations, and exposure represent important preconditions to personal victimization. This lifestyle model will be explained, followed by a set of propositions about how this might apply to street-walkers' victimization experiences and their worries about crime.

Demographic Characteristics

The authors (Hindelang, Gottfredson, & Garofolo 1978) use the example of age to illustrate how much time a child, as compared to an adult, spends outside of the immediate family. Associating with peers and becoming involved with extracurricular activities, for example, allow the adolescent greater autonomy than younger children. According to Hindelang and colleagues (1978), one's lifestyle becomes increasingly determined by adaptations to the economic structure. Accordingly, the occupation that a person assumes will have an impact on that person's lifestyle (Smith & Hill 1991). This impact manifests itself with respect to where, when, and with whom time is spent (Hindelang, Gottfredson, & Garofolo 1978, 247). The authors further state that as age increases, so does the fear of crime. In addition, as people age, they tend to associate with people more like themselves. The occupation of prostituting along the streets appears to indicate that the person will spend a great deal of time out-of-doors. Given these conditions, to what extent will they be victimized or be fearful of victimization?

Although females usually spend more time inside their homes than males (Webb & Hall 1989; Warr 1990), female street-walkers necessarily spend a lot of time outside. It appears, then, that their occupation will dictate the amount of time spent outside, the number of interpersonal contacts, and the probability of encountering strangers (Band 1991).

Hindelang and colleagues (1978) also suggest refering to marital status, family income, and race as important demographic characteristics of the lifestyle model of victimization. Persons who are married have more structure in their lives and spend more time in the home than single people. Past research on prostitutes reveals that most of the female street-walkers are not married (Pearson & Toby 1991) and spend most of their time outside, either unaccompanied or in the company of other unattached persons. Thus, marital status is another indicator of lifestyle.

Family income and race are variables closely related to life changes and life experiences. As income increases, so does one's ability to choose his or her lifestyle—namely, where to live, the mode of transportation, the time spent in public versus private places, and leisure-time activities. The literature on prostitution claims that street-walkers tend to live in urban areas of social disorganization and erosion, and generally is a group that is not wealthy (Box, Hale, & Andrews 1988; Thompson, Bankston, & St.

Pierre 1992). Finally, race is associated with lifestyle because most blacks live in segregated housing and/or financially heterogenous areas more than whites do (Cohn, Barkan, & Halteman 1991; Taylor & Covington 1993). Coupled with income factors, race determines the exposure to victimization risk: nonwhites living under limited financial conditions in urban areas and thus are high-risk targets for crime victimization.

The Probability of Victimization

The likelihood of becoming the victim of a crime varies across the population. Hindelang and colleagues (1978) explain the variations in victimization based upon lifestyle and exposure to victimization risk. Furthermore, they set forth a series of propositions that point to ways that particular lifestyles can expose people to victimization experiences.

Their first proposition is that suffering a victimization experience is directly related to how much time a person spends in public places, particularly at night. Research has shown that most crime occurs late at night and during early morning (Pearson & Toby 1991; Madriz 1992). Street-walkers spend most of their time in public places and primarily at night (Feucht 1993). Therefore, it would seem that street-walkers have a high probability of being victimized.

The second of Hindelang and colleagues' (1978) propositions is that the likelihood of being in public places at night is a function of lifestyle. Street-walkers work at night and in public places as a function of their occupation more than they work during the day and in private places.

"Social contacts and interactions occur disproportionately among individuals who share similar lifestyles" is Hindelang and colleagues' third proposition (1978, 245). Research has discussed the varied types of individuals whose lifestyles and interactions overlapped with other criminal types (Vrig & Winkel 1991; Smith & Hill 1991). Some of those types of individuals in the above research were prostitutes, drug dealers, pimps, gamblers, and thieves. According to Hindelang and colleagues (1978), an individual's chances of personal victimization are dependent upon the extent to which the individual shares demographic characteristics with offenders. This is their fourth proposition, which also is illustrated in Coston's (1993) research of homeless women.

Street-walkers usually try to keep their occupations away from family members (Taylor & Covington 1993). This fact is consistent with Hindelang and colleagues' (1978) fifth and sixth propositions. The fifth proposition is that "[t]he proportion of time that an individual spends among nonfamily members varies as a function of lifestyle" (p. 259). Their sixth proposition asserts that the chances of personal victimization also increase when one spends time around nonfamily members. It appears that the lifestyle associated with the occupation of street-walking would be full of stories of the high degree of crime. This fact, supported by the general social disapproval associated with prostitution, further isolates this group of women from familial contact.

Street-walkers cannot isolate themselves from people with offender characteristics. This is Hindelang and colleagues' (1978) seventh proposition. Therefore, the probability of personal victimization increases as street-walkers mix with other criminal types.

Hindelang and colleagues' eighth proposition focuses on the desirability of targets for criminal victimization. Offenders who victimize prostitutes probably believe that prostitutes will be unwilling or unable to call the police due to their lifestyle. Therefore, crimes against prostitutes may be perceived as holding a degree of impunity for the offender. Suitable targets, according to Felson and Cohen (1980), focus on visibility, access, value, and inertia.

These propositions are not independent of one another and thus are difficult to test. But, given this theoretical model of personal victimization, some exploratory and descriptive data were sought to illustrate street-walkers' personal victimization experiences. In addition, the data reflect prostitutes' worries about crime in relation to other worries that they might have while working predominantly in public, high-crime places at night, and how interacting with potential offenders is reflected in their victimization experiences.

METHODOLOGY

Site and Sampling Procedures

The data in the present study are derived from interviews conducted with female street-walkers who had been arrested for solicitation between 20th and 50th Streets on the west side of Manhattan in New York City and who were in custody awaiting arraignment when interviewed one-on-one. Each interview lasted about 30 minutes and was conducted in the New York County Criminal Court lockup unit.

Of the 77 streetwalkers approached for this study over a two-month period during the summer, 59 acknowledged that they were selling sexual services along the streets and agreed to be interviewed free-of-charge. The remaining 18 refused to be interviewed either because they were not going to receive financial compensation for it or because they denied that they were soliciting money for sexual services.

Measures

Street-walkers were asked a number of demographic characteristics: their age, race, city of origin, length of time living in New York City, sources and amount of income, frequency of working as a prostitute on the streets each week, highest level of education completed, and whether they had any vocational or technical training. They were also asked for their self-perceptions of health, if they see a doctor regularly, and/or had been in the hospital since working along the streets.

In addition to these demographic items, respondents were asked about the nature and extent of their direct and indirect criminal-victimization experiences before and while working on the streets. They were asked questions about their self-perceptions of vulnerability to criminal victimization, such as "How likely do you think it is that you could be the victim of personal crime?"; and "How likely do you think it is that you could be the victim of a property crime?" Answers to these items ranged from (1) not likely, to (7) extremely likely; and women were also asked, "Compared to other working girls, do you think that you are more, or less, or just-as-likely to be victimized?"

The subjects were asked about their use of precautionary behaviors. Did they avoid certain places and people due to the threat of criminal victimization, and if they did, the types of places and customers avoided? Street-walkers were also asked if they carried anything to protect themselves, and if so, the types of protection utilized.

Subjects were asked to name their five biggest worries that they have while working, and then to rank-order those worries. The last question asked them to indicate on a five-point scale (0 = not worried, to 4 = extremely worried), "How worried are you about becoming the victim of a crime?"

RESULTS

Table 11.1 shows the demographic characteristics of the sample. On average, the 59 street-walkers in this sample were 26 years old. Most of them were black ($n = 33$); 26 were white. Most were originally from New York City ($n = 37$). Most of those who were not from New York City replied that they were originally from outside of the United States. Four reported being from the Midwest, two reported that they were originally from Southwestern states, and six were from New England. Of those not originally from New York City, 11 subjects reported selling sex for money when they arrived and that it had been their reason for coming to New York City. The remaining 11 reported having been in New York City anywhere from two months to five years before selling sexual services. The average length of time spent street-walking in New York City was 31 months, with the range being from two months to seven years.

About half of the prostitutes in this study reported that selling sex was their only source of income. Other reported income sources from food stamps, welfare, both welfare and food stamps, and receiving disability income from the government. When asked how much income they receive from legitimate income sources, the median was \$500 a week. The range of income received weekly from legitimate sources was \$165 to \$1,000. Street-walkers reported having earned a median of \$1,500 each week by selling sexual services, with the range being from \$200 to \$5,000. A factor associ-

Table 11.1
Demographic Characteristics of the Sample

Characteristic	*N*
Race	
white	26
black	33
Origin	
New York City	37
Midwestern states	4
Southwestern states	2
New England states	6
outside of the United States	10
Primary source(s) of income	
selling sex	30
selling sex and receiving government aid (welfare, food stamps)	19
selling sex and receiving disability checks	10
Education	
completed college (BS)	4
completed some college	12
completed high school	37
completed eighth grade	4
completed ninth grade	3
completed tenth grade	2
completed eleventh grade	13
completed vocational training	34
Types of vocational training	
bartending	13
cosmetology	11
data entry	4
landscaping	3
medical-laboratory training	3
Perceptions of health	
excellent	12
good	18
average	24
fair	6
Hospitalization	
no	37
yes	22

ated with the amount of money earned weekly was how often they would sell their sexual services. The average number of hours spent working the streets was 30 hours, and the range was from two hours to 70 hours each week. Those whom spent more time on the streets earned more money.

The highest level of education completed by most prostitutes of this study was high school ($n = 37$). Four reported having completed the eighth grade, three reported having completed the ninth grade, two reported having completed the tenth grade, and 13 reported having completed the eleventh grade. Most prostitutes reported having had no college education. Of the 16 who reported having had some college, only four had earned a Bachelor's degree. Over half the subjects in this sample reported having had some vocational training (n = 34). Most of those with vocational training reported that they had either formal or informal training in bartending (n = 13). Other vocational skills reportedly obtained included cosmetology (n = 11), data entry (n = 4), landscaping (n = 3), and medical-laboratory training (n = 3).

Fifty-four percent of the subjects in this study consider their health to be average, while 24 percent perceived it to be good. Seventeen percent shared perceptions of excellent health, and 5 percent replied that they were in fair health. Most street-walkers in this sample stated that they see a doctor regularly (64 percent); most had not been in the hospital within the last year (54 percent). Of the 46 percent who reported having had been in the hospital, most said it was because they had been physically assaulted. Other visits to the hospital reported by these women were for sexually transmitted diseases, pneumonia, chemical dependence, and/or for psychiatric reasons.

Table 11.2 depicts the victimization experiences reported by prostitutes—most of these subjects reported having been the victim of a crime while working on the streets. The number of times victimized while working on the streets ranged from 1 to 20. Rape was the type of victimization experienced most often, followed by robbery. Other types of victimization experiences suffered by these women include assault, theft, and a combination of victimization experiences—that is, more than one type of crime happening in a single criminal event; for example, rape and robbery, or robbery and assault.

When the subjects were asked about their victimization experiences while not working, most of them reported having had been the victim of a crime during the past year, with the number of times ranging from one to three. Incidents of rape, robbery, and vehicle theft were reported.

Ninety-six percent of the subjects in the study reported vicarious victimization experiences; they had heard that both males and females had been victimized. When the subjects were asked how likely they think it is that they could be the victim of a crime, the average response was a (6)—"extremely likely." All of the subjects reported avoiding certain places and types of customers due to the threat of victimization. Some reported avoiding deserted areas and avoiding the piers. Other places avoided due to the likelihood of victimization were other boroughs (they reported that they only worked in Manhattan), places where no other prostitutes worked, and places suggested for sexual relations by the customer. Most prostitutes, regardless of race, reported that they would avoid young black

Table 11.2
Past Victimization Experiences

Characteristic	*N*
Victimized while working	
no	10
yes	49
Type of victimization	
rape	17
robbery	18
assault	7
theft	9
combination victimization:	
rape and robbery	2
robbery and assault	4
Victimized while not working (within the past year)	
no	22
yes	37
type of victimization:	
rape	27
robbery	5
theft	5
Vicarious victimization experiences	
no	9
yes	50
Types of places and people avoided*	
deserted areas	17
piers	16
boroughs outside Manhattan	5
places where no other prostitutes work	6
places suggested by the customer for sexual relations	11
minority customers	10
intoxicated customers	5
persons who were vulgar or aggressive	15
teenagers	20
Weapons	
no	10
yes	49
Types of protection	
knife	15
scissors	12
guns	12
karate	8
lye	2

Note: *Some subjects mentioned more than one type of place or person avoided.

or Hispanic customers. Other types of customers avoided that were reported by the women in this sample were intoxicated customers, vulgar or aggressive customers, and teenagers.

Most of the subjects reported always carrying a weapon. Some reported carrying a weapon only "sometimes." Only a few reported never carrying a weapon. Of those who carry a weapon all of the time, most carry a knife. This percentage was closely followed by those who reported carrying scissors most often. Guns and karate were weapons carried and a method of protection for those in the sample. A few reported carrying some form of chemical for protection—for example, lye or ammonia.

Street-walkers were asked to indicate their five biggest worries, and then to rank-order these worries from the biggest (1) to the least (5). Their top five responses, in order, were:

1. Being killed
2. Being mugged
3. Getting arrested
4. Serving jail time
5. Being identified if they were injured or killed.

Other worries reported by the subjects in this sample, in numeric order, included being raped, not making enough money, getting AIDS, "other prostitutes taking my customers," "my kids finding out about the kind of work I do," and "obtaining enough money to buy drugs." When the women were asked about how much they worry overall about becoming the victim of a crime, their average response indicated that they were "somewhat unworried." Sixty-four percent of the street-walkers reported that they did not have a pimp or someone who managed their prostitution.

Concluding Remarks

Prostitutes are crime victims. These findings provide empirical support for their victimization experiences in relation to their risky lifestyles and vulnerabilities. These women appear to be easy targets because of their attracting motivated offenders. Future research should focus on comparing female street-walkers to the average female citizenry. This chapter provides additional groundwork for the study between and among uniquely vulnerable populations.

References

Band, T. (1991). "The effectiveness of a police-initiated fear-reducing strategy." *British Journal of Criminology 31*:1–13.

Box, S., C. Hale, and G. Andrews. (1988). "Explaining fear of crime." *British Journal of Criminology 28*:340–56.

Cohn, S., S. Barkan, and W. Halteman. (1991). "Punitive attitudes toward criminals: Racial consensus or racial conflict?" *Social Problems 38*:287–95.

Coston, C. (1993). "Vulnerable populations: Homeless women." *Journal of Social Distress 2*:1–21.

Felson, M., and L. Cohen. (1980). "Human ecology and crime: A routine activity approach." *Human Ecology 8*:389–406.

Feucht, T. (1993). "Prostitutes on crack cocaine: Addiction, utility, and marketplace economics." *Journal of Deviant Behavior 14*:91–108.

Hindelang, Michael, Michael Gottfredson, and James Garofalo. (1978). *Victims of personal crime: An empirical foundation for a theory of personal victimization.* Cambridge, MA: Ballinger Publishing Company.

Madriz, E. (1992). *Fear of crime and victimization of women: A real paradox?* Ph.D. dissertation, University of Michigan. Ann Arbor: Dissertation Abstracts.

Pearson, F., and J. Toby. (1991). "Fear of school-related predatory crime." *Sociology and Social Research 75*:117–25.

Smith, L., and G. Hill. (1991). "Victimization and fear of crime." *Criminal Justice & Behavior 18*:217–39.

Taylor, R., and J. Covington. (1993). "Community structural change and fear of crime." *Social Problems 40*:374–93.

Thompson, C., W. Bankston, and R. St. Pierre. (1992). "Parity and disparity among three measures of fear of crime: A research note." *Deviant Behavior: An Interdisciplinary Journal 13*:373–89.

Vrig, A., and F. Winkel. (1991). "Characteristics of the built environment and fear of crime: A research note on interventions in unsafe locations." *Deviant Behavior: An Interdisciplinary Journal 12*:203–15.

Warr, M. (1990). "Dangerous situations: Social context and fear of victimization." *Social Forces 68*:891–907.

Webb, V., and I. Hall. (1989). "Response to criminal victimization of older Americans." *Criminal Justice and Behavior 16*:239–59.

CHAPTER TWELVE

AIDS, Violence, and Matters of Respect

family and peer relations of African-American and Latino convicted felons

LAURA T. FISHMAN

THE ADVENT OF THE AIDS pandemic has had a profound impact on the rapidly accelerating disintegration of African-American and Latino families within impoverished urban neighborhoods; that is, those neighborhoods that have an increasing number of adults as well as children involved in the street-level drug-using/selling economy, are frequent clients of the criminal-justice system, and are stricken by the HIV/AIDS virus. Given this, extended family life all-too-frequently takes on devastatingly tragic proportions. It has become the norm, within these neighborhoods, for extended family-kin networks to suffer the loss of one or more family members to alcoholism and drug addiction, to the jails, and/or to premature death from overdosing on drugs, homicide, and the AIDS virus. Whenever the plight of these poor and working-class African-American and Latino families has become public, the public discourse frequently has focused upon how the future of this urban population is indeed a bleak one. For instance, a common response made by the media and professional literature is that this population can be considered as "at risk for extinction," as the "most vulnerable Americans and Latinos," or as "victims of genocide" as well as some other catastrophic descriptions. As this public discussion continues, poor African Americans and Latinos seldom are invited to express their concerns about their futures and the futures of their communities. This ethnographic study, however, will look at some African-American and Latino male convicted-offenders' experiences with

AIDS, a life-threatening disease. In particular, I will examine some consequences of this disease on the men's abilities to survive within various prison systems and within their family-kin networks.

HIV/AIDS-infected African-American and Latino convicted-offenders' struggle to survive can be described as difficult at best. The lives of these men reveal how they have struggled, sometimes desperately, to survive the constant barrage of illnesses and emotional issues as well as the social and bureaucratic hostility that comes with diagnosis. Compounding the difficulties, another contributing factor to the men's struggles is their association of AIDS with stigma and multiple losses: namely, the loss of respect and loss of masculine dignity around sexual promiscuity, the willingness to fight, and participation in the illicit drug economy. To do this, I will look at how some HIV/AIDS-infected African-American and Latino prisoners and parolees believe that maintaining their reputations as men deserving to be treated respectfully is a most pressing problem.

Their battle to survive the virus along with the constant struggle to maintain their reputations is to be explored within three social contexts: (1) the New York State prison system; (2) the illicit, underground drug economy within poor New York City neighborhoods; and lastly (3) within family extended-kin networks. A common thread that runs through the men's accounts is that the major playing fields for obtaining respect and dignity are the streets and prisons, whereas the family and extended-kin networks setting are of secondary importance. A variety of ways are used to obtain and maintain respect, but my major focus is on how men anticipate disrespectful encounters as a response to their HIV/AIDS status. The extent to which they engage in violence to reduce the risk of reprisals and to maintain their reputations that they believe to be a deterrent to potential violence will be described. Lastly, I will look into how various New York prisons as well as inner-city neighborhoods reinforce fears and anxieties about violent encounters.

The literature has documented that violence is an almost daily occurrence within some prison systems, as well as within some poor inner-city communities. Given this, interpersonal violence and aggression can be powerful stressors that impact on African-American and Latino offenders' perceptions that disclosure of their HIV/AIDS status can undermine their status as men who are to be treated respectfully.

A number of recent studies have offered important insights into how AIDS, as a life-threatening disease, has the capacity to not only threaten the infected men's physical well-being, but also their social well-being. A consistent theme in these studies is that the diagnosis of AIDS carries a massive stigma, which, in turn, starts the emotional upheaval that is faced by HIV/AIDS-infected people. "Stigma" is considered here as a pattern of social prejudice, discounting, and discrediting an individual's experiences as a result of others' judgments about his personal characteristics or group membership (Goffman 1963; Herek 1990; Herek & Glunt 1991). Studies by several researchers (Dalton 1990; Herek & Glunt 1991) suggest that AIDS-related stigma primarily results from the properties of AIDS as a disease. First, it is stigmatized for its tendency to disfigure one's appearance and impair one's ability for social interaction, its communicability, and its lethality. Within inner-city ghettoes and barrios (for example, Diaz 1998; Boyd-Franklin, Alemán, Jean-Gilles, & Lewis 1995; Singer et al. 1990), AIDS is linked to "weakness" that undermines machismo and manliness.

Although AIDS is no longer primarily seen as the "gay men's disease," some researchers have noted that African Americans and Latinos still maintain the misperception that HIV/AIDS is a disease mainly dangerous to white gay men (Boyd-Franklin, Alemán, Jean-Gilles, & Lewis 1995; Dalton 1990). Such homophonic terms given to gays as "faggot," "sissy," "bitch" especially call men's masculinity and heterosexuality into question, and perhaps also the status of HIV/AIDS-infected African-American and Latino men into question. As noted by Nightingale (1993), African-American and Latino men are not necessarily afraid of being called such epithets as "sissy" when their HIV/AIDS status is known. Instead, they are concerned about the possibility of being victimized by other males "on the streets" and within prison communities. These fears are well-founded, since they are fully aware that "sissies" are fair game for exploitation.

Documenting the conditions under which prisoners, gays, and intravenous (IV) drug-users with HIV/AIDS become stigmatized has only begun (Christ & Wiener 1985; Foster 1988; Kowalewski 1988). There is evidence that prisoners with AIDS receive treatment different from that afforded the general prison population (Olivero 1990; Potler 1988). Such treatment may include the segregation of prisoners with AIDS/ARC (AIDS related complex) from the general prison population, lack of programming for AIDS/ARC prisoners, lack of outdoor recreation, and inadequate health care. Potler (1988) found that inmates have commented that the prison should get rid of "them" (AIDS/ARC prisoners) or have complained of having to "deal with scum."

According to more recent research findings, only a small number of the gay population with HIV/AIDS recalls experiencing stigmatization of any form within their communities (Stallworth 1994). They anticipated workplace hostilities, familial rejection, police harassment, antigay violence, and health-care difficulties, but little ostracism has occurred. Within this context, however, little is known about HIV/AIDS-infected African American and Latino encounters with stigmatization within their communities. A few investigators (Boyd-Franklin, Alemán, Jean-Gilles, & Lewis 1995; Dalton 1990) have found that HIV/AIDS-infected people of color *do* anticipate and sometimes experience similar forms of stigmatization, as do gay men. However, it also is noted that Latinos more often than African Americans are commonly not rejected by their families, at least not for IV drug-use and for the virus (Diaz 1998; Fitzpatrick 1990).

To date, there has been little systematic investigation of African-American and Latino offenders' reactions to having contracted a disease that places into question their manliness. The literature on masculinity may be useful here, which has noted that male participation in the illegal drug economy generally demands an adherence to the "code of the streets" (Bourgois 1995; Anderson 1994; Horowitz 1995; Butterfield 1996; Erlanger 1979; Oliver 1994) as a route towards male dignity and respect. This code amounts to a set of informal rules governing interpersonal behavior, including violence. A central feature of the code, adhered to by both African Americans and Latinos, is the concept of "manhood" or "machismo." According to Anderson (1994) and White and Cones (1999), manhood in the inner-city means taking the prerogatives of men with respect to strangers, other men, and women. It suggests physicality and a certain ruthlessness. As was so aptly stated by Stallworth (1994, 51), young African Americans "lived hard, died hard, and talked plenty of trash in between."

However, among some investigators, there is consensus that manhood and respect (*repeto*) are flip-sides of the same code. Respect can be defined as being treated right, or granted the deference one deserves. Signs of *dis*-respect (to be *dissed*) are typically defined as deliberate insults or aggressive actions (Anderson 1994; Horowitz 1995; Majors & Billson 1992; Nisbett & Cohen 1995; Oliver 1994) such as making derogatory remarks, slurs, insults, jostles, bumps directed at a man, and threats with a weapon in the hands of an adversary. In the face of these affronts, it is believed that men have to stand up for their rights and not back down or hide if attacked. Though one might escape safely and avoid the necessity of fighting or killing, it would be cowardly and dishonorable to flee. Instead, a "real man" (i.e., to be "*baad ass*" or "*loco*"[1]), note several investigators (Erlanger 1979; Horowitz 1995; Mirande 1997; Stallworth 1994), will show a willingness to fight by more than physical prowess.

It is important to note here that several researchers suggest that some aspects of the rules of the street for achieving a "baad" reputation have changed (see Stallworth 1994; Nightingale 1993; Conner 1995). For instance, since the 1980s, young men of color adhere to new rules that de-emphasize the importance of possessing women and appear to take women and sex for granted. Drugs, making money, and power are their predominant concerns. Of relevance here is the observation that young men make it clear that they redefine their manhood by finding that the "way to get paid" is by involvement in drug distribution. It seems to pay-off: the greedier they are, the more they get paid. And if they have to be cold to make big money, then cold they are going to be. Thus criminality is linked to coldness.

Second, when confronted with disputes or acts of disrespect, these young men are believed to be less likely than the older men to talk it out or get into a fistfight. Now, according to Stallworth (1994), respect is forged on having a gun and using it at the slightest provocation. The intent, however, is the same when fists are used: to prevent others from messing with them, to prove their masculinity. In addition, Stallworth (1994) points out that reputations are made on the basis of a cavalier attitude toward death, which shows "heart" and earns respect. The goal of many young African-American men is to develop an image as ruthless, devious criminals who are capable of and willing to do anything to the fullest to be known as "baad ass niggers" or "loco." This reputation conveys that these men do not care about anything and will stop at nothing to acquire what they want.

Almost no work has been directed explicitly at how adherence to the street code has important consequences for African-American and Latino convicted offenders who are diagnosed as being HIV/AIDS infected. This chapter intends to fill a gap in the literature by examining the extent to which a diagnosis of HIV/AIDS can be perceived as jeopardizing these young men's reputations as "baad-ass," "loco," cold, virile, tough, and physically strong players on the streets and within prison settings. A variety of strategies are employed by these offenders as they cope with this disease simultaneously as they cope with anxiety about being "dissed" (shown disrespect) and with others perceiving them as "sissies," "queers," and "faggots."

To date, there has been some investigation into factors accounting for the domination of violence in the prison setting as a daily occurrence. A number of researchers appear to agree that those African-American and Latino prisoners primarily incarcerated in maximum-security prisons import a general "criminal subculture" that fosters high levels of both violent and nonviolent prison misconduct (Nightingale 1993; Silberman 1995; Sim 1994). Both the inner-city impoverished community and the prison constitute settings that can evoke acts of physical exploitation and protective violence.

It is expected that the drive for respect will have some consequences for African-American and Latino male convicted offenders who are coping with the stigma of AIDS as well as the pervasive misconception that HIV/AIDS infection can jeopardize men's physical strength and mental agility as well as virility. The literature points out that respect is primarily based on peers conferring deference within such social milieus as "the streets" and various prison systems. Little mention is given to looking at the extent to which African-American and Latino convicted offenders also look to their family and kin networks for a sense of manly dignity. This chapter describes how the men's important women as well as other family members are crucial to their concepts, manhood, and dignity as well as their sense of well-being for surviving the HIV/AIDS virus.

It therefore is important in describing the everyday struggles of HIV/

AIDS-infected prisoners to examine closely not only the importance of maintaining relations with family and kin networks, but the importance of these relations as an alternative toward searching for respect within the urban street and prison cultures. Finally, it is also important to consider that how these men handle their contacts with family and friends can influence their abilities to handle this life-threatening illness and stressors associated with the illness. However, whether they are interacting in the underground drug-economy setting, within prison settings or within the family- kin settings, the ways in which they cope are shown as differing between their willingness or unwillingness to employ violent strategies to ensure personal safety and/or to convince themselves and others of their manliness.

Methodology

The preliminary findings reported here were based on my research-in-progress, which focused on two populations of African-American and Latino male prisoners with HIV/AIDS infection. One consisted of 67 HIV/AIDS-infected African-American and Latino prisoners incarcerated in four maximum- and one medium-security upstate New York correctional facilities. Within each facility, arrangements were made by health-care providers who knew the identity of prisoners with HIV/AIDS. Prisoners who had ongoing contact with a significant woman (e.g., mother, sister, female partner, or aunt) and who had served at least six months were informed about my research project and their cooperation was elicited.

The second population to be discussed here consisted of 20 African-American and Latino male parolees who were clients of a community-based AIDS service organization and re-entry drug-treatment program located in the South Bronx, New York City, which primarily serviced parolees who were residents of the South Bronx. I followed a similar method in requesting clients' cooperation. They, too, were informed about the project by those staff members who knew their HIV/AIDS status. In turn, they also had to agree to meet with me before I even attempted to interview them. Interviews were limited to those men who maintained their relations with at least one female member of their families and who had been incarcerated within upstate New York correctional facilities for at least six months.

In-depth, unstructured interviews were conducted with each prisoner and parolee. All the men who participated in this study did so voluntarily. Each man was informed about the project, and his informed consent was obtained. The participants were assured of confidentiality and all interviews were conducted in a private space in the prison health clinics or in a private room at the agency or at the men's apartments. Interviews were generally several hours long. The length of the sessions depended upon the health and willingness of the participants. The interviews were structured to obtain information regarding the man's family background, prior arrests and convictions, how he learned that he had contracted HIV/AIDS, and how he coped with the illness. In keeping with the tradition of qualitative research, the specific content of the interview was determined, to a great extent, by the responses from each man I interviewed. Therefore, while the interview followed no rigid structure, an interview guide was used to ensure that the same basic topics were raised with each prisoner and parolee.

The collected data was analyzed with the "grounded theory" and "constant comparative" procedure developed by Glaser and Strauss (1967) and Charmaz (1983). Since the grounded-theory method emphasized discovery and theory development, data collection and analysis proceeded simultaneously so that a theoretical understanding of the phenomenon was constantly revised as more data were collected. On the basis of the constant-comparative method, information from data sources would be subjected to rigorous comparisons, cross-checking, and validation with respect to the experiential frame and life-space of the prisoners with HIV/AIDS.

A Profile of African-American and Latino Male Convicted Offenders

Of the final study population, all 87 African-American and Latino prisoners and parolees had lived within the metropolitan New York City area. Forty-five of the men were African American, and the remaining 42 were Latino. Virtually all of the men lived marginally—that is, most were poor, badly educated, and chronically unemployed. Only a few actually experienced short periods of employment, which generally alternated with longer periods of unemployment. Some men were getting money by petty crime and drug dealing.

According to the men's accounts, they reported that during their growing years, they had experienced three types of family arrangements: a home with two natural parents; a home with a natural mother but without a father; or a family headed by a close relative, usually a grandmother or sister. Some who began using drugs in their early adolescence indicated another pattern, however: they were raised on the streets of New York City, less frequently in Puerto Rico, or in state institutions.

Before their most recent incarceration, seldom had the men, as adults, established for themselves domestic households independent from their family members. For the most part, these convicted offenders continued living within female-based households headed by their mothers, adult sisters, or grandmothers. Only a few men reported that they continued to live with both parents; rarely had the men lived by themselves at some time during their adult years. However, most of these men upon occasion had formed short-term living arrangements with at least one woman. It was clear from their stories that these short-term living arrangements with women were based on the exchange of money, drugs, and/or sex for shelter. Whenever these relationships dissolved, these men moved back into a family member's household. In contrast, some men actually lived for extended periods of time with women whom they described as their "wives" or "girlfriends" (i.e., female partners). It appeared to be the norm among these men that they changed domiciles in quick succession from their mother's home, to a female partner's home, and sometimes to various siblings' homes. Several men related how they had "hit bottom." Since their consumption of alcohol and/or drugs had spiraled out of control, they had no home, no job, no family they were close to, and, all too often, nowhere to go. These men alternated between living on the streets or in the apartments of women, friends, associates, and homeless shelters. Few provided steady economic support for their children and/or made some monetary contribution to their extended families.

One major factor contributing towards the men's inability to be reliable income providers was their extensive absences from their households as a consequence of arrest and imprisonment. All the men had extensive criminal histories and reported that they had spent time in prison prior to their current incarceration. During their most recent incarceration, these prisoners and parolees told me that they were serving sentences ranging from three years to life. According to these men, they were charged with a variety of crimes against persons, ranging from simple assault, aggravated assault, rape, robbery, and homicide. Others reported that they were charged with such crimes against property as stealing cars, burglarizing homes, pharmacies, and small stores, as well as committing grand larceny. Many claimed that their involvement in these crimes was drug-related. Only a few were charged and/or convicted solely for possession of drugs and drug dealing.

This background of marginalization strongly suggested that most of my study population paid a price for being poor and nonwhite—the price being the use and abuse of drugs. A sizeable number consumed drugs, with the drug of choice tending to be cocaine-crack or heroin. Given this, the majority of men were heterosexual IV drug-users, and only a few were homosexual IV drug-users. The preponderance of IV drug-users indicated the effects of both geographical concentration and the tendency for drug-users to be arrested for crimes punishable by imprisonment. Both prisoners and parolees also lived within an area of New York City with relatively high incidence of AIDS among IV drug-users. It should be noted that among these men, drug dealing and drug addiction were closely linked. For instance, once addicted, many users sold drugs to support their habits. In contrast, many who were not addicted when they began to sell drugs for profit became so.

Most of these men were aware of their risky behavior while on the streets but postponed getting an HIV antibody test until they were incarcerated. Some incarcerated men were more willing to be tested once the symptoms of HIV infection started to appear (e.g., rashes, fevers, night sweats, and swollen lymph nodes). A few were tested upon being hospitalized for some opportunistic infection that suggested AIDS. Only a few of the men on the streets sought testing at an earlier stage of the HIV infection.

This chapter, as a preliminary exploration, presents some important insights into how African-American and Latino male convicted offenders perceive the diagnosis of HIV/AIDS as making them vulnerable to disrespect from their peers and social-control agents and therefore being exposed to possible victimization. The men's accounts disclose how their responses are influenced by such external social phenomenon as prisons, the illegal drug-using/selling economy, and family and kin networks.

LIFESTYLES

> *If you want to get your outcasts out-of-sight, first you need a ghetto and then you need a prison to take pressure off the ghetto.*
>
> —**Kozol (1995, 142)**

During the 1990s, a consistent theme had emerged within the subcultural literature and prison literature. It noted that the inner-city ghettos and barrios (especially those located in New York City) increasingly came to resemble the structures and cultures of prison systems. Several investigators (Harer & Steffensmeier 1996; Kozol 1995) cited some common characteristics of these impoverished communities, which approximated those characteristics of prisons as "total institutions." First, Kozol (1995) specifically reported that the South Bronx as well as other poor neighborhoods served as a form of quarantine, not just of people who had AIDS but also of people who were feared because of their race and poverty. Suggested here was the contention that these neighborhoods were "hypersegregated" insofar as residents were isolated from the dominant white community, neglected by the business community, and were recipients of inadequate health and social services.

Most troublesome of all, both Abu-Jamal (1995) and Ianni (1975) contended that this state of segregation was likened to the imprisonment of members of these communities. In response to this felt sense of imprisonment, they further argued, the segregated population had been induced to accept a caged condition that it had not chosen but knows no way by which to escape. As within various prisons, movement out of these communities became restricted for many of the residents. Rather than facing the barriers of walls, noted Kozol (1995), most residents were further restricted by poverty that prevented them the sufficient monies to travel throughout the city. Most accepted these arbitrary borders and subsequently utilized those services within their communities. In turn, only those workers employed by services and the police came into these communities. The fact that few leave willingly and few from the more affluent classes entered willingly re-enforced that poverty stigmatized the poor people of color and kept them in their place—namely, within the ghettoes and barrios.

Lastly, as noted earlier, both upstate New York prisons systems and poor New York City neighborhoods were characterized as environments enmeshed in danger and violence. Ianni (1975) pointed out that both environments mirror each other as approximations of high-rise housing projects that "contained" residents, who responded to the oppressive and over-crowded conditions with anger and aggression that heightened the likelihood of participation in various forms of drug-related property crimes, drug-related homicides, and assaultive behavior. Specifically, the male residents were killing themselves either with needles or by guns.

Most men in my study group found that imprisonment was the continuation of a process of marginalization and exclusion. Within this context, the reports of most convicted offenders indicated that the codes of behavior for survival in the street culture were taken with them into the prison setting and subsequently imported back with them into their communities. These codes of behavior, however, were shaped by a diagnosis of HIV/AIDS. For virtually all these men, having a diagnosis of HIV/AIDS impacted on behavior in the following ways: (1) maintaining the impression of a willingness to fight to death if necessary, (2) maintaining the public front of a commitment to death before dishonor, and lastly (3) not acting in a disrespectful manner.

It must be noted here that the men's abilities to adhere to these forms of behavior became increasingly unlikely as the disease progressed to the terminal stage. Almost all the men bragged to me about how respected they were before they were infected. For instance, they reported that they were respected because they had shown considerable courage and did not back down and were ready to fight, regardless of the seriousness of the confrontation. Many gave the impression that their masculinity was rooted in "machismo" or in the images of the "baad ass nigger" or "loco." Almost all the young men, growing up in the streets, reflected an adherence to the new rules of the new generation. In addition to living hard and dying hard, they continually disclosed that prior to their diagnosis, they did not give "a fuck about anything." Tied to their not caring was a cold disregard for the value of human life, much less their own. Many maintained a cold-hearted, mean-spirited outlook. Intermittently, they frequently tried to convince me and perhaps themselves that they were the baddest dudes to come out of the ghettos and barrios since Superfly.[2] Some wore their prison sentences as badges of honor. The more time they had done, the more respect they achieved among their peers because they were then viewed as "hardcore." In some instances, tied to being perceived as tough, ruthless, and cold was the ability to endure any harm inflicted upon their bodies. Unlike the older men in my study group, the young ones spoke about hanging tough as being able to survive gun and knife wounds.

Frequently, these men shared with me their tales of death and injury on the streets as well as within the prison settings. With great pride they recounted their war stories about each injury inflicted on them and did not hesitate to show me each scar they received from gunshot and knife wounds. Respect, therefore, was forged upon the injuries received and their abilities to survive them.

Unique to the urban street culture, however, was the importance of "taking care of the business" of drug dealing, which could provide an additional route of respect. An important symbol of "taking care of the business" was to use the proceeds from getting paid for involvement in drug-distribution activities to partying, spending lavishly on peers, to aggrandize oneself by spending monies on gold chains, sneakers, clothes, expensive cars, loud music, and so forth. In this manner, they were considered by their peers within the illegal drug economy as one of those who were "making it."

Involvement in the urban street culture also frequently led to multiple sexual partners. Some African-American men admitted that they had achieved the status of "players of women" by using women solely as sexual objects. Oliver (1994) noted that African-American men acted as "players of women" as an acceptable alternative to the traditional definitions of manhood. Most men opted to redefine manhood in terms of toughness, sexual conquest, and thrill-seeking.

DISCLOSURE OF HIV/AIDS AND VULNERABILITY TO BEING DISSED

Another common theme emerged within the accounts elicited from African-American and Latino male prisoners and parolees. A diagnosis of HIV/AIDS infection was believed to place these men in situations in which they were more likely to encounter stigmatizing events and consequently were treated by their peers as being "weak" or as deserving of disrespect. Potential acts of disrespect were considered to be a challenge to everything they cherished—their reputations, honor, and their ability to appear as "somebody" to their peers (Stallworth 1994).

According to most men, fears and anxieties about disclosure of their now "tainted identities" was far more intensified within various prisons than on the streets. Since various prisons systems were dominated by a culture of masculinity, it became difficult for most men to hide their newly acquired status, and consequently there was no escape when disclosure occurred.

African-American and Latino prisoners with HIV/AIDS were not unfamiliar with being labeled "them" or "other." They had experienced similar labeling repeatedly as economically oppressed minorities and as members of cultures whose traditional values hold them inferior: that is, as people of color, these prisoners had already been stigmatized by poverty, race, and IV drug-use and had repeatedly been the targets of social-control measures. Under these circumstances, prisoners understandably wished to avoid new forms of stigmatization, which were likely to accompany the disclosure of their health status.

In the communities of color in New York City, those most likely to be designated as "others" were gays, bisexuals, and IV drug-users. The pervasive negative attitude of both African Americans and Latinos towards homosexuality was reinforced by religious beliefs that viewed homosexuality and drug use as deviant or sinful behavior. The stigmatization directed against persons with HIV/AIDS was based on the common perception that "they" chose to have AIDS by participating in deviant behavior. Furthermore, both Latino and African-American communities responded to AIDS from the perspective of manliness (or machismo). Manliness, a pervasive belief in these communities, encouraged virtually all the men in my study population by virtue of their gender to participate in dominance, authoritarianism, aggressiveness, heavy drinking, excessive sexual activity, and violence. As in these communities, convicted offenders of African-American and Latino descent were likely to associate AIDS with unmanliness, unnaturalness, and weakness. Whether within the various prison systems or within the African-American and Latino communities, this perception of AIDS as being another example of "bad behavior" or "otherness" was a subject not to be openly discussed.

The silence that existed within the various prison systems regarding the presence of infected prisoners was a response to the social and racial stereotypes that surrounded AIDS on the streets. Prisoners' accounts disclosed that the dominant reactions of prisoners to the situation of those prisoners living with HIV/AIDS was to act cool, indifferent, or unresponsive. Aside from an occasional derogatory statement, the bulk of prisoners continued to absorb themselves in their own round of activities, keeping their mouths shut and expressing little concern for those whose illness was readily apparent. These accounts suggested that a "culture of silence" had emerged based on denial and fear.

This culture of silence could best be characterized as presenting a closed-awareness context (Glaser & Strauss 1965)—namely, one interactant did not know either the true identity or the other's view of his identity. In this context, the stigmatized was confronted with creating a "normal" identity and playing down his deviant identity. Within the prison community, the closed-awareness context was maintained as long as the unaffected prisoners did not know the status of the prisoners with HIV/AIDS. This culture could only be maintained if prisoners with HIV/AIDS allowed it to exist. If they kept their status to themselves, then the other prisoners could continue to maintain "normalcy" and hence reduce their fears of contamination. African-American prisoners were more likely than Latino prisoners to be fearful about disclosing their status primarily in anticipation of the loss of respect. Underlying this anticipation of loss of respect, they feared physical harm, stigma, abandonment, and rejection. Some men reported that a lot of HIV/AIDS-infected prisoners did not want to be looked at as gay or that they had indulged in homosexual activity; they'd rather be considered as IV drug-users.

Of relevance here, Latinos noted that the Latino prison community had more solidarity than the African-American prison community. Therefore, they were less likely to be "dissed" by their fellow Latino prisoners or ostracized by their "amigos." On the other hand, the African-American community tended not to form tightly knit peer groups. Consequently, ostracism was more likely to be keenly experienced among African Americans who were without a solid support group to buffer the hostility that emanated from the larger prison community. Those prisoners who did not disclose their condition believed that disclosure was fraught with danger, knowing that so many prisoners and correctional personnel feared and/or despised those who had the illness.

Accordingly, the reactions of noninfected prisoners had some serious consequences for prisoners in my study population. Noninfected prisoners were quick to act in a demeaning manner towards the infected ones, who were treated as "lepers." They were discriminated against and avoided. Noninfected prisoners refused to eat with them. They were recipients of derogatory statements and treated in a disrespectful manner. Frequently, they were ostracized and subjected to petty forms of harassment or to violent encounters. Occasionally, prisoners threatened to riot if a prisoner with HIV/AIDS was placed within their cellblocks. Some had been known to torch the cells to convince the administration to remove the infected prisoner.

HIV/AIDS-infected prisoners incarcerated within maximum-security prisons were more likely than HIV/AIDS-infected prisoners incarcerated in medium-security ones to worry about the possibility of encountering hostile reactions from other prisoners, and had to remain continually alert to possible hostility and violent reactions from fellow inmates. Prisoners incarcerated within the maximum-security prisons appeared to have few clues as to how to respond in a nonstigmatizing manner. AIDS education in these prisons was woefully inadequate. By contrast, within the medium-security prison, AIDS education was ongoing and pervasive and hence the illness was treated as a more ordinary event.

VULNERABILITY TO VIOLENCE ON THE STREETS

Within poor, inner-city communities, African-American and Latino convicted offenders infected with HIV/AIDS also reported that they were exposed to a new sense of vulnerability to violence not previously experienced. More of these men pointed out, however, that they believed that the prison milieu was not as safe as their communities. A number of these men indicated that living within their communities meant experiencing fear as a predominant factor in their daily lives, but unlike in prison, there was a wider range of alternatives available for managing their safety on the streets. Many recalled that on the streets they were less likely to be caught up with drug-related violence or with those groups of men who had an investment in reputations based on respect.

In many instances, the accounts indicated that vulnerability to emotional and physical victimization increased concomitantly with the progression of the disease to its terminal stage. As long as men appeared to be healthy, physically strong, and mentally alert, they could easily hide their HIV/AIDS status. Conversely, when the disease became physically visible, these men reported being assaulted, mugged, and receiving derogatory comments in public places. Suggested here is that these men were additionally aware for the first time that they were more likely to be a *victim* rather than the *victimizer*.

The effects of this fear were profound. The dishonor that a number of convicted offenders perceived being conferred upon them as a consequence of their spoiled identities could also be perceived as a loss of their manhood. Many defined this loss as the inability to assume a dominant position among peers and to resist similar claims by others. To be able to resist others' claims demanded a physical agility and stressful vigilance over the potential to be victimized. Physicality was continually demanded. In addition, a negative consequence of this drive for public affirmation of manhood meant a weakening of their immune systems—an invitation to AIDS-related illnesses and quicker ride to death.

Through AIDS education, many prisoners and parolees learned how to survive with the illness. Most of these men were presented with guidelines for establishing lifestyles that were more positive-oriented, affirmative of life, and urgent about the necessity to give up the "real bad dude" images. To live, therefore, meant disassociating themselves from the illegal drug economy, their criminally inclined peers, and from the code of the streets and prisons.

Another consequence of an HIV/AIDS status was the fears and anxieties men felt about disclosure, especially when disclosure occurred within the prison environment. Maintaining a group of buddies was more crucial to surviving within the prisons than on the streets for this reason. It was through the buddy network that men could relieve material deprivations that were a common "pain of imprisonment"; that is, on many occasions prisoners would gain some access to such scarce material goods as drugs, cigarettes, and other contraband as well as additional foods to supplement prison fare. Given this, the men in my study population complemented Frazier's (1995) observation that "everyone had to ride with someone for self-preservation." Lone prisoners, especially those lone prisoners living with HIV/AIDS, found that survival was difficult without close buddies. In addition, the accounts strongly suggested that in the atmosphere of prisons or impoverished New York City communities where nearly everybody is suspected to be capable of aggression, survival generally depended on the convicted offenders' abilities to have someone to cover their backs. Any likelihood of potential loss of the mutual protection of membership in small groups of buddies was quite disturbing.

MAINTAINING RELATIONS WITH SIGNIFICANT WOMEN AND OTHER FAMILY MEMBERS

Telling their significant women that they had been diagnosed with HIV/AIDS was not an easy task for most prisoners. Nevertheless, most of the men included in the study population chose to reveal their condition. Latinos were more likely than African Americans to disclose to a small network of trusted friends and family members, because they wanted to ensure some insulation from potentially threatening interactions as well as to receive the support they needed. Both Latinos and African Americans frequently told their women and other family members when they felt most vulnerable to emotional and physical victimization and/or needed some relief from their fears about the illness. The most opportune time for sharing their status appeared to be during their time served in various prisons. Whether or not their important women were suspicious that their loved ones were infected with the virus, the notification of their diagnoses of HIV/AIDS infection came as a rude awakening. Most women initially expressed shock, disbelief, grief, and a willingness to lend some comfort and assistance.

In this section, men's accounts revealed that their significant women's support had important effects on how they coped with a life-threatening illness. Attention is given to how significant women's support was most crucial under three circumstances: (1) during incarceration, (2) during the early stage of re-entry, and lastly (3) when the disease progressed to its last stages. Within this context, then, maintaining contacts with family members had some benefits for easing men's multiple fears about dying, rejection, and abandonment and the loss of respect and manliness.

Prior to incarceration, almost all the men spoke about drying up the goodwill and resources of their important women and other family members. In many cases, men spent household money for their own purposes, stole anything and everything that was saleable within their households, ate up the household's food, ran up telephone bills, and so on. Many significant women found this behavior intolerable and responded by hiding their money, putting locks on refrigerators, doors to bedrooms, and telephones and in some instances, demanding that the men find separate domiciles. However, separate domiciles did not mean dissolving their relations with their loved ones, but only meant that they could establish some kind of peace and predictability for themselves. Latina women were more likely than African-American women to keep their men at home and bear the financial costs, crises, and aggravations their men caused them. Although African-American women were more likely to encourage separate domiciles, none of their men listed these women as completely severing ties with them. All the women, instead, informed their men that whenever they overcame their drug habits and committed themselves to more conventional lifestyles, they would be welcome back into their homes.

All the men reported that arguments with their mothers, aunts, and sisters *did* erupt but seldom led to violent episodes. These men, especially Latino men, claimed to adhere firmly to the highly regarded normative expectation that "real men" did not physically abuse their mothers or sisters who acted as co-participants in rearing them. The particular role of the mother was important to most of the African-American and Latino men. Mothers were to be revered, to be treated honorably and respectfully. To respect mothers meant to adhere to their mothers' rules of behavior within their homes. For instance, to come home high on drugs and/or drunk and disorderly was a sign of lack of respect, hence mothers were expected to discipline their adult sons. Lastly, stealing from siblings and fathers was perceived by many men as rather acceptable behavior, but to take money from their mothers was to act not only disrespectfully but to call their manhood into question.

In contrast, the men's accounts revealed that such treatment was not usually accorded their female partners. As their alcohol and drug addictions became chronic, confrontations between men and their partners often lead to violent episodes. Physically battering their female partners reinforced men's sense of power and effectively ended what men perceived to be their partners arguing and nagging and/or taught them a lesson.

From the interviews with the men, it appeared that they were far more reluctant to threaten the viability of relations with their female relatives than with their female partners. Whether mothers or close sisters, their important female relatives remained the central and most stable feature within their lives. Men in the study group were more likely to depend on these female relatives for nurturance, emotional support, and active assistance, especially during times of crisis. And it was expected that the men's important female relatives, in times of emergencies, would assist them by drawing together the necessary resources within a network of extended kin. Wives and girlfriends generally did not have sufficient access to their extended kin to request assistance for their male partners.

Through telephone calls, letters, and sometimes prison visiting, men in my study population maintained contact with their female relatives and/or partners. The number of times they called depended on the willingness of the women to pay for these telephone calls. Whenever these men made contact with their important women, they attempted to maintain their goodwill in order to maximize receiving monetary assistance, information about the management of the virus, "care packages" of food to supplement the prison diet, approved vitamins, and so forth. Most of these prisoners complained that prison food was substandard and sometimes inedible and that they needed to supplement their food, cook for themselves, or to cook and share food with their associates. Others expressed interest in acquiring a diverse range of vitamins to supplement their holistically oriented AIDS program whenever the prison system approved their requests for vitamins. Lastly, those prisoners located in upstate New York near the Canadian border indicated that they especially needed additional clothing to provide warmth during the long, cold winters. It was their female relatives and sometimes their female partners whom they relied upon to send them such monies and approved goods.

According to the men's accounts, it was primarily mothers, sisters, and aunts who struggled to maintain their connections with their men. Although severely financially strained, most of these important women (and a few wives) attempted to function from a distance, working to close the gap of enforced separation and ensure their men's well-being. Men received some satisfaction from these contacts. Maintaining ties could have a direct bearing on their health, longevity, and sense of well-being. For instance, by placing orders for financial and/or material assistance, these men were at least able to know that they had retained remnants of their former roles as family members who occasionally were able to tell other family members what to do and how to do it. In these instances, it was not uncommon to not only make requests but to offer their women advice concerning the appropriate style and quality of the goods, where to make the purchases, the appropriate price to pay for the items requested, and so forth. In turn, these men received some necessities to alleviate their discomfort, to help them delay the progression of the HIV/AIDS virus, and, lastly, to mitigate their diminished sense of autonomy.

However, the fact of imprisonment placed prisoners living with HIV/AIDS in a situation in which they were unable to reciprocate in any significant ways. It was rare that the men were able to give their female relatives or partners money for their provisions, much less money to ease their important women's financial difficulties. Resources generally flowed to the men. And in the case of this new crisis (i.e., the men's confrontations with a life-threatening illness), men frequently were able to encourage additional resources from their women. The major reason provided for needing these resources was that the lack of these provisions would hasten their death. And the women certainly did not want to see themselves as contributors to their loved one's deaths, especially their dying alone in their cells or in some upstate hospital. From the men's accounts, it was clear that many of these women felt great pressure to meet their needs because of their own guilt about their men having contracted the virus and/or realistic worries about their men's present situations.

What is particularly interesting here is that whenever prisoners interacted with their important women, they strove to maintain their familial relations. Within this context, then, prisoners commonly projected images of themselves that were so encouraging that their important women would continue to accept their long-distance telephone calls, travel exceedingly long distances to visit them, and/or most crucially, continue to send them some money and fill their orders for approved goods and food. For instance, acting contrite and repentant rarely occurred. Aware that most of their important women had previously heard such contrite remarks and promises to stay out of trouble, men reported that they believed their women would respond to the like with cynicism. Few men made such traditional promises as wanting to settle down, obtain regular employment, remain drug-free, and to stay out of trouble. Instead, many of them expressed a willingness to turn their lives around to deter the disease from progressing so that they could be released from prison before they became terminally sick and died. Underlying this promise was a concern about their health. They also tended to reassure their women that they were now committed to living drug-free lives. Furthermore, according to the prisoners' reports, they conveyed how they were now living in virtuous moderation by eating nutritious foods every day, getting plenty of sleep, dressing warmly when necessary, and reducing the stress in their lives. Others even disclosed to their important women, sometimes for the first time, that they were avoiding violent confrontations, drug consumption, and getting into trouble to ensure their early release. These prison lifestyle changes were motivated by their HIV/AIDS status.

Plans were made for release from prison. Many men utilized HIV/AIDS as the starting-off point to convince their women that they had reflected on the errors of their ways: namely, how "druggin', stealin', muggin', and drug-related shootings had devastated their children as well as their women." The living with a life-threatening disease had lastingly altered their conduct. They made plans to leave prison and become involved in drug recovery and to continue to live with HIV/AIDS rather than succumb to it. Believing themselves to be at the edge of death and dying, most intended to be the kind of men their women always knew they could be. These future plans generally were sufficient to assure the women's commitment to assist them whenever they were released to their communities.

Implications

During imprisonment, it became beneficial to HIV/AIDS-infected African-American and Latino prisoners to become the kind of men their mothers, sisters, aunts, and wives always knew they could be. For perhaps the first time, they shared with their women a common concern and goal that they could attempt to achieve; they could all be concerned about the men's health status, the progression of the disease, the goal of surviving a life-threatening disease, and of avoiding dying alone within the various upstate prison systems. Lastly, with the onslaught of HIV/AIDS and imprisonment, most of the men cited that their women felt perhaps that they could, this time, turn their lives around. In turn, women generally responded by encouraging their men, providing them with essential information about the virus, and often doing whatever they could do to make their men's lives more bearable within the constraints of the various prisons.

RE-ENTRY: SETTING THE STAGE FOR LIVING WITH HIV/AIDS

After months and sometimes years of planning, the African-American and Latino parolees in the study population were reunited with their significant women and other family members. Although reunions could be joyful events, the ensuing period immediately after re-entry posed some difficulties for parolees, especially if they were HIV/AIDS infected. The problems and dilemmas of re-entry after imprisonment, however, were basically similar to the problems encountered by prisoners in general, but had some unique aspects stemming from the HIV/AIDS infection. In this section, particular attention is given to looking at some experiences of African-American and Latino parolees with HIV/AIDS during the immediate aftermath of their re-entry into their communities.

The upstate New York prison systems did not prepare most men who were infected with the virus for re-entry. In varying degrees, prison communities *did* introduce men to some coping strategies that assisted them to live with HIV/AIDS within the prison environment. As many men reported, even though they attended prisoners' AIDS support groups, they took what they learned and acted on this information within the constraints of the prison system. After release, however, the men experienced a sharp discontinuity between their HIV/AIDS-infected prisoner status and that as parolees infected with HIV/AIDS. They also cited that their status as HIV/AIDS-infected sons, husbands, and friends bore little relationship to their "tainted" status in prison.

According to the men's accounts, the impact of HIV/AIDS had some consequences for the roles accessible to them upon returning home. Prior to their recent incarceration, as a direct consequence of their involvement in the street-level illegal-drug-selling/using economy, they typically encountered a narrowing of the options they could engage in; that is, many experienced a loss of such options as access to the occupational world, the loss of female partners and their children, loss of some of their roles as brothers, nephews, family members, loss of access to the educational world, and so on. What was unique among the men described here was how upon re-entry, HIV/AIDS further narrowed their options in some important ways but in some other ways simultaneously broadened their options. How options continued to be narrowed could be due to the following: (1) mandates of the rules of parole, (2) the recommended regime for surviving HIV/AIDS, and (3) receiving some forms of governmental assistance.

With parole papers in hand, prisoners immediately were informed by their parole officers that some conditions of their parole were to remain drug-free, to avoid criminal behavior, to attend a community-based AIDS service organization, and to establish conventionally oriented lifestyles. In turn, their participation at a community-based AIDS service organization (located in the South Bronx) was contingent upon adherence to the parole rules and regulations as well as such basic procedures for managing the virus: to specifically dissociate themselves from their criminally inclined friends; to cease drinking and drugging; to avoid sexual promiscuity and practice safe sex; and, lastly, to follow a regime similar to the one they followed within their prison environments (eating nutritionally, getting sufficient rest and exercise, seeing their doctors on a regular basis, and avoiding stress-inducing situations). In effect, both parole officers and social-service workers demanded that the men in my study population should disassociate themselves from what many men still considered to be their most satisfying roles as "gangstas," "players of women," and chronic alcohol- and drug-users.

Conversely, the community-based organization's goals were to assist men to widen their options by providing services so that they could perform successfully in more conventionally oriented roles such as fathers of their long-neglected children, husbands, volunteers in community-based activities, and so forth. In addition, this organization provided assistance in obtaining legitimate incomes, stable residences, access to medical care, and so forth.

As with any parolee, re-entry meant an extension of living on the margins due to parolees' unemployed status, their past criminal records, poor schooling, and drug problems. Marginalization became more intensive for the men in my study group because they were living with HIV/AIDS and subsequently forced to participate daily with other parolees similarly labeled within the recovery program. Another contributing factor to living on the margins was the need to establish some form of legitimate income almost immediately upon returning to the streets. Without employment but reluctant to remain financially dependent upon their families, most men faced the reality that they needed to apply to some governmental agency for financial assistance. The first reality, then, for most men was that they needed to learn how to navigate the many systems of welfare agencies, housing agencies, Supplemental Security Income (SSI), the New York City Division of AIDS Services (DAS),[3] Medicaid, and so forth. In addition, they also had to learn how to negotiate their health care. For most of these men who were historically marginal, these agencies bewildered them, sometimes intimidated them, and reinforced a sense of impending dependency that symbolized a lack of manliness since they, as "real men," had never received any kind of handout from governmental and/or social agencies. But now, to minimize stressors linked to lacking the resources for living independently, they needed to obtain assistance from their case managers to begin to apply for entitlements and find apartments for themselves as soon as they entered the program.

However, the men's accounts suggested that not only did participation in recovery programs, but also the entitlements accorded to them, impacted on the breadth of the roles they could successfully play that would accord them respect. They wanted to establish lifestyles on the basis of legitimate income, but were forced to *not* work because they could lose their benefits or else experience a drastic reduction in those benefits. However, the income available to the men in my study group (for example, public assistance in the form of some cash, food stamps, and medical assistance) made it possible for them to barely keep their heads above water and further constrained them in terms of the roles they could play.

Within this context, then, a striking feature of parolees' accounts was that most returned to their home communities to live with their significant women. Those significant women who were their female partners expected their men to move back into the family circle and resume their familial responsibilities. Most of the others returned to the home of those significant women who were their mothers, sisters, and aunts. According to the men's reports, these women were willing to provide them only with temporary shelter until they were able to live on their own. In contrast, two men were placed by their parole officers into homeless shelters because their family members, including their significant women, were unable to shelter them.

For those men who were living on their own or temporarily living with female kin, finding their own apartments became a central focus of their daily lives. It was clear that having their own living space would serve to enhance the image of themselves as approximating "real men" who had the capacity to take control of their own lives and avoid being dependent on others for their well-being. Unfortunately, these men reported that finding an apartment to live in, furnishing these apartments, and managing to provide for their other necessities forced them to become dependent upon the government. Many felt demeaned by their imputed status as AIDS clients. It has been well-documented that both community-based programs (as well as treatment programs) and governmental-assistance programs provided a ready-made support network for recovering addicts, but also revealed the well-established identities of ex-cons or ex-addicts living with AIDS. These statuses informed the men's view of themselves—a view that placed their manhood into question.

Implicit here, then, was that staying alive, to survive with AIDS meant being dependent on entitlements, being poor, being regarded by former peers as "weak," and being caged within their impoverished communities. At the very best, however, these bare-boned entitlements merely made life possible, not necessarily tolerable or livable. Furthermore, many men reported that serious problems remained. Being dispossessed of their former, more satisfying roles left them with an enforced conventional lifestyle that gave them few satisfactions. It should be pointed out here that a major consequence of exiting out of their drug-related careers was the lack of knowledge that there were alternative ways of being "real men."

The decision to stop their involvement in nonconventional lifestyles appeared to be preceded by a variety of factors, most of which were negative social sanctions. Health problems, difficulties with maintaining their former lifestyles, the termination of entitlements, and the threat of being returned to prison with an increased likelihood of serving longer sentences and dying there were antecedents of their initial decisions to quit.

Work and the identity that stemmed from working were not accessible to most. Work, nevertheless, had marginal expressive value to most men. Historically as well as currently, most of them mentioned that there was little incentive to take jobs that would provide little more than economic subsistence. Aware of the low status of available jobs and how little respect they would achieve from working, they easily opted to survive by receiving governmental assistance that demanded that to receive a stipend, they not work or work less hard than those above them on the economic ladder. Unlike before incarceration, the meaning of work or that "real men" should work was less rooted in the code of honor (see Horowitz [1995] for example). Most men did not feel inclined to work even when they had children who were economically dependent upon them.

By attempting to follow the regime for conventional lifestyles, most men observed that these constraints on their behavior only reinforced what others believed about AIDS. It was the disease of the weak that took away one's manhood. To follow a conventional way of life was what they avoided for most of their lives; for them, the conventional life meant to follow a very narrow and exacting path. A similar path was enacted during re-entry into the community. When I asked the men to describe a typical day, they reported that as recovering addicts, they had to attend daily Alcoholics Anonymous or Narcotics Anonymous meetings as well as the community-based organization's activities. When not attending these programs, they spent most of their time at home watching television or listening to their stereos. If they *did* drink alcoholic beverages or consumed drugs, they did so moderately. The most difficult problem of re-entry confronting most men was spending time by themselves and being "straight." The difficulty lay in their having too much time to think; many of these men's thoughts at this time were unpleasant, making a return to drug use with its possibility of blocking out such thoughts very attractive. Many remarked that they spent countless nights and weekends at home with no company except for their own thoughts. Intermittently, they reported that they looked to their important women and conventionally oriented family members and friends for support.

Furthermore, for many men, especially those living independently from their families, a life of accepting government handouts and focused on daily attendance at the community-based program became increasingly boring, especially during nights and weekends. Nevertheless, there were some satisfactions. For the first time as adults, they had their lives in order. Thanks to the entitlements and the community-based program, they were straight, legal, and were able to provide for themselves and had a modicum of respect. But something was missing: their participation in what their peers considered to be manly activities such as adherence to the code of the streets, to publicly demonstrate their physical abilities to withstand insults as well as violent confrontations, to maintain their reputation as men deserving of respect, and, lastly, to victimize others.

Avoiding these activities placed many men in a social vacuum. They were unsure of themselves as defined by the urban street culture's notions that manhood was to be achieved through use of the knife and gun. This uncertainty about their manliness had first emerged with their diagnosis of HIV/AIDS. A further sense of unease was tied to the fact that most of these men who received entitlements noted that their newly experienced dependency simply did not conform to the street culture's notions of manliness. Men without money tended to be "real men" when they did not accept handouts—and a "real man" did not go on welfare or receive SSI or become a client of drug-treatment programs nor allowed his failures to be probed by social workers in order to qualify for a bare-bones subsidy.

In response, a number of parolees turned to other ways of getting money, quasi-legal and/or illegal hustles for some gold, some gangsta clothes, and some sneakers, which continued to be the street culture's symbols of manliness. Others, to avoid getting money quasi-legally or illegally, went to their significant women and/or other family members and asked for contributions.

What these preliminary findings implied was that there could be a decrease in violent behavior, drug consumption, and criminality along with an increased reliance on the state. Nevertheless, the dilemma of the HIV/AIDS-infected African-American and Latino parolees was how to be men when both the traditional ways and the street culture's ways towards manliness and respect appeared to be stripped from them.

RE-ENTRY: ESTABLISHING RELATIONS WITH FEMALE PARTNERS

Although some men could successfully perform their parole guidelines as well as guidelines for living with HIV/AIDS, many still found something missing in their lives to affirm their manliness. What was missing was a steady relationship with a woman. To convince themselves and others of their manliness at the same time as being severely stressed by their status as HIV/AIDS clients, many men searched to obtain symbolic proof that they were still deserving of respect as men. Such proof could be established by demonstrating their ability to establish a long-term relationship with a woman. Such a relationship had some benefits: it offered sexual gratification, companionship, reinforced their masculinity, and deflected attention away from their perceived "tainted identities" as HIV/AIDS-infected dependents on governmental handouts. Many men reported that they chose women who themselves were former addicts and parolees who also were clients of the community-based program. Other women were met within the drug culture and could be characterized as being heavy users of drugs, prostitutes, "mules" or small-time drug dealers. Occasionally, I was told how some men preferred to have relations with "non-tainted" female partners, but this seemed impossible under the circumstances of their lives. Instead, their chosen partners were perceived by the men in my study population to have permanently fallen and to be essentially damaged goods.

All the men linked to female partners expressed their belief that they would not be perceived as "eligible" by more conventionally oriented women because they lacked full-time employment, had criminal records, drug problems, and, lastly, were HIV/AIDS infected. In response to their belief that the doors were closed to them of conventionally oriented women, their choices were deliberate because they did not want to risk rejections, hence further affronting their manliness. In addition, it was difficult to achieve intimacy with women who had no understanding of their past lives nor could identify with their current status as HIV/AIDS-infected ex-cons, drug abusers, and criminals.

Initially, according to the men, having a female partner to counter the loneliness and boredom they were experiencing brought them elation, pleasure, and some satisfactions. However, the euphoria usually did not last long. After their initial weeks together, couples encountered some unique problems typical of any newly wed couples and some problems unique to couples sharing past histories and current stigmatized statuses. Most of these men specifically experienced some strains and stresses because either one partner was in recovery and the other was not, or both partners were in recovery. Several men reported that when both were in recovery, they frequently had different agendas. For instance, one day one partner would suffer severe mood swings based on the need to get high; another day, the other partner would go through similar changes. Arguments erupted and in some cases resulted in physical confrontations. Other men living with women who were actively using drugs expressed discomfort when their partners continued their drug consumption, sometimes working as mules, prostitutes, and so on to support their habits. In these cases, arguments centered around these women's disinterest in pursuing more conventional lifestyles as well as how the women's drug use tempted the men to resume their own addictions.

Another major source of partner arguments stemmed from one or both partners' mood changes centering around fears and anxieties about the possibilities of getting progressively sicker and dependent upon the other partner. A last source of frequent arguments focused on the men's attempts to control their women's behavior. These arguments all-too-frequently led to violent reactions. Many of these men reacted violently to their women's active resistance to their demands. At times, both partners acted violently.

Control and power became central issues in these relationships. To retain their positions as heads of household, some men demanded that their women stay more or less confined to their homes and check in with them when they went to the doctor, their friends, or their families. If the women left their homes or the community-based agency unexpectedly, accusations of infidelity would inevitably ensue. Men indicated that whenever their partners obeyed them, this obedience demonstrated loyalty, love, and faithfulness.

Some of the women attempted to accept their partners' authority in these matters, but the cost of compliance was high. Eventually, many of these women who had gained a sense of independence, assertiveness, and aggressiveness as a consequence of surviving in the illegal drug economy and managing their own addictions began to resist this imposed control, being unwilling to relinquish their hard-fought independence. Challenging their men's authority became increasingly more frequent during their relationship; hence they were less likely to seek their men's permission to do things nor to defer to them and rely upon the men's judgments in handling their own recovery and illness. From the men's interviews it was apparent that these forms of resistance threatened their already-diminished sense of masculinity. Such threats then generally led to feelings of resentment and anger on their part. To relieve these feelings of powerlessness and impotency, some men frequently retaliated violently.

IMPACT OF THE HIV/AIDS VIRUS ON INTIMATE PARTNERS' HETEROSEXUAL RELATIONSHIPS

Along with a mutual determination to exit from the drug culture, the HIV/AIDS virus could provide a common focus and strengthen marital relationships. It provided a form of mutual interest, and partnerships were at times characterized by joint support in recovery and living with the disease. The mutual concern with each other's health, with restructuring the entire patterns of their lives to avoid drug use, and the debilitating effects of the virus became the commonality shared by couples. They had some common interests: they could share their passage through recovery, shape future plans, express faith in their union, and perhaps deflect attention away from daily anxieties and fears based on their experiencing this life-threatening disease.

These relationships served as a welcome reprieve from having to assess how this disease devastated them physically—a reprieve from worrying about who would care for them, and, lastly, from anxieties about their abilities to remain drug-free. In this way, intimate relations for some men served to minimize stress, and hopefully, by minimizing stress, the progression of the disease itself would be halted.

On the other hand, many of these accounts pointed out that the men's illnesses also had some nonbeneficial impacts on their relationships with their chosen partners. As several men pointed out, the virus physiologically affected their manhood. Some, confronting the later stages of AIDS, complained of impotency, impaired sexual needs, and decreased energy to engage their own as well as their mate's sexual needs. Consequently, these men grieved over their loss of manhood and its implications for maintaining steady relations with their women. Others complained about how such AIDS-related dementia caused quickening of their tempers, lowered their tolerance for stress and frustration, as well as increased their argumentative behavior that could result in physically abusive behavior. These preliminary findings suggested that aspects of the HIV/AIDS virus made difficult the everyday functioning and coping of these men and their steady partners.

In addition, most of the men in my study group had experienced a sense of diminished masculinity as a consequence of their newly acquired role as recovering HIV/AIDS-infected parolees dependent on governmental handouts that was brought into their relationships with steady females. In response to what they perceived as a diminished capacity as "real men," they recalled their expectations that their women would continually reassure them that they were still such. With these expectations in mind, the men were eternally vigilant to any signs of their partners' disrespectful behavior directed at them, which then motivated them to reassert their power and authority as men—not as "sick men," but as "well men." Typically, these men resorted to battering because it worked; it gave them immediate control over their partners because they felt strong and powerful enough to terrify their women, especially since physicality and its rewards were no longer available to them or played out on the streets.

Within this context, then, HIV/AIDS *did* contribute to weakening already fragile relationships. It became an important factor in giving rise to domestic violence. On the other hand, it was an important factor in motivating men to avoid participating in physical victimization to impress their peers and strangers with their willingness to fight; all were more aware that violence in the public sphere was more easily detected and therefore increased the likelihood of arrest and imprisonment. In contrast, domestic violence enacted within the private sphere would be less noticeable, and as batterers, they were less likely to be rearrested and imprisoned.

Most important was the finding that establishing intimate relations did not necessarily help to stabilize African-American and Latino parolees with HIV/AIDS, nor necessarily motivate them to remain drug-free, avoid crime, and establish stress-reduced lifestyles. Instead, the findings suggested that HIV/AIDS could be a contributory factor to weakening relationships by escalating conflicts and thereby motivating one or both partners to resort to drug consumption as the most familiar means of medicating their pain, anxieties, and fears. As the drug needs of one or both partners began to supersede their concern for each other, conflicts persisted. Under these circumstances, conflict and battering appeared to erode men's sense of powerlessness and diminished sense of masculinity. Ultimately, some men went back to what they did best—the drug life and resuming their more familiar and satisfying roles as men of honor, or as "baad ass niggers" or "locos."

CONCLUSIONS

My findings strongly suggested that a good number of African-American and Latino men battered their partners from a position of powerlessness and marginalization. Most of these men had a history of feeling powerless. As HIV/AIDS-infected parolees without sufficient money, access to leisure, dependent upon governmental financial assistance and health benefits, and under the supervision of social workers, parole officers, and HIV/AIDS workers, they were conscious of being ground down by not only poverty, but also a lack of autonomy and powerlessness. Whichever way they turned, they seemed to come up against additional constraints on their behaviors so as to ensure that they remained drug-free, dissociated from the street-level drug-using/selling networks, and managed the threat of dying from AIDS-related diseases. Having a history of resistance to such constraints, it was not surprising that in many instances the battering of women was a direct response to their feelings of resentments, rage, and powerlessness and to the losses they believed they were experiencing—the loss of the satisfactions of drug life, loss of cherished roles as "gangstas," "men of honor," "players of women," and so forth.

NOTES

1. "*Loco*" translates into English as meaning "crazy."

2. Occasionally during interview sessions and informal conversations with convicted offenders in my study group, Superfly was mentioned as a valid standard for how men should go about conducting themselves in a respectful manner. Superfly, a character in a 1970s' blaxploitation film, was created as a glorified stereotypical image of the "real black man." To convey this image, Superfly was portrayed as possessing an array of characteristics such as: being a trash-talking "bad-ass," physically imposing, quick-tempered, taking no shit from anyone, and not hesitating to "get one over" (outwit) his enemies. Essentially he was one *baaaad* dude (see Pouissant and Alexander [2000]). Given this, to make such a

comparison then was to emphasize that other men's conduct was not only worthy of elevating to a similar status as Superfly, but was to be respected.

3. DAS provided immediate housing assistance and entitlements for people with HIV/AIDS, especially for infected parolees leaving prisons without addresses. SSI, in turn, granted benefits to people who met its criterion, which included a diagnosis of HIV and at least two HIV-related symptoms. Grants provided a bare-bones living allowance for the duration of the disability or the person's life. To continue receiving welfare assistance and to participate in the treatment programs meant that clients were scrutinized by the programs for any signs of drug use and criminal activities and constantly warned that returning to drugs and to the interpersonal aggression and violence of street life could only lead to a speedy death.

References

Abu-Jamal, M. (1995). *Live from death row.* Reading, MA: Addison-Wesley Publishing.

Anderson, E. (1994). "The code of the streets." *Atlantic Monthly* (May):80–94.

Bourgois, P. (1995). *In search of respect: Selling crack in el barrio.* New York: Cambridge University Press.

Boyd-Franklin, N., C. Alemán, M. M. Jean-Gilles, and S. Y. Lewis. (1995). "Cultural sensitivity and competence: African-American, Latino, and Haitian families with HIV/AIDS," in *Children, families and HIV/AIDS: Psychosocial and therapeutic issues*, ed. N. Boyd-Franklin, G. C. Steiner, and M. G. Boland (pp. 53–77). New York: Guilford Press.

Butterfield, F. (1996). *All God's children: The Bosket family and the American tradition of violence.* New York: Knopf.

Charmaz, K. (1983). "The grounded theory method: An explication and interpretation," in *Contemporary field research: A collection of readings*, ed. R. M. Emerson. Boston: Little, Brown.

Christ, G. H., and L. S. Wiener. (1985). "Psychosocial issues in AIDS," in *AIDS: Etiology, diagnosis, treatment, and prevention*, ed. V. T. DeVita, S. Hellman, and S. A. Rosenberg (pp. 275–97). New York: Lippincott.

Conner, M. K. (1995). *What is cool? Understanding black manhood in America.* New York: Crown Publishers.

Dalton, H. L. (1990). "AIDS in Blackface," in *Living with AIDS*, ed. S. R. Graubard. Cambridge, MA: MIT Press.

Diaz, R. M. (1998). *Latino gay men and HIV: Culture, sexuality, and risk behavior.* New York: Routledge.

Erlanger, H. S. (1979). "Estrangement, machismo, and gang violence." *Social Science Quarterly 60*:235–48.

Fitzpatrick, J. P. (1990). "Drugs and Puerto Ricans in New York City," in *Drugs in Hispanic Communities*, ed. R. Glick and J. Moore (pp. 195–202). New Brunswick, NJ: Rutgers University Press.

Foster, Z. (1988). "The treatment of people with AIDS: Psychosocial consideration," in *AIDS*, ed. D. Corless and F. Pittman (pp. 33–42). Washington, DC: Hemisphere Publishing.

Frazier, M. B. (1995). *From behind the wall: Commentary on crime, punishment, race, and the underclass by a prison inmate.* New York: Paragon House.

Glaser, B. G., and A. L. Strauss. (1965). *Awareness of dying.* Chicago: Aldine.

———. (1967). *The discovery of grounded theory: Strategies for qualitative research.* Chicago: Aldine.

Goffman, E. (1963). *Stigma: Notes on the management of spoiled identity.* Englewood Cliffs, NJ: Prentice Hall.

Harer, M. E., and D. J. Steffensmeier. (1996). "Race and prison violence." *Criminology 34*:323–56.

Herek, G. M. (1990). "Illness, stigma and AIDS," in *Psychological aspects of serious illness*, ed. P. Costa and G. R. Vanden Bos (pp. 103–50). Washington, DC: American Psychological Association.

Herek, G. M., and E. K. Glunt. (1988). "An epidemic of stigma: Public reactions to AIDS." *American Psychologist 43*:886–91.

Horowitz, R. (1995). *Honor and the American dream.* New Brunswick, NJ: Rutgers University Press.

Ianni, F. A. (1975). *Black mafia: Ethnic succession in organized crime.* New York: Pocket Books.

Kowalewski, M. R. (1988). "Double stigma and boundary maintenance: How gay men deal with AIDS." *Journal of Contemporary Ethnography 17*:211–28.

Kozol, J. (1995). *Amazing grace: The lives of children and the conscience of a nation.* New York: Crown Publishers.

Majors, R., and J. M. Billson. (1992). *Cool pose: The dilemmas of black manhood in America.* New York: Lexington Books.

Mirande, A. (1997). *Hombres y machos: Masculinity and Latino culture.* Boulder, CO: Westview Press.

Nightingale, C. H. (1993). *On the edge: A history of poor black children and their American dreams.* New York: Basic Books.

Nisbett, R., and D. Cohen. (1995). *Culture of honor: The psychology of violence in the South.* New York: Westview Press.

Oliver, W. (1994). *The violent social world of black men.* New York: Lexington Books.

Olivero, J. M. (1990). "The treatment of AIDS behind the walls of correctional facilities." *Social Justice 17*:113–25.

Potler, C. (1988). *AIDS in prison: A crisis in New York State corrections.* New York: Correctional Association of New York.

Pouissant, A. F., and A. Alexander. (2000). *Lay my burden down: Unraveling suicide and the mental health crisis among African-Americans.* Boston: Beacon Press.

Silberman, M. (1995). *A world of violence: Corrections in America.* Belmont, CA: Wadsworth Publishing.

Sim, J. (1994). "Tougher than the rest: Men in prison," in *Just boys doing business? Men, masculinities, and crime*, ed. T. Newburn and E. A. Stanko (pp. 100–17). New York: Routledge.

Singer, M., C. Flores, L. Davison, G. Burke, Z. Castillo, K. Scanlon, and M. Rivera. (1990). "SIDA: The economic, social and cultural context of AIDS among Latinos." *Medical Anthropology Quarterly 4*:72–114.

Stallworth, R. (1994). "'Gangster' rap: Music, culture and politics" (unpublished manuscript), rev. ed., Utah Division of Investigation, Murray, UT.
White, J. L., and J. H. Cones III. (1999). *Black man emerging: Facing the past and seizing a future in America.* New York: Routledge.

PART THREE

The Uniquely, Uniquely Vulnerable

CHAPTER THIRTEEN

Worries about Crime among Foreign Students Studying in the United States

a comparative study

CHARISSE T. M. COSTON

THIS EXPLORATORY AND DESCRIPTIVE study examined the salience of the role that worries about crime occupy in the lives of nonnative students who are studying in the United States. Two groups of foreign students were interviewed and compared: one group from an urban campus on the East coast, and one from a rural campus in the Midwest. Additionally, those factors that might influence foreign students' worries about criminal victimization were assessed in order to determine if any of them have explanatory power. The terms *foreign students* and *international students* are used interchangeably in this chapter to refer to those pupils from another country who are enrolled in an institution of higher education in the United States—not to U.S. natives or U.S. citizens.

Although broad generalizations about the worries of all foreign students studying at all universities in the United States cannot be made from this study, results indicated here can be used by college deans and counselors of foreign students in international and students' services. These findings provide administrators and counselors with information about some of the worries of their clients and can be used to help prepare counselors to deal with potential problems that foreign students might have while studying in the United States. They also can aid in the development of programs for handling such worries of foreign students should they arise. These preliminary data could be used by U.S. embassy personnel in foreign countries as a tool in preparing the foreign student for study in the

United States. Finally, these results extend the literature on worries about crime and victimization experiences to a little studied and what objectively would appear to be a truly susceptible subgroup for criminal victimization in the United States.

BACKGROUND

Potentially, foreign students may be a group that is especially susceptible to criminal victimization because they may not be well-versed in the English language or assimilated into the American culture. Difficulties of coping with an alien, culturally different population and a general fear of strangers can make foreign students feel helpless and especially vulnerable to crime—thus making them worry about the possibility of crime happening to them. Worrying about crime results from the experience of helplessness in the face of harm (Merry 1981; Coston 1991).

Researchers have noted that acts of criminal victimization are not random (Hindelang, Gottfredson, & Garofalo 1978; Sparks 1982; Garofalo 1987). There are certain attributes of victims and the situations they are involved in that makes them high-risk targets for criminal victimization. In short, there are high-risk persons, high-risk locations, and high-risk time periods.

Researchers suggest that an individual's perception of danger in a community is really a fear of strangers (Merry 1981; Lewis 1982; Lodhi & Tilly 1983; Roberts 1989; Lynch 1990; Wirth 1991). Merry (1981, 125) defines strangers as "persons who are potentially harmful, and whose behavior seems unpredictable and beyond control." Foreign students would appear to have the potential of being exceptionally worried about crime victimization, because so many more people are strangers to them. They are, as Merry (1981, 125) describes, foreign immigrants "lost in a sea of strangers."

Merry (1981, 94) defines two types of strangers that typically are encountered. One type are those passersby "who appear fleetingly, but never participate in the social life of the community." Simmel (1950, 402) refers to these types of strangers as "those who come today and go tomorrow." The second type are those "kind of strangers who have lived down the street for 5–10 years, but who are still not known as individuals with names or personal histories—these people share public spaces, walkways, stores, yet remain anonymous." This kind of stranger has been described by Simmel (1950, 403) as the "person who comes today and stays tomorrow, but never becomes part of a social system." Foreign students are more likely to encounter strangers of Merry's first type at an urban university, and the second type at a rural university—thus feeling more vulnerable and worried about becoming the victim of a crime at the former rather than the latter type of institution.

Foreign students on an urban campus on the East coast (a high crime environment) would appear to be at a higher risk for criminal victimization when compared to those foreign students on a rural campus (a low crime environment) in the Midwest. People who live in large urban cities may live next door to others and still remain strangers, even though they use the same laundromat and walkways and so on. They cross paths without ever touching (Merry 1981). People who live in small towns with large universities still have a "sense of a cohesive local social unit to which residents feel identification and belonging" (Merry 1981, 94).

Most research in the area of concerns, worries, or fears about crime have analyzed the correlates of these emotions among mainstream segments of the general population, for example, females, the elderly, racial minorities, and urban residents (Yin 1980; Meithe & Lee 1984). Recent studies suggest that the rank-ordering of fears, worries, and concerns about crime in relation to other fears, worries, or concerns should be the initial direction of research prior to any assessment of the correlates of these emotions (Yin 1980; Stein, Linn, Slater, & Stein 1984; Gibbs 1986; Hanrahan 1990; Coston 1991). For example, Yin (1980) revealed that the elderly were not fearful of crime to the point of being prisoners within their own homes, but that their lack of money and poor health were greater concerns.

Little has been written about the concerns of foreign students studying outside of their native countries. Spaulding and Flack (1976) and Brown (1980) have mentioned that foreign students are worried about loved ones back home and/or are homesick. They are concerned about economic well-being as well as the physical health condition of parents, other relatives, spouses, and perhaps their own children who were left behind in their home country. Another worry of foreign students is their ability to read, write, speak, and comprehend the host country's language (Moumen 1985). Moumen elaborates on this by saying that the learner, in a foreign environment, needs and depends on the English language more than anything else to communicate to the people of that foreign culture his or her views about himself or herself, his or her identity, the world, and his or her feelings or thoughts. Failing in school has been mentioned by Brown (1980) as a constant worry of foreign students. Brown (1980) and Hossain (1983) believe that foreign students studying abroad are at times worried about their legal obligations to return to their native country. Many foreign students, according to Hossain (1983), have signed agreements promising to return to their home country or old job after school. There also is the worry about returning to a new job that is waiting for the foreign student after finishing school. Another worry of some foreign students is the political instability within their native country (Spaulding & Flack 1976). Other worries briefly mentioned by researchers are: continuing to be morally right, practicing their religion, not having enough money, finding friends who are morally right, and finding romantic love (Spaulding & Flack 1976; Brown 1980; Hossain 1983; Moumen 1985). Conspicuously absent from this literature is research that focuses on foreign students' worries about being victimized by crime.

A secondary goal of the present research was to explore the correlates of foreign students' worries about crime. A review of the results of past research on the correlates of the general (United States) population's worries and fears about crime has shown that urban residents are more fearful of crime than rural or suburban ones (Sundeen & Mathieu 1976; Wiltz 1982; Stein, Linn, Slater, & Stein 1984; Gordan & Riger 1989). Diverse samples of people who were living in large urban cities (cities having a population of over one million) have revealed that they are afraid of walking alone in their neighborhoods at night and during the day (Hindelang 1974). Those people who are the most afraid of crime are not those who are the most victimized—for example, females and the elderly (Conklin 1975; Yin 1980; Riger, LeBailley, & Gordon 1981; Gordan & Riger 1989). The literature shows that people who have been victimized and those who have been victimized a greater number of times are more fearful than those who have only heard about the victimization experiences of others (Meithe & Lee 1984). Some research shows that people who have high perceptions of vulnerability also have greater fear of crime (Miethe & Lee 1984; Perloff 1986), while other studies have found a negative correlation between self-perceptions of vulnerability and the fear of crime (Coston 1988; Taylor 1990). Existing literature indicates that those people who utilize self-protective behaviors deprioritize worries about crime (Riger, LeBailley, & Gordon 1981).

Fear-of-crime literature does not reveal the impact of marital status, having children living within the household, or self-perceived abilities to speak, read, write, and comprehend the English language. Foreign students are not mentioned by past researchers who have studied the correlates of worries or fears about crime. The present study assessed whether all of the correlates above culled from past studies apply to foreign students' worries about crime at both urban and rural universities.

CONTEXT

The two universities in this study had nearly equal numbers of total students and foreign students in 1990 (the year data were collected). The Midwestern university had approximately 34,000 total students and 1,727 foreign students registered in 1990, while the East coast university had approximately 40,000 total students and 1,940 foreign students registered during the same year.

Data from the 1990 FBI's *Uniform Crime Report* indicate that the urban university and its host city had higher numbers of crimes reported (716,403) than did the Midwestern city and its university (4,991). However, rates of reported crime for the two cities were very close: the rate per 100,000 people for the urban city in 1990 was approximately 9,814, while the rate per 100,000 people for the Midwestern city was 8,182.

Methods

The registrar at the Midwestern university generated a random sample of 200 from the 1,727 full-time foreign students who were registered for the spring semester of 1990. Packets of materials containing the survey instrument and instructions were sent to these 200 foreign students selected. These students were advised to call and schedule a meeting with researchers if they wanted to have each question read and explained to them. Twenty respondents availed themselves of this service. Students were read the question in their native language if they requested.

Thirty-seven sample respondents returned the original questionnaire through the mail. Three follow-up mailings resulted in ten more completed surveys. Six of these respondents attended another meeting to have the questionnaire explained to them; four of these latter respondents mailed in the completed questionnaire. The total number of respondents in the sample from the rural university was 67, a 33.3 percent response rate.

Likewise, a random sample of 200 foreign students who were registered full-time during the spring semester of 1990 was generated by the registrar at the urban university. These 200 foreign students selected to be in the sample were mailed copies of the questionnaire, instructions, and a list of meeting times from which to choose to meet with researchers and have the survey read or explained to them. Due to budgetary constraints, students at the urban university were not given the option of mailing in their answers to the survey instrument. A total of 77 respondents in the sample came to three group meetings and had the survey read and explained to them. Their native languages were used to explain questions and provide English responses when the subjects requested. Several follow-up mailings resulted in one additional group meeting that yielded five additional completed interviews. The total sample size of foreign students at the urban university was 82, a 41 percent response rate.

The Survey Instrument: Demographic Characteristics of the Sample

Table 13.1 shows the personal characteristics of the foreign students at each university. Of those interviewed, the average age of a foreign student at the rural university was 28, while the average age of a foreign student at the urban university was 25. The students from the rural campus reported having been in the United States for an average of 24 months, while students at the urban university reported a shorter stay of 13 months. Most of the respondents at the rural university were male, while females were more prevalent at the urban university.

Students reported their native countries. Students in the sample who were from the rural campus were most often from the Far East, followed by the Middle East and Africa, respectively. Foreign students in the sample from the urban university were represented most often by the Far

Table 13.1

Personal Characteristics

Characteristics	*Rural Midwestern university (N = 67)*	*Urban Eastern university (N = 82)*
Mean age	28	25
Time spent in U.S., mean (in months)	24	13
Gender (in percentages)		
male	56	45
female	44	55
Native country (by region of the world)		
Africa	12	6
Far East	17	35
Middle East	13	4
Europe	9	13
South America	5	12
Canada	5	2
Australia	4	3
USSR/Eastern Europe	2	7
Marital status (in percentages)		
not married	49	60
married	37	37
married and living with spouse	34	35
married and living with spouse and children	31	31
Primary income source (in percentages)		
U.S. fellowship/assistantship	21	2
parents/relatives	37	34
fellowship/assistantship from native country	13	9
sponsored by foreign employer	22	20
working	3	24
personal savings	3	1
Educational level* (in percentages)		
undergraduate	50	48
Master's degree	22	40
law	10	6
medical	4	1
doctorate degree	14	5
joint graduate degrees	2	—
Major areas of study (in percentages)		
social sciences	40	43
natural sciences	33	27
humanities/arts	27	30
Areas of residence in the city (in percentages)		
urban	44	76
suburban	31	18
rural	25	6

Note: *Two students mentioned double majors: J.D./M.A. (sociology and psychology).

East, followed by Europe and South America. Most of the foreign students attending school on both campuses reported being single, although many of them were married. Most of those subjects who were married reported living with their spouse while here in the United States, although most of them did not have children living with them within their households.

Most foreign students from both samples reported that their primary income source while studying in the United States came from their family and relatives back in their native country, although 24 percent of foreign students from the urban university reported that they were working and that this was their primary income source. Table 13.1 lists other primary income sources reported by each group.

The educational objective reported most often by foreign students in both groups was the undergraduate degree, but the Master's degree closely followed as second. Other educational goals included law, medical, and Ph.D. degree goals; two students mentioned a double major in law and psychology and law and sociology. Table 13.1 lists the major areas of study for both groups. The social-science area dominates over the humanities and natural sciences.

Most foreign students have not spent time in any other city in the United States or its territories. Table 13.2 describes the travel experiences of those foreign students from both universities who have spent time traveling outside of their host university. As the table shows, most foreign students, regardless of the university, reported having only stayed in those other locales a few days for a short vacation.

Table 13.2

Time Spent in Other Locales within the United States (in percentages)

Characteristic	*Rural Midwestern university (N = 67)*	*Urban Eastern university (N = 82)*
Numbers having spent time in places other than the university city		
no	79	55
yes	21	45
Other places*		
Alaska	1	—
Arizona	—	2
California	10	13
Colorado	1	1
Connecticut	—	1
Delaware	8	—
Florida	3	1

continued

Table 13.2 (continued*)*

Characteristic	*Rural Midwestern university (N = 67)*	*Urban Eastern university (N = 82)*
Georgia	3	3
Hawaii	3	1
Idaho	5	—
Illinois	10	—
Indiana	5	1
Iowa	1	1
Kansas	1	—
Louisiana	3	—
Maine	—	3
Massachusetts	1	6
Michigan	1	—
Mississippi	1	—
Montana	—	1
Nebraska	—	1
Nevada	1	—
New Jersey	13	—
New York	—	6
North Dakota	1	—
Ohio	1	—
Oregon	3	—
Texas	—	1
Virginia	—	1
Washington, D.C.	3	7
other U.S. territories	1	6
Length of time spent in other locales		
airport only	15	—
a few days	35	44
a few weeks	11	9
a few months	6	7
six months to one year	3	1
one year	3	—
one year or more	5	—
Purpose of visit		
short vacation	70	78
extended visit	20	15
lived	10	7

Note: *Some students mentioned more than one other place.

Description and Selection of the Sample

This cross-sectional study utilized self-report data. The questionnaire was pilot-tested on a selected sample of foreign students from both universities. These students were asked to identify possible problems with interpretation and other general problems with the design of the instrument. The pilot-tested interview results were not included in the final results reported here.

Personal Characteristics. Respondents were asked their age, sex, region of the world from which they came, and length of time spent in the United States to date. If all of their time spent in the United States was not spent at their university, they were asked where else they had lived or visited, the length of time that they spent at each one of the locations that they listed, and the purpose of their visit.

Respondents also were asked if they were married and, if they were, if their spouse and any children were living with them. They were asked about their primary source(s) of income, their year in school, and major. They also were asked to indicate the type of neighborhood in which they lived in the United States (i.e., urban, suburban, or rural). Subjects were asked about their ability to read, write, comprehend, and speak the English language. The wording of the question was: "On a scale of 1 (not fluent) to 5 (fluent), how would you rate your abilities in the following four areas of the English language: speaking, reading, writing, and comprehension?" Results of this question were aggregated into an index. The index for samples of subjects at both universities showed a high degree of reliability (a = .90). In other words, there was no difference within either sample in the ability to speak, read, write, and comprehend the English language. Therefore each foreign student in both samples was given an average self-perceived ability in the English-language score. The mean for all foreign students at the Midwestern university was 4. The mean for all foreign students at the urban university was 3. In short, the urban group believed that they were less fluent in the English language than the rural group.

Crime-Related Variables. Foreign students were asked if they had ever been the victim of a crime while in the United States or in any other country where they had ever lived or visited. If they had been victimized, they were asked about the nature and extent of their past victimization experiences (including attempts). Respondents also were asked about the nature of their vicarious victimization experiences—namely, only hearing about the victimization experiences of other foreign students.

Perceptual Variables. The foreign students were asked about their perceptions of vulnerability. The two specific questions were: "How likely do you think it is that you could be the victim of (1) a property offense (theft, burglary), and (2) a personal crime (rape, robbery, murder) while studying in the United States?" Response categories ranged from 1 (not likely) to 7 (extremely likely). Results for the two questions were aggregated into an index. The reliability for this index was high for subjects at each university (a = .81 for the rural university, and a = .96 for the urban university). In other words, foreign students in both samples made no distinction between the likelihood of personal or property victimization. The index was then collapsed for both samples, and each foreign student was given an average vulnerability-to-criminal-victimization score. The means for foreign students at the rural university (4) and the urban university (5) show that subjects at the rural university felt less vulnerable than subjects attending the urban university.

Anticipatory Variables. Foreign students were asked about their use of protective behaviors. Specifically, they were asked whether they avoided certain places and, if they did, what types of places they avoided and why. They also were asked whether they carried anything to protect themselves and, if they did, what they carried.

Identifying and Rank-Ordering Worries. Each person in the sample was asked to list the five biggest worries that they had in their lives while living in the United States. After having given them time to list their worries, they were asked to rank-order the worries that they had listed ranging from 1 (the biggest worry) to 5. This initial list of worries was generated by the foreign students; that is, they were not given a prepared list from which to choose.

Worries about Crime. The last question on the survey instrument asked foreign students to indicate on a five-point Likert-type scale the degree to which they worry about becoming the victim of (1) a property offense, and (2) a personal crime while studying in the United States. For both samples of students there was high reliability among these two variables (a = .88 for the rural sample, and a = .97 for the urban sample).

Next, each foreign student in each of the two groups was given an average worry-about-criminal-victimization score. The mean scores for each group—the rural university and urban university foreign students—were 2.2 and 3.4, respectively. In other words, there was no difference in worries about property or personal victimization for subjects in these samples. Subjects attending the urban university worried more about becoming the victim of a crime than subjects at the rural university. This variable was the dependent variable in the regression analyses.

RESULTS

As table 13.3 shows, most foreign students on both campuses reported not having been the victim of a crime while in the United States. Only 37 percent of the foreign students on the rural campus and 28 percent of the foreign students on the urban campus reported being the victims of crime. Of those who reported having been victimized while attending the rural university, 56 percent reported being victimized once; 20 percent reported being twice the victim of a crime; 16 percent reported being victimized three times; and 8 percent of them reported having been victimized four times. Foreign students attending the rural university who had been victimized regardless of the number of times reported burglaries and thefts most often.

Foreign students attending the urban university reported having been the victim of a crime ranging from one (35 percent) to four times (17 per-

Table 13.3

Criminal Victimization History in the United States*

Characteristics	*Rural Midwestern university (N = 67)*	*Urban Eastern university (N = 82)*
Past criminal victimization (in percentages)		
no	63	72
yes	37	28
Frequency of past victimization (in percentages)		
once	56	35
twice	20	35
three times	16	13
four times	8	17
Nature of victimization for those victimized once		
robbery	2	5
assault	3	—
theft	4	2
burglary	5	1
Nature of victimization for those victimized twice		
robbery	—	9
assault	1	3
theft	8	4
burglary	1	—
Nature of victimization for those victimized three times		
robbery	—	4
assault	3	3
theft	7	2
burglary	2	—
Nature of victimization for those victimized four times		
robbery	—	4
theft	8	12

Note: *No one mentioned more than four past victimization experiences. Past experiences are counted only once.

cent). The type of crime most often reported by foreign students attending the urban university was robbery, although reports of theft, burglary, and assault were reported. No foreign students in either sample reported more than four victimization experiences.

Table 13.4 depicts criminal victimization experiences suffered by foreign students in their native countries and/or outside of the United States and its territories. Most foreign students reported no past victimization experiences. Of those who did, 34 percent of foreign students at the rural university reported incidents, while 23 percent of foreign students on the

Table 13.4

Criminal Victimization History in Native Country and/or Outside the United States*

Characteristics	*Rural Midwestern university (N = 67)*	*Urban Eastern university (N = 82)*
Past criminal victimization (in percentages)		
no	66	77
yes	34	23
Frequency of past victimization (in percentages)		
once	60	32
twice	22	42
three times	10	16
four times	8	10
Nature of victimization for those victimized once		
robbery	3	2
assault	4	1
theft	5	3
burglary	2	—
Nature of victimization for those victimized twice		
robbery	1	4
assault	2	2
theft	—	9
burglary	7	1
Nature of victimization for those victimized three times		
robbery	—	3
assault	—	4
theft	6	2
Nature of victimization for those victimized four times		
robbery	—	2
theft	4	6
Vicarious victimization experience (in percentages)		
no	15	15
yes	85	85
male	12	6
female	13	13
both	60	66

Note: *No one mentioned more than four past victimization experiences. Past experiences are counted only once.

urban campus reported incidents. As table 13.4 shows, the types of victimization experiences include theft, burglary, assault, and robbery. Most foreign students, at both universities, had heard of past victimization experiences of both male and female foreign students in the United States.

Table 13.5

Self-Protective Behaviors (in percentages)

Types of behavior	*Rural Midwestern university (N = 67)*	*Urban Eastern university (N = 82)*
Avoid places?		
no	27	5
yes	73	95
Situations avoided		
outside (walking or driving) alone after midnight	21	17
big cities (walking or driving)	14	—
outside (walking or driving) alone after sunset	12	10
ghettos	29	26
nightclubs	20	7
mass transit (day and night)	4	20
parks	—	13
scaffolding	—	7
certain streets	—	9
Carry a weapon?		
no	57	47
yes	43	53
Means of protection		
knife	14	17
mace	76	33
blackjack	6	10
stun-gun	4	6
handgun	—	10
street sense	—	14
whistle	—	10

Five percent of the foreign students who had been victimized while attending the rural university had been the victim of a crime in their native country. Eleven percent of the urban university's foreign students who had been victimized while attending school also had been victimized in their native country.

The urban university foreign students' predictions of future victimization were slightly higher than were those of students at the rural university (the means are 5 and 4, respectively). As discussed earlier, the means for both universities show that foreign students attending the rural university are less worried about victimization than their urban counterparts (2.2 and 3.4).

Table 13.5 shows the behaviors used by foreign students to insulate themselves from criminal victimization. Of those students attending the rural university who reported avoiding situations (73 percent), most reported avoiding ghettos (29 percent). The second and third types of situations avoided by foreign students at the rural university were walking or driving alone after midnight (21 percent), then nightclubs (20 percent). Other places avoided are listed in table 13.5. Ninety-five percent of the foreign students attending the urban university reported avoiding places due to the threat of criminal victimization. The situation avoided by the largest percentage of these foreign students was ghettos (26 percent). The second and third type of situations avoided were mass-transit stations (20 percent), then parks (13 percent). Other types of places avoided by foreign students at the urban university are listed in table 13.5.

As might be expected, a larger percentage of foreign students at the urban university reported carrying weapons (53 percent versus 43 percent). Table 13.5 indicates these results. Foreign students who carry a weapon report carrying mace most often, irrespective of the type of university they attend. Referring to table 13.5, one can see that the other means of protection utilized by foreign students are: knives, blackjacks, stun-guns, handguns, "street sense," and whistles, although only foreign students at the urban university used the latter three measures.

Tables 13.6 and 13.7 list the worries of foreign students who attend both the rural and urban universities. Table 13.6 shows foreign students' worries (in raw numbers), in order of magnitude, ranging from (1) the

Table 13.6

Rank-Ordering of Worries among Students at a Large Rural Midwestern University[1]

Worry	*1*	*2*	*3*	*4*	*5*[2]
Failing in school	22	5	7	4	3
Racial attacks	10	9	4	13	3
Poor health	7	12	3	5	2
Family here in the United States	6	6	7	2	2
Getting mugged	5	8	2	3	27
Lack of money	3	11	11	6	2
Family back home	4	7	6	9	3
Job satisfaction upon returning home	2	3	1	10	1
Being morally good	1	2	4	2	2
Contracting AIDS	2	1	6	1	2
Becoming addicted to drugs	1	—	—	—	—
Choosing the right friends	—	—	9	8	4
Breaking up with a boy- or girlfriend	—	—	3	—	3

Notes: [1]*N* = 63; four students indicated "no worries." [2]Eight students listed no fifth worry.

Table 13.7

Rank-Ordering of Worries among Students at a Large Urban Eastern University[1]

Worry	*1*	*2*	*3*	*4[2]*	*5[3]*
Failing in school	13	17	6	3	8
Racial attacks	2	5	10	15	7
Poor health	3	12	19	9	5
Family here in the United States	—	6	8	8	8
Getting mugged	32	11	14	6	4
Lack of money	5	6	5	10	5
Family back home	8	1	1	7	11
Job satisfaction upon returning home	4	4	3	4	6
Being morally good	2	2	2	3	3
Contracting AIDS	6	8	7	5	8
Becoming addicted to drugs	2	5	5	—	3
Choosing the right friends	2	1	9	—	1
Breaking up with a boy- or girlfriend	—	1	—	1	—

Notes: [1]$N = 79$; three students indicated "no worries." [2]$N = 71$; eight students listed no fourth worry. [3]$N = 69$; ten students listed no fifth worry.

most serious to (5) the least serious of the five worries listed at the rural university. They are: (1) failing in school ($N = 22$); (2) poor health ($N = 12$); (3) the lack of money ($N = 11$); (4) racial attacks ($N = 13$); and (5) getting mugged ($N = 27$). The rank-ordering of worries by foreign students attending school on the urban campus is located in table 13.7 and shows that, in order of magnitude, their worries are: (1) getting mugged ($N = 32$); (2) failing in school ($N = 17$); (3) poor health ($N = 19$); (4) racial attacks ($N = 15$); and (5) about their family back home ($N = 11$).

Multivariate Analysis

Multiple regression was used in the analysis of both groups to assess the influence of fourteen predictor variables on the dependent variable: worries about crime. The predictor variables were: age, sex, whether all of their time in America was spent at their present university, length of time spent in the United States, marital status, if children lived within the household, the average self-perceived ability in the English-language score (see the methods section for a more detailed analysis of this variable), past victimization experiences before and while living in the United States and the numbers of past victimization experiences, their self-perceived vulnerability score, whether they avoid places, and whether they carried a weapon. All of the predictor variables were entered at one time. Partial correlation

Table 13.8

Significant Variables Influencing Foreign Students' Worries about Crime: The Rural University

Variable	*b*	*SE b* *ß*	*Stdz*	*t-score*
Sex	–3.2	1.4	–.42	–2.2[1]
Age	–.35	.15	–.50	–2.2[1]
Victim of crime in native country	–3.1	1.5	–.45	–2.1[1]
Number of times a victim of crime in native country	.99	.50	.40	2.0[1]
Kids	–2.6	1.4	–.40	–1.8[2]

Notes: [1]= .05. [2]= .10. R^2 = 6; *F* = 2.7.

coefficients were used to assess the contribution of the predictor variables by controlling the effects of other variables in the equation.

Table 13.8 contains the regression results for the foreign students at the rural university. Multiple-regression results reveal five significant variables that together explain 6 percent of the variance in these foreign students' worries about crime. The significant variables that were negatively correlated with worries about crime were: age, sex, whether they had been the victim of a crime in their native country, and whether they had children living with them in the United States. The independent variable that had a positive relationship with worries about crime was the number of times victimized in their native country. Females and younger foreign students were more worried about criminal victimization (ß = –.42 and –.50). If a foreign student had not been the victim of a crime in his or her native country, that individual was more worried about crime (ß = –.45). The more often a foreign student had been the victim of a crime in his or her native country, the more worried that individual was about becoming the victim of a crime in the United States (ß = .40). The above-mentioned variables were all significant at the .05 level. If a foreign student had children living within the house, he or she was not worried about victimization (ß = –.40—possible reasons for this finding will be explored later). This variable was significant at .10. Because this was an exploratory study, the more liberal significance level was included. The null hypotheses were rejected in the *t*- and *f*-tests. The conclusion is that the independent variables as well as the overall regression equation are helping to predict rural foreign students worries about crime (*f* = 2.70 at .05).

Nine predictor variables were not significant in explaining rural foreign students' worries about becoming the victim of a crime in this preliminary study. They were: whether all of their time in the United States had been spent at their present university, the length of time spent in the

Table 13.9

Significant Variables Influencing Foreign Students' Worries about Crime: The Urban University

Variable	*b*	*SE b* *ß*	*Stdz*	*t-score*
Self-perceived vulnerability	.46	.15	.12	3.0[1]
Self-perceived ability in the English language	–.78	.32	–.14	–2.4[2]
Vicarious victimization experience	1.56	.82	.12	2.0[1]
Victim of a crime in native country	.50	.34	.21	1.65[3]

Notes: [1]= .01. [2]= .05. [3]= .10. R^2 = 31; *F* = 9.5.

United States, self-perceptions of their ability in the English language (this group felt more adept in English than their urban counterparts), the occurrence and frequency of past victimization experiences in the United States, self-perceptions of vulnerability (this group felt that criminal victimization experiences were less likely than did foreign students at the urban university), whether they avoided places, and whether they carried weapons.

Table 13.9 shows regression-analysis results from subjects at the urban university. The percentage of variance explained by the four statistically significant independent variables is .31. Those subjects who had heard about the victimization experiences of other foreign students also tended to be more worried about becoming the victim of a crime, and this relationship was positive (ß = .12). A subject's perceptions about his or her ability in the English language was correlated with the subject's worries about victimization (ß = .14). The less comfortable the subject was with his or her ability to master the English language, the greater he or she worries about a victimization experience. Foreign students who had been the victim of a crime outside of the United States were more worried about becoming the victim of a crime while in the United States (ß = .21). Those foreign students who believe that future victimization experiences were likely were also more worried about a victimization experience occurring (ß = .12). The null hypotheses in both the *f*-test (*f* = 9.5 at .05) and *t*-test were rejected. The overall equation is significant, and the independent variables have explanatory value for predicting foreign students', from an urban university, worries about crime.

Ten predictor variables were not significant in predicting urban foreign students' worries about becoming the victim of a crime. They were: age, sex, whether all of their time had been spent at their present university, the occurrence and frequency of past victimization experiences in the United States, whether they avoided places, length of time in the United

States, whether they carried a weapon, whether children lived within their household, and the number of previous victimizations suffered in their native countries.

DISCUSSION, IMPLICATIONS, AND SUGGESTIONS FOR FUTURE RESEARCH

Overall, foreign students from the urban university felt more vulnerable to and worried about becoming the victim of a crime than foreign students at the rural university. Urban foreign students ranked getting mugged as their biggest worry, while rural students ranked getting mugged as only their fifth biggest worry. Regression results showed different predictor variables influencing foreign students' worries about crime that depended upon the type of university: urban or rural. Although the following explanations of findings were not tested in this exploratory study, they may form the groundwork for more rigorous studies in the future.

Results among the foreign students at the rural university reveal that younger subjects were more worried than older subjects. A review of the past literature stresses that older people are more worried about becoming the victim of a crime. Perhaps younger foreign students feel less emotionally prepared to study abroad. Consistent with past studies was the finding that females are more worried about becoming the victim of a crime than males. Those international students at the rural university who had been the victim of a crime in their native countries might have desensitized themselves about the likelihood of its occurrence, and thus worried less about its occurrence. But the greater the number of times that they had been victimized in their native country, the greater their worries about becoming the victim of a crime in the United States. Past literature focusing on the general population reveals that the occurrence and frequency of past victimization experiences result in greater worries about becoming the victim of a crime. The occurrence and frequency of past victimization experiences while in the United States were not significant predictors of rural foreign students' worries about becoming the victim of a crime. Those foreign students at the rural university who had children living within their households were not as worried about becoming the victim of a crime as those students who did not have children living with them. Foreign students at the rural university ranked worrying about getting mugged as only their fifth biggest worry. Perhaps those with children worried more about other, more immediate concerns that may or may not be related to their children.

Among foreign students attending school at the urban university, four predictor variables revealed having a greater impact on their worries about becoming the victim of a crime, compared to the much lower percentage of explained variance of the significant predictor variables among rural foreign students. Urban foreign students who *believed* that it was likely that they could become the victim of a crime also tended to *worry more* about it. Foreign students who considered their mastery of the English language to be poor also tended to worry more about becoming the victim of a crime. Perhaps U.S. embassies could test foreign students' ability in English so that the lack of being able to articulate in the language will not be so apt to result in higher worry levels. Those foreign students who had heard about the victimization experiences of other foreign students were correspondingly more worried about becoming the victim of a crime. International students attending the urban university who had been the victim of a crime in their native country were more worried about becoming the victim of a crime in the United States. A review of past literature shows that the findings in this study of urban foreign students are consistent with previous studies, with the exception of self-perceptions of ability in the English language. This variable was absent from this literature.

There are several implications that can be drawn from this study. These ramifications are incorporated here into practical suggestions that can be used by U.S. embassy personnel in foreign countries, counselors of international students in this country, and the general population. Embassy personnel can prepare foreign students for study in this country by informing them of possible worries that they might have that could interfere with their studying. In addition, these personnel might offer strategies for handling such worries if they occur. In so doing, embassy personnel can offer an obligatory orientation program to assist foreign students' preparedness to travel and study abroad. These data also could be used by counselors in international services and by college deans to develop policy for addressing the potential worries of foreign students once they arrive and begin studying in the United States. Finally, these study results, from a little-studied subgroup, should assist those U.S. citizens who come into contact with foreign students regularly (such as service-delivery personnel) as well as the general population in becoming sensitized to the nature of the potential problems of non-U.S. citizens studying at universities in the United States. Every citizen should be sensitized with the awareness of the potential worries of foreign students, and thus strive to make foreign students feel comfortable in a culture that may be strange to them.

In conclusion, there are many suggestions for future research. This study could be replicated on samples of foreign students who are stratified by native country so that the worries of foreign students can be refined by their countries of origin. Results focusing on worries among college students native to the United States could be compared to results of worries among nonnative students studying here to determine if there are any differences between these two groups. Results comparing the worries of U.S. college students studying abroad with those worries of U.S. college students studying in the United States could be compared. As a result, the host country where U.S. students are studying could provide orientation programs that address potential worries these students might have.

Finally, researchers may want to develop and validate a single variable representing the different dimensions of fear, such as the concern, worry, and anxiety associated with becoming the victim of a crime. To date, researchers studying in this area use one-dimensional variables tapping only singular dimensions of the concept that do not provide as comprehensive an understanding of the phenomenon as would a multidimensional variable.

ACKNOWLEDGMENTS

The author would like to acknowledge the support of Adel Ali Helal (employed by The Arab Security Studies and Training Center, in Riyadh, Saudi Arabia) who assisted with the interviews of the subjects in this study, and Robert M. Bohm who edited drafts of this chapter.

REFERENCES

Brown, D. (1980). *Principles of language learning and teaching.* Englewood Cliffs, NJ: Prentice Hall.

Conklin, J. (1975). *The impact of crime.* New York: Macmillan.

Coston, C. (1988). *Fear of crime among New York City's shopping-bag ladies.* Unpublished doctoral dissertation, Rutgers University, Newark.

———. (1991). "Worries about crime: Rank-ordering survival concerns among urban transient females." Paper presented at the annual meeting of the American Society of Criminology, November.

DuBow, F., M. Edward, and G. Kaplan. (1979). *Reactions to crime: A critical review of the literature.* Washington, DC: U.S. Department of Justice.

Erskine, H. (1974). "The polls: Fear of violence and crime." *Public Opinion Quarterly 38*:131–45.

Garofalo, J. (1987). "Reassessing the lifestyle model of criminal victimization," in *Positive criminology*, ed. M. R. Gottfredson and T. Hirschi. Newbury Park, CA: Sage Publications.

Gibbs, J. (1986). "Fear of crime: A concept in need of clarification." Paper presented at the annual meeting of the American Society of Criminology.

Gordon, M., and S. Riger. (1989). *Female fear.* New York: Free Press.

Hanrahan, K. (1990). *Exploring fear of crime among elderly urban females.* Unpublished doctoral dissertation, Rutgers University, Newark.

Hindelang, M. J. (1974). "Public opinion regarding crime, criminal justice, and related topics." *Journal of Research in Crime and Delinquency 11*:101–6.

Hindelang, Michael, Michael Gottfredson, and James Garofalo. (1978). *Victims of personal crime: An empirical foundation for a theory of personal victimization.* Cambridge, MA: Ballinger Publishing Company.

Hossain, M. (1983). "Social determinants of foreign students' length of stay in United States." *International Journal of Contemporary Sociology 20*, nos. 3–4.

Lewis, Oscan. (1982). "Urbanization without breakdown: A case study." *Scientific Monthly 75*:31–41.

Lodhi, Abdule, and Charles Tilly. (1983). "Urbanization, crime and collective violence in nineteenth-century France." *American Journal of Sociology 79*:296–318.

Lynch, Kevin. (1990). *The image of the city.* Cambridge, MA: MIT Press.

Meithe, Terrance, and Gary Lee. (1984). "Fear of crime among older people: An assessment of the predictive power of crime-related factors." *Sociological Quarterly 16*:397–414.

Merry, S. (1981). *Urban danger: Life in a neighborhood of strangers.* Philadelphia: Temple University Press.

Moumen, F. (1985). *Attitudes, motivation, and orientation in learning English as a second language.* Unpublished Master's thesis, Indiana University, Bloomington.

Perloff, Linda. (1986). "Self–other judgments." *Journal of Personality and Social Psychology 50*:502–10.

Riger, Stephaine, Robert LeBailley, and Margaret Gordon. (1981). "Community ties and urbanites' fear of crime: An ecological investigation." *American Journal of Community Psychology 9*:74–77.

Roberts, Bryan. (1989). *Organizing strangers.* Austin: University of Texas Press.

Simmel, G. (1950). *The sociology of Georg Simmel.* Glencoe, IL: Free Press.

Sparks, R. (1982). *Research on victims of crime: Accomplishments, issues.* New York: National Institute of Mental Health.

Spaulding, S., and M. Flack. (1976). *The world's students in the United States: A review and evaluation of research on foreign students.* New York: Praeger.

Stein, Shayna, Margaret Linn, Elisa Slater, and Elliott Stein. (1984). "Future concerns and recent life events of elderly community residents." *Journal of the American Geriatrics Society 16*:306–11.

Sundeen, Richard, and James Mathieu. (1976). "The fear of crime and its consequences among elderly in three urban communities." *Gerontologist 16*:211–17.

Wiltz, C. J. (1982). "Fear of crime, crime victimization, and elderly blacks." *Phylon 43*:283–94.

Wirth, Louis. (1991). "Urbanism as a way of life." *American Journal of Sociology 44*:1–29.

Yin, Peter. (1980). "Fear of crime among the elderly: Some issues and suggestions." *Social Problems 27*:492–504.

CHAPTER FOURTEEN

Victims in Underdeveloped Countries

DIANE C. BATES
JOANNE ARDOVINI-BROOKER

THE TERM "VICTIM" IS OFTEN USED to place a number of people into a very small rubric that limits the scope of *victimology*. The opening of Doerner and Lab's book, *Victimology* (1998), exemplifies the myopic nature of the majority's view of victims. They state: "Something not very funny happened on the way to a formal system of justice. The victim got left out. As strange as it may sound, the bulk of history has seen crime victims become further removed as an integral part of dealing with criminals" (Doerner & Lab 1998, 1). The error that this statement demonstrates is that *individuals* can only fall victim to crime. However, there are many categories of victimization. Individuals may fall victim to natural disasters or be victimized by social structures. Types of victimization subsumed under the rubric of *structural victimization* range from industrial/technological and corporate to institutional. Other categories of victimization include collective, multiple, and random. In other words, *victimology* is intended to study the victims, the offenders, and societies (Wallace 1998, 3). It is not intended to focus solely on the impact of crime on an individual. Moreover, we must not perpetuate the false image that victimization occurs to one person at a time.

Victimization can occur to a collective—most often, marginalized groups. One commonality that applies to virtually all uses of the term "victim," no matter what the category, is that the victim suffers injury and harm by forces beyond his or her control and not of his or her personal responsibility (U.S. Department of Justice 2002). This commonality opens the field of study to a variety of social phenomena that are injurious to societies. In this chapter, we examine oppression within Third World countries that results from social, cultural, or global processes as a form of victimization. In developing countries, the focus of the field shifts from the individual victim of crime to the victimization of vulnerable classes. Victimization in developing countries thus represents a structural problem, linked to the processes of modernization and globalization.

Conditions of chronic underdevelopment have recently intensified due to the debt crisis in Latin America, Africa, and Asia. During the 1960s and 1970s, First World advisors and international lending institutions encouraged developing countries to take out massive loans to build up social and economic infrastructures. It was assumed that this investment would stimulate Rostow's economic "take-off" and countries could then repay their debt (Rostow 1964). When the world economy entered into recession during the 1980s, however, many of these countries found themselves saddled with debts (and budgets) that they simply could not pay. Development institutions then changed their models to structural adjustment and austerity, in which social programs (such as education, health care, and agricultural subsidies) were eliminated in order to meet loan obligations. Standards of living declined accordingly; the 1980s is known in development circles as "The Lost Decade" because most social indicators at the end of the 1980s were lower than they had been at the end of the 1970s. The 1990s and early 2000s have recorded few improvements. This situation has deepened the vulnerability of the most vulnerable in developing countries, and has thus increased the number of people who potentially belong to victimized classes.

To examine forms of victimization in these regions, we use a comparative approach. We cite examples from our own research, but also draw from other literature. We report details of specific cases to highlight the individualized processes of victimization, even within conditions of collective oppression. These stories, we believe, assist in our understanding of the structural victimization and social reality of oppression (Elias 1986) that occur in Third World countries.

Instead of attempting to systematically measure rates of victimization in developing countries, we intend for this chapter to introduce readers to the types of victimization unique to this position within the global economy. While victims of violence, corruption, and substance abuse can be easily found in developing countries, and often with considerably fewer resources and less access to social services than do their counterparts in wealthier countries, we have chosen to focus on classes of victims who find themselves in circumstances unfamiliar to the global North. Among these, we examine three broad classes of victims: indigenous and traditional peoples, the urban poor, and the rural poor.

INDIGENOUS AND TRADITIONAL PEOPLES[1]

The victimization of tribal peoples in North America has been extensively covered elsewhere (cf. Brown [2000]). Traditional cultures in Asia, Africa, and Latin America have only recently gained international attention to their situation. The work of activists such as Chico Mendes, a rubber-tapper from the Brazilian Amazon, and growing militancy in places like Chiapas, Mexico and Borneo, Indonesia have pushed the continued victimization of indigenous and traditional people into international human-rights debates. Small in number and largely relegated to marginal and frontier areas, indigenous people have never figured centrally in national development agendas. Economic-development strategies pit national interests against the lifestyles of indigenous and other traditional peoples. Development-oriented national governments often treated indigenous peoples as backwards and impediments to modernization, and they encouraged assimilation (at best) or genocide (at worst).

Typically, conflicts erupt over land and natural resources and, until very recently, indigenous interests have been subverted in favor of the "national good." In the past, victimization was often sudden and violent, with the national military or local militias called out to eliminate or repress indigenous peoples. Survivors faced ethnocide, either intentional or de facto, as their traditional lifestyles were rendered incompatible with modern land uses. In more recent times, governments and nongovernmental organizations (NGOs) have increased their sensitivity to the situation of indigenous and traditional peoples. Consequently, contemporary victimization tends to be more complicated than straightforward violence. Of course, this is not to suggest that the old-style forms of victimization do not take place, as they most certainly do. To investigate new forms of victimization of traditional and indigenous peoples, we discuss four different cases: the game reserves of Kenya, the Dayak and Penan of Borneo, the *caboclo* rubber-tappers in the Brazilian Amazon, and the Chiapas rebellion in Mexico.

The Game Reserves of Kenya

Kenya is an ethnically diverse country, in which the government is culturally dominated by English- and Kiswahili-speaking people, primarily of African origins. The influence of British colonization is quite strong, both in terms of culture and land use. The interior savannahs of Kenya have long captured the imagination of non-African people, inviting explorers, game hunters, and wildlife enthusiasts. Initially developed to protect large game (such as elephants and lions) for elite hunters, the Kenyan national park and wildlife refuge system now attracts thousands of tourists annually, and tourism has grown into one of the most important sectors in the nation's economy. As the Kenyan government has come to recognize this asset (and, to a lesser extent, the ability of wildlife protection to gather international development aid), it has increased both the size and regulation of these (nominally) public lands. Under the leadership of Richard Leakey, Kenya made its park guard into a paramilitary organization during the late 1980s. Game wardens patrolled the parks in Jeeps armed with mounted machine guns and the authority to shoot to kill. And kill they did; wardens killed over a hundred poachers within two years of the institution of Leakey's regime (Peluso 1993, 205). These efforts have reduced the amount of poaching that has occurred in Kenyan parks, and environmental organizations have commended the efforts of the Kenyan government.

The indigenous people in and around these parks do not share in this enthusiasm. Reserves have removed vital resources from local uses for the benefit of wealthy tourists. One of the current authors visited a traditional village adjacent to the Tsavo National Park in 1995 and was told that school children in the village had visited the park for the first time in 1994, and then only thanks to a grant from the U.S. Peace Corps. In a better-known example, the nomadic Maasai people were forcibly removed from their traditional land and told that they could no longer range cattle in areas where national parks were developed. Their removal from these territories began at the turn of the twentieth century, but by the 1960s, the Maasai were refused access to traditional lands for grazing. Moreover, they were warned that if they killed predators that threatened their herds or hunted lions in a rite of passage for Maasai men, they would be subject to arrest and prosecution as poachers (Hamisi 2002). In other words, park boundaries made traditional nomadic uses of the land impossible and criminalized traditional cultural practices. In this case, the Maasai have become victims of national and international interests that will devastate their traditional culture.

The Dayak and Penan of Borneo

In Borneo, indigenous groups have taken a direct approach to fending off threats from outside incursions. Borneo contains one of the largest remaining contiguous rainforests on the planet, divided between the countries of Indonesia and Malaysia.[2] The Penan and Dayak are rainforest peoples who had maintained their traditional ways until quite recently. In the 1970s, Japanese and other Asian lumber companies began to threaten these groups' traditional homelands. By 1991, the Penan of Malaysian Borneo began to organize roadblocks to prevent the harvest of forests that sustained their traditional economy, resulting in arrests and violence (Environment News Service 1991; Sahabat Alam Malaysia 1992). Similar events occurred in Indonesian parts of the island, although there, the Dayak have been accused of using violence, especially against settlers from other islands (see below). Conflict with the Dayak led the central government of Indonesia to send its army to Borneo to (in theory) stem the violence. In actuality, the Indonesia army has been repeatedly linked with repressive ethnic violence. In the case of the Penan and Dayak, victimization continues because the national military and court system defend outside interests over those of traditional peoples.

The Caboclo *Rubber-tappers of the Brazilian Amazon*

The victimization of indigenous and traditional peoples by national governments became headline news in December 1988 when labor activist and environmentalist Chico Mendes was assassinated in the Brazilian state of Acre. Mendes was a *caboclo*, an ethnic group of mixed European, Native American, and/or African descent that lives in the interior reaches of the Brazilian Amazon and has formed the backbone of the rubber economy since the late 1800s. During the 1970s and 1980s, the Brazilian government granted large land claims to wealthy Brazilian ranchers, who began to clear the forests, with little concern over the situation for the *caboclo* and indigenous peoples who lived and worked there. Mendes, who had considerable experience as a labor activist for the Brazilian Workers' Party (PT), negotiated a coalition between *caboclo* rubber-tappers and indigenous groups to stop these incursions. The ranchers responded with militias that resulted in the deaths of several activists and countless acts of violence (Revkin 1990). Despite international attention to Mendes's campaigns, including awards from the World Bank and United Nations, local ranchers waged an open campaign of terror and violence in Acre. Among other acts, Acre ranchers put a price on Mendes's head. The national government in Brasilia remained silent, even after Mendes's murder. Mendes's assassins—ranchers Darly and Darcy Alves da Silva—openly bragged of their involvement in the murder throughout Acre. Only after international outcries did the Brazilian courts convict the ranchers (Revkin 1990). In this case, the lack of action by the national government allowed for decades of victimization of *caboclo* and indigenous activists in Acre and other Amazonian states.

The Chiapas Rebellion in Mexico

Lack of government action has also been a root-cause of victimization of the Maya in southern Mexico. The victimization of indigenous peoples is a recurring theme in modern Mexican history, with the Mexican Revolution and Emiliano Zapata, a Nahua revolutionary, serving as icons for the struggle against this oppression. The southern states of Mexico contain high proportions of indigenous populations, including the Nahua, the Oaxaqueño, and the Maya. Despite the modernization of the Mexican economy during the 1960s and 1970s, most indigenous populations continue to depend on subsistence agriculture and receive few services from the federal government. In the late 1980s and early 1990s, the central government of Mexico negotiated the North American Free Trade Agreement (NAFTA), which eroded communal rights to land and subsidies that protected traditional agriculture. When NAFTA went into effect on January 1, 1994, the Zapatista National Liberation Army (EZLN), consisting primarily of Mayan people from the state of Chiapas, took up arms against the central government. Mexico City responded by sending the army to quell the rebellion, resulting in violence perpetrated primarily by the Mexican army (Collier 1999). The EZLN complaints focused on the central government's long-standing neglect and disenfranchisement of Mayan and other indigenous groups in southern Mexico. While peace agreements have stemmed much of the violence in Chiapas since 1994, EZLN concerns have not been fully addressed, despite widespread national and international concern for the situation of the Maya.

In all of the previous case studies, victimization of indigenous and traditional peoples stems from two general processes: (1) institutional racism in the political, legal, and military structures of developing countries that privileges national interests over indigenous and traditional ones; and (2) internal colonialism, inasmuch as indigenous and traditional peoples are not granted authority over their traditional resources, which are instead treated as goods that can be privatized and utilized for national interests. The Maasai, the Dayak, the Penan, the Amazonian rubber-tappers, and the Zapatistas have all become part of a worldwide resistance to victimization under the banners of indigenous, environmental, and human rights. This resistance uses information as its most powerful weapon, relying on media coverage and the Internet to gather worldwide condemnation of their victimization. In this sense, indigenous and traditional peoples have been somewhat successful in curbing the more acute forms of victimization. Nonetheless, the future for indigenous and traditional movements is bleak: the dire financial situation of most developing countries and the relatively small numbers of indigenous and traditional peoples push their concerns to low priorities on national agendas.

THE URBAN POOR

Unlike indigenous and traditional peoples, the urban poor in developing countries do not enjoy international status as a *cause celèbre*. Roughly since World War II, the urban population in developing countries has exceeded the rural population, despite the lack of sanitation, utilities, and transportation in cities. Shortages of land and stagnation in traditional rural sectors drove millions of migrants from the countryside to burgeoning Third World cities, which are characterized by substandard housing, low levels of social services, poverty, and a growing dependence on informal economic structures. Uncontrolled urban growth has created new social problems and new vulnerabilities. Each year, a growing number of people in Asia, Africa, and Latin America find themselves in overcrowded living conditions, subject to high levels of crime, violence, corruption, and health risks. Urbanization has also contributed to the development of new classes of victims. In this section we will address three such forms of victimization related to the economy of Third World cities: working in the informal economy, working in the sex trade, and working in export-processing zones.

Among the urban poor in developing countries, the informal economy is larger and more important than the formal economy in terms of employment. Informal employment includes illegal activities such as prostitution and the drug trade, but is more typically ordinary work that is external to formal economic structures. Since, by definition, these people work outside the weak regulatory protections afforded by labor laws, informal workers find themselves subject to harassment, violence, and exploitation. To examine these problems in detail we will describe the situation of ambulant vendors in the Andean countries of South America.

In the cities of South America, a large number of ambulant retailers roam the streets selling just about anything they can carry. Many of these vendors are women and children, but adult men also find themselves in this informal retail sector. All ambulant vendors face the same problems: higher likelihood of theft, harassment by law-enforcement officers, and exposure to unhealthy working conditions. In an oral history, one elderly woman who sold food on the streets of a Peruvian city describes her victimization at the hands of city workers:

> One day, just when my little food business was going along well, the city hall employees, all dressed up in uniforms like policemen, came around asking for our municipal licenses. I didn't know what a municipal license was all about, and I kept on going there to sell, till one day those same municipal police began confiscating our pots and plates. . . . I kept on going there after that happened, quietly selling my food where those municipal dogs wouldn't see me. . . . [O]ne day I let myself get caught. I'd just gotten there that day and was waiting around for my steady customers to arrive, when suddenly a municipal policeman came around the corner, and there just wasn't enough time to get away with my pot. Then he told me: "Dammit! What are you, deaf? No good, fucking Indian!" Boom! Boom! He kicked my pot over and stomped up and down on my plates, which were all made of red pottery. (Valderrama Fernandez & Escalante Gutierrez 1996, 132–33)

Florence Babb, who conducted an ethnography of marketwomen in Huaraz, Peru, wrote that ambulant retailers reported "greater risks at night, when customers may be drunk and threaten the sellers" (1989, 90). Babb observed an increase in the number of children accompanying ambulant retailers over the course of her fieldwork (1989, 189).

In another example of risks to ambulant workers, Rudel (1998) describes how in Quito, Ecuador, poor mothers and their children beg from the medians of busy streets. Since Ecuador still uses leaded gasoline, poor women and children are exposed to dangerous levels of toxic lead. We can confirm that begging not only occurs on the streets of Quito, but so does the selling of everything from fruit to newspapers to basic toiletries. Heavily congested and contaminated streets have become an important marketplace for ambulant retailers throughout Latin America and the Caribbean, increasing the health risks borne by this already vulnerable class of workers.

Another category of urban victims in the developing world involves the sex trade, which is most prominent in Southeast Asia but exists worldwide. In Asia, most of the "clients" are Japanese and Western businessmen and tourists, who pay relatively little money to have sex with women, boys, and girls. The United Nations Children's Fund (UNICEF) (2001) reports that as many as a million women and children are subject to sexual exploitation in developing countries, especially Southeast Asia. In Thailand alone, monetary transfers from urban female sex workers are estimated to remit nearly $300 million each year to the countryside (UNICEF 2001, 7). Many of the women involved in the sex trade are minors, who are desirable sex partners because of the perception that they do not carry HIV. In fact, sex workers of all ages have much higher than average exposures to HIV and other sexually transmitted diseases.

Many sex workers do not choose their trade; instead, they are coerced or forced into it. The president of the Philippines estimated that some of the 100,000 children involved in the sex trade in her country find themselves in the trade "through the influence of peers, others through deception or force" (Macapagal Arroyo 2001, 4). UNICEF (2001) describes the common process of debt bondage, in which girls work until they have paid off money given to parents or guardians that have "sold" them into service. As the girls must also work to pay expenses such as rent and food, the debt cannot often be paid quickly, if at all. UNICEF described the way in which one young girl was deceived into the sex trade:

> Srey Kanya was sitting outside her home weaving rush mats for her mother when Mrs. Ith approached her. Mrs. Ith was well-dressed and spoke kindly to Srey Kanya. "You're too smart to be tucked away in this village," said Mrs. Ith. "You should be in the town working in a good job that pays a high salary. I can help you if you like." Srey Kanya was flattered. She was 15 years old and knew life in the village didn't hold a bright future for her. She had also had many disagreements with her mother and she felt that her parents might be glad if she left and got a job through which she could send them back some money. But there was no decent, well-paid job for Srey Kanya. Instead, she ended up in a brothel in Phnom Penh [Cambodia]. (UNICEF 2001, 26)

In another example of interest to the victimization of women workers in developing countries, we now turn to industrial sweatshops. Factories in export-processing zones (also known as *maquiladoras* or *maquilas*) throughout the developing world take advantage of low wages, limited labor and environmental regulation, and the desperation of the urban poor to assemble inexpensive products. In most cases, the preferred workers are young women, who are seen as much easier to control and less like to unionize. In Mexican *maquiladoras*, workers are subject to low pay, hazardous working conditions, sexual harassment, and toxic contamination of their communities (Iglesias Prieto 1997). In El Salvador, a female worker told a foreign human-rights delegation about treatment in apparel factories:

> [I]n the D—— *maquila*, every Monday [we] have to sing the Korean national anthem in Spanish, and if the workers don't know the words, they have to stand facing the wall for the day and do not get paid. There were eight spontaneous abortions in the factory in one year, and none of the women were given permission to go to the doctor. The . . . factory doesn't respect human rights. On August 12, they buried one woman who worked at D—— because she didn't get medical attention. She had a headache and asked to go to the hospital, but they wouldn't let her go. She kept working, got up to go to the bathroom, vomited, and fell. (Bates 1996)

Adding insult to these injuries, *maquila* workers are regularly paid below the legal minimum wage. A panel of Salvadoran *maquila* workers explained that despite the legal minimum wage of $4.41 per eight-hour shift, workers were paid considerably less. These workers passed around pay stubs to corroborate their assertions. One woman was paid $109.51 for 31 days' labor, an average of $3.51 per day (Bates 1996).

Maquilas in El Salvador have actively prevented the formation of labor unions to alleviate the conditions in these factories (Bates 1996). The panel of Salvadoran *maquila* workers described their attempt to unionize a Taiwanese-owned factory simply to have more than two opportunities to go to the bathroom on each 12-hour shift. The organizers were fired, but reinstated after a 28-hour strike. The organizers eventually gained the support of 450 workers, *all* of whom were fired when the *maquila* owners recognized that they might have to collectively bargain with the workers. Workers fired for organizing were placed on a blacklist and barred from working in the other factories. They then had to seek work in the informal economy, including prostitution.

The situation of the Salvadoran *maquila* workers, like that of sex workers, draws attention to the international economic linkages that create classes of victims in Third World cities. For *maquila* and sex workers, victimization stems from the inequality in social power between the global wealthy, with their demands for cheap products and prostitution, and the global poor. In the case of ambulant vendors, victimization results from their lack of protection by domestic institutions. We have emphasized victimization in work in order to highlight the pervasive and structural nature of urban victimization in developing countries: major sectors of the urban labor force could be classified in toto as victims.

THE RURAL POOR

Although by proportion, developing countries have shrinking rural populations, the absolute number of people living in rural areas continues to grow. Rural poverty currently reflects less the inadequacies of traditional production than the uneasy relationship between rural, traditional peoples and modern capitalist systems. Among the categories of vulnerable people in the rural areas are: landless rural workers, small holders, and colonists (or transmigrants).

The landless have no independent means to support themselves. Landless workers usually work in one of three arrangements: as occasional day laborers, in which case their livelihood is insecure almost by definition; as regular workers, usually on large plantations or ranches; or as renters and sharecroppers. Occasional day laborers compete for whatever paid work is available, usually working for less than the legal minimum wage and often subject to dangerous working conditions. Rural areas in general have less access to health care and education, and landless occasional workers have the least amount of access to even these scarce facilities. Occasional workers often must migrate (sometimes great distances) to obtain work, which may disrupt family organization and promote abandonment. Sharecroppers and renters fare a little better, but have little flexibility in terms of their rent or share. If a crop fails, they still must pay rent or compensate for the landlord's share. All types of landless rural workers suffer from high levels of insecurity, both in terms of residence and income.

The case of Zimbabwe highlights the precarious position of landless farm workers. Zimbabwe is a poor country of about 11 million residents, in which over a quarter of the adults are currently infected with HIV/AIDS (Central Intelligence Agency 2001). Two-thirds of the country's population works in agriculture, with a concentration in export crops such as tobacco. White farmers have historically dominated this sector. Despite their history of poor treatment of African workers, these white farmers employed hundreds of thousands of landless workers. In the wake of Zimbabwe's 1980 independence and subsequent war with the Democratic Republic of Congo,[3] Zimbabwe's president Robert Mugabe promised to redistribute land to his supporters (primarily ex-combatants and members of the ZANU-PF[4] party). When the occupations of white farms began, the frontline of the occupation became a locus of violence between Mugabe's supporters and farm workers. In its annual report on Zimbabwe, Amnesty International describes the situation of farm workers:

> Up to 70,000 black farm workers were estimated to have been assaulted and forced to abandon their homes by state-sponsored militia composed of "war veterans" and other ZANU-PF supporters. Many were destitute after losing both their livelihoods and all their belongings when their houses were razed to the ground. Farm invasions were stepped up during

> 2001 and reports indicated that 90 percent of the commercial farms in the country were on a government list of farms for acquisition. In Mashonaland West Province, for example, some 7,000 farm workers were reported to have been forcibly evicted from their homes in August alone. There were increasingly grave warnings of a looming crisis in the country when staple crops ran out. (Amnesty International 2002, 1)

Landlessness is often closely linked to the shortage of available land in developing countries. Due to population growth, consolidation of agricultural land by large producers, and division of small farms, even those people who own land are likely to own less than can support their families. This condition has been aggravated by the so-called Green Revolution, in which extension agents attempted to increase production on small plots through biotechnology and chemicals. As genetically modified grains (such as rice and corn) are engineered to be sterile, farmers cannot save seeds from one harvest to plant in the next, thus obligating them to purchase seeds for each harvest. This process saddled small holders with debt and led to foreclosures. Nonspecific pesticides advocated during the Green Revolution killed insect predators as well as insect pests, allowing for chemical-resistant plagues to devastate crops that are not treated with increasing amounts of expensive pesticides. Despite its intentions, the Green Revolution has been associated with growing rural poverty, especially in Asia (cf. Shiva 1989).

Small holders are often victims of powerful agents that intend to help them. In Ecuador, for example, farmers were issued plots of land to develop small-scale cattle ranches and commodity farms for national markets. Funding for these programs came from the Inter-American Development Bank and the U.S. Agency for International Development, along with assistance from the Ecuadorian government (Rudel 1993). The National Development Bank (BNF, or Banco Nacional de Fomento) issued loans to small holders and colonists to develop these enterprises. With the help of these outside agents, over 90 percent of farmers in one community had agricultural loans (Rudel 1993, 118). These loans were initially a bargain for poor farmers, as they had fixed interest rates that ran below rates of inflation. As bank policies changed under structural adjustment during the 1990s, the BNF changed its interest policy to a floating rate, which rose to a high of over 60 percent during the mid-1990s (Bates 2000). Farmers found that they could not generate enough cash income on their land to meet loan obligations. As farmers defaulted on their loans, the BNF foreclosed on hundreds of farms throughout Ecuador. In a 1997–1998 survey of the farmers in the same community cited above, 41 of 59 farm-owning households still had loans. All but one reported difficulty in repaying these loans, and several other farmers had already lost their land to foreclosure or sold under threat of it. One former farmer, who sold his land to cover the loan payments, described a typical situation:

> The farm wasn't good for anything. Nothing grew, especially naranjilla.[5] We quit growing everything. We didn't cultivate anything because nothing produced. We had pests in the pasture grasses and in the bananas that made it so I couldn't harvest them. I had loans from the bank, and we had to pay them even though we didn't sell anything. (Bates 2000)

After selling his farm, this informant then moved to a small city where he found work in the informal sector. His situation is common among small holders; their vulnerability makes it likely that they will become landless rural workers or will migrate to urban areas, where they face urban forms of victimization, as described above.

The shortage of land in rural areas of developing countries is also linked to the insecure position of colonist farmers. During the 1960s and 1970s, many developing nations sought to solve the problems of rural poverty by opening up (or "colonizing") new agricultural frontiers. The two largest examples of this are the Brazilian Polonoroeste Program and the Indonesian Transmigration Program, although similar colonization projects took place in many other countries. Using national and international funds, colonists were relocated to places that (we now know) are totally inappropriate for intensive agriculture, usually tropical rainforests. Ample evidence exists about the rapid degradation of these environments, often at the same time that funding for these projects dried up (cf. Hecht & Cockburn 1989). This degradation leaves colonists in a bad position: they are geographically isolated from their traditional support networks, but cannot survive on the land to which they relocated.

The experience of Indonesian transmigrants provides a good example of how colonists become victims of their circumstances. With financial help from the World Bank, the Indonesian government has moved 3.6 million people from the densely settled "inner" islands such as Java and Madura to less populated "outer" islands such as Sumatra and Borneo. Most transmigrants were landless rural workers (World Bank 1994, 13). The World Bank's (1994) audit of the transmigration projects found that they had performed well below expectations, largely because of the lack of expertise in farming on fragile rainforest soils. In effect, transmigration stranded poor settlers on outer islands with limited opportunity for agricultural development and few nonfarm options.

In addition to the poverty and isolation of transmigrants, they also faced hostility from the indigenous populations of the outer islands, who understandably resent the relocation of large numbers of outsiders onto their traditional homelands. On February 18, 2001, violence broke out again between Madurese transmigrants and the indigenous Dayak following decades of conflict. By April, the *Jakarta Post* reported at least 500 Madurese settlers had been killed in the violence, and another 80,000 fled or evacuated the region (*Jakarta Post* 2001). In other words, transmigrants experienced landlessness on their home islands, the precariousness of small-holding agriculture in their new locations, and a whole new breed of problems associated with being unfamiliar and unwelcome in their new surroundings.

The state of the rural poor in developing countries mirrors the structural vulnerability found in urban areas; namely, that the nature of work and survival in rural areas increases peoples' vulnerability. Whether victimized by powerful national agents, as in the case of Ecuadorian farmers, or by other desperate segments of their own national population, as in the case of Zimbabwean farm workers and Madurese transmigrants, the rural poor face a grim future. As colonization has slowed due to the failure of programs such as the Indonesian Transmigration program, the potential for opening up new land for the rural poor appears as limited as the prospect of meaningful land reform. As a consequence, more and more rural residents will find themselves landless or near-landless, increasing the number of people in these classes of victimization.

CONCLUSION

All the cases discussed in this chapter demonstrate the variation and complexity of victimization that occurs in Third World countries. We must add that many of the circumstances described above may also be relevant to classes of victims in more developed countries. As global cities and vast disparities in wealth, health, and security become typical of the so-called First World, we expect that many of these classes of victims are already or will become prevalent in more affluent regions of the world. Given this trend, our main purpose in this chapter has been to open victimology to a discourse of global and structural victimization.

Although our intent is not to offer solutions to these situations, we do feel an obligation to extend at least one basic recommendation. In the promotion of healing, we would advocate a fundamental proposition upon which restorative justice is built; that is, the concept that "victims, offenders, and communities should have opportunities for active involvement in the restorative justice process as early and as fully as possible" (Tobolowsky 2000, 290). This would only empower those that are oppressed by the disenfranchisement of their country and the victimization that ensues.

NOTES

1. The difference between *indigenous* and *traditional* is blurry and often ideologically based. *Indigenous* here refers to largely pre-industrial cultures that existed in Asia, Latin America, and Africa prior to European contact. *Traditional* cultures refer to largely pre-industrial people with long-standing cultural ties to regions mainly within Latin America and the Caribbean whose origins are linked to European economic expansion, such as the *maroons* of the Caribbean, the *quilombos* and *caboclos* of Brazil, and the Garifuna of Central America. Generally,

both *indigenous* and *traditional* peoples are separated from the mainstream national populations by ethnicity and geography, as well as being disadvantaged in terms of social power.

2. The country of Brunei is also located on the island of Borneo, but the Dayak/Penan conflicts have not occurred within the sultanate, which has a very small indigenous population.
3. Formerly Zaïre.
4. Zimbabwe African National Union-Patriotic Front.
5. A commercial fruit crop (*Solanum quitoense*).

References

Amnesty International. (2002). *Country report: Zimbabwe (Republic of)*. Available at <http://web.amnesty.org/ai.nsf/countries/zimbabwe?OpenView&Start=1&Count=30&Expandall>. Retrieved September 3, 2002.

Babb, Florence E. (1989). *Between field and cooking pot: The political economy of marketwomen in Peru*. Austin: University of Texas Press.

Bates, Diane C. (1996). *Partners across borders: August 1996 delegation to El Salvador* (unpublished internal document). St. Cloud, MN: Partners Across Borders.

———. (2000). *Environmental refugees?: Colonist migration from the Ecuadorian Amazon*. Doctoral dissertation, Rutgers University.

Brown, Dee Alexander. (2000). *Bury my heart at Wounded Knee: An indian history of the American West*. New York: Henry Holt.

Central Intelligence Agency (CIA). (2001). *World fact book*. Washington, DC: CIA.

Collier, George A., with Elizabeth Lowery Quaratiello. (1999). *Basta!: Land and the Zapatista rebellion in Chiapas*. Oakland, CA: Food First.

Doerner, William G., and Steven P. Lab. (1998). *Victimology*, 2nd ed. Cincinnati: Anderson Publishing.

Elias, Robert. (1986). *The politics of victimization: Victims, victimology, and human rights*. New York: Oxford University Press.

Environmental News Service. (1991). "Native logging victims arrested (Sarawak, Malaysia)." Available at <www.nativenet.urthscsa.edu/archive/nl/91b/0016.html>. Retrieved August 20, 2002.

Hamisi, Kakuta. (2002). "Maasai and agents of change." Available at <http://www.maasai_infoline.org>. Retrieved August 20, 2002.

Hecht, Susanna, and Alexander Cockburn. (1989). *The fate of the forest: Developers, destroyers, and defenders of the Amazon*. New York: Verso.

Iglesias Prieto, Norma. (1997). *Beautiful flowers of the Maquiladora: Life histories of women workers in Tijuana*. Austin: University of Texas Press.

Jakarta Post. (2001). "C. Kalimantan violence claims five more lives" (April 4).

Macapagal Arroyo, Gloria. (2001). "Getting our act together: A president's campaign against the sexual exploitation of children," in *Profiting from abuse: An investigation into the sexual exploitation of our children*, ed. UNICEF (pp. 4–7). New York: UNICEF.

Peluso, Nancy Lee. (1993). "Coercing conservation?: The politics of state resource control." *Global Environmental Change* (June):201–17.

Revkin, Andrew. (1990). *The burning season: The murder of Chico Mendes and the fight for the Amazon rainforest*. New York: Plume.

Rostow, W. W. (1964). "The takeoff into self-sustained growth," in *Social change*, ed. Amitai Etzioni and Eva Etzioni (pp. 285–300). New York: Basic Books.

Rudel, Tom. (1998). "Streetcorner environmental injustice: Begging and lead intake among small children in Quito, Ecuador." *Environment, Technology, and Society: Newsletter of the Section on Environmental Technology, American Sociological Association 89*:1.

Rudel, Thomas K., with Bruce Horowitz. (1993). *Tropical deforestation: Small farmers and land clearing in the Ecuadorian amazon*. New York: Columbia University Press.

Sahabat Alam Malaysia. (1992). "Sarawak update from SAM." Available at <www.nativenet.uthscsa.edu/archive/nl/9212/0126.html>. Retrieved August 20, 2002.

Shiva, Vandana. (1989). *Staying alive: Women, ecology, and development*. Atlantic Highlands, NJ: Zed Books.

Tobolowsky, Peggy M. (2000). *Understanding victimology*. Cincinnati: Anderson Publishing.

United Nations Children's Fund (UNICEF). (2001). *Profiting from abuse: An investigation into the sexual exploitation of our children*. New York: UNICEF.

U.S. Department of Justice. (2002). "National victims assistance academy." Available at <http://www.nvaa.org>. Retrieved September 2, 2002.

Valderrama Fernandez, Ricardo, and Carmen Escalante Gutierrez, eds. (1996). *Andean lives: Gregorio Condori Mamani and Asunta Quispe Huamán*. Austin: University of Texas Press.

Wallace, Harvey. (1998). *Victimology: Legal, psychological, and social perspective*. Needhan Heights, MA: Allyn & Bacon.

World Bank. (1994). *Indonesia transmigration program: A review of five bank-supported projects*, report no. 12988. Washington, DC: World Bank.

CHAPTER FIFTEEN

Low Crime Rates in Bahrain

Islamic social control— testing the theory of "synnomie"

CHARISSE T. M. COSTON
ADEL A. HELAL

THIS PIONEER WORK BUILDS UPON the systems of social control (*synnomie*) developed by Freda Adler (1982). Its intent is to assess the low-crime profile of Bahrain and in so doing, to offer explanations for this country's low-crime rates. While there *is* crime in Bahrain, this country appears to be the exception to the rule that rapid industrialization breeds high crime. The unique situation in Bahrain will be analyzed by first giving an overview of the country of Bahrain, then examining recent crime statistics reported by official agencies in the country, the United States, and, in addition, the state of Vermont. The official sources of these data are not considered to be the most reliable indicators of crime, but they are the most *comparable*. Vermont is used for the comparison of numbers, since it has an approximate population to that of Bahrain.

The low statistics of the amount of crime reported for Bahrain form the foundation for this chapter. This chapter offers possible explanations of low crime by using as its base the theory of *synnomie* (the consistency of norm and values sharing); it summarizes its main points and draws conclusions that point indicate the future of Bahrain, its citizens, and incidences of reported crime as the country continues on its mission of modernization.

INTRODUCTION: THE THEORY OF "SYNNOMIE"

Using Adler's (1982) development of the theory of *synnomie* to explain why some countries have low crime rates, this chapter focuses on an explanation of low crime rates in Bahrain, an island country located in the Persian Gulf. Adler (1982) defines the concept of *synnomie* as the opposite of *anomie* (a concept developed by Emile Durkheim). According to Durkheim (1951), *anomie* is a system of norm-erosion caused by a breakdown in the regulation or control of society. Durkheim used *anomie* to explain a particular cause of suicide. This theory was later applied to criminal behavior by Merton (1938), who claimed that people become frustrated when their goals are not achieved by institutionalized means, therefore blaming society for the occurrence of criminal behavior. Adler refers to the opposite of norm erosion as *synnomie*, and defines it as "congruence or togetherness of norms and values" (1982, 57). She says that inherent in *synnomie* is the assumption that all subcultures and individuals themselves will coexist with a harmony of norms.

It was this theory that compelled the authors to undertake a project that focuses on explanations for low crime rates in Bahrain. In particular, it is the aim of this project to assess the social-control system in this Islamic country in an effort to determine why Bahrainis do not have a preoccupation with crime nor why they do not have high rates of crime. In carrying out the intentions of this project, the authors would like to explore the formal and informal social-control systems in Bahrain. For example, religious teachings of the Muslim tradition dominate every element of life in Bahrain, and these religious teachings are interwoven into the law and criminal-justice system. Albert Reiss (1950) asserted that the failure of social and personal controls made individuals more susceptible to committing a crime. Bahrain is a *Gemeinschaft*-type of society in which its citizens hold loyalty to family members as tantamount to existence. Everyone looks out for one another. Even though Bahrain has foreigners who have migrated to the country, most of them and Bahraini citizens are homogeneous in terms of ideologies and beliefs. It appears that Hirschi's (1969) basic propositions for insulation against crime have been addressed by both formal and informal social-control systems in Bahrain. For example, Hirschi talks about strong parental attachment, positive goals, involvement in conventional activities, and beliefs in favor of law-abiding behavior. The Islamic religion that has formed the underlying current for harmony and norm-sharing is largely responsible for the law-abiding behavior that results in low crime rates. The authors agree with Ali (1985, 54) when he says that "this [the Islam religion] provides individuals with certainty and stability, social solidarity, a sense of belongingness and basic securities."

BACKGROUND: BAHRAIN, THE COUNTRY

According to official documents (Ministry of Information of Bahrain, circa 1970), Bahrain was protected by a treaty established with the United Kingdom. On August 15, 1971, Bahrain gained its independence from the

United Kingdom. The country of Bahrain (*Bah-Rain*) is located in the Persian Gulf (Arabian Gulf) and consists of 33 islands that occupy a total of approximately 678 square kilometers (260 square miles).

Bahrain, although basically hot and humid, has three distinct seasons. It is hot and humid from May to mid-October. From December to March the weather is the coolest, with the average temperature being about 40 degrees Fahrenheit. From March until May there is considerable rainfall, although, comparatively, rainfall is light. This is also the windiest period. Bahrain is too sandy, rocky, and bare to support much natural vegetation.

The largest island is Manama; it is the capital, with a population of 122,000. The second largest city is Al-Murharraq, which has a population of 95,000. Other principal islands in the group are Sitra, Nabih Saleh, Jidda, Umm Al-Nassan, and Hawar Islands. The total population of the State of Bahrain is 417,000 (66 percent indigenous) according to the Ministry of Informationm of Bahrain (1988). The Bahraini Arabs constitute 73 percent of the total population (Ministry of Information of Bahrain, circa 1970). Because of the geographical location of the state of Bahrain and its center of commerce, foreigners have been attracted to the area and have affected the composition of the Bahraini population (Monroe 1972). According to a U.S. Department of State bulletin, the ethnic groups are divided into Arab (73 percent), Iranian (9 percent), and Pakistani and Indian (the remainder). The major religion is Islam. Although Catholic and Protestant religions exist within the country, Bahrain adopted both the civil law and the *Sharia* (Islamic law). Bahrain has also adopted portions of English law in order to adapt to modernity. The official language is Arabic, and the second language is English. Other ethnic groups, such as Iranians, speak Farsi.

Bahrain has been governed by the Khalifa family since the late seventeenth century. The ruler of Bahrain entered into relations with the United Kingdom in 1905 (Cressey 1960). After World War II, Bahrain became the center for British administration of treaty obligations in the lower Persian Gulf area. Bahrain demanded independence as a separate entity, and finally achieved complete independence as the state of Bahrain. It announced at the termination of the treaty between itself and Great Britain that their relationship would be one built upon mutual respect and friendship (Cressey 1960).

The ruler is the executive and chief of the state of Bahrain. The prime minister is the head of government; the cabinet consists of a council of ministers. The judicial branch is composed of an independent judiciary with the right of judicial review (Cottrell 1970). There are no political parties. The type of government is a monarchy. Since Bahrain's independence from the United Kingdom, it has become a member of the United Nations, the Arab League, and the Gulf Cooperation Council.

The Ministry of the Interior is one of the cabinet units and has the responsibility for guaranteeing the security and stability of the country. The criminal investigation department, under the Ministry of the Interior's basic function, comprises several sections: investigations, administration and planning, criminal records, vice squad, drug squad, Interpol, homicide, and the crime laboratory.

The oldest industry on which Bahrain was economically dependent was pearl-diving (Long 1976). The exceptional quality of Bahrain pearls is thought to be due to the many fresh-water springs in the seas around the country. The start of pearl production in Japan during the 1930s led to a reduction in the demand of pearls from Bahrain, and today, even though the government encourages pearl-diving, virtually no boats are operating (Long 1976). Lime production, pottery, fishing, boat-building, and weaving are other traditional industries that still survive and exist alongside twentieth-century industries.

Bahrain's economy, along with other Arab countries, is oil-based (Whelan 1978). Bahrain became a member of OPEC (Organization of Arab Petroleum Exporting Countries) in 1970. Although Bahrain was the first oil-producing country in the Arabian Gulf area, its oil production is limited today, because other Arab countries have begun the massive distribution of this product (Arab Communicators 1982). Bahrain does not export crude oil, unlike other Gulf states. The country's domestic oil output is processed on Sitra Island at a refinery. Light oil is imported through the Arabia-Bahrain pipeline, according to a United States report published in 1986. Bahrain has a diversified economy through which it has prepared itself for the reduction in natural oil supplies. However, oil remains its largest single source of income—78 percent of the total Bahraini economy (Whelan 1978).

As a result of economic diversification, Bahrain has two alternative major industries. Aluminum Bahrain (ALBA) went into production in 1971, with Japan being its chief customer (Raban 1979). The other major industry is ship-repairing and dry-docking (ASHRY). This developing country has also entered into the services sector (Makdisi 1979). Emphasis is now being placed upon developing Bahrain as a regional center for business and banking. Light and service industries are also being developed. An offshore banking center has been established in Bahrain and many international banks have been given licenses (Raban 1979). Makdisi (1979) claims that the banking community will invest extensively in housing and real estate and provide employment locally.

According to Wright (1983), the Amir (Al Kalifa) has provided for the better welfare of his people in three vital areas: education, medical care, and housing. Before the Amir's rule took effect in 1961, education was provided primarily by home tutors. The Amir has developed a sophisticated educational system. The authority for this educational system now lies in one of the cabinet units, the Ministry of Education. The system of education in Bahrain consists of four levels:

1. *Primary level*: duration is six years; children at age six.
2. *Intermediate level*: for graduates of the primary level; graduation is in three years.
3. *Secondary level*: for graduates of the intermediate level, who enter and graduate in three years.
4. *Higher education*: open to all students who have graduated from secondary school.

The education in Bahrain includes religious study in the Muslim tradition. Tuition is free. The Bahraini government's goal is to provide free educational opportunities for all children and to develop an educational system that will promote the socioeconomic needs of the country. Private schools exist in Bahrain for primary and secondary education (Ministry of Information of Bahrain 1988). So far, the largest educational project in this region is the Arabian Gulf University, which is located in Bahrain. This educational project joins the efforts of Kuwait, Bahrain, Iraq, Oman, Qatar, Saudi Arabia, and the United Arab Emirates.

According to Long (1976), Bahrain has one of the most "advanced medical-welfare services in the Middle East" (p. 172). Health centers are provided to cater to all villages and towns. Free primary medical care is provided for those who cannot pay. There are dentists and psychiatrists in Bahrain who cater to those who can afford the services. These services come under the cabinet unit of the Ministry of Health. This ministry also consults with United Nations agencies—for example, the World Health Organization. The directorate of public health is active in "the prevention of communicable diseases, in protecting and improving the work and general environment, in enhancing health consciousness of the population by vigorous health education, and in general the promotion of health" (Monroe 1972, 136).

In 1974, the Ministry of Housing was established. Its responsibility was to develop housing and housing policies (Wright 1983). The goal of this cabinet unit was to provide housing for every Bahraini family. The rent for housing cannot exceed more than a quarter of a family's monthly income (Raban 1979). The ministry has also implemented a policy that establishes loans for anyone wishing to buy a house or buy land on which to build their own house.

Even though other types of religions exist in Bahrain, there are few Protestants and Catholics. The foundation for Bahrain laws is rooted in the religion of Islamic tradition (Raban 1979). Eighty-five percent of the population is Muslim (Ministry of Information of Bahrain 1988). Relationships between people are close. Most Bahrainis know one another and look out for one another's personal interests. The governmental units and industries in Bahrain are as much concerned with the spiritual wealth as the material wealth of their employees. All governmental units and most of the industries regularly receive the word of God and teachings of the Prophet Muhammad during the course of each workday. Religious instruction is available to everyone either directly or by radio and television. Broad government planning, mostly through the strictures of Islam, has resulted in the sharing of norms and morals during modernization and Bahrain's exposure to other cultures.

As a result of Bahrain's unique geographical location as an island between the Far East and the West (Whelan 1978), transportation and communication have developed considerably. Bahrain's national airport is located in Muharraq and as far back as the 1930s was used for "refueling and supplies for planes traveling to India" (Whelan 1978, 79). Today, the airport in Bahrain can handle up to ten jumbo jets and 15 other planes simultaneously (Ministry of Information of Bahrain 1988). The airport handles approximately 40,000 flights a year and directs planes over a large part of the Gulf. It was the first in the world to receive the supersonic Concorde from Britain in 1976 (Arab Communicators 1982). Gulf Air is the national airline of Bahrain, Qatar, Oman, and United Arab Emirates. Its headquarters is located in Bahrain. According to Makdisi (1979), Bahrain's position in maritime communications was "greatly enhanced by the Mina Sulman Port." A number of companies linking the Far East, Europe, and the United States operate from Bahrain.

Bahrain has four main roads that connect most of its towns and villages. A causeway connects the country to Saudi Arabia. There is a public-transportation system that utilizes 150 buses covering 70 routes per day.

Bahrain has a postal service. The postal department issues both regular and commemorative stamps. The telecommunications services in the country are run by both cable and wire (Ministry of Information of Bahrain 1988). There are direct lines between Bahrain and most other countries. There are also Telex services.

Bahrain radio first went on the air in 1955 for two hours a day. Most of its programs (65 percent) are produced locally. Programming includes religious, literary, and scientific subjects and music. Radio broadcasts are now on the air 24 hours a day. Arabic, English, and even French radio programs are broadcast in Bahrain (Ministry of Information of Bahrain 1988).

There are two television stations: one Arabic, the other English. Color transmission began in 1975. Bahrain television transmits for an average of eight hours per day. Channel 4 transmits a mixture of recorded Arabic material and cooperates with other Gulf states for joint programming (Ministry of Information of Bahrain 1988), while Channel 55 is the English-language television station.

The Ministry of Information publishes a weekly magazine called *Bahrain* that has been distributed worldwide since 1974 and covers local, Gulf, Arab, and international news. Bahrain has a number of newspapers. The

Ministry of Information publishes a daily newspaper, while other newspapers are published by the private sector, including two English-language ones. The government archives retain all documents, official records, and clippings of all articles on Bahrain. This includes maintaining a file about Bahrain collected from Arab Gulf local, regional, and national papers. It also stocks literary, cultural, and technical as well as reference works.

According to the Ministry of Information (1988), a special effort has been made over the past few years to record Bahrain's traditional and popular music before they disappear. There are now some "20,000 tapes in the archives" (p. 138).

Bahrain, while being the smallest of the Arab countries in terms of land and population, is a leader of the Gulf states in terms of education, health care, and social-welfare reforms. The next section will focus on crime rates in Bahrain. Specifically, the authors will report on crime rates in the country and compare them to crime rates in the United States, and more specifically, to the rates in the state of Vermont. As Bahrain continues to develop, it will be interesting to determine if there is a corresponding increase in its crime rates.

Crime Rates in Bahrain Compared to Crime Rates in the United States

This section focuses on crime statistics from official crime-reporting agencies in both Bahrain and the United States. Crime statistics quoted about Bahrain were supplied by the Ministry of Interior. This annual report of crime rates is prepared by the Ministry of Interior from the criminal investigation unit, which compiles these statistics from all police department's reports of arrests. Individual police departments' participation in this program is compulsory. Neither the numbers of convictions nor the final dispositions on the cases are reported. Likewise, official statistics on the amount of crime in the United States derive from the Federal Bureau of Investigation's (FBI) *Uniform Crime Reports* system. Although this service reports crime statistics prepared from local police departments' records of arrests and participation is voluntary, nearly 95 percent of all police departments supply information annually (Cole 1984). There are no reports of convictions or final dispositions of the cases listed in the FBI's statistics of crime.

There is a murky figure of crime in both Bahrain and the United States. The true amount of crime continues to elude us. With these limitations, including the limitations of the crime-rates reporting systems, we are dependent upon estimates prepared by these two sources. Estimates of crimes committed against persons and property are believed to be the most accurate because they are the most frequently committed, most serious, and have the highest probability of being reported to the police

Table 15.1

Number of Crimes Reported in Bahrain during 1986 and 1987

Type of crime	*Number, 1986*	*Number, 1987*	*Percent increase*
Crimes against the person	3,408	3,790	11
Crimes against property	6,684	7,413	11

Source: Adapted from Bahrain, the Ministry of Interior (1987).

(Sourcebook of Criminal Justice Statistics 1988). Therefore, statistics for these types of crimes will be reported for comparison. To date, there have been no victimization surveys conducted in Bahrain. While there have been victimization surveys conducted in the United States that indicate higher crime rates than the Uniform Crime Reporting system, the statistics from these sources will not be used.

Crime Rates in Bahrain

The Ministry of Interior reports the statistics for the crimes listed below. Crimes against the individual are rank-ordered according to their seriousness: murder (the intentional killing), attempted murder, murder by error (an accidental killing), assault (including all types of assaults), threatening (it is this type of crime that is most commonly referred to as "harassment" and/or "verbal assaults"), and others (any type of crime against the person that does not fit into one of the other five categories). Crimes against property are listed here in their order of seriousness: theft/larceny (includes robbery, burglary, car theft, and grand larceny), fraud and breach of trust, destruction of property, and arson.

Table 15.1 illustrates the general increase in 1987 from 1986 in both crimes against the person and crimes against property. There is an increase of 382 cases of crime against individuals, and 729 cases of crime against property in 1987. The general increase in the number of crimes in 1987 occurred throughout the year and not in a particular period of the year or in a specific geographical area of the country (Ministry of Interior of Bahrain 1988). This fact may support the idea that there are no environmental reasons for the crime-rate increase. The development of the country, including an increasing population, could be the reason for this increase in crime. According to the Ministry of Information, the population increased from 358,000 in 1983 to 417,000 in 1985. We have no estimated population increase after 1985.

The total number of crimes against the person increased to 3,790 in 1987 from 3,408 in 1986. The amount of increase is 382 cases, which is equal to 11 percent. From table 15.2 and figure 15.1, we see that there were

Table 15.2

Rates of Increase and the Percentage for the Types of Crime against the Person Reported in Bahrain during 1986 and 1987

Type of crime	Number, 1986	Number, 1987	Increase	Percent increase
Murder	2	2	—	—
Attempted murder	2	7	5	250
Murder by error	56	75	19	34
Assault	2,782	3,069	287	10
Threatening	327	393	66	20
Others	239	244	5	2
TOTAL	**3,408**	**3,790**	**382**	**11**

Source: Adapted from Bahrain, the Ministry of Interior (1987).

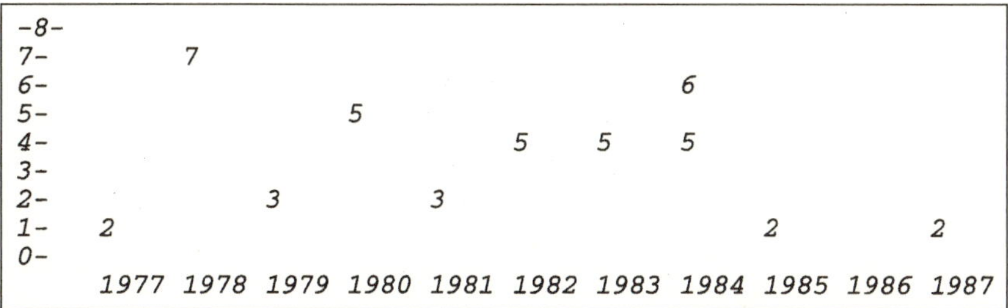

Figure 15.1 The frequency of willful murder in Bahrain from 1977 to 1987. *Source*: Adapted from Bahrain, the Ministry of Interior (1987).

two cases of willful murder in 1986, and two cases in 1987, there being no increase in this most serious crime.

Table 15.2 further shows that only two cases of attempted murder occurred in 1986, compared to seven cases in 1978. If we look at attempted-murder statistics for the last three years, we see that only one case occurred in 1985, two cases occurred in 1986, and seven cases in 1987. Murder by error (accident), according to the Ministry of Interior and indicated in table 15.2, occurred 56 times in 1986. This statistic increased to 75 in 1987—an increase of 19 cases (34 percent). This type of crime mostly occurred by traffic accident.

Assault, which includes all types of assault and also robbery, burglary, car theft, and grand larceny, rose from 2,782 cases in 1986 to 3,069 cases in 1987, an increase of 287 cases (10 percent). Figure 15.2 illustrates the

```
500-
3000-                                 2664                         3069
2500-                     2333                              2782
2000-                                        2425
1500-
1000-1102          1189
500-
0-
     1981     1982      1983     1984      1985     1986      1987
```

Figure 15.2 Total number of assaults per year for seven years (1981 to 1987). *Source*: Adapted from Bahrain, the Ministry of Interior (1987).

Table 15.3

Rates of Increase and the Percentage for the Types of Crime against Property Reported in Bahrain during 1986 and 1987

Type of crime	*Number, 1986*	*Number, 1987*	*Increase*	*Percent increase*
Theft/larceny	2,236	2,569	333	15
Fraud/breach of trust	2,742	2,864	122	4
Destruction of property	1,360	1,487	127	9
Arson	346	493	147	42
TOTAL	**6,684**	**7,413**	**729**	**11**

Source: Adapted from Bahrain, the Ministry of Interior (1987).

numbers of assaults during the last seven years. In 1981, there were only 1,102 assaults; in 1987, assault cases reported by the Ministry of Interior reached 3,069.

Referring to table 15.2, we see that threatening has increased from 327 cases in 1986 to 393 cases in 1987. Figure 15.3 depicts the increasing trend of threatening in Bahrain for the past seven years. Table 15.3 shows that crimes against property have increased in 1987 over 1986. Figure 15.4 illustrates the trend of this type of crime over a seven-year span, from 1981 to 1987.

Note the large increase in property offenses from 1985 to 1986. The theft/larceny and fraud/breach-of-trust cases were largely responsible for this increase. There were 1,961 cases of theft in 1985, compared to 2,236 cases in 1986. And there were 623 cases of fraud/breach-of-trust cases reported in 1985, compared to 2,742 cases of this crime reported in 1986. Since these two categories contain a number of different types of offenses, the numbers of offenses in this category, although rising, would not be as startling.

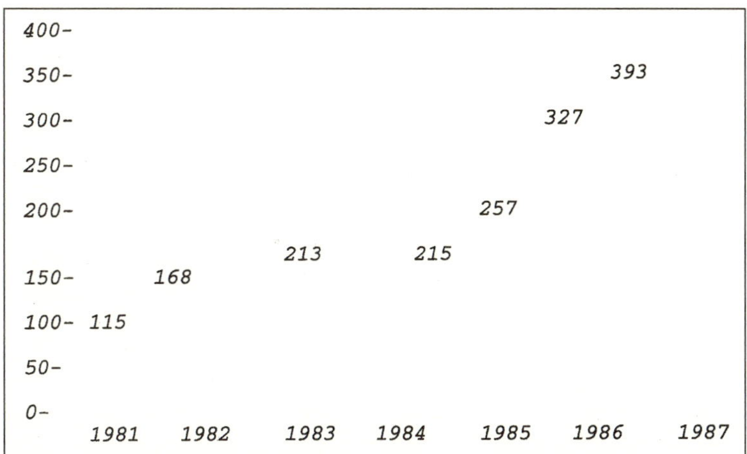

Figure 15.3 Total number of cases of threatening per year for seven years (1981 to 1987). *Source*: Adapted from Bahrain, the Ministry of Interior (1987).

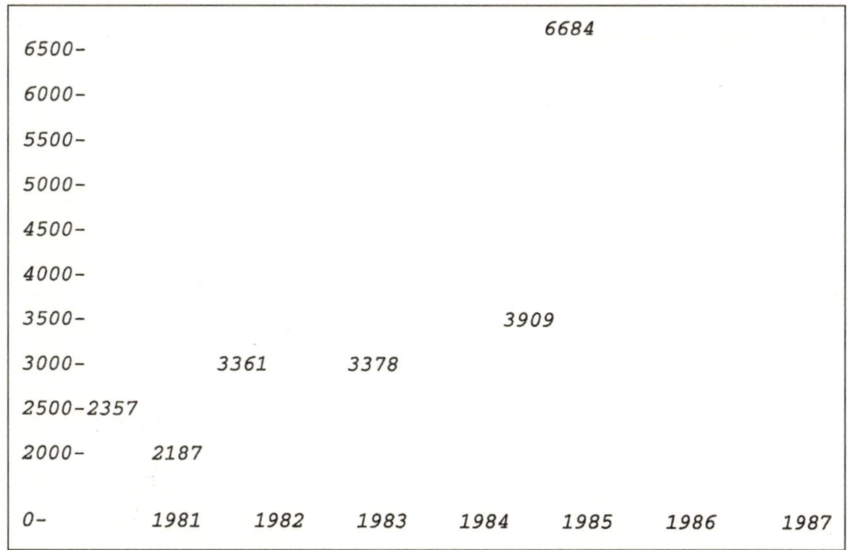

Figure 15.4 Frequency of occurrences of crimes against property over a seven-year period (1981 to 1987). *Source*: Adapted from Bahrain, the Ministry of Interior (1987).

Crime Rates in the United States

The specific arrest rates in the United States, using the FBI's *Uniform Crime Reports* and the *Sourcebook of Criminal Justice Statistics*, for those index offenses reported to the FBI by local police departments that will be used here are crimes against persons (i.e., homicides, robberies, assaults) and crimes against property (i.e., arson, grand larceny, car theft, burglary). These crimes were selected on the bases of their comparability with Bahrain and seriousness and likelihood of being reported to the police. Bahrain does not report crimes of rape as a single category. No reports of rape have been sent to the Ministry of Interior from the criminal investigation unit. The closest category into which rape would fall would be the "crimes against morals" section. Bahrain places robberies, burglaries, and larcenies into one category called "theft/larceny." Given these differences, including differences in the population size between the United States (population estimate 240,000,000 [U.S. Census Bureau 1988]) and Bahrain (population estimated at 417,000 [Directorate of Statistics 1985]), we will also use the state of Vermont, which has a population of 556,000, hence closer to the population of Bahrain.

The FBI's *Uniform Crime Reports* indicate that 13,508,700 crimes were reported to U.S. police departments in 1987, which is 21 percent higher than the numbers of crimes that occurred in 1978. *Uniform Crime Reports* indicate that in the United States as a whole, there were 20,096 murders and nonnegligent manslaughters reported in 1987. Murder and nonnegligent manslaughters represented 1 percent of all the violent crimes reported in 1987. This statistic for 1987 reported 3 percent fewer murders and nonnegligent manslaughters than in 1986. There was a 4 percent rise nationally in these cases from 1983 to 1987. Robbery accounted for 4 percent of all index crimes, and 35 percent of violent crimes, in the United States in 1987. The estimated robbery total in 1987 was 517,704. The robbery rate decreased 6 percent from the 1986 rate. The robbery rate for 1987 was 2 percent lower than the robbery rate for 1983. Aggravated assault increased from 834,322 cases in 1986 to 855,088 cases in 1987, which was a 3 percent increase. Aggravated assaults were up 31 percent over the 1983 level.

In terms of crimes against property, there were 3,241,410 burglaries reported by police departments in 1986. The number of cases decreased by 2 percent in 1987 (the numbers decreased by 7 percent from 1978). There were 7,257,153 cases of theft reported to the FBI in 1986, compared to 7,449,851 cases in 1987 (a 12 percent increase over the 1983 statistics). Motor vehicle theft cases totaled 1,244,137 cases in 1986, and increased by 5 percent, to 1,288,674 cases, for 1987. The number of motor vehicle theft cases reported to the FBI in 1987 increased 28 percent over the number of cases reported in 1983. Only 12,000 police departments reported arson figures for 1987, which totaled 102,410 cases. Based upon these limited data sources, arson cases decreased 5 percent from 1986 to 1987. It might be possible that these figures stem from improved arson-reporting procedures.

Vermont, the state within the United States that has the approximate equivalent population of Bahrain, reported 23,406 index offenses to the FBI (excluding forcible rape) for 1987 (Vermont Criminal Information Center 1987). This 1987 statistic represents a 9 percent increase over 1986 crime rates for Vermont, which totaled 21,515 (excluding forcible rape). Of the 23,406 index offenses reported to the FBI, 748 cases of violent crime (excluding rape) were reported. Of the 748 cases of violent crime reported in Vermont, 558 cases were aggravated assaults. Crimes against property accounted for 22,535 cases of reported crime in Vermont in 1987, larceny/theft accounting for 15,485 of these.

In 1987, Bahraini crime statistics, reported by the Ministry of Interior, totaled 11,203 cases. This includes both crimes against persons and crimes against property. This statistic for crimes committed in 1987 is higher than the crimes reported for 1986. There were 10,092 crimes against persons and property in 1986 (1,111 cases lower than in 1987). Likewise, crime statistics for the United States have increased overall. Most particularly, the state of Vermont's index offenses, excluding rape, increased by 1,891 cases, from 21,515 cases in 1986 to 23,406 cases in 1987. It appears that both Bahrain's and Vermont's reported crime statistics are increasing at about the same rate, but the amount of crime in Vermont is twice as high as the amount of crime reported in Bahrain.

The next section will focus upon possible explanations for the low crime rates in Bahrain. The basis for this explanation is derived from a theory of social control (*synnomie*) that was developed by Freda Adler in 1982.

Possible Explanation for Low Crime Rates in Bahrain

Bahrain, while one of the most cosmopolitan countries in the Persian Gulf region, still follows the teachings in the Holy Koran and its codes for prescribed standards of conduct. The Holy Koran makes up the very fabric of life for the people of Bahrain, and its influence can be observed and felt in the economic, political, and social paths of life within this culture. According to symposium proceedings on the "Effects of Islamic Legislation on Crime Prevention in Saudi Arabia," the word for Muslim law (*Sharia*) has the teachings of the Holy Koran and the Prophet Muhammad tightly interwoven into it. The religion of Islam is the most important social structure in Bahrain. Islam has opposed wrongdoing in all of its forms, claiming that wrongdoing can lead to the downfall of all societies. Islamic teachings attempt to eradicate the commission of crime before it happens by influencing the human conscience. The Prophet says that the power of the conscience is much stronger than any other external force.

Perhaps it is that this Islamic society internalized its Muslim tradition, and as an outgrowth of this internalization of religion comes law-abiding behavior. Hence a violation of the law is not only a crime against society, but a violation of the principles of God. Bahraini citizens are encouraged to pray five times a day. There are moral police officers who regulate the dress and public behavior of its citizens. Even in the wake of rapid industrialization, the norms of the Muslim religion are adhered to.

Ordinary citizens are given access to the ruler (Amir) of Bahrain, Sheikh Isa bin Sulman Al Kalifa. This present Amir is the tenth member of the Al Kalifa family to rule Bahrain, dating back to 1783 A.D., and this shows the consistency of governing for over 200 years. This ruler is available to the peoplt for a couple of days each month, and it is this practice that makes people feel that they are in touch with the head of their government and have a voice in the concerns and issues that face their country.

The effects of the Muslim religion can be seen in other informal social-control aspects of life in Bahrain. Those that will be discussed in this section are the *family* (it takes the responsibility for the less fortunate within society—namely, the poor, widows, orphans, the sick, and aged), the *neighborhood*, *education*, and *social affairs* that most often revolve around family activities.

No discussion of the low crime rates in the wake of rapid industrialization of Bahrain would be complete without a historical discussion of the criminal-justice/legal system of the country, its criminal procedures, and ideological principles of crime control. Bahrain, a British protectorate until 1971, has developed its own legal system since attaining independence (Amin 1983). The *Sharia* or Islamic law is the legal system of Bahrain. Its basic principles are contained in the Holy Koran, which provides the roots for which legal solutions are based. Along with other Gulf states, Bahrain adheres to the Orthodox Sunni schools of law rather than those of the Shi'a. Bahrain adopted the British codes simply by translating the English texts into Arabic. Only laws relating to marriage, divorce, and succession remain under the complete influence of the *Sharia*. All other areas of law have been imported from the West (Souryal 1988).

The Islamic penal code is formally enforced in Bahrain. It is enforceable against all Muslims and non-Muslims (Amin 1983), though the penalty for committing a crime is harsher on perpetrators who are Muslim and on those committing crimes against Muslims. The judges are almost exclusively Sunni and generally apply the Sunni schools of thought to the law unless the litigants are Shi'a.

According to Souryal (1988), since firearms, alcohol, and drugs are banned, the opportunity for violence is reduced. Most disputes are swiftly settled informally by passersby. The motivations of these arbitrators are in both by being upset by its occurrence, and the reward of acting as peacemakers from God. When serious violations occur, the law is applied formally, forcefully, and punishments are meted out swiftly and severely.

Another reason proposed for the low crime rates in Bahrain is that, while rarely imposed, the country has the authority to execute violators in public (Amin 1983). The *Sharia*, unlike in the United States, contains a mixture of church and state. The principles are based upon "prevention, conditioning, bonding, moralizing, and punishment" (Souryal 1988, 23).

Bahrain's ideological principle of crime control is the presumption of innocence. Criminal procedural safeguards include that the defendant must be given a notice of the charges and reasonable time to prepare a defense; while there is no right to an attorney, one can be discretionarily appointed. The defendant must be confronted by witnesses against him, and has the right to present witnesses on his own behalf. Trials are not open to the public, and even though permission to attend can be requested, it is rarely given. Amputation, stoning, lashing, flogging, and death are forms of punishment in the *Sharia* (Moore 1987).

The Influence of the Family

The earliest influence on a child is his or her primary relationship: the family. The family, more specifically the parents, has the responsibility of rearing the child. Bahrain's family structure has not shifted as much as family structures in the West, most notably in the United States. Young adults are encouraged to marry and form a family early in their lives. This tradition is encouraged in order to add stability to an individual's life.

Loyalties, after the loyalty to God, include the loyalty to family and country. Bahrainis place a high value on taking care of their families. Parents often arrange the marriages of their children and act in their best interests. Arranged marriages are conducted in order to ensure family tradition and economic well-being.

It is worth mentioning that women are considered to be very important members in Bahraini culture. Bahrain has made every attempt to give women the same rights as men by integrating them into the country's developmental process. Bahraini women are allowed to own, buy, and sell property, to work, and to own their own businesses. As a way of showing their commitment to this endeavor, the government has provided facilities such as kindergartens, nursery schools, child-welfare centers, and houses for families with low incomes. Today, Bahraini women occupy positions in government ministries and banks. The Social Security Law and the Civil Service Law of 1976 made the equal opportunities for women more accessible through the use of engagement salaries, promotion, and advanced training. These female labor forces increased from 5.44 percent in 1976 to 7 percent in 1978 (Nugent & Thomas 1985).

The Influence of the Neighborhood

This sense of belonging and obligation towards family logically extends to the neighborhood. Bahrainis have a strong sense of obligation that not only exists within the family, but also to neighbors as well as to the citizen (passerby) on the street. Islamic teachings also dictate how the common man and woman are to be treated. Bahraini residents are often seen carrying food to one another, and neighbors constantly watch out for one another's property. Property is extended not only to material goods, but also to spiritual health and well-being. Even neighborhood children become the responsibility of everyone. There are welcoming customs that each new neighbor receives when moving into the community—for example, food. There are social classes in Bahrain, but people who are more fortunate are required to share their wealth with others who are less so. It is a general custom that the wealthier residents in the community give money, clothing, and food to the less fortunate community residents. The giving of money and other necessities of life to the less fortunate extends not only to community residents, but is a responsibility that is true of all those residents who are financially more able than others. There are formal mechanisms for providing charity (*Zakat*), which is an obligation that a certain amount of money be given each year.

Thus the idea of the neighborhood in itself forms an extended family that is built upon primary relationships among people (*Gemeinschaft*). Bahrain society consists of close, tightly knit families who rely upon one another for support and friendship.

The Influence of Education

The Islam religion manifests itself in the area of education. Children receive the teachings of the Islamic religion at all levels of education. By the time the child reaches school age, he or she has already been trained by parents in the conduct that is expected at school. As the result of a poem by Ahmad Shauqi ("Nations are their ethics. They endure only as long as their ethics do"), Bahrainis feel a strong obligation to include teachings of ethics in every subject. Education, in Bahrain, is compulsory for all children. Adult literacy centers are available throughout the country for adults who missed the opportunity of a formal education.

Bahrain has acknowledged that there is a crucial link between education and the economic development of its country (Sadik & Snavely 1972) and recognizes education as one of its basic institutions. The annual report that Bahrain submitted to the conference of Arab Ministers of Education held in Yeman in 1972 stated that the output of the educational system far exceeds the capacity of the industries of the island to absorb the school graduates. There is no minimum-wage policy and this also frustrates the graduates. The government has become the largest employer, superseding the oil companies, by creating new jobs to address this problem. In addition, Bahrain has started new technical-trade offerings at vocational schools, because the compulsory general education did not prepare those students who wanted to enter into a trade upon leaving high school. Bahrain has recently, during the 1980s, started vocational programs that stress agriculture and farming. The island does not lend itself to much natural vegetation, and for a long time the government did not focus on developing manpower to address this need. Now the Bahraini government wants to limit the numbers of foreigners imported for this reason and provide its own citizens this opportunity for performing agricultural duties (Rumaihi 1978).

During the 1950s, the ruler of the country was upset by students leaving Bahrain to study abroad, especially in non-Arab countries, because the citizens who were returning had lost their sense of patriotism and were even criticizing the government (Rumaihi 1978). This changed, however, during the 1970s, when Bahrainis were allowed to pursue their education in foreign lands. Now the Bahraini government even grants scholarships to distinguished students to study abroad.

Social Activities

The purpose of social activities is to reaffirm the belief system that is embedded within the Muslim tradition (Khuri 1980). Social activities mostly take place within the family, but because political parties are banned in Bahrain, men and women jointly and sometimes separately congregate in religious centers. These religious centers are paramilitary institutions where men and women discuss current social, political, and economic issues that face their country. Tea and coffee are served and smoking is allowed, but no dancing, music, and/or joyful activities are allowed (Khuri 1980).

Marriage ceremonies are held in hotels or in cultural and sports clubs. Cultural and sports clubs originated in Bahrain in 1953 to accommodate the newly emerging groups. These clubs were attacked during the 1960s on the basis that they corrupted morality, and "the participation of women and girls in club activities opposed custom and religious teachings" (Khuri 1980, 172). Theologians in Bahrain soon reacknowledged the necessity of these clubs but asserted that they should be kept free of frivolities and antireligious practices. Today, these clubs are simply places where people meet after work and pass time socializing and exercising. The government tolerates these clubs as long as they accept, or at least do not undermine, the politics and ideologies of the state.

The consumption of alcohol is allowed in Bahrain, although strict Muslims avoid this indulgence. The bars that can be found there mainly attract foreigners who are working in or visiting the country.

The Bahraini government is particularly interested in sporting activities. The Council for Youth and Sports was established to "encourage the development of all aspects of youth" (Ministry of Information of Bahrain 1988). This council has provided sports fields, centers, and trainers and fosters social and cultural interests among the young. It also publishes a weekly student magazine that highlights upcoming events.

The sharing of these values appears to suggest that the formal and informal systems of social control are intertwined. These offerings of formal and informal social-control practices in Bahrain appear to have merit for explaining why the crime rates, although rising at about 1 percent annually, remain relatively low. In spite of the population increase of foreigners in Bahrain, it appears to have maintained a homogeneous society. Bahrainis appear to have a strong sense of obligation towards family and the neighborhood. The institution of education has continued to reinforce the values of Islam and family tradition. Even social activities reinforce traditional values. However, Bahrain is a peculiar country, having its own indigenous system of transmitting values whose utility for use by other countries is limited. The explanations set forth in this chapter for low crime rates in Bahrain are not exhaustive, but are an attempt to highlight those characteristics that are most responsible. Bahraini citizens have internalized the traditions of Islam—Islam has become a way of life for most citizens. Therefore, the religious solidarity in Bahrain can be credited as being the most powerful social-control agent in the country and the major reason why crime rates have remained relatively low.

The following section summarizes the points stated in this chapter and points toward this rapidly industrializing country's future.

SUMMARY AND CONCLUSIONS

Bahrain is in the process of rapid industrialization and urbanization. Rumaihi (1978) stated that Bahrain is increasing in population size at a rate of "4 percent per annum" (p. 135). It has been estimated that the crime rate has increased by "1 percent from 1985 to 1988" (Ministry of Information of Bahrain 1988). According to Nakhleh (1976), most of the violent crime and thefts (about 65 percent) are committed by foreigners who are working in Bahrain.

Although the true amount of crime is impossible to ascertain, reported crime statistics were used in this chapter to illustrate the point that crime in Vermont, a state that is close in equal population to Bahrain, has twice as much reported crime. Even more startling are the overall reported statistics of crime for the United States as a whole. Due to the merging of some categories, some of Bahrain's crime statistics appear to be larger than they actually are. For example, if it had been possible to separate the crimes of theft into auto thefts, robberies, and burglaries, the crimes in these categories would be even smaller. Although it would be unsound to compare these two countries due to their peculiar characteristics and unique features, the amount of reported crime demonstrates that there is a large variance between the two countries in terms of their crime rates. This chapter described the impact of social controls in Bahrain.

Even in the wake of rapid industrialization, away from traditional village society whose economy was based upon pearl-diving, Bahrain has remained relatively stable. The formal and informal social-control mechanisms appear to be interwoven throughout Bahraini society. The Islam religion lays the foundation for life; its influence can be seen in several critical areas within Bahrain: the family, neighborhood, education, and social activities. Bahrainis place a high value on their responsibility towards their families. As stated earlier, Bahraini men are encouraged to marry early, which is believed to aid the country's stability. Sadik and Snavely (1972) revealed that 66.5 percent of Bahraini males 21 years of age and over were married; only 2.2 percent were divorced. This concern for others extends to the neighborhood and to passersby. The poor, the ill, the aged, and widows are cared for by individual citizens and governmental agencies. The more fortunate members (in terms of finances) of Bahraini society have the responsibility for donating resources to care for those less so.

Religious instruction forms the foundation for education in Bahrain, and these religious teachings begin in primary school and extend into higher education. The Bahraini government, within the past decade, has installed vocational programs aimed at agricultural and technical trades. It is its hope that graduates of these schools will work in Bahrain.

Since there are no political parties in the country, Bahraini citizens often meet informally at religious centers to discuss the social, political, and economic issues that face the country. In addition, Bahraini citizens can address their concerns about these issues directly to the Amir. The Amir has a special fund to finance necessary operations for citizens who cannot afford to pay for them, either within the country or abroad. The Ministry of Education sponsors distinguished students to study abroad. Cultural and sports clubs also exist in Bahrain and are places to which people go to relax, socialize, and exercise.

The violation of the law, according to Long (1976), as considered by Bahrainis is perceived as a violation against Muslim teachings. Bahrainis have a very strong bond to their religion, including the teachings of the Prophet Muhammad. In Bahrain there exists a religious solidarity, which dictates how people should live. It is this social structure that has been credited as the cause for why there is low crime in Bahrain. Bahrain is certainly one of those countries that is not obsessed with crime.

Mourad (1976), in the proceedings of the symposium on "Effects of Islamic Legislation on Crime Prevention in Saudi Arabia," commented that "scientific and technological progress is concentrated on the material aspects, ignoring the social and human viewpoints." Characteristics of this condition as stated by Mourad include the deprivation of moral and social values that lead to the corruption of social relationships and the instability of the family. It appears that Bahrainis have maintained their system of personal controls so as not to morally degenerate. National cohesion and social allegiance to the values contained in the Holy Koran are evident throughout the country.

What implications can be drawn from the situation as it exists in Bahrain? This work makes a contribution to Adler's (1982) theory of *synnomie*. The situation of low crime in Bahrain extends her theory to that country. This contribution demonstrates the validity of the theory of *synnomie*. *Synnomie*, as defined by Adler, is the "state of sharing of norms or customs and, beyond that, a system of intact social controls capable of assuring such a sharing" (1982, 157). This system of formal and informal controls exists in Bahrain; there is a system of values-sharing. The common denominator that is required for a state of *synnomie* is evident in Bahrain: it is the religion of Islam.

We need more cross-cultural research to further test the theory of *synnomie*. Perhaps there are more countries with low crime rates than there are with high rates. It would be particularly interesting to assess the role that religion plays in reports of low crime; that is, to what extent do the effects of Muslim law and Islam influence the commissions of crimes? The United States has a system of separation of church and state; in Bahrain, the two are combined. As Ali (1985) states, "sin and crime are particularly the same thing" (p. 46). It would be impossible to transplant the practices of Bahraini society into the practices of the United States. But the Bahraini example sheds light on how the country has managed, in the face of rapid development, by its melding of church and state to keep crime low.

What other mediating variables (e.g., other formal and informal controls) are there that might affect crime statistics? Or is the religion of Islam the only factor that contributes to the low crime volume in Bahrain? One might consider this latter proposition, because it has been demonstrated that Islam filters down and affects the family, neighborhood, education, social activities, and its governing force extends itself into everyday life. It will be interesting to follow the crime trends in Bahrain, as this country continues to develop, in an effort to determine if there occur higher rates of crime. It might also be enlightening to correspondingly assess this country's fear of crime at various points in time.

ACKNOWLEDGMENTS

An earlier version of this chapter was presented at the 1990 annual meeting of the American Society of Criminology in Baltimore. We wish to thank Professors G. O. W. Mueller and Freda Adler for their direction, support, and guidance with the preparation of this manuscript. Additionally, we would like to thank Dr. Tariq Almoayed, Minister of Information of the State of Bahrain, for the use of official statistics.

REFERENCES

Adler, Freda. (1982). *Nations not obsessed with crime*, vol. 50. Littleton, CO: Rothman.

Ali, Bader-El-Din. (1985). "Islamic law and crime: The case of Saudi Arabia." *International Journal of Comparative and Applied Criminal Justice 9*, no. 2.

Amin, S. H. (1983). *Legal systems in the Gulf states.* London: London Press.

Arab Communicators. (1982). *Bahrain business directory.* Bahrain: Shams Offset.

Cole, Robertson. (1984). *Order under the law.* Prospect Heights, IL: Waveland Press.

Cottrell, Alvin. (1970). "British withdrawal from the Persian Gulf." *Military Review* (June).

Cressey, George B. (1960). *Crossroads: Land and life in Southwest Asia.* Chicago: Lippincott.

Durkheim, Emile. (1951). *Suicide.* Glencoe, IL: Free Press.

Federal Bureau of Investigation. (1987). *Uniform crime reports* (1981–1987). Washington, DC: U.S. Government Printing Office.

Hirschi, Travis. (1969). *Causes of delinquency.* Berkeley: University of California Press.

Khuri, Fuad. (1980). *Tribe and state in Bahrain.* Chicago: University of Chicago Press.

Long, David. (1976). *The Persian Gulf: An introduction to its people, politics, and economics.* Boulder, CO: Westview Press.

Makdisi, Samir. (1979). "Arab economic cooperation," in *Arab industrialization and economic integration*, ed. Roberto Aliboni. London: Croom Helm.

Ministry of Information of Bahrain. (1988). *Bahrain: Profile.* State of Bahrain: Government Press.

Monroe, Elizabeth. (1972). "The changing balance of power in the Persian Gulf." *International Affairs* (January).

Moore, Richter. (1987). "Courts, law, justice, and criminal trials." *International Journal of Comparative and Applied Criminal Justice 2*, no. 1.

Nakhleh, Emile. (1976). *Bahrain.* Lexington, MA: Lexington Books.

Nugent, Jeffery, and Theodore Thomas. (1985). *Bahrain and the Gulf.* New York: St. Martin's Press.

Raban, Johnathan. (1979). *Arabia through the looking glass.* London: Collins.

Reiss, Albert. (1950). "Delinquency as the failure of personal and social controls." Paper presented at the annual meeting of the American Sociological Society, Denver, 7–9 September.

Rumaihi, M. G. (1978). *Bahrain: Social and political change since the First World War.* London: Bowker.

Sadik, Muhammad, and M. Snavely. (1972). *Bahrain, Qatar, and United Arab Emirates.* Lexington, MA: Lexington Books.

Souryal, Samuel. (1988). "The role of the *Shariah* law in deterring criminality in Saudia Arabia." *International Journal of Comparative and Applied Criminal Justice 12*, no. 1.

U.S. Census. (1988). *Statistical abstracts of the United States.* Washington, DC: U.S. Government Printing Office.

Vermont Criminal Information Center. (1987). *Vermont crime report.* Waterbury, 1987.

Whelan, John. (1978). "Bahrain," in *Middle East economic digest* (March).

Wright, Marcus. (1983). "Bahrain," in *Middle East economic digest* (September).

CHAPTER SIXTEEN

Teacher, Actor, Candlestick Maker

victims all looking at government-sanctioned victimization of its citizenry

BABETTE M. PROTZ

As someday it may happen that a victim must be found,
I've got a little list, I've got a little list . . .

—Ko-Ko, Lord High Executioner, *The Mikado*

IT WAS A TIME OF ECONOMIC expansion and nickel candy bars; a period often referred to as the "happy days." It was the 1950s, when bomb shelters were advertised as readily as cars and emergency bomb drills were as prevalent as fire drills in American schools. For some, it was a time of personal prosperity; however, for others it was a time of victimization by their government in its pursuit of Communists—known largely by the interchangeable terms of "McCarthyism" or the "Red Scare." The Red Scare, identified with the name of Senator Joseph McCarthy, was the progeny of the political dichotomy—democracy and communism—vocalized by Woodrow Wilson and Joseph Stalin in 1917. The geopolitical and ideological contests that transpired throughout the world following World War II set in motion the development of the anticommunist movement within the United States in the 1950s. Governmental mandates (i.e., House of Un-American Activities [HUAC]) spawned the growth of the Red Scare. Officials in the Truman administration, the Federal Bureau of Investigation (FBI), and right-wing zealots in Congress supplied the HUAC the weapons to use against the citizenry of the United States (Hellman 1977; Patterson 1996). This national and international witch-hunt led to unsubstantiated attacks against political activists, common citizens, and industry. According to Zinn (1980), conservative and fearful reactions to communism circulated throughout the country. Americans became convinced of the need for absolute security—the price, curtailment of a most precious American commodity, civil liberties.

Several times in the history of the United States the government reacted to perceived threats by violating the civil liberties of its citizens. The Alien and Sedition Act of 1798 provided that any person writing, uttering, or publishing false, scandalous, and malicious writings against the government, Congress, or the president would be liable to a fine and imprisonment. The first Red Scare began in the closing of the nineteenth century as a reaction to the socialist movement and trade unions. Police departments were enlarged, the National Guard was formed, and employers mobilized law-and-order leagues and private-detective agencies as a means of repressing organized labor. Justification for the harsh repression of organized labor was made by claims that the country was under attack by the Red Menace. During World War I, Congress passed the Espionage Bill in 1917. Prisons filled with antiwar protestors, striking workers, and immigrants deemed Communists. Citizens were sentenced to prison for things they wrote or said. The Immigration Act of 1918 provided for the exclusion of anarchists and the deportation of immigrants holding radical or revolutionary ideas. Sedition laws were passed by states, and thousands of citizens were arrested under these laws. Raids on homes, meeting places, and pool halls during the 1920s resulted in thousands of citizens being arrested—most without warrants or probable cause.

In 1942, shortly after Pearl Harbor, President Roosevelt issued Executive Order 9066 establishing defense zones within the United States and gave military commanders the authority to exclude persons from such zones. While it did not give the military the authority to confine people after their exclusion, it became the basis for rounding up and confining thousands of Japanese Americans who lived on the West Coast; internees were tested on their loyalty before being released. A perceived threat that Japanese Americans would assist the enemy became the basis for Congress to unanimously pass a law making resistance to Executive Order 9066 a criminal offense. In *Hirabayashi v. United States* (1943), the U.S. Supreme Court upheld the evacuation order despite the fact that no evidence was produced that Fred Korematsu, a native-born U.S. citizen, was disloyal. Although the United States was also at war with Germany and Italy, citizens of German or Italian ancestry were not treated in this fashion—indicating a strong motivation on the part of the government for retribution after the Pearl Harbor attack. Executive Order 9066 was not rescinded until 1976. Enter the second Red Scare.

Probably the most powerful weapon against the perceived threats to American security in the government's arsenal according to Schrecker (1994) was the criminal-justice system. Putting communists on trial transformed party members from political dissidents into criminals. Victimization of individual citizens by their government may be the most insidious in its course of development and vicious in its lifespan. Important, therefore, is a historical look at the state of affairs within the body politic responsible for creating victims during the Red Scare of the 1950s.

The first official list of organizations considered to be subversive was issued in 1947 by then Attorney General Tom Clark and became quickly adopted by state and local governments. The Supreme Court, deeply divided over the list, never ruled on its constitutionality (Walker 1990). It can be reasonably assumed that the failure of the Court to rule on the constitutionality of the list resulted from the Court's own divisive position. The clear-and-present-danger test[1] as set forth in *Schenck v. United States* (1919) enjoyed, according to O'Brien (1997), a renaissance during the 1940s. Knappman (1995) stated that this was the first case in which the Supreme Court ruled directly on the extent in which the federal government may become involved with limiting speech. During this period, the clear-and-present-danger test became a standard by which to review a wide range of restrictions on speech and the press, including handbill distributions, solicitations, and individuals' speeches before public assemblies. At the same time, a more libertarian approach to viewing the scope of the First Amendment was advocated by Chief Justice Stone and Justices Black, Douglas, Murphy, and Rutledge. The Court, although divided, affirmed the Smith Act in *Dennis v. United States* (1951) and the McCarran Act in *Communist Party v. Subversive Activities Control Board* (1961).

Schrecker (1998) states that the force of the Red Scare came from men in powerful positions willing to condone serious violations of citizens' civil liberties in order to remove what they believed to be the danger of communism. The "blacklist," as it became known, was a list consisting of individuals who had been censured, discriminated against, and refused employment because of their past, present, or alleged Communist Party affiliations and/or their use of the First or Fifth Amendments. Individuals fell prey to the blacklist when they refused to dignify the blatantly anti-constitutional activities being carried out by their own government. The actual number of individuals who were blacklisted is unknown. Schrecker (1998) states that hundreds or perhaps thousands of workers lost their jobs. The web of those blacklisted caught authors, producers, academicians, and government employees, as well as the average citizenry. The tentacles of the membership ban placed on communists and noncooperative witnesses by the Screen Actors Guild (SAG) reached out across the nation: writers and others within the entertainment industry in New York were equally impacted as those in California.

Ironically, the media, which relies heavily on the freedoms guaranteed by the First Amendment, were the sources for much of the information concerning the danger of communism. The government, through the media, broadcasted the alarm that communism was threatening to envelop the United States. Fear dominated daily life and loyalty oaths were the order of the day. Americans in all walks of life were swearing oaths of loyalty, including a troupe of Las Vegas strippers who took the solemn vow that they had never conspired to overthrow the government (Fariello 1995, 25). In retrospect, strippers swearing allegiance to their government may seem to border on the eccentric; however, the consuming fear that led to this should give pause. Equally absurd was the requirement by the state of New York that students graduating from high school sign the loyalty oath to receive their diploma. The American Civil Liberties Union (ACLU), formed to protect dissenters after World War I, did little to nothing to assist those citizens under attack by their government. Communists were excluded from membership as early as 1941; and during the 1940s and 1950s Morris Ernst, the head of the ACLU, corresponded with J. Edgar Hoover, passing along information about alleged communists within the organization (Patterson 1996; Zinn 1980).

Individuals suspected of Communist Party involvement endured constant harassment. Both state and federal investigators grilled those suspected of communism on their church attendance, reading habits, and voting patterns. Thousands of government employees were suspended without pay, denied access to the evidence that was being used against them or the opportunity to confront anonymous informers, a clear violation of their Sixth Amendment rights. According to Walker (1990), cases of questionable loyalty based on secretly collected evidence and testimony was an all-too-common scenario. Numerous citizens were detained and questioned regarding their loyalty and their possible threat to national security based solely on secretly collected testimony and evidence. The charges against them were for the most part not relevant or ambiguous.

Targets

Those tagged as communists were many and varied. Throughout the United States, especially in the South, an overall undercurrent existed that viewed individuals as subversives who supported racial equality. Whitfield (1996, 21) purported that "If someone insists there is discrimination against Negroes in this country, or that there is inequality of wealth, there is every reason to believe that person is a Communist." The *Brown v. Board of Education* (1954) decision added fuel to the racist fire. Segregationists under the guise of anticommunists used this case as a pillar to support their claims that integration was part of the communist plot (Schrecker 1998). Racists within such organizations as the HUAC damaged the civil rights movement and further victimized those individuals repressed under the Jim Crow laws (Patterson 1996; Schrecker 1998). The National Association for the Advancement of Colored People (NAACP) was outlawed in several Southern states. Attacks on the civil rights movement forced some within the organization to leave, and others on the verge of joining to reconsider, most often abandoning their beliefs out of self-preservation. As offered by Patterson (1996), the Red Scare influenced the civil rights movement from the start by narrowing the movement's agenda and separating it from potential allies.

Some of the most racist and anti-Semitic men in public life were attracted to the HUAC, such as John Rankin who, in 1950, stated that the activities of the civil rights movements were part of the communist program. Navasky (1980, 112) reports that there was a measure of anti-Semitism in the hysteria over communism and that the general mood of this period was that people felt that if "you scratch a Jew, you can find a communist." The arrest, prosecution, and conviction of Ethel and Julius Rosenberg as spies created a generalized fear within the Jewish community that a link would be established between being a Jew and being a communist. According to Carmichael (1993), the conviction and execution of the Rosenbergs played a crucial role in the creation of the cold war. In 1950, the Rosenbergs were arrested and charged with belonging to a spy group that was passing atomic bomb secrets to the Soviets. The only witness at trial able to tie Julius Rosenberg to the communists was Harry Gold who, according to Hellman (1977), had been prepared for trial by over 400 hours of interviews with the FBI. The prosecution encouraged its witnesses to embellish their testimony, besides scheming directly and illegally with Judge Kaufman to ensure a death penalty. When convicted and sentenced to death, the Rosenbergs appealed the decision to the Supreme Court, which declined to hear their appeal. In June 1953, Justice William O. Douglas, unsure of Kaufman's power to issue the death sentence, granted a stay of execution. In a special session, the Supreme Court removed the stay by a vote of 6 to 3. The Rosenbergs were executed in June 1953. It was felt by some in the Jewish community that had the Rosenbergs not been Jewish, they would have not received the death penalty (Navasky 1980).

By the mid-to-late 1940s any threat of communism was largely contained, having lost whatever influence it may have once had in the United States (Carmichael 1993; Schrecker 1998; Whitfield 1996). Consequently, the hunt and measures employed come into question. Were the actions that severely devalued civil liberties a response to an authentic threat of a communist invasion of the United States, or were they more a means to prohibit individuals whose views were seen as opposing the government from voicing their societal concerns? No one was safe from government scrutiny: housewives, librarians, nurses, factory workers—any citizen was an equal target for victimization. Hundreds of elementary and high school teachers lost their jobs, as did social workers and university professors. The fear on the part of attorneys to take on these cases prohibited many citizens from exercising their Sixth Amendment right of legal counsel. Lawyers who defended people in anticommunist proceedings were perceived as sharing the beliefs of their clients, and the few who would take these cases did so at the risk of losing their livelihoods, the possibility of going to jail, and/or of being disbarred (Fariello 1995; Navasky 1980; Schrecker 1998; Walker 1990).

An individual's livelihood, their place in society, or the avoidance of prison was contingent upon his or her willingness to name names. By resisting the demands of the times (i.e., HUAC hearings, loyalty oaths) an ordinary individual could kiss goodbye a career and often a secure identity in mainstream American life (Buhle 1995, 35). Between March 1947 and December 1952, some 6.6 million persons were investigated through Truman's security programs, and roughly 500 people were dismissed from their jobs in debatable cases of questionable loyalty. While not one case of espionage was found, the official nature of the hunt lent credence to the impression that the government was overrun with spies (Zinn 1980).

Navasky (1980) stated that those individuals required to appear before the HUAC hearings were subjected to a type of degradation ceremony, thereby causing the individual(s) stigmatized by the communist label to be greeted with considerable apprehension and distrust by their fellow community members. From the viewpoint of Lemert's status-degradation theory, the actions by the state could theoretically create criminality by stealing an individual's place in society and/or their means of support. The theory of status degradation indicates that the process may take place formally; however, greater emphasis is placed on the label when the process occurs publicly, and when labels are attached, an individual undergoes a fundamental identity change (Schrecker 1982). Such was the case with the HUAC hearings. Communist labels stigmatized the individuals, subjecting them to blacklisting and therefore a loss of income and social isolation. Those individuals labeled as communist were seen as sinister and/or untrustworthy. Congressional degradation ceremonies created crimes, criminals, and their punishments.

Navasky (1980, 328) stated that the blacklistees reversed the irreversible by eventually resuming a normal life. However, several questions are prompted by this statement: At what cost? How many of the blacklisted were able to actually return to mainstream American life? What, if any, where the repercussions and did the inability of those individuals who were not able to return to their former societal or professional workplace pave their entry into illegitimate activities?

Whitfield (1996) suggests further research into what the late Speaker of the House, Thomas P. O'Neill, referred to as "politics being local." How did the fears of the 1950s affect American communities? Did the pervasive fears of the time, when neighbor would turn against neighbor, affect crime? Failing to recognize and understand the forces that produced this period makes repetition, in some fashion, likely.

THE PERPETRATORS: MCCARTHY ET AL.

In the early 1950s, Wisconsin Senator Joseph A. McCarthy spoke to the Republican Women's meeting in West Virginia. Holding up some papers, he announced that he possessed a list of 205 names of known members of the Communist Party who were working in the State Department (Carmichael 1993; Fariello 1995; Halberstam 1993; Patterson 1996; Schrecker 1998; Walker 1990; Zinn 1980). The next day in another state, the number on the list changed to 57. Throughout his meetings and hearings, the number of known communists within the government changed repeatedly (Halberstam 1993; Patterson 1996; Zinn 1980). When McCarthy appeared on the senate floor, some of the dossiers from which he read were three years old and most of the individuals were no longer employed with the government. According to Zinn (1980, 422), relevant or not, he used them and changed the descriptions as he went along (i.e., "liberal" changed to "communistically inclined," "active fellow traveler" became "active communist").

McCarthy, as well as other members of the government, relied on the media to impart information to the American public. The collusion of the media and public-relations firms that used sophisticated public-relations tools to impart unreliable information provided McCarthy the means by which lives were successfully ruined (Shapiro & Sparks 1995). Reporters rarely made McCarthy produce evidence. He was skillful at making charges in smaller towns, timing his statements to meet the deadline of the wire service, knowing that the local Associated Press (AP) representative would use it to create new headlines (Halberstam 1993; Schrecker 1998). Truth or even verification of the facts did not appear to be relevant. The media became the most reliable weapon in McCarthy's arsenal. His spree of accusations, charges, and threats lasted for four years, ending with his attack on the U.S. Army with allegations that it was also filled with communists.

LAWS AND TRIBUNALS

Schrecker (1994) purports that the transformation of the communist threat into a national obsession came about through the involvement of the federal government. Its actions helped to construct and legitimize the anticommunist concordance. From the 1940s to 1950s, almost every governmental agency became involved: the State Department, Congress, and the Supreme Court. Bureaucrats within the executive branch wielded the most influence. M. W. Swearingen was a special agent with the FBI from the 1950s through the 1970s. He was assigned to Chicago, where he was involved in the political machinery that encompassed surveillance, illegal break-ins, and maintenance of the Security Index (Fariello 1995). The Supreme Court in 1937 handed down a decision that prohibited wiretapping. In 1940, President Roosevelt overrode that decision by stating that the Court did not intend to have its decision against wiretapping apply to grave matters involving the defense of the nation (Schrecker 1998, 106).

Roosevelt himself interpreted the decision by the Supreme Court and empowered the FBI with the freedom to use electronic surveillance against those individuals *suspected* of subversive activities. The FBI director, J. Edgar Hoover, disregarded the 1943 decision by the attorney general to end the program by simply changing its name from Custodial Detention List to Security Index.

Other committees, boards, and laws created victims of the Red Scare as well. Established in 1938, the HUAC was originally expected to concentrate on agents of Nazi Germany and the Soviet Union within the United States. In 1945, the HUAC turned its attention to communism. In that same year, the HUAC had compiled several thousand files on individuals allegedly engaged in, or *likely* to engage in, subversive activities (Carmichael 1993). Although years later Truman would privately concede it had been a terrible mistake, in 1947 he signed Executive Order 9835 that put the Federal Employees Loyalty Program into effect. It was the most extensive loyalty inquiry in the history of the country. In January 1951, Truman felt that his loyalty program was infringing on civil liberties; however, in April 1951, he signed Executive Order 10241, which altered the grounds for dismissal of an individual believed to be disloyal, from "reasonable grounds" to "reasonable doubt," thereby shifting the burden of proof upon the accused (Fariello 1995; Patterson 1996). Now the innocent had to prove their innocence. The most important federal legislation concerning subversive acts were contained in three laws: the Smith Act, the Internal Security Act of 1950 (aka the McCarran Act), and the Communist Control Act of 1954.

The Smith Act, approved by Congress in 1940, forbade any person to advocate the violent overthrow of the government, to organize or be associated with any group having that intent, or to teach or encourage such violence. Individuals accused of violating the Smith Act had only to have *talked* about an action—to have shown that the individual engaged in illegal activities was not required (Patterson 1996; Schrecker 1998; Zinn 1980). The Internal Security Act of 1950, also known as the McCarran Act, provided, among other things, fines and punishments for anyone who contributed substantially to the establishment within the United States of a totalitarian dictatorship, the direction and control of which was to be vested in any foreign government, organization, or individual. A Subversive Activities Control Board (SACB) was formed with the mandate to identify these groups. The SACB attempted to cripple communist activity by forbidding communists to secure passports, to work in defense plants, or to hold nonelective federal offices. The SACB also authorized the detention of accused spies and saboteurs during any national emergency (Fariello 1995; Patterson 1996). The Communist Control Act of 1954 declared that the Communist Party of the United States constituted a conspiracy to overthrow the government, and that its role as the agency of a hostile power made it a danger to the security of the country.

Consequently, all rights and privileges generally possessed by political parties under federal and state laws were denied to the Communist Party, and any willful or knowing member of that party was subjected to the punishments and penalties of the McCarran Act. Countless individuals that were brought in for hearings and/or put on trial were charged with conspiracy. According to Belfrage (1973), this device was useful in those cases where it had been decided that someone should go to jail for his or her politics despite weak evidence of any wrongdoing—the individual was accused of *talking* about doing something, a charge that made innocence unproveable. It became a criminal offense in many states to merely advocate governmental change or to even join any organization so advocating governmental change. Numerous federal, state, and local laws were passed prohibiting subversive activities: for example, in Texas, membership in the Communist Party carried a penalty of 20 years in prison; in Michigan, the act of writing or speaking subversive words brought on a life sentence; Tennessee punished unlawful advocacy with the death penalty; and Virginia proposed execution for anyone caught lurking about with intent to spy (Fariello 1995, 41).

The intentions of these antisubversive laws were to protect the country from communism, with their basic purpose being to punish espionage or armed uprisings against the government. The argument in their defense was that for the government to wait for the communists to strike the first blow was an open invitation to disaster. While this may have been true, to accomplish this protection by deflating the First Amendment rights of free speech and association to the point of extinction should be viewed as abhorrent, especially since it is now believed that the Soviet Union did not have the capability to launch such an attack at that time.

FIRST AMENDMENT—FIFTIES STYLE

The antisubversion laws previously stated stripped members of the Communist Party in the United States of their constitutional rights, or as Whitfield (1996, 14) stated, "the right to have rights." The fear of communism permeated American culture during this period, appearing to override the Constitution as well as acting as a catalyst in the erosion of the First Amendment. One of the basic tenants of the First Amendment provides that Congress will make no law that would abridge the freedom of speech, the press, or the right of the people to peaceably assemble or petition the government for redress of grievances. These basic fundamental rights were quashed by the state as countless individuals were deprived of their livelihoods when careers were destroyed, marriages broken, and when artistic works, plays, books, and movies were censored and/or banned. The First Amendment's guarantee of freedom of association and free speech as well as the Fifth Amendment's guarantee against self-incrimination ironically worked against the individual. By invoking either of these rights, the individual was seen as being guilty of subversion. Schrecker (1986) stated that on questions of guilt, *silence meant guilt.*

The Supreme Court in the case of *Dennis v. United States* (1951) redefined freedom of speech. In this case, Eugene Dennis along with ten codefendants were charged with and convicted of violating the Smith Act, namely, conspiring to form groups advocating an overthrow of the government and conspiring to form groups that taught this same overthrow. The only evidence provided at these trails came from FBI informants and ex-communists, many of whom were professional informants—no overt criminal act was ever alleged (Knappman 1995; Navasky 1980). The Supreme Court upheld the conviction by expanding the clear-and-present danger formula to "grave-and-probable" danger. In agreement with Congress, the Court stated that "freedom of speech is not an absolute, nor above control by the legislature when its judgment is that certain kinds of speech are so undesirable as to warrant criminal sanction" (*Dennis v. United States* 1951). The Court, with this ruling that allowed speech to be permissibly constructed, collapsed one of the most fundamental rights provided to the citizenry under the Constitution. The *Dennis* case upheld the Smith Act, causing Eugene Dennis and his fellow appellants to serve time in prison; it also became the model for further Smith Act trials. According to Knappman (1995), between the years 1951 and 1956 every case tried under the Smith Act resulted in convictions that were upheld by the Court of Appeals and denied review by the Supreme Court. It was not until 1957 while revisiting the Smith Act that the Supreme Court began to establish guidelines for congressional inquiries. In *Watkins v. United States* (1957), the Supreme Court held that "[t]he Bill of Rights is applicable to congressional investigations, as it is to all forms of governmental action," as well as stating that "[n]o inquiring is an end in itself; it must be related to, and in furtherance of, a legitimate task of Congress." Watkins was convicted for refusing to answer questions "pertinent to the question under inquiry." Summoned to testify before the HUAC, Watkins spoke freely about his own activities and association with the Communist Party. He refused, however, to answer questions about whether he had known others to be members of the party. He based his refusal on the stance that the questions were out of the scope of the committee's activities and not relevant to its work. As there was no clear understanding of the "questions under inquiry," the Supreme Court overturned the conviction, thereby modifying the Smith Act to apply only to those who advocate a concrete course of illegal action.

Discussion

The Emergency Civil Liberties Committee in 1954 warned that the threat to civil liberties in the United States was the most serious in the history of the country (Fariello 1995). Karmen (1996, 295) stated that "[t]he human costs of crime cannot be measured in dollars and cents." The same can be said for the victims of the Red Scare. The victims were not only individual members of society—American society as a whole was victimized. Navasky (1980) stated that the social costs of the period were extensive and have yet to be determined; he said further that the individuals subjected to the loyalty oaths were plagued by worry, depression, fatigue, fear, insomnia, drinking, headaches, indigestion, suspension, and loss of self-respect.

It is impossible to know what intellectual losses were suffered by the pervasive insistence of the loyalty oaths. The president of Yale University stated that there would be no witch-hunt at Yale because there would be no witches; Yale would not hire communists. President Conant of Harvard and Eisenhower, then president of Columbia, concluded in 1949 that communists were unfit to teach (Patterson 1996). Anticipating an attack from the Senate Internal Security Subcommittee, Schrecker (1986) reported that Rutgers University passed bylaws that advised scholars to remain within their fields of competence. Speculating on new research was condoned only if he or she could legally prove competence in the area. The American Association of University Professors (AAUP) opposed loyalty oaths, and also opposed the firing of teachers; however, it was not until 1956 that the AAUP censured those universities that violated the civil liberties of its professors (Patterson 1996).

In *Dennis v. United States* (1951), the Court stated that Congress did not intend to eradicate the free discussion of political theories or destroy the traditional rights of Americans to discuss and evaluate ideas without fear of governmental sanction. Yet, according to Buhle (1995), university environments hardened, becoming places that simply dispensed information to students on how to succeed and curbing any responses students may have had to the influences shaping the country. Thus faculties became defenders of the status quo.

Samuel Stouffer of Harvard University attempted to measure the magnitude of thought concerning communism in 1954 through a national poll and found that 80 percent agreed with President Eisenhower in his 1954 State of the Union Address that proposed stripping admitted communists of their citizenship; 52 percent favored sending them to prison; 77 percent wanted communists banned from radio; and 42 percent believed that the press should not be permitted to criticize the American government (Whitfield 1996).

The religious right and moral crusaders also joined the McCarthy bandwagon. Billy Graham spoke to "enormous and enthusiastic crowds" during 1950 and 1951, warning against "over 1,100 social-sounding organizations that are communist or communist-operated in this country"; he further stated that the communists control the minds of a great segment of our people, and that the educational and religious culture is almost beyond repair (Patterson 1996, 237). In his opening prayer for the Senate in 1952, Graham echoed McCarthy's spirit when he referred to "barbarians beating at our gates from without and moral termites from within" (Navasky 1980, 24). He backed Senator McCarthy's demand that witnesses appearing before his committee not be permitted to shield themselves behind the Fifth Amendment; further, he aligned communism with satanism (Whitfield 1996). During the 1950s, formal church attendance was the highest it had been in the country to date. Churches were the most trusted institution in American culture and figures such as Billy Graham were highly respected (Whitfield 1996). At his peak in 1954, Bishop Fulton Sheen reached an estimated 25 million people a week via television. The abuse of constitutional rights and vacuous allegations of subversion were not only excused but also backed by members of the "moral police," thereby providing moral validation.

Could This Happen Again?

According to Schrecker (1998), this couldn't happen again in the same way, but American politics has never lacked for supposed enemies from within; and when the anticommunist crusade withered away, no barriers were erected to prevent its recurrence. Hence it is reasonable to believe that it could. The demonization of some groups and the use of state power to repress them occurs all the time, as does the willingness of those in power to collaborate with the process. While the cold war produced its own structure, the process through which McCarthyism came to dominate American politics is infinitely replicable. Post–Red Scare examples include, but are not limited to:

- Government surveillance and attacks throughout the 1950s, 1960s, and 1970s against Vietnam War protestors, Students for a Democratic Society (SDS), women's groups, and the destruction of the Black Panthers.
- While he was president during the 1980s, Reagan expanded the powers of the FBI and Central Intelligence Agency (CIA) in domestic surveillance, brought the McCarran-Walter Act back to life by excluding critics of the United States from entering the country and banning films considered as being anti-American.
- During the late 1980s and 1990s, topics concerning military spending, the Gulf War, and the use of polarized projections to support politically and economically motivated agendas for the maintenance of the domestic status quo were reminiscent of the 1950s political rhetoric (Carmichael 1993).

Remembering that the state was assisted in creating victims through rhetoric and the media, should the aforementioned incidents be taken simply as political oratory, since the cold war is now over?

The theft during the 1950s of artistic works never written, published, or produced due to fear of the writers, producers, and artists and the theft of discussion and debate within American institutions of higher learning were crimes perpetrated upon American society as real as any on a court docket today. The mechanism that allowed the creation of victims during the 1950s appears to still be in operation, given the recent controversy over freedom of speech on college campuses since the terrorist attack on September 11, 2001. Equally alarming is the passage of the Patriot Act on October 26, 2001. Much of the language of this act is hauntingly familiar: expansion of the ability of the government to conduct secret searches; broad access given to the FBI to sensitive business records without having to show evidence of a crime; neighbors encouraged to spy and report on neighbors; minimization of judicial supervision of federal telephone and Internet surveillance by law-enforcement authorities. These provisions parallel those acts passed during the period prior to and during the onslaught of the government's 1950s victimization of American citizenry.

Passage of new laws, political rhetoric, demands for personnel files, liberal-baiting, and/or the hunt for conspiring demons based on elusive, unproven evidence should not be simply overlooked. The fact that the blacklist was not abolished until 1974 should be a sobering indicator of the government's continued interest in regulating citizens' constitutional rights—a blight on the criminal-justice system. The phenomenon of governmentally sanctioned victimization should be studied from the criminal-justice standpoint and, most importantly, it should serve as a reminder of an American inquisition and its victims—which would be all of us. Perhaps the final question becomes why should we, citizens of the United States, accept attempts by the government to cut back on civil liberties when the government has never made the case that this is truly necessary?

NOTE

1. Words that, ordinarily and in many places, would be within the freedom of speech protected by the First Amendment, may become subject to prohibition when of such a nature and used in such circumstances as to create a clear-and-present danger that they will bring about the substantive evils that Congress has a right to prevent. The character of every act depends upon the circumstances in which it is done.

REFERENCES

Belfrage, C. (1973). *The American inquisition.* New York: Bobbs-Merrill.

Buhle, P. (1995). "The Hollywood blacklist and the Jew: An exploration of popular culture." *Tikkum 10*(5):35.

Carmichael, V. (1993). *Framing history: The Rosenberg story and the cold war.* Minneapolis: University of Minnesota Press.

Dennis v. United States, 341 U.S. 494 (1951).

Fariello, G. (1995). *Red scare: Memories of the American inquisition.* New York: Avon Books.

Gilbert, W. S., and A. Sullivan. (1885). *The mikado.*

Halberstam, D. (1993). *The Fiftes.* New York: Ballantine Books.

Hellman, L. (1977). *Scoundrel time.* New York: Bantam Books.

Hirabayashi v. United States, 320 U.S. 81 (1943).

Karmen, A. (1996). *Crime victims*, 3rd ed. New York: Wadsworth Publishing.

Knappman, E. E. (ed.). (1995). *American trials of the 20th century.* Canton, MI: Visible Ink Press.

Lieberman, R. (1995). "Communism, peace activism, and civil liberties: From the Waldorf conference to the Peekskill riot." *Journal of American Cultures 18*(3):59.

Navasky, V. (1980). *Naming names.* New York: Viking Press.

O'Brien, D. M. (1997). *Constitutional law and politics*, vol. 2: *Civil rights and civil liberties*, 3rd ed. New York: W. W. Norton.

Patterson, J. T. (1996). *Grand expectations.* New York: Oxford University Press.

Schenck v. United States, 249 U.S. 47 (1919).

Schrecker, E. (1986). *No ivory tower: McCarthyism and the universities.* New York: Oxford University Press.

———. (1994). *The age of McCarthyism: A brief history with documents.* Boston: St. Martin's Press.

———. (1998). *Many are the crimes.* New York: Little, Brown.

Shapiro, S., and S. Sparks. (1995). "Political correctness—the new McCarthyism." *Public Relations Quarterly 40*(4):25.

Walker, Samuel. (1990). *In defense of American liberties: A history of the ACLU.* New York: Oxford University Press.

Watkins v. United States, 354 U.S. 178 (1957).

Whitfield, S. J. (1996). *The culture of the cold war*, 2nd ed. Baltimore: Johns Hopkins University Press.

Zinn, H. (1980). *A people's history of the United States.* New York: Harper & Row.

CHAPTER SEVENTEEN

Nonhuman Animals as Victims

victimology and the animal-rights movement

BONNIE BERRY

NONHUMAN ANIMALS HAVE BEEN HISTORICALLY, and continue to be, victimized in many ways. They are starved, beaten, and exploited for their labor. They are used for recreation and entertainment (circuses, cockfighting, fishing, movies, zoos, to name a few). They are hunted by traditional means and in canned-hunting ranches. They serve unwillingly as experimental subjects in testing products and medical procedures to be used by and on humans. They are murdered for their flesh, their fur, their hides, their feathers. They are humiliated. They are confined against their will in overly crowded conditions and yet are alone.

The settings in which these cases of abuse occur are numerous: laboratories, factory farms, private homes, "pet" stores, racetracks, puppy mills, and so on. The people involved in the abuse run the gamut of individuals to large organizations, the latter constituting, as we will see below, institutionalized species-ism, committed by corporations and governmental entities (notably the military).

EXPLANATIONS FOR NONHUMAN VICTIMIZATION

For those who are aghast at nonhuman animal abuse, explanations are required. For those who see nothing wrong with this nonhuman abuse, and indeed do not define animal abuse as *abuse*, no explanation is required, because the issue of animal abuse seems a foolish one. Since this chapter proceeds from the point of view that animal victimization is a problem, let us consider explanations for it.

A substantial reason why nonhuman animals are treated badly on all levels, individually and organizationally, is the false assumption that nonhumans do not have the same capacity to feel and think as do humans; for example, it has long been inaccurately claimed that nonhumans do not feel pain and are not intellectually endowed (Berry 1997). Consider, for instance, a recent news article headlined "Study Suggests Monkeys Have Ability to Think" (Wade 1998). Of course monkeys can think, but it is beyond the comprehension of many species-ists that monkeys and other nonhumans can think. Thinking and feeling, in the same manner as human animals think and feel, is an accepted assumption by nonspecies-ists but a truly remarkable concept for species-ists. The point is: if humans believe that nonhumans are not intellectually capable or sensate, abuse is permitted; namely, abuse is not abuse. Similarly, sexists and racists have abused women and racial minorities, justifying their abusive treatment of less powerful humans on the basis of their supposed insensate-ness and their supposed deservedness.

Even if it were allowed that nonhuman animals feel and think, they may still be subject to exploitation because, as Singer (1990) asserts, species-ists believe that their most trivial interests outweigh the vital interests of other (nonhuman) species. In short, humans are superior, according to the homocentric attitude, and nonhumans are doomed to be sacrificed for human needs and desires (see also Rachels 1990; Pluhar 1995). Stephen Jay Gould (1999) writes of the human refusal to see ourselves as other than "separate and superior" to nonhuman animals. We have an unfortunate tendency to dichotomize, to divide human and nonhuman animals as good versus bad, higher versus lower, and (I would add) powerful exploiters versus powerless exploitees. These dichotomies allow the use of certain strategies to justify oppression.

To put a finer point on it, we hierarchically arrange nonhuman animals, with some privileged for protection and others not. Animal companions, for example, are seen as more worthy of protection because they "belong" to us. Endangered species are more protected that those species not deemed endangered by virtue of their scarcity and symbolic imagery useful to humans (the American Bald Eagle comes to mind). Other nonhumans are greatly stigmatized, however, and subject to abuse in the forms of murder and loss of habitat. Wolves are murdered because they harm livestock—that is, they harm nonhuman animals worth money to humans (Lopez 1978; Antonio 1995; Sink 1998). Spotted owls are deprived of habitat because they get in the way of timber-industry profits. The stigma assigned to these and other nonhumans is "justified" on the basis of a human perspective of needs and desires.

Another related, but more intractable, reason for nonhuman victimization is the inconceivability of nonhuman animals as having equal worth to human animals (Berry 2001a, 2002a). The *very idea* that nonhumans are equally deserving of rights, compared to humans, is not within the realm of species-ist consideration. This brings us to a discussion of overlapping "isms." Once upon a time, it was inconceivable that women were equal to men and that nonwhites were equal to whites. The inconceivability of equality across and within species accounts for victimization of nonhumans and human minorities.

OVERLAPS WITH OTHER "ISMS"

Species-ism often overlaps with sexism and racism, allowing and encouraging abuse leveled at nonhumans, women, and nonwhites. On the topic of thinking and feeling abilities, for instance, Adams and Donovan (1995) have pointed out that nonhumans, women, and nonwhites have long been excluded from membership in the moral community on the basis of all three groups' alleged absence of rationality, thereby precluding the "rights of public citizenship" (p. 1). This interlocking oppression of nonhuman and minority human animals speaks, obviously, to power—specifically, the power to exploit, the power to profit from oppression (Kappeler 1995) derived from a myriad of motives, from culinary to scientific and beyond (Pluhar 1995).

Beings without power are more likely to be victims, to be victimized and assigned the status of victims. Being made a victim—of crime, unfair treatment, abuse, and so on—can make even a once-equal human into a less-than-equal human. Victimization itself brings about power loss, in other words. The circumstances of being made a victim are very specific: Without the victimizing event, a white, straight, U.S.-born, Christian male (that is, a majority member) is not a victim or even typically considered to be victim material. Criminal victimization can make a white male a victim, but even so, his victim status is entirely particular to that (crime) event and outcome. Whereas human minorities (women, homosexuals, ethnic and racial minorities, the differently labeled, the poor, immigrants, and so forth) and nonhuman animals are more likely to be placed in the victim role because they already occupy a minority role. Human minorities and nonhumans start out with a massive disadvantage in the world of victimization: they have few or no rights. Nonhumans do not, for the most part, possess even a modicum of rights. They can be starved, mistreated, murdered, assaulted, and so on with impunity and with no legal recourse.

"Interlocking oppression" (Adams & Donovan 1995) has proved a fruitful way to consider the common experiences of nonhuman animals and human minorities, particularly women, in terms of their relative powerlessness (Adams 1995, 1996; Berry 1997). Similar experiences with oppression can provide the catalyst for sympathy as well as activism on the part of (unlike) victims. Broadly, it is well-documented that women constitute the majority of animal-rights advocates, perhaps because of their shared experiences with oppression. More specifically, I have noted the shared experiences and sympathy that women prisoners feel for nonhuman animals. Like nonhuman animals, prisoners live in cages, have been experimented upon, many have been brutalized (raped, assaulted), and at all times are at the mercy of their keepers (Berry 1996).

What Constitutes Victimization? Definitions

Essentially, the loss of or never having possessed autonomy and the external perception of equal worth constitute risk of victimization. Being subject to assault, murder, starvation, and/or the infliction of psychological trauma all speak to powerlessness to control one's own destiny and therefore being subject to victimization. Nonhumans, in relation to humans, have no say about how they are treated. They lose their homes and habitats, their families and their family structures, and (in short) their control. Plus, they have no voice, except those of human animal-rights advocates.

The issue of crime definitions as they pertain to nonhuman animals is intellectually intriguing albeit disheartening. For the most part, all societies, with variation, do not view offenses against nonhuman animals in the same way as they do offenses against human animals. That is, what constitutes a criminal offense, complete with criminal punishment, against a human animal is not so considered in the case of nonhuman animals. The United States has advanced, ever so slowly and minimally, against criminal offenses as perpetrated upon nonhuman animals, yet we cannot state that the crime definitions and penalties are equal across species.

Comninou (1995) writes that "[a]lthough no animals have legal standing, game animals are excluded from even the minimal protection afforded by anticruelty legislation" (p. 135). Again, we find issues of hierarchy, with some arguing that domesticated animals have greater "moral status" than "wild" or free-roaming animals; in other words, domesticated animals have greater value to humans and are thus more likely to be subject to protection. We are more considerate, explains Davis (1995), of domesticated animals. If so, why is this? Probably the answer lies in Belknap's (2001) remarks on property and Coston's (1992) addressing homelessness as an aggravating factor in victimization. This then leads to a comparison of homeless animals and animal companions, as protected or not.

Viewing nonhuman animals as property and offenses against them as property offenses will be discussed in more detail in the following section on reactions to nonhuman victimization, but let me describe here the similarities in views of victimized nonhumans and women as human and male possessions. We are reminded of Belknaps's (2001) treatment of rape of human women as a property offense. She writes: "Laws historically defined rape as theft, and rape laws were designed to protect upper- and middle-class white men in the case of their 'property' (daughters and wives) being devalued by rape" (p. 210). Perhaps with time, we will see nonhuman animals not as property and violations of nonhuman animals as crime instead of a property offense, much as we have with human women and the crime of rape.[1]

Some nonhuman animals, like human animals, are especially vulnerable to crime victimization. For example, Belknap (2001) and Coston (1992) describe homeless women, relative to women with homes, as uniquely vulnerable to attack. Their vulnerability is particularly marked, as Coston found, if they are nonwhite, and they are particularly targeted as rape victims. Homeless nonhuman animals, who don't "belong" to human "owners," are likewise especially vulnerable. This would be true of free-roaming wildlife as well as homeless dogs, cats, and other nonhumans.

One might suppose that animal companions, then, would be safe (or relatively so) from mistreatment. According to a study by Irvine (2002), however, animal companions are by no means safe from abuse, and here we find the class issue rearing its ugly head. Animal companions were originally only the property of the wealthy. Theoretically, the nonwealthy could have animal companions if they had the luxury of extra food and shelter to provide them, but these companions were not protected as were those of the wealthy. By law, the nonwealthy could be, and were, forced to abandon their animal companions, partly for reasons of ensuring class distinction.

In sum, one might assume that homeless women and homeless animals are doubly victimized—because of their homeless state and because of their status as minorities with relative powerlessness. However, one cannot assume that women and nonhuman animals who have homes are also not victimized. It may even be the case that women and nonhumans who are connected with men and human "owners" are covertly and therefore more successfully victimized. The issues of homelessness/belonging and of property are embedded in the discussion below about criminal and civil responses to victimization, along with broader issues of cross-species deservedness and social movements against victimization.

RESPONSES TO NONHUMAN VICTIMIZATION

Animal-rights violations—starvation, leaving animals homeless, physical abuse, fur-trapping, factory-farming, unnecessarily inhumane slaughtering, or any number of other abuses—are not typically considered deserving of public shame, public disgust, and criminal penalties and are not punished as they would be if perpetrated against humans. Occasionally, really awful crimes against nonhuman animals come to light, such as the making of "crush videos"—crush videos being films of nonhumans being tortured, usually killed, in a horrific manner; for example, snakes and rodents being killed by a woman's spike heel.[2] Abuses such as these are indisputably terrible and public horror might dictate that criminal penalties are appropriate for the perpetrators; however, a common punishment for making crush videos is a fine.

The lopsidedness of the penalties imposed for nonhuman animal abuse compared to human abuse is quizzical and disturbing. Imagine the response to an impaling of a human with a human-sized spike; obviously, a harsher penalty than a fine would be in order. Consider also a road-rage incident in which a man became enraged at a fellow motorist, got out of his car, approached the other motorist, yelled at her, grabbed her dog out of her car, and threw the dog into traffic where he was run over and killed. Surprisingly, the murderer was sentenced to three years in prison (*New York Times* 2001). Imagine the same scenario but with a human child being thrown into traffic and killed.

Much of the strain that animal-rights advocates experience stems from our feeling that nonhuman animal abuse is punishment-worthy, yet knowing that criminal penalties for animal-rights violations are rife with inequalities (Berry 2001b). Not only is there the aforementioned disparity in penalties exacted for human and nonhuman victimization, but there is the disparity across penalties imposed for nonhuman victimization depending on the identity of the perpetrators. People who hurt their animal companions or who run small-scale but heinous cockfighting operations are more likely than large-scale corporate violators of being arrested and facing criminal penalties. These penalties are not onerous, usually fines and community service, but they are occasionally applied to individual-level and small-scale abusers and are growing in severity due to animal-rights advocates' activities. Large-scale abusers—slaughterhouses, testing corporations, fur-producers, factory farms, and so on—are rarely subject to criminal penalties.

Punishment can take a number of forms; they can be informal or formal, criminal or civil. Informal punishments may be more effective but have less public reach than formal punishments; alternatively, formalized social controls, backed by legal clout, apply to all relevant jurisdictions and (theoretically) to all violators. Criminal and civil sanctions are both legally based but with, simplistically put, different rules for determining fault and different punishment outcomes. The Animal Legal Defense Fund (ALDF) champions the use of civil remedies rather than, or in addition to, criminal actions for animal abuse. The ALDF has been measurably successful in animal-protection litigation; its work has proved highly useful in legally defining animal abuse, spelling out the wrongfulness of animal abuse, and in exacting punishment for animal abuse through civil routes (Wise 2000). One aspect of its strategy in winning animal-abuse cases that may give one pause, however, is the depiction of the abused animal as damaged property and the abuse as harm to property. Civil penalties *do* elicit the question of monetary worth of a life, as though nonhuman animals are objects or property. But we use this same curious remedy with humans: we set an economic value on a human life and exact that value from the person who harmed or took that human life. This strategy has worked well in cases of human-rights violations; witness the Southern Poverty Law Center's successes at bankrupting the White Aryan Resistance, the Aryan Nation, and various Klan organizations via criminal and civil routes (Berry 2001b).

Human rights are not only similar to nonhuman rights, but further that human rights can evolve into nonhuman rights. Glaberson (1999) offers that

> [m]ore than a generation after civil rights and environmental lawyers took their battles to the courts, there are now lawyers who are [defending animal rights]. . . . Fighting for creatures like performing orangutans and dogs used in experimentation, the lawyers are creating a new field of animal law with far more ambitious goals than traditionally weak anticruelty laws. They are filing novel lawsuits and producing new legal scholarship to try to chip away at a fundamental principle of American law that animals are property and have no rights. These lawyers . . . are influenced by developing scientific and ethical scholarship showing animals to have far higher levels of cognition and social development than previously believed. (p. 16)

Harvard and Georgetown Universities, among the most prestigious U.S. law schools, are offering courses in nonhuman animal law. And legislatures across the country have given animal-rights lawyers a potent new tool in upgrading animal-cruelty crimes from misdemeanors to felonies. Animal-rights lawyers have also been successful in battling what they call "execution orders, the sort of routine euthanasia that occurs when dogs bite people" (Glaberson 1999, 16). And they file cases against mistreatment of circus animals and farm animals, as well as cases against hunting. Not surprisingly, these lawyers defending nonhuman victims face ridicule, much as did civil rights and environmental lawyers in their fights for integration and clean air.

In addition to legal remedies, social movements effect change. Animal-rights social-movement organizations such as PETA (People for the Ethical Treatment of Animals), ALF (Animal Liberation Front), HSUS (Humane Society of the United States), and others have made quite a bit of headway on raising public awareness as to animal rights and animal victimization, but also have aided more concretely in creating changes in legislation, shutting down abusive facilities (through economic boycotting, exposure of cruel practices, and so on), and ending or reducing abusive traditions (such as cockfighting). Animal-rights activities vary on a continuum of active to passive, from letter-writing, contribution-sending, and other more-or-less private and passive behaviors to more public and drastic advocacy behaviors such as eco-sabotage (monkey-wrenching bulldozers and so on), setting laboratory and farmed animals free, and other similar actions (see Lyall 1998; Brooke 1998, 1999).

A conceptual framework to explain animal abuse and animal rights has proved useful, but it is not enough to list the atrocities. Many of us have done so (notably Adams & Donovan 1995; Adams 1995, 1996; Berry 1996, 1997, 2001a; Nibert 2002) and, while such knowledge heightens awareness and probably advances the evolution of animal rights, societies are also moving forward in concrete activities aimed at prohibiting nonhuman abuse. For example, it is now a federal offense to transport birds across state lines for sport-fighting purposes (Berry 2002a). And "exotic" game farms have been banned in Oregon (*New York Times* 1999a), although the practice continues in some states (West 1999). The news remains mixed over criminal punishments. Nine men were charged in the shotgun slayings of more than a thousand federally protected birds in 1998. They pled guilty and, for the largest mass killing and wounding ever, via shotgun slaughter of an endangered species, they were "punished" with home confinement and a fine (*New York Times* 1999b). And the work of nonhuman-rights movements continues, partly to enlighten the masses about the more covert hateful crimes against nonhumans, as we see in guaranteed-kill ranches (West 1999) and hunts (Sink 1998; Chen 1998). Even less obvious to some are the ranching of fur-growing animals and the buying of fur, taken from nonhumans in horrifyingly painful ways (Lyall 1998; Herring 1999).

Institutionalized Species-ism: Individual and Systemic

Our biggest battle in the struggle against nonhuman victimization is against institutionalized species-ism. As with sexism, racism, and homophobia, nonhuman animal victimization can occur on an individual level or on an organizational level. In fact, this is how we usually think of nonhuman victimization—as occurring on a case-by-case basis, as committed by individuals or organizations. Individualized abuse corresponds to types of abuse: beating, starving, rape, and other abuses against nonhumans, as Coston and Protz (1998) have analyzed it. But species-ism, like sexism and racism, is more difficult to remedy when it is committed organizationally and when it is institutionalized. Organizational abuse is better represented by animal testing, ranching, and so on, occurring on a grand scale, with policy as the backdrop and as perpetrated by organized collections of humans.

Institutionalized racism, sexism, homophobia: species-ism refers to a deeply engrained *system* of prejudice and discrimination. For example, because institutionalized racism operates within the criminal-justice system, housing markets, employment, and in many aspects of American life, racists feel justified in their racist attitudes and behaviors. In the same way that institutionalized sexism has operated in the economic sector (through denial of jobs and equal pay), familial institutions (role expectations and so on), and legal (criminal and civil) systems, sexists feel justified in their sexism. Species-ism and the other "isms" can, and often do, occur willfully or without thought; nonhuman animals and human members of powerless classes represent victims of a lack of consciousness. To the extent that we don't think about the wrongfulness of our abuse, or if upon brief consideration we do not see our abuse as wrong, our abuse is institutionalized—deeply embedded within the social structure.

In sum, nonhuman victimization can result from large and powerful social forces that superficially "legitimize" their abuse, because the sources of this victimization are superficially legitimate and powerful, such as a military entity or corporation. Let me leave you, my reader, with a clear example of institutionalized nonhuman abuse, discrimination, victimization, exploitation. The Bush administration's attempt to destroy the Alaska National Wildlife Refuge and thereby destroy nonhuman habitat and thereby destroy nonhuman lives was couched in terms of keeping us safe from terrorist countries and their oil reserves upon which we are dependent. In fact, the desire of the administration to drill in a fragile environment has to do with capitalist pursuits and energy profit (Berry 2002b).

Conclusion

Much of what this chapter has been about, and what this edited collection is about, is power and oppression. Clearly, the less powerful are victimized by the more powerful. Mills (1997), writing of cockfighting and dog-fighting in his treatise on societal-level meanness, believes that there has been an increase in animal cruelty, corresponding to increases in social meanness during the 1990s. Moreover, he states: "What is happening in the animal world is not . . . an isolated occurrence. Very much part of the nineties culture is the rise of a new savagery in which violence is chic and the winner-take-all ethic of the economy has become part of sports and entertainment" (p. 43). I am not sure that I can agree with him. While I have chronicled the phenomena of social rage in my 1999 analysis (Berry 1999), I remain unsure that rage against nonhuman animals is on the rise. Rather, it may be the case that social rage against animal victimization is more the case.

Our recent events of terrorism serve as a distraction from an administration bent on destroying the environment as well as destroying all manner of human and nonhuman rights. It is up to those of us who are concerned about victimization—of nonhuman animals, women, and all categories of the oppressed—to end the abuse, globally and locally.

Notes

1. Upper- and middle-class white men were in a better position to protect "their" property (women) than minority and poor men. Moreover, upper- and middle-class white women were more socially valued than poor or nonwhite women.

2. The presence of crush videos brings forth the question of why such videos exist, and who supplies the market for such videos. As far as is known, there has been no demographic profile of who desires such videos, but it may be surmised that watchers of crush videos are motivated by the desire to view cruelty. While it

is confusing to those of us who are not attracted to viewing cruelty, it remains an ugly truth that some people like to observe torture of humans and nonhumans.

REFERENCES

Adams, Carol J. (1995). *Neither man nor beast: Feminism and the defense of animals*. New York: Continuum.

———. (1996). *The sexual politics of meat: A feminist-vegetarian critical theory*. New York: Continuum.

Adams, Carol J., and Josephine Donovan (eds.). (1995). *Animals and women: Feminist theoretical explorations*. Durham, NC: Duke University Press.

Antonio, Diane. (1995). "Of wolves and women," in *Animals and women: Feminist theoretical explorations*, ed. Carol J. Adams and Josephine Donovan (pp. 213–30). Durham, NC: Duke University Press.

Belknap, Joanne. (2001). *The invisible woman: Gender, crime, and justice*, 2nd ed. Belmont, CA: Wadsworth.

Berry, Bonnie. (1996). "Solidarity among the oppressed." *Prism 9*(1–2):23–25.

———. (1997). "Human and non-human animal rights and oppression: An evolution toward equality." *Free Inquiry in Creative Sociology 25*(2):155–60.

———. (1999). *Social rage: Emotion and cultural conflict*. New York: Garland.

———. (2001a). "On intolerance: Social emotions, behaviors, and biases." *Humanity and Society 25*(1):19–39.

———. (2001b). "To punish the punishers: The animal rights advocates' dilemma." Paper presented at the annual meeting of the American Society of Criminology, November, Atlanta.

———. (2002a). "Cumulative constructions of animal rights: Different routes to equality." Paper presented at the annual meeting of the American Sociological Association, August 17, Chicago.

———. (2002b). "Animal rights in a time of terror." *Animals and Society 2*:3–4.

Brooke, James. (1998). "Group claims responsibility for blazes at Vail resort." *New York Times* (October 22):A14.

———. (1999). "Environmentalists battle growth of ski resorts." *New York Times* (January 19):A10.

Chen, David W. (1998). "Landowner and animal lovers fight tradition of the gentry." *New York Times* (December 28):A22.

Comninou, Maria. (1995). "Speech, pornography, and hunting," in *Animals and women: Feminist theoretical explorations*, ed. Carol J. Adams and Josephine Donovan (pp. 126–48). Durham, NC: Duke University Press.

Coston, Charisse T. M. (1992). "The influence of race in urban homeless females' fear of crime." *Justice Quarterly 9*:721–30.

Coston, Charisse T. M., and Babette M. Protz. (1998). "Kill your dog, beat your wife, screw your neighbor's kids, rob a bank?: A cursory look at an individual's vat of social chaos resulting from deviance." *Free Inquiry in Creative Sociology 26*(2):153–58.

Davis, Karen. (1995). "Thinking like a chicken: Farm animals and the feminine connection," in *Animals and women: Feminist theoretical explorations*, ed. Carol J. Adams and Josephine Donovan (pp. 192–212). Durham, NC: Duke University Press.

Glaberson, William. (1999). "Legal pioneers seek to raise lowly status of animals." *New York Times* (August 18):A1, A16.

Gould, Stephen Jay. (1999). "The human difference." *New York Times* (July 2):A19.

Herring, Hubert B. (1999). "Getting out the vote in 90210." *New York Times* (May 16):D2.

Irvine, Leslie. (2002). "Rethinking the human/animal boundary: The historical role of pets in the construction of social class." Paper presented at the annual meeting of the American Sociological Association, August 17, Chicago.

Kappeler, Susanne. (1995). "Speciesism, racism, and nationalism . . . or the power of scientific subjectivity," in *Animals and women: Feminist theoretical explorations*, ed. Carol J. Adams and Josephine Donovan (pp. 320–52). Durham, NC: Duke University Press.

Lopez, Barry Holstun. (1978). *Of wolves and men.* New York: Scribners.

Lyall, Sarah. (1998). "Set England's minks free! Oops. That's killing them." *New York Times* (October 15):A12.

Mills, Nicolaus. (1997). *The triumph of meanness: America's war against its better self.* New York: Houghton Mifflin.

New York Times. (1999a). "Oregon bans hunting on exotic-game farms." *New York Times* (April 25):A22.

———. (1999b). "Nine plead guilty in bird killings." *New York Times* (April 9):A21.

———. (2001). "Man gets three-year term for dog's death." *New York Times* (July 14):A12.

Nibert, David. (2002). *Animal rights/human rights: Entanglements of oppression and liberation.* Lanham, MD: Rowman & Littlefield.

Pluhar, Evelyn B. (1995). *Beyond prejudice: The moral significance of human and nonhuman animals.* Durham, NC: Duke University Press.

Rachels, James. (1990). *Created from animals.* Oxford: Oxford University Press.

Singer, Peter. (1990). *Animal liberation.* New York: Random House.

Sink, Mindy. (1998). "Coyote hunt splits animal advocates and ranchers." *New York Times* (November 16):A14.

Wade, Nicholas. (1998). "Study suggests monkeys have ability to think." *New York Times* (October 23):A14.

West, Debra. (1999). "One person's hunt, another's slaughter: Guaranteed-kill ranches thrive, but opponents want them banned." *New York Times* (May 11): A23.

Wise, Steven M. (2000). *Rattling the cage: Toward legal rights for animals.* Cambridge, MA: Perseus Books.

CHAPTER EIGHTEEN

The Exploitation, Victimization, and Unique Vulnerabilities of Native Americans

COURTNEY C. PETERSEN

When told no alternative remained to them as a nation but death or removal, they seemed not to hesitate saying, "It is death anyhow. We may as well die here."

—**Unknown**

THERE HAS BEEN A LONG HISTORY of oppression toward Native Americans. As we look back, Native Americans have had to endure a number of social, political, and medical problems not limited to the introduction of fatal diseases by the Europeans, removal and relocation, warfare and genocide, the breakdown of culture through the forced application of European influences and traditions, the destruction of the environment, and the decrease in fertility as a result of disease, forced migrations, and intermixture with Europeans (Lester 1999).

Native Americans are of interest to study for a number of reasons (Nielsen 1996a, 12). First, they have special historical and political status in this country. Second, the United States has an ideal of equality of opportunity and justice, but the history of Native Americans, in addition to the past and present conditions of this population's lives, is a complete contradiction to this idea. Third, Native Americans have a special legal status, with its own body of law. Further, they are the only minority group specifically mentioned in the U.S. Constitution. Fourth, Native American cultures are historically different from European cultures and thus have resulted in an innovative criminal-justice system from which the dominant society could learn a great deal. Finally, Native Americans are overrepresented within the criminal-justice system in the United States.

Native Americans remain a generally invisible population in the study of crime. For example, Young (1990) surveyed 12 introductory crime-justice textbooks used in the late 1980s and found no mention of crime concerning Native Americans. Much of the research on minorities in criminal justice tends to focus on African Americans, while other minority groups are designated as "other." Native Americans are deserving of attention because they provide both opportunities to test the adequacy of current criminological theories and current intervention strategies used to reduce and prevent criminal behavior.

The current treatise will examine the criminal behavior of Native Americans to show that Native Americans are disproportionately represented within the criminal-justice system. It will also be shown that the crime rate of this population is due to special social and personal conditions experienced by Native Americans. In order to critically explore criminal behavior and its possible causes, this chapter will include a number of sections. Section 1 will provide a context in which to place Native American crime and criminal-justice involvement through a brief examination of the plight of the Native American population in history. Section 2 will ascertain and discuss the rates of Native American victimization, in addition to crime and incarceration rates for youth and adults. Section 3 will examine the implications of the findings and discuss the possible root-causes for crime using three data sets. Finally, Section 4 will examine the policy implications as a result of the disproportionate arrest and confinement of Native Americans in relation to these risk factors.

SOCIAL AND HISTORICAL CONTEXT

The arrival of Europeans in North America severely damaged the culture, economic systems, and social structures of Native Americans (Nielsen 1996a). Some changes, such as those involving culture, law, and politics, were caused by intentional governmental policy. However, these changes did not happen rapidly, but rather were more gradual due to the differential rate of European settlement within the United States (Nielsen 1996a, 13).

Europeans used ideologies based on Social Darwinism and paternalism to justify their treatment of Native Americans (Nielsen 1996a). More specifically, Europeans felt that they had the right to impose their own culture, economy, laws, and religion upon any "inferior" person (Nielsen 1996a, 14). For example, Native Americans were expected to give up their land, children, beliefs, and, in some cases, their lives. Laws were passed that forbade the practice of ceremonies, and children were taken from families and placed in boarding schools, often referred to as "Indian Schools," run by Europeans to assimilate the children into the dominate culture (Nielsen 1996a). In addition, reservations were created to protect Native people from both whites and also from themselves. Finally, Native American women were subject to forced sterilization in order to prevent the continued propagation of "savages" (Glauner 2002).

After the Revolutionary War, the U.S. government was left with the "Indian Problem" (Glauner 2002). This problem dealt with the Native American lands that were deemed desirable to the settlers. The government concluded that the best course of action was to remove the Native American nations from the east to the west, moving them from their sacred lands to the foreign lands west of the Mississippi (Glauner 2002, 930). Native Americans attempted to fight the government based on the constitutional decree that "once treaties are ratified they are the supreme law of the land" (Glauner 2002). They held that if these treaties were the supreme law, the government must recognize the past treaties granting Native Americans specific rights to the land they possessed (Jackson 1995). The Native Americans also referred to a Congressional Act called the Northwest Ordinance,[1] passed in 1787, which stated that "Land and property shall never be taken from [Native Americans] without their consent and, in their property, rights, and liberty, they shall never be invaded or disturbed, unless in just and lawful wars authorized by Congress." The government claimed that as discoverers of the new land, their rights superseded those of the Native Americans.[2] It was at this point that the United States began breaking treaties and taking Native American lands until the passing of the Indian Removal Act of 1830.

The Indian Removal Act of 1830 provided the legal basis for the isolation of tribes to reservations (Lester 1999). As the Anglo population continued to travel westward, the tribes west of the Mississippi were forced to give up much of the land that had been granted to them by the government. One basis for taking the land was John Locke's theory that man's right to land stems solely from his use of it; the government reasoned that Native Americans lost all rights to the land because they had failed to cultivate it (Glauner 2002). The reservations they received in exchange were often placed on land that had few natural resources and were long distances from urban areas. One of the strongest illustrations of the result of the Indian Removal Act was the "Trail of Tears."

The Major Crimes Act of 1885 provided federal jurisdiction over seven crimes committed by Indians in Indian country, including murder, manslaughter, rape, assault with intent to kill, arson, burglary, and larceny (Snyder-Joy 1996). Indians became less able to define and enforce criminal law, while the federal jurisdiction over Indian country was expanded to also include some state authority. The Dawes Act of 1887 then forced Native American to assimilate by permitting the land controlled by the Native Americans to be split into small parcels and given to individual Native Americans with the aim of turning them into ranchers and farmers (Lester 1999). Other land that had been decreed to Native Americans was sold to whites. In 1953, Public Law 280 granted some states (California, Minnesota, Nebraska, Oregon, and Wisconsin) criminal and civil jurisdiction over Indian lands, while providing that any state that wished to gain jurisdiction over tribes could do so by state law or by amending their state constitution (Snyder-Joy 1996, 41). In other words, states could gain jurisdiction over Native American lands without the consent of the tribe.

In 1934, Congress passed the Indian Reorganization Act, which was intended to loosen the grip of the federal government on the management of internal affairs on Indian reservations (Vicenti 1995). The Act allowed a tribe to organize under two different forms of government: section 16 allowed tribes to adopt a constitution that governed the newly organized tribe, while section 17 provided that the tribe could organize a business committee to manage the tribe's affairs. Many tribes did not take advantage of either section, choosing to accept mandates of federal law.

In 1953, legislation was passed to remove reservations from their status as independent political entities. The goal was to start employment and relocation programs to encourage Native Americans to leave reservations and move to other parts of the country (Lester 1999). After the passing of this legislation, the proportion of Native Americans living on reservations declined from roughly 50 percent to about 25 percent in 1980 (Lester 1999, 7). In addition, the growth of Native Americans in urban areas grew from about 10 percent in 1930 to about 48 percent in 1970 (Gundlach, Reid, & Roberts 1977). The possible consequences of this urbanization have been declining birth rates, more intermarriage with non-Native races, and reduced tribal cultural practices (Lester 1999). For example, in 1980, over half of all Native Americans were married to non-Native Americans, compared to about 1 percent of whites and 2 percent of African Americans who married outside of their races (Lester 1999, 9).

The Major Crime Act of 1885 was modified in 1968 with the passing of the Indian Civil Rights Act of 1968 (ICRA), which amended Public Law 280 to include that Indians must vote to approve the extension of state civil and criminal jurisdiction (Snyder-Joy 1996). In addition, the ICRA extended most of the provision of the Bill of Rights to Indian tribes. However, many Indian people view the passage of this act as bringing about the demise of traditional Native American values and practices (Vicenti 1995).

The Supreme Court has substantially narrowed the authority of Indian tribes to maintain jurisdiction over many criminal-justice activities within their communities (Snyder-Joy 1996). Although an examination of all cases that have defined and redefined criminal laws and jurisdiction is beyond the scope of this chapter, it is important to briefly examine some general findings that have impacted the Native American people. In 1832, the Supreme Court decided that state laws were not enforceable in Indian Country.[3] It would appear from this ruling that a precedent was set for federal Indian policy. However, the expansion of settlers west of the Mississippi only increased the effort to dislocate Native Americans. This expansion, combined with the federal encroachment into Native American land, only established stronger government control over Native land (Snyder-Joy 1996).

In the 1955 case of *Tee-Hit-Ton Indians v. United States*,[4] the Supreme Court held that the United State may lawfully take the land and other property of Indian and Alaskan Native tribes without due process and without compensation. This is due to a lack of federal statute recognizing the right to unrestricted possession, occupancy, and use of the land.[5] In addition, the United States can extinguish, at will, the legal existence of any tribe or tribal government. In essence, the Court has ruled that Congress has plenary power over Indian tribes (Coulter 2001).

In 1978, *Oliphant v. Suquamish Indian Tribe*[6] held that due to a tribe's domestic, dependant status, Native American government does not have jurisdiction over non-Indians unless such power is granted by Congress. Finally, in 1990, *Duro v. Reina*[7] held that a tribal reservation does not have jurisdiction over nonmember Indians by holding that there was such diversity among tribal social and cultural structures that the assumption should not be made that all tribes are alike. Justices William Brennan and Thurgood Marshall, in their dissent, criticized the Court's opinion, holding that the Court created a jurisdictional void in which neither federal nor tribal jurisdiction exists over nonmember Indians who commit minor crimes against another Indian.[8]

In response to the *Duro* decision, Congress passed Public Law 102-137 to legislatively reinstate the power of Indian tribes to exercise criminal jurisdiction over non-Indians (Snyder-Joy 1996). In general, it appeared that the Supreme Court was employing contradictory approaches to Indian issues and ignoring mandates of Congress. However, the conflict between the Congressional legislation and Supreme Court decisions such as *Duro* resulted in even more anxiety about the future of federal Indian law. And of even more concern is the resulting complexity that exists for criminal and civil jurisdiction on Native American lands (see appendix A at the end of this chapter).

At no time has the U.S. government issued a comprehensive, official acknowledgment or apology for transgressions committed against Native Americans by citizens and government officials (Weston 2001). Disputes to the facts continue, with those who defend the repression and annihilation of Native Americans due to ruthless attacks by "blood-thirsty savages" against "innocent settlers" who were forced to use violence to defend themselves and their families (Weston 2001, 1042). And throughout the country, we continue to see monuments and statues that praise the heroism of settlers against the "savages." It is clear that the effects of past abuses of human rights continue to both oppress and marginalize Native American people.

AN EXAMINATION OF NATIVE AMERICANS AND CRIME

This section will examine Native American involvement in crime. This will include an assessment of victimization rates of Native Americans in addition to the arrest and incarceration rates of both youth and adults in jails and prisons. Native Americans, based on the 1998 Census, account for approximately 1 percent of the U.S. population (2,357,000 persons). Native Americans include Alaska Natives, Aleuts, and American Indians.

Victimization

According to the National Crime Victimization Survey (NCVS), American Indians have higher per capita rates of violent victimization than whites, blacks, or Asians in the United States (Greenfeld & Smith 1999). For example, from 1992 to 1996, there were approximately 124 violent victimizations per 1,000 persons age 12 and older (p. 2). In comparison, African-American victimization rates are 61 and whites are 49, with all races having a rate of about 50 per thousand persons. Violent crime rates among American Indian males were 153 per 1,000 males, with rates for females reported at 98 per 1,000 (p. 4). In general, American Indians are overrepresented among victims of violent crime compared to their share of the general population (Greenfeld & Smith 1999).

Violent crime victimization rates were highest among American Indians living in urban areas (207 per 1,000), with the lowest rates for those in rural areas (89 per 1,000) (Greenfeld & Smith 1999, 5). In addition, the highest rates of victimization occurred in the 18–24 age range, with 232 per 1,000 persons age 12 and older, with about 52 percent of violent crimes committed against American Indians occurring among this age group.

The relationship between the offender and victim is important to analyze. Strangers were reported to have committed 46 percent of the violent crimes against American Indians (Greenfeld & Smith 1999, 6). In addition, over half of all crime involved offenders with whom the victim had a prior relationship: 15 percent committed by intimates and family members, and 38 percent committed by an acquaintance. The race of the offender also has an impact on victimization of American Indians: approximately 60 percent of American Indians reported that their victimizer was white, while 30 percent were likely to have been other American Indians; only 10 percent were reported as being black (Greenfeld & Smith 1999, 7).

For murder in particular, there are about 150 American Indians murdered each year, with rates proportionate to their population (Greenfeld & Smith 1999, 19). Approximately 13 percent were killed during a brawl involving alcohol or drugs (p. 21). Moreover, about 45 percent were victims killed during an argument. In almost 57 percent of the cases, the race of the murderer was American Indian, with 84 percent of the cases having a victim and an offender with a prior relationship (p. 22). In general, the murder rate among Native Americans is seven per 100,000, which is simi-

Table 18.1

Number of Arrests per 100,000 Population

	ALL AGES		YOUTH	
	All races	*Native Americans*	*All races*	*Native Americans*
TOTAL VIOLENT	**275**	**291**	**445**	**294**
murder	7	7	9	5
rape	13	16	19	14
robbery	59	37	165	67
aggravated assault	197	231	252	208
TOTAL PROPERTY	**1,039**	**1,369**	**2,783**	**3,026**
TOTAL ALCOHOL VIOLATIONS	**1,079**	**2,545**	**649**	**1,341**
driving under the influence	553	1,069	61	98
liquor laws	255	727	510	1,108
drunkenness	271	749	78	135

lar to that found in the general population. It is important to note that murder rates of Native Americans are dropping at similar rates to the murder rates of other populations throughout the country.

Arrests

It is rarely acknowledged that Native American prisoners are the largest group per capita for growth in the prison population (Lindesmith Center 2002). Native Americans appear to have high rates of arrest for certain types of crimes. For example, the rate of arrest for alcohol violations, including DUI, liquor-law violations, and public drunkenness were more than double the national rate (Greenfeld & Smith 1999, 25) (see table 18.1). Crime among Native Americans has been found to differ from the general population, while other figures show a remarkable similarity. For example, the following highlights findings from a Bureau of Justice Statistics report on American Indians and crime (Greenfeld & Smith 1999):

- Native American arrest rates for violence were about the same as the rates among white youth in 1996.
- The 1997 arrest rate for Native Americans for alcohol-related offenses was more than double that found among all races.
- There are fewer Native Americans than blacks, but more than whites, under correctional supervision at any given time.
- About 1,000 out of every 100,000 adult Native Americans are held in jail—the highest rate of any racial group.

- On a per capita rate, Native Americans have a rate of prison incarceration that is about 38 percent higher than the national average.

These previous statistics provide a background within which an examination of Native American crime can take place. These previous points are quite telling in terms of the troubles that Native Americans face. The following section will examine the arrest and incarceration of both Native American youth and adults.

Native American Youth. Native American youth are growing up without support and with limited opportunities. For example, it was estimated that approximately 43 percent of the Native American population is under the age of 20 (Coalition for Juvenile Justice 2000). The result is that many of them are not progressing well due to a lack of positive role models, poor health and social services, failing schools, and a lack of youth social and treatment programs. In addition, Native American youth are not protected by the U.S. Constitutional protection against double jeopardy; these youth can be tried for the same offense in tribal and state or federal court (Coalition for Juvenile Justice 2000).

Native American youth have been found to be overrepresented in the juvenile-justice system. For example, Native American youth are 1 percent of the U.S. population aged 10 to 17, but they comprise 2 percent of total juvenile arrests for larceny-theft (Coalition for Juvenile Justice 2000). Although the difference between 1 and 2 percent appears miniscule when thought of in terms of percentages, it still means that Native American youth are arrested twice as often as statistically they should be. Table 18.2 presents arrest data for juveniles in 1998 by race of the offender (adapted from Office of Juvenile Justice and Delinquency Prevention [1999a] and Federal Bureau of Investigation [1999]). The overrepresentation of African-American youth is quite clear. Arrests rates for Native American youth show less disproportionality. However, Native American youth are clearly overrepresented for the crime of murder and for offenses that involve alcohol.

The actual sentencing of Native American youth to residential placement shows a similar story. For example, in 1997, Native American youth comprised approximately 1 percent of the general population of youth, yet they accounted for 2 percent of youth actually placed in a public or private facility (Office of Juvenile Justice and Delinquency Prevention 1999b). In general, minority youth are overrepresented in residential placement for all offense types, comprising approximately 63 percent of all youth in residential placement in 1997. Table 18.3 presents the racial proportions of youth in residential placement (adapted from Office of Juvenile Justice and Delinquency Prevention [1999b]).

It may be more useful to examine the residential custody rates per 100,000 youth. Nationally, in 1997, there were 204 white youth in custody

Table 18.2

Juvenile Arrests in 1998 by Race

Most serious offense charged	*Estimated number of juvenile arrests*	PERCENT OF TOTAL ARRESTS *White (79)**	*African American (15)**	*Native American (1)**
VIOLENT CRIME INDEX	**112,200**	**55%**	**42%**	**1%**
murder	2,100	47	49	3
rape	5,300	59	39	1
robbery	32,500	43	54	1
aggravated assault	72,300	61	37	1
PROPERTY CRIME INDEX	**596,100**	**70**	**27**	**1**
burglary	116,000	73	24	1
larceny-theft	417,100	70	26	1
motor vehicle theft	54,100	61	36	1
arson	9,000	80	18	1
NONINDEX	**1,895,000**	**73**	**25**	**1**
driving under the influence	21,000	91	6	2
liquor laws	157,300	92	5	3
drunkenness	24,600	89	7	3

Note: *Proportion of youth in general population.

Table 18.3

Proportion of Juveniles in Residential Placement in 1997 by Offense Type

Most serious offense	*White*	*African American*	*Latino*	*Native American*
TOTAL JUVENILES IN RESIDENTIAL PLACEMENT	**37%**	**40%**	**18%**	**2%**
person	31	43	21	1
property	43	35	17	2
drug	23	56	19	1
public order	38	38	20	2
technical violation	40	37	19	2
violent crime index	27	45	23	1
property crime index	43	35	17	2
status offense	59	30	7	2

Table 18.4

Residential Custody Rates by Race and State, 1997

	CUSTODY RATE (PER 100,000)			
State	*White*	*African American*	*Latino*	*Native American*
U.S. TOTAL	**204**	**1,018**	**515**	**525**
Alaska	289	1,055	372	734
Arizona	244	975	515	214
Idaho	139	—	160	330
Iowa	239	2,250	736	1,700
Minnesota	155	1,676	515	1,690
Montana	221	—	768	524
Nebraska	234	1,754	716	1,417
Nevada	382	942	448	1,250
New Mexico	169	905	498	220
New York	152	886	394	603
North Dakota	261	—	391	1,203
Oregon	326	1,505	681	1,046
South Dakota	356	—	2,401	1,204
Washington	246	1,592	520	787
Wyoming	454	—	846	1,243

for every 100,000 youth in the population, compared to 1,018 African-American youth, 515 Latino youth, and 525 Native American youth. But the disparity becomes even more clear upon the examination of placement rates for specific states with larger Native American populations (see table 18.4, adapted from Office of Juvenile Justice and Delinquency Prevention [1999b]). The proportions of Native American youth in custody are clearly disproportionate and even eclipse the custody rates for African-American and Latino youth in some states.

The waiver of youth to adult court or the exclusion of certain crimes from juvenile court has also resulted in a number of minority youth being placed in adult prisons. An examination of the number of new youth commitments to adult prison uncovers a very clear pattern. Table 18.5 reveals the overrepresentation of minority youth, including Native Americans, and the underrepresentation of white youth in almost every state reporting data on admissions to prison (adapted from Poe-Yamagata and Jones [2000]).

The implications for the arrest and placement of Native American youth are disheartening. Youth who commit their crimes on the reservations can be subject to federal prosecution (Coalition for Juvenile Justice 2000). However, the federal government does not own or operate any juve-

Table 18.5

New Prison Commitments, 1996

Most serious offense	*White*	*African American*	*Latino*	*Native American*
Arkansas	41%	59%	0%	0%
population	75	21	2	1
California	11%	38%	50%	1%
youth authority	9	29	49	1
population	42	7	40	1
Colorado	25%	26%	46%	2%
population	73	5	19	1
Minnesota	48%	37%	4%	11%
population	88	4	2	2
Missouri	48%	51%	0%	1%
population	82	14	2	0
Nebraska	33%	27%	23%	17%
population	87	5	6	1
Nevada	31%	28%	33%	6%
population	66	8	20	2
North Carolina	22%	74%	1%	3%
population	67	27	3	2
North Dakota	40%	0%	20%	40%
population	89	1	1	8
Oklahoma	33%	33%	7%	27%
population	74	10	5	10
Oregon	64%	12%	16%	1%
population	84	2	9	2
South Dakota	45%	9%	0%	45%
population	84	1	1	13
Utah	23%	9%	50%	9%
population	88	1	7	2
Washington	48%	22%	19%	2%
population	79	4	9	2
Wisconsin	31%	56%	7%	5%
population	85	8	4	1

nile-detention facilities; the result is that youth are often shipped to public and private facilities hundreds of miles from their homes (Coalition of Juvenile Justice 2000, 11). Contact with family is often limited and the result can be frightening. The cumulative disadvantages minorities, and Native Americans in particular face will continue to spiral as states continue to pass more punitive laws affecting youth.

Native American Adults. Native Americans aged 18 and older comprise approximately 1 percent of the general population. In 2001, there were 119,281 arrests of Native Americans in the United States (Federal Bureau of Investigation 2002, 252), representing approximately 1.3 percent of all arrests. Of those arrests, there were 11,046 made for liquor-law violations, representing 2.7 percent of all arrests for this crime. In addition, there were 9,703 arrests for drunkenness, representing 2.3 percent of arrests of Native Americans. In an examination of arrests in cities, Native Americans again represented 1.3 percent of all arrests: 2.9 percent of arrests for liquor-law violations, and 2.3 percent of arrests for drunkenness. A small yet significant disproportionate arrest pattern is visible in arrests for rural areas, where Native Americans make up approximately 2.5 percent of all arrests: 3.8 percent of arrests for drunkenness, 5.7 percent of arrests for vagrancy, and 3.6 percent of arrests for murder/nonnegligent manslaughter and aggravated assault (Federal Bureau of Investigation 2002, 270, 279).

On average, there are annually about 9,000 felony convictions in states courts, with Native Americans accounting for just over one-half of 1 percent (0.6 percent) of felony convictions across the nation (Greenfeld & Smith 1999, 25). More specifically, in 1996, there were an estimated 7,000 felony convictions of Native Americans, a rate of approximately one felony conviction for every 200 Native Americans aged 18 and older. In comparison, among blacks the rate is about one for every 51 adults, while rates for whites are about one per 300 (Greenfeld & Smith 1999, 25).

In 1997, there were 1,126 federal district court cases against Native Americans (Greenfeld & Smith 1999). Almost half of these cases involved a violent crime (see table 18.6, adapted from Greenfeld and Smith [1999, 30]). The majority of these cases were filed in South Dakota, Arizona, New Mexico, and Montana. Federal court cases clearly show that Native Americans are overrepresented in violent and property offenses, although they are consistently charged less for drug offenses.

Native Americans comprised almost 3 percent of the persons in local jails nationwide (Greenfeld & Smith 1999). In addition, they accounted for

Table 18.6

Types of Offenses Charged in Federal Court, 1997

Type of offense	*All cases*	*Native American cases*
Violent	7%	48%
Fraud	18	9
Property	5	13
Drugs	40	15
Regulatory	3	2
Other	27	14

Table 18.7

Native Americans in Jail by Offense and Status, 1996

	UNCONVICTED JAIL INMATES		CONVICTED JAIL INMATES	
Offense	*All races*	*Native Americans*	*All races*	*Native Americans*
VIOLENT OFFENSES	**37%**	**27%**	**22%**	**22%**
homicide	7	3	2	.2
sexual assault	4	—	3	7
robbery	9	2	6	8
assault	15	16	10	10
other	2	6	2	2
PROPERTY OFFENSES	**26%**	**27%**	**29%**	**27%**
burglary	8	12	8	8
larceny	6	2	10	6
motor vehicle theft	3	7	2	5
other	9	6	9	8
DRUG OFFENSES	**20%**	**7%**	**24%**	**16%**
PUBLIC-ORDER OFFENSES	**17%**	**40%**	**26%**	**35%**
weapons	2	8	2	1
driving while intoxicated	4	14	10	13
other	12	18	14	22

2.5 percent of those offenders who had not been convicted of crimes, and 3 percent of those serving shorter sentences or awaiting transfer to other institutions. When the statuses of conviction are combined, Native Americans are less likely to be jailed for a violent or drug offense (see table 18.7, adapted from Greenfeld and Smith [1999, 28]). However, it is clear that Native Americans are more likely to be in jail, charged with or convicted of offenses involving driving while intoxicated. In 1996, Native Americans accounted for an estimated 10 percent of unconvicted jail inmates charged with DWI, and just over 4 percent of convicted DWI offenders (Greenfeld & Smith 1999).

The correctional population in 1997 shows that Native Americans accounted for about 1 percent of the more than 5.7 million adults under the correctional care, custody, or control (see table 18.8, adapted from Greenfeld and Smith [1999, 26]). This compares to about 2 percent of white and 10 percent of black adults under correctional supervision.

In addition, in 1997, just under half of the Native American offenders under the care, custody, and control of the department of corrections were confined to prisons or jails (Greenfeld & Smith 1999, 27). In contrast,

Table 18.8

Correctional Population by Race and Status, 1997

	White	*African American*	*Native American*
Probation	67%	32%	1%
Local jails	53	43	3
State prisons	43	55	1
Federal prisons	60	37	2
Parole	53	46	1

less than one-third of correctional populations nationwide were confined in prisons or jails (figure 18.1). For example, among the nationwide criminal-justice population, approximately 57 percent were on probation, 12 percent on parole, and 32 percent were being held in prisons or jails. One conclusion that could be drawn is that Native Americans adults are discriminated against concerning placement in correctional facilities rather than the use of alternative means such as probation and parole. However, without further information, this can only be implied from the data.

The following question remains: "Are Native Americans discriminated against in the criminal-justice system?" As with research on discrimination of African Americans, the research is not always conclusive. It has been shown that Native Americans are in prisons with higher frequency than their proportion in the general population, and that they have higher arrest rates for some crimes. In general, some reports have found discrimination (Lundman 1974; Hall & Simkus 1975; Hood & Lin 1993; Wordes & Bynum

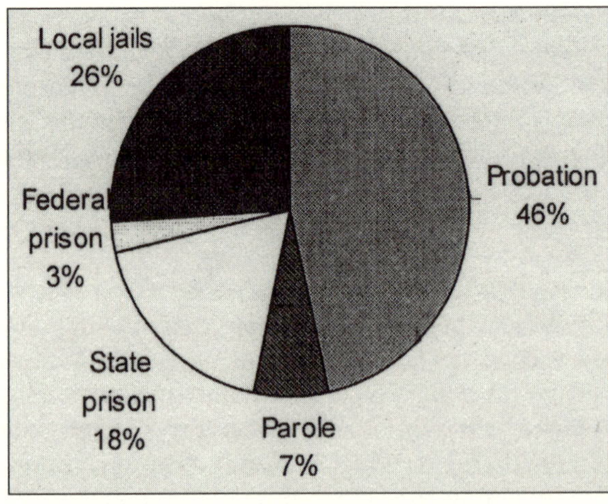

Figure 18.1 Native Americans in the correctional population.

1995), while other reports have also found reverse discrimination (Leiber 1994; Feimer, Pommersheim, & Wise 1990), mixed results (Bynum & Paternoster 1984; Alvarez & Bachman 1996; Feld 1995), or no differences (Pommersheim & Wise 1989; Hutton, Pommersheim, & Feimer 1989).

It is clear that further investigation needs to be done to assess discrimination at different points in the criminal-justice system. However, it may be concluded that any discrimination faced by Native Americans varies greatly from region to region (Lester 1999). This may be dependent upon the population of Native Americans within the region. However, the treatment of any group within the criminal-justice system should *not* vary upon the region where the crime is committed. In addition, particularly when speaking of Native Americans, the kind of jurisdiction and punishment should *not* be dependent upon the Native American or non-Native America status of the offender or victim.

An Evaluation of Special Issues for Native Americans

In 1998, there were approximately 2,357,000 Native Americans in the United States residing in about 550 federally recognized tribes (Siedschlaw & Gilbert 2000). Unemployment, assaultive crime, substance abuse, and child abuse within Indian reservations all occur far out of proportion to non-Indian populations (p. 137). The process of colonization has led to Native Americans being marginalized; they have been placed at the economic and political edges of society. For example, Native Americans only received the right to vote in national elections in the United States in 1920 (Nielsen 1996a). Economically, about 23 percent of Native Americans live below the poverty line, compared to 7 percent of whites and 26.5 percent of African Americans (p. 16). In addition, 17 percent of Native American men are unemployed, and they are less likely to finish school and more likely to work in lower-income jobs such as manual labor.

The following section will examine risk factors for Native Americans using data from the Bureau of Justice Statistics' "Survey of Inmates of Local Jails, 1996" and "Survey of Inmates in State and Federal Correctional Facilities, 1997" (see appendix B at the end of this chapter for descriptions of data sets) and the general literature on Native Americans and crime.

The American Criminal-Justice System

Native Americans who commit their crimes off of the reservation face serious legal problems. For example, Native Americans who are tried off of the reservation are rarely tried by juries with any Native Americans members and thus are not tried by their "peers" (Mann 1993). In addition, there are rarely any Native American defense counselors available to defend them, and rarely are there any Native American judges in the court system (Lester 1999).

Opposing Value Concepts

The Native American culture has been found to be diametrically opposed to the Euro-American culture. For example, among Native Americans, the concepts of "community," "family," and "self" are held in that order of importance. However, among Euro-Americans, the order is "self," "family," and "community" (Siedschlaw & Gilbert 2000, 143). Native Americans emphasize faith, reason, and logic, while Euro-Americans value logic, reason, and finally faith. The concept of *freedom* also poses value conflicts. Native Americans contribute the meaning of life through obligations and responsibilities at home, while Euro-Americans strive to be free and independent from others (Siedschlaw & Gilbert 2000, 144).

These differences in values have an impact in how each group will function in the community and how each will generate institutions, structures, and codes to foster and maintain harmony and well-being (Dumont 1996). This includes unique modes of decision-making and the enforcement of rules. Native Americans are driven by their inner conscience to respect the same in others, with the goal being the common good. These values will shape behavior and may cause conflict, as the Native American is forced to adapt his behavior to the expectations of the dominant culture.

Influence from the Dominant Society

"Influence from non-Indian cultures, lifestyles, and negative peer influence has diminished the authority of parents to discipline their children, provide guidance, and instill the cultural values, lifestyle, and traditions of their tribal communities" (NVAA 1999, 14). As more Native Americans move off the reservation, families break down and the communal lifestyle is slowly replaced with more individualized ways of life. Native Americans, particularly youth, may have a lack of heritage identification that can contribute to low self-esteem and negative Indian identities, making them more vulnerable to engaging in criminal behavior (NVAA 1999).

Poverty

While 26 percent of whites are low income,[9] the rate is 49 percent for blacks and 54 percent for Native Americans (Staveteig & Wigton 2000). In addition, across income levels, Native Americans are twice as likely as whites to report housing hardship, measured by asking adults whether they had been unable to pay the rent, mortgage, or utility bills during the previous year (Staveteig & Wigton 2000). In addition, approximately two-thirds of all rural Indians live in houses without running water.

Native American communities are usually located in rural areas that are geographically isolated (NVAA 1999). This limits the resources, including employment opportunities, which come into the community. However, many Native Americans lack both the financial and family resources to leave their community. For example, a Bureau of Indian Affairs (1974) report found that in 1970, the average per capita annual income for rural

Table 18.9

Inmate's Parent or Guardian Abused Alcohol or Drugs

	Jail	*Federal prison*	*State prison*
White	35	36	20
African American	26	28	21
Native American	46	38	36

Indians was $1,140, compared to $2,108 for urban Indians. Both figures are well below the poverty level.

Family Structure

Approximately 33 percent of Native American children live in one-parent families (Staveteig & Wigton 2000). Data from jail and prison surveys confirm the high number of offenders who grew up in one-parent families. For example, 29 percent of state prison inmates, 45 percent of jail inmates, and 38 percent of federal prison inmates lived with their mother only. In addition, many inmates were raised by grandparents (17 percent of state inmates, 7 percent of jail inmates, and 10 percent of federal inmates). In addition to growing up in a single-parent home, Native Americans had high rates of having a parent or guardian who abused alcohol or drugs (table 18.9). Across all offenders, Native Americans were more likely to have a substance-abusing parent or guardian. In addition, approximately half of Native American offenders report having an immediate family member who was incarcerated.

Native Americans are unique in another sense: they are large because they are often comprised of more than the traditional family members; the immediate family also includes grandparents, aunts, uncles, and cousins (NVAA 1999). Although a large family can provide support, care, shared responsibility for children, and pass on traditions, the entire family can be rendered dysfunctional due to the effects of child maltreatment, substance abuse, and poverty (p. 11).

Physical and Sexual Abuse

"Child abuse and neglect are clear manifestations of family dysfunction in Indian Country and are often a prelude to Native American juvenile delinquency" (Armstrong, Guilfoyle, & Melton 1996, 87). There is no definitive research to determine the extent of child abuse and neglect within Native American populations or any correlates between abuse and other forms of delinquent behavior. However, it appears from jail and prison data that both physical and sexual abuse are a part of the history of inmates (table 18.10).

Table 18.10

Inmates Reporting Physical- and Sexual-Abuse Histories

	PHYSICAL ABUSE		SEXUAL ABUSE	
Inmates	*Federal prison*	*State prison*	*Federal prison*	*State prison*
White	20%	9%	10%	4%
African American	11	6	6	3
Native American	18	15	7	5

Education and Employment

Difficulties in adjustment to educational settings have contributed to the high dropout rate of Indian students (Latham 1985). Native American youth may have difficulty in coping with the contrast between the culture in which the youth was raised and the school culture in which the youth is placed (Armstrong, Guilfoyle, & Melton 1996). One risk factor in schools that can lead to isolation and adjustment problems and can later contribute to delinquency behavior is the presence of learning disorders. Data from the jail and prison surveys reveal that Native Americans (10 percent), whites (10 percent), and African Americans (9 percent) in jails and federal prisons have similar rates of learning disorders, although rates for Native Americans were much higher in state prison (11 percent), versus 6 percent for whites and 4 percent for African Americans.

It is clear from table 18.11 that state and federal inmates have comparable rates of educational attainment. This is true across race. Only about one-quarter of offenders of all races actually complete high school or attain their GED, with nearly two-thirds of offenders reporting having attended some high school. These low rates of attaining a high school diploma and very low rates of attending and completing college add to the frustration of Native Americans, because their ability to obtain employment may be dramatically decreased.

The survey of jail and prison inmates also examined employment sta-

Table 18.11

Highest Grade Completed by Prison Inmates

	SOME HIGH SCHOOL		HIGH SCHOOL DIPLOMA/GED		SOME COLLEGE OR MORE		COMPLETED COLLEGE	
Inmates	*State*	*Federal*	*State*	*Federal*	*State*	*Federal*	*State*	*Federal*
White	62%	43%	24%	27%	11%	18%	2%	5%
African American	62	46	26	33	10	16	2	3
Native American	65	50	22	35	10	14	2	1

Table 18.12

Inmates Who Were Employed Prior to Arrest

	Jail	*Federal prison*	*State prison*
White	71%	74%	75%
African American	57	63	66
Native American	55	67	71

Table 18.13

Type of Employment Prior to Arrest

	JAIL INMATES			STATE PRISONERS			FEDERAL PRISONERS		
	Full-time	*Part-time*	*Occa-sional*	*Full-time*	*Part-time*	*Occa-sional*	*Full-time*	*Part-time*	*Occa-sional*
White	81%	13%	6%	86%	10%	4%	87%	9%	3%
African American	70	21	8	77	19	4	79	18	3
Native American	80	13	7	77	14	9	81	14	5

tus prior to arrest (table 18.12). It appears that employment rates do not differ substantially among races, although white offenders in all groups were more likely to be employed prior to their current arrests. It is also important to examine if the inmates had full-time, part-time, or occasional work (table 18.13). Again, the type of employment did not vary dramatically among racial groups. It may be valuable to further examine the kinds of jobs inmates are employed in, such as low-skill or manual-labor work.

Substance Abuse

Alcohol fuels both adult and youth crime. For example, 2 percent of all juveniles nationwide arrested for both public drunkenness and driving under the influence in 1997, as well as 3 percent of all juveniles arrested for liquor-law violations, were Native Americans (Coalition for Juvenile Justice 2000). In addition, in 1996, nearly 49 percent of convicted Native American adult jail inmates reported use of alcohol at the time of their offense. If violent offenders are analyzed separately, alcohol use at the time of offense jumps to 71 percent (Greenfeld & Smith 1999, 29).

Drinking behaviors of Native Americans in jails and prisons tell a very sad story. For example, 12 percent of state inmates, 7 percent of federal inmates, and 14 percent of jail inmates began drinking alcohol before age 10. The mean age for beginning to use alcohol was lower for Native

Table 18.14

Mean Age When Inmates Began Drinking Alcohol

	Jail	Federal prison	State prison
White	15.98	16.72	15.29
African American	16.86	17.23	16.16
Native American	14.74	15.70	14.94

Americans than for other racial groups (table 18.14) in correctional facilities. Approximately 64 percent of federal inmates and 57 percent of state inmates report drinking regularly at some time in their lives. In addition, 71 percent of federal inmates, 68 percent of state inmates, and 83 percent of jail inmates drank regularly in the year prior to arrest. Native American offenders who report drinking at the time of their offense was 46 percent for federal inmates and 33 percent for state inmates. Approximately 48 percent of federal inmates and 40 percent of state inmates report that they were arrested because of drinking.

Alcohol use also plays another role in the lives of Native Americans. Approximately one in 99 Native Americans is born with Fetal Alcohol Syndrome (FAS), compared to approximately one in 500 babies born in the general population (Coalition for Juvenile Justice 2000, 13). Children with FAS can have a range of problems, including hyperactivity and erratic behavior, which can put them at risk for criminal-justice involvement. These youth may also be susceptible to being introduced to alcohol at an earlier age.

Illegal drug use also presents a risk for Native Americans. In a study of Native American youth on reservations, 54 percent of seventh to twelfth graders had used marijuana during 1988 to 1990 (Beauvais 1996). In addition, 23 percent reported some lifetime use of cocaine. Research has also shown that Native American youth have consistently higher rates of drug use, especially of marijuana (Beauvais 1996). And although drug use has been decreasing gradually since 1981, cocaine and psychadelics are increasing in this population. Illegal drug use by Native Americans in prisons and jails is very disheartening. For example, nearly 74 percent of federal inmates had used any illegal drug in their lifetime, while that number jumps to 86 percent for state inmates. In addition, 55 percent of federal inmates and 73 percent of state inmates report using illegal drugs regularly. Lastly, 61 percent of federal inmates and 44 percent of state inmates report using drugs or alcohol at the time of their offense (table 18.15). However, the arrest and incarceration rates for drug offenses by Native Americans remain relatively small.

Table 18.15

Inmates Using Drugs or Alcohol at the Time of Offense

	Federal prison	*State prison*
White	57	35
African American	47	32
Native American	61	44

Policy Implications

The relationship between the criminal-justice system and Native Americans must be critically examined. Of primary importance is finding a way through the confusion in interpreting the range of criminal-jurisdiction questions. In many cases, the various police and prosecutorial agencies leave a feeling of frustration for offenders, victims, and criminal-justice professionals. Tribal, federal, and state jurisdiction can and often do apply to a case simultaneously. This becomes even more difficult in cases where law enforcement attempts to cross reservation lines. Some tribal governments do not allow extradition of their members until complex procedures are met, while others allow for an expeditious process based upon a warrant (Martinez 2002). In some cases, however, these practices are well-known but are not always formally written. An effort must be made by both Native American and non-Native American law-enforcement agencies to be aware of jurisdiction issues to avoid the confusion. In addition, an understanding of the historical context that frames issues surrounding jurisdiction would foster both cooperation and good police practices.

A second concern for criminal justice and reporting practices is the collection of race and ethnic identity. For example, in 1997, the Bureau of Justice Statistics reported that only 1.47 percent of adult inmates in federal prison were identified as Native Americans, while only 0.85 percent of inmates in state prisons were identified as being ones (Abril 2002). However, according to the surveys conducted by the Bureau of Justice Statistics, Native Americans made up 3.3 percent of inmates in state prisons, 3 percent of inmates in local jails, and 3.7 percent of inmates in federal prisons during that same year. This may reflect intake processes at arrest or incarceration that may not allow for an accurate accounting of the Native American population. In other words, self-identification may be a more appropriate means for collecting race and ethnic data. Eliciting more detailed demographic data may provide a more accurate picture of the ethnic composition of criminal-justice populations at each stage. This data can then be used to place inmates in culturally appropriate programs or programs that take into consideration the large range of Native American cultural characteristics (Abril 2002).

Substance abuse in general, and alcohol abuse specifically, are a serious problem for Native American youth and adults. Treatment on reservations may be sparse, and there simply aren't facilities in which to house drunk Native Americans. Not only must programs evaluate the mental-health issues connected with substance use, but there must be an emphasis on treating the family, including communicating openly with family members, offering treatment options, and developing after-care plans (Coalition for Juvenile Justice 2000).

"To recognize and consider the value, quality, and spirituality of other cultures is inherent in the positive aspects of multiculturalism" (Siedschlaw & Gilbert 2000, 149). Native Americans often receive little support for local solutions because insiders and outsiders may hold the image or belief that Native American groups cannot handle their own problems. Problems within the Native American community should be viewed from the context of the tribe rather than from programs created by criminal-justice experts with no focus on specific cultural concerns (Nielsen 1996b). In addition, there must be awareness that, due to geographic location and other economic difficulties, these communities may need more focused support to incorporate long-term and comprehensive services.

It would be advantageous to adapt current reservation-based services to urban areas. As more and more Native Americans are pushed or pulled away from home communities by government relocation policies, lack of employment, politics, and violence related to drug and alcohol use, they become a forgotten minority (Nielsen 1996b). There are very few Native American–specific criminal-justice services to help overcome serious disadvantages such as language barriers, lack of knowledge about the legal system, and discrimination (p. 298). Needed services could include the creation of Native American centers as resources to help Native Americans connect with needed services, but also to provide recreational, social, and traditional cultural programs.

The lack of criminal-justice data as a result of poor or nonexistent management and collection system makes it difficult to establish the nature of crimes committed by Native Americans both on and off the reservations (NVAA 1999). Much of the current data is created by the combination of fragments of information from a wide variety of different sources. Basic information about types of crimes committed, victimization, risk and protective factors, and policy evaluation are in dire need. In addition, criminologists must examine the utility of current criminological theories for understanding criminal behavior within this population. The omission of Native Americans from this discourse must be rectified.

SUMMARY AND CONCLUSIONS

The previous treatise examined victimization, crime rates, incarceration rates, and risk factors for criminal-justice involvement of Native

Americans. Native Americans do not commit a great deal of crime, and much of the crime they do commit is related to alcohol use and abuse. However, there is a tremendous need to pay attention to this population. It is clear that based on this information, alternatives to incarceration must be found for Native Americans. Due to the criminalization of alcohol consumption and drunkenness, a large proportion of Native Americans are filling the country's jails and prisons. The use of community resources and detoxification centers may be less expensive and provide better rehabilitation than simply locking them up.

It is also quite obvious that little research has been conducted on Native American crime and its correlates. Specific areas that should be examined include a focus on risk and protective factors, the increasing formation of gangs on and off Native American reservations, substance-abuse treatment programs targeted toward this specific population, and the application of tribal court procedures within the traditional criminal-justice system. The continued treatment of Native Americans as inferior and incapable of solving their own problems must end. We must establish Native Americans as a legitimate group worthy of attention by both the government and general population.

Appendix A
Summary Table of Criminal Jurisdiction in Indian Country (NVAA 1999)

Persons involved	*Federal jurisdiction*	*Tribal jurisdiction*	*State jurisdiction*
Indian offender versus Indian victim	Major Crimes Act, the United States can prosecute 16 listed offenses. Among these, burglary, involuntary sodomy, and incest are defined and punished in accordance with the state law, all others are defined by federal statute.	Tribal courts may have concurrent jurisdiction over crimes under the Major Crimes Act. All other offenses, tribal courts have *sole* jurisdiction (except where federal statute specifically provides otherwise).	None, except under PL 280 as amended, or other federal statute or by tribal vote pursuant to 25 U.S.C. §1321. The tribe *may* retain concurrent jurisdiction.
Indian offender versus non-Indian victim	Major Crimes Act; General Crimes Act; Assimilative Crimes Act.	Tribal courts may have concurrent jurisdiction over crimes under the Major Crimes Act. They do have concurrent jurisdiction over offenses, which can be prosecuted by the United States under the General Crimes Act. Except for major crimes, tribes may preempt federal prosecution.	Same as above.

continued

Persons involved	*Federal jurisdiction*	*Tribal jurisdiction*	*State jurisdiction*
		For any other offenses (as defined by tribal codes), tribal courts have exclusive jurisdiction.	
Indian offender, victimless crime	The United States probably can prosecute under the General Crimes Act as explained above or the Assimilative Crimes Act.	Same as above.	Same as above.
Non-Indian offender versus Indian victim	General Crimes Act, plus a substantive offense defined by federal statute or a substantive offense defined by state law incorporated by the Assimilative Crimes Act.	Tribal courts have no jurisdiction to prosecute non-Indians, unless Congress delegates such power to them.	Probably no state jurisdiction except under PL 280, as amended or with tribal consent pursuant to 25 U.S.C. §1321.
Non-Indian offender versus non-Indian victim	No federal jurisdiction except for distinctly federal offenses.	Same as above.	State courts have jurisdiction over all offenses defined by state law and involving only non-Indians.
Non-Indian offender, victimless crime	General Crimes Act, plus a substantive offense defined by federal statute or a substantive offense defined by state law incorporated by the Assimilative Crimes Act. The law is still questionable whether federal jurisdiction is exclusive or concurrent with the state.	Same as above.	State courts probably have concurrent jurisdiction with the United States, although the law is unclear.

APPENDIX B
DESCRIPTION OF DATA SETS

1. *Survey of Inmates of Local Jails, 1996*

Conducted by the Bureau of the Census in conjunction with the Bureau of Justice Statistics, this collection provides nationally representative data on persons held prior to trial and on those convicted offenders serving sentences in local jails or awaiting transfer to state prisons. Data were collected on individual characteristics of jail inmates, current offenses and sentences, characteristics of victims, criminal histories, jail activities and programs, prior drug and alcohol use and treatment, and health-care services provided while in jail.

2. *Survey of Inmates in State and Federal Correctional Facilities, 1997*

Conducted by the Bureau of the Census in conjunction with the Bureau of Justice Statistics, this survey provides nationally representative data on state prison inmates and sentenced federal inmates held in federally owned and operated facilities. Through personal interviews from June through October 1997, inmates in both state and federal prisons provided information about their current offense and sentence, criminal history, family background and personal characteristics, prior drug and alcohol use and treatment programs, gun possession and use, gang membership, and prison activities, programs, and services.

NOTES

1. Stat. 50 (1787).
2. 1 Stat. 50 (1787).
3. *Worcester v. Georgia* 31 U.S. [6 Pet.] 515 (1832).
4. 348 U.S. 272 (1955).
5. 348 U.S. 272 (1955).
6. 435 U.S. 191 (1878).
7. 110 S.Ct. 2053 (1990).
8. 110 S.Ct. 2053 (1990), 2070.
9. Low income calculated by comparing family income in 1996 to the Federal poverty level in 1996. Those who fell 200 percent below the federal poverty level were considered low income.

REFERENCES

Abril, J. C. (2002). "The Native American identity phenomenon." *Corrections Compendium 27*(4):1–4.

Alvarez, A., and R. D. Bachman. (1996). "American Indians and sentencing disparity." *Journal of Criminal Justice 24*:549–61.

Armstrong, T. L., M. H. Guilfoyle, and A. P. Melton. (1996). "Native American delinquency: An overview of prevalence, causes, and correlates," in *Native Americans, crime, and justice*, ed. M. Nielsen and R. Silverman (pp. 75–95). Boulder, CO: Westview Press.

Beauvais, F. (1996). "Trends in Indian adolescent drug and alcohol use," in *Native Americans, crime, and justice*, ed. M. Nielsen and R. Silverman. Boulder, CO: Westview Press.

Bureau of Indian Affairs. (1974). *The American Indian.* Washington, DC: U.S. Department of the Interior, Government Printing Office.

Bureau of Justice Statistics. (2002). *Compendium of federal justice statistics, 2000.* Washington, DC: U.S. Department of Justice, Office of Justice Programs, Bureau of Justice Statistics.

Bynum, T. S., and R. Paternoster. (1984). "Discrimination revisited." *Sociology & Social Research 69*:90–108.

Coalition for Juvenile Justice. (2000). *Enlarging the healing circle: Ensuring justice for American Indian children.* Washington, DC: Coalition for Juvenile Justice.

Coulter, R. T. (2001). *Racial justice lawyering on behalf of Indians and other indigenous peoples.* Available at <http://www.indianlaw.org/body_racial_justice.htm>.

Dumont, J. (1996). "Justice and Native peoples," in *Native Americans, crime, and justice,* ed. M. Nielsen and R. Silverman (pp. 20–33). Boulder, CO: Westview Press.

Federal Bureau of Investigation. (1999). *Crime in the United States, 1998.* Washington, DC: Federal Bureau of Investigation.

———. (2002). *Crime in the United States, 2001.* Washington, DC: Federal Bureau of Investigation.

Feimer, S., F. Pommersheim, and S. Wise. (1990). "Marking time." *Journal of Crime and Justice 13*(1):86–102.

Feld, B. C. (1995). "The social context of juvenile justice administration," in *Minorities in juvenile justice,* ed. K. K. Leonard, C. E. Pope, and W. H. Feyerherm (pp. 66–97). Thousand Oaks, CA: Sage Publications.

Glauner, L. (2002). "The need for accountability and reparation: 1830–1976. The United States government's role in the promotion, implementation, and execution of the crime of genocide against Native Americans." *DePaul Law Review 51*:911–59.

Greenfeld, L. A., and S. K. Smith. (1999). *American Indians and crime.* Washington, DC: U.S. Department of Justice, Office of Justice Programs, Bureau of Justice Statistics.

Gundlach, J. H., P. N. Reid, and A. E. Roberts. (1977). "Migration, labor mobility, and relocation assistance." *Social Service Review 51*:464–73.

Hall, E., and A. Simkus. (1975). "Inequality in the type of sentences received by Native Americans and whites." *Criminology 13*:199–222.

Hood, D. L., and R. L. Lin. (1993). "Sentencing disparity in Yakima County." *Explorations in Ethnic Studies 16*:99–114.

Hutton, C., F. Pommersheim, and S. Feimer. (1989). "I fought the law and the law won." *New England Journal of Criminal and Civil Confinemen 15*:177–201.

Jackson, H. H. (1995). *A century of dishonor.* Norman: University of Oklahoma Press.

Leiber, M. J. (1994). "A comparison of juvenile court outcomes for Native Americans, African Americans, and whites." *Justice Quarterly 11*:257–79.

Lester, D. (ed.). (1999). *Crime and the Native American.* Springfield, IL: Charles C. Thomas.

Lindesmith Center. (2002). *The U.S. war on drugs: Political economics of a new slavery.* Available at <http://www.lindesmith.org/about/position/race_paper_econ.cfm?printpage=1>.

Lundman, R. J. (1974). "Routine police arrest practices." *Social Problems 22*:127–41.

Mann, C. R. (1993). *Unequal justice.* Indianapolis: Indiana University Press.

Martinez, L. (2002). "Policing Indian country." *Law and Order 50*(7):124–31.

Nielsen, M. (1996a). "Contextualization for Native American crime and criminal justice involvement," in *Native Americans, crime, and justice,* ed. M. Nielsen and R. Silverman (pp. 10–19). Boulder, CO: Westview Press.

———. (1996b). "Major issues in Native American involvement in the criminal justice system," in *Native Americans, crime, and justice*, ed. M. Nielsen and R. Silverman (pp. 293–302). Boulder, CO: Westview Press.

NVAA. (1999). *Specific justice systems and victims' rights*. Available at <http://www.ojp.usdoj.gov/ovc/assist/nvaa99/chap3-4.htm>.

Office of Juvenile Justice and Delinquency Prevention. (1999a). *Juvenile arrests, 1998*. Washington, DC: Office of Juvenile Justice and Delinquency Prevention.

———. (1999b). *Juvenile offenders and victims, 1999 national report*. Washington, DC: Office of Juvenile Justice and Delinquency Prevention.

Poe-Yamagata, E., and M. Jones. (2000). *And justice for some*. Washington, DC: Building Blocks for Youth.

Pommersheim, F., and S. Wise. (1989). "Going to the penitentiary." *Criminal Justice and Behavior 16*:155–65.

Siedschlaw, K., and J. N. Gilbert. (2000). "Native Americans and criminal justice," in *Multicultural perspectives in criminal justice and criminology*, ed. J. Hendricks and B. Byers (pp. 131–50). Springfield, IL: Charles C. Thomas.

Snyder-Joy, Z. K. (1996). "Self-determination and American Indian justice," in *Native Americans, crime, and justice*, ed. M. Nielsen and R. Silverman (pp. 38–45). Boulder, CO: Westview Press.

Staveteig, S., and A. Wigton. (2000). *Racial and ethnic disparities: Key findings from the National Survey of America's Families*. Washington, DC: Urban Institute.

Vicenti, C. N. (1995). "The reemergence of tribal society and traditional justice systems." *Judicature 79*(3):134–41.

Weston, R. (2001). "Facing the past, facing the future: Applying the truth commission model to the historic treatment of Native Americans in the United States." *Arizona Journal of International and Comparative Law 18*:1017–59.

Wordes, M., and T. S. Bynum. (1995). "Policing juveniles," in *Minorities in juvenile justice*, ed. K. K. Leonard, C. E. Pope, and W. H. Feyerherm (pp. 47–65). Thousand Oaks, CA: Sage Publications.

Young, T. J. (1990). "Native American crime and criminal justice require criminologists' attention." *Journal of Criminal Justice Education 1*:111–16.

CHAPTER NINETEEN

Removal of the Southwest Michigan Potawatomi

government crimes of oppression and cultural genocide

LINDA ROBYN

WHEN TWO DIFFERENT RACES OF PEOPLE come together, lives are changed; sometimes for the better, but often for the worse. The Europeans' search for lands rich in resources demonstrates such a meeting with an outcome that adversely transformed a region and people through social conflict that is still occurring today. The French who came to the Great Lakes region during the sixteenth century, followed by the British and then the American settlers, did not respect or try to understand the culture and ways of native peoples they encountered. The history that developed between Europeans and tribes from the Great Lakes region led to the perception of the Native people being an exploitable group, or disposable resource. The cultural genocide that resulted is one reason why exploitation is still occurring today.

Cultural genocide has been perpetrated against American Indian tribes since the first Europeans landed on these shores, which were also known as "Turtle Island" to many First Peoples. One of the tribes from the Great Lakes region encountered by the French, British, and American settlers is known as the Potawatomi. Removal of the Potawatomis from their home in and around the area of Kalamazoo, Michigan is one of many stories recounting the experiences of tribal people nationwide as the government appropriated Native lands in its quest for wealth and power. Although their land was not taken through force by the U.S. government as was the horrific experience of many other American Indians, this account of the removal of the Potawatomis from their homeland is an example of cultural genocide that continues to victimize American Indian people today.

During the 1960s, thousands of school-aged children visited the "pioneer room" housed inside a museum located in the Kalamazoo Public Library. Students visited the display to learn about the hard-working, industrious pioneers who settled in this region during the early-to-mid-1800s. Part of the display included a wall mural depicting a group of Indian men, also living in the area at the time, dressed in loin cloths, faces decorated with war paint, placing a canoe in the water. We were left to our own imaginations to figure out what these men were setting off to do, but the lasting impression included visions of raids on the peaceful settlers. Left out of the presentation and display was any mention of the rich and fertile land around the area of Kalamazoo that was becoming the central point of a struggle between settlers and the Potawatomis during the 1800s.

In those days, many questions were left unanswered about the Potawatomi people who lived in the area before the first settlers arrived. Stories were told from time-to-time about a large Indian population in the area who were known as the Potawatomis, but where were they now? As young students, we were also told that the name of our town, "Kalamazo," was an old Indian word translated as "land of the boiling pots," or something like that—no one knew for sure at the time. Looking in current history books and encyclopedias during the 1960s gave little clue as to who the Potawatomis were and why they left the area.

Years later, archival research for a history project began to uncover some of the mystery surrounding questions raised decades earlier. Young students were and are still being taught to this day by most teachers and history books that the United States is a model of freedom and democracy. Our country served as a beacon of light to those searching for an example of a humanitarian nation that would never dream of practicing policies of conquest and aggression toward those who lived within its boundaries. Archival research into why the Potawatomi "moved away" from the Kalamazoo area painted a much different picture of the "truth" as it was told to those of us growing up and being educated in the public school system during the 1960s.

Research conducted uncovered the reality of the crimes of genocide committed by the U.S. government against American Indian tribes since the arrival of the first Europeans. An even bigger discovery was learning that these practices are still occurring today, as Indian people are criminalized for resisting huge multinational corporations in their war of aggression against native peoples and the natural world (Churchill 1997; Deloria 1969, 1995, 1996; Fixico 1986; Gedicks 1993; Jaimes 1992; Maybury-Lewis 1997). As a student growing up and learning about our history, nothing was taught about the millions who died and were killed during forced marches in the dead of winter, starving and freezing to death under unspeakable conditions, as well as an assortment of other horrendous methods used to annihilate the indigenous people who stood in the way of progress and the ideal of Manifest Destiny.

From the highest elected officials in our land to the most humble workers, American Indian people were described as squalid savages subject to the "superior race" because of their inferiority and propensity to subsist from the forest (Diamond 1992, 308–9). Hundreds of campaigns were carried out to exterminate indigenous peoples in this country. Officers later reveled in the fact that they instructed troops attacking defenseless native communities to "kill and scalp all, little and big [because] nits make lice" (Churchill 1997, 2). Churchill writes that "body parts taken by soldiers in such slaughters remain prized possessions, discretely handed down as trophies through the generations of all too many American families" (1997, 2).

What most children learned in school was a history of conflicts falsely framed as "Indian wars" by Native people from aggressive tribes. After all, Hollywood gave the American public images and stereotypes of John Wayne protecting these good and well-meaning settlers against ruthless, blood-thirsty savages. Most students have not been taught that these "wars" were actually futile efforts to stave off thousands of "pioneers" and "peaceful settlers" who were illegally taking over Native homelands. These battles were always taught from the point of view of the conqueror, as being justified and maybe even regrettable, but never as being criminally reprehensible.

THE POTAWATOMIS AS VICTIMS

Economic advancement of the dominant culture meant that the people and region would be shaped and changed as part of colonial struggles. The Potawatomi people of southwestern Michigan were not able to escape this advancement, falsely framed as an effort to "civilize" and "Christianize" tribes throughout the United States. These hypocritical and devastating practices were seen as being well-intended by most, to create a "superior" way of existence, but in fact resulted in the virtual disappearance of this vital, thriving tribe.

Theories of Social Darwinism and the concept of Manifest Destiny gave "scientific" support and justification for the outright prejudice of European settlers and their descendants in Kalamazoo at the time toward the Potawatomi people. Based on these European notions, the Potawatomis were considered "backward" and "uncivilized." To overcome this "backwardness," the settlers felt it incumbent on themselves to help, or force, the Potawatomi to overcome this flaw and progress toward civilization. To overcome this backwardness, settlers urged the Potawatomis to accept Christianity and abandon their traditional ways of life and language, all the while hoping that they would cease to exist altogether as a society. With members of this tribe no longer embedded within their backward society, they could then assimilate into the population of the rest of the community (Maybury-Lewis 1997, 13–15). The Potawatomis were extremely loyal to the white settlers of Kalamazoo during the 1800s, but their progression toward civilization and assimilation as defined by the white settlers were slow. There were also stories of atrocities being committed by tribes in "Indian" wars close by that began filtering into the region, thus ensuring a rising tide of resentment and fear by the settlers toward the Potawatomi.

The Potawatomis were part of a great nation of people. So numerous were they, and so large a territory did they cover, that they can be separated into four distinct groups: the Ojibwa of the Lake Superior region, the Missisauga of Manitoulin Island and of the mainland around the Mississagi River, the Ottawa of the Georgian Bay region, and the Potawatomi on the west side of Lake Huron within the state of Michigan, some of whom moved across into Ontario during the eighteenth and nineteenth centuries. Three of these four tribes—the Lake Superior Ojibwa, the Ottawa, and the Potawatomi—formed a loose confederacy that became known in the eighteenth century as the "Council of the Three Fires" (Jenness 1932).

In writing about the history of Kalamazoo County in 1880, S. W. Durant states that the Ojibwas, "or as they were more commonly called, Chippewas, occupied that portion of the state of Michigan known as the upper peninsula" (Durant 1880, 74). Potawatomi tradition states that the Ottawas, Chippewas, and Potawatomis were one tribe, being part of Algonquian-speaking peoples who came to the Great Lakes region from the north and east (Edmunds 1978, 3–6). Since the Potawatomis continued to keep the "council fire" of the originally united tribes, they became known as the "Keepers of the Fire," or Fire Nation (Edmunds 1978, 3–6). It is suggested that the three tribes separated at the Straits of Mackinac no later than the sixteenth century, the Ottawas remaining at the strait, the Chippewas migrating to the north and west, and the Potawatomis moving down the eastern shore of Lake Michigan.

With the Iroquois conquest during the mid-1600s and a war of extermination by the Illinois Confederacy, the Algonquian tribes, including the Potawatomi, fled from Michigan and sought refuge in the Green Bay area and in southern Wisconsin (Edmunds 1978, 5). Then, at the beginning of the eighteenth century, they moved to the Chicago area. Soon after that they occupied the country in the valleys of the St. Joseph and Kalamazoo Rivers. When Samuel de Champlain first visited the area between Lakes Huron, Erie, and Ontario, he found the different branches of the great Huron–Ottawa nation densely populated, "their numbers being variously estimated at from 10,000 to 35,000" (Durant 1880, 74). It seems odd that such a large population could not stop the destruction of their culture that began with the arrival of Champlain. But this great nation of people did not have the means to stand up against men like Champlain who later came along with all the power and control of the U.S. government at their disposal. As a result, the Potawatomi were one of many tribes who disappeared into obscurity as part of an effort to settle a land that appeared to be largely vacant and therefore open to whomever might wish to lay claim to it.

As with other groups of people who had not developed their own states and were not considered full members of the dominant society through equal opportunities and treatment, the Potawatomis were referred to as "tribal." Because they were a "tribal" people and not an integral part of the U.S. government that ultimately ruled them, settlers laying claim to this vacant land were justified in their actions for the progress of society and the realization of Manifest Destiny. The word "tribe" is an unfortunate term used to refer to small, preindustrial societies that govern themselves without any centralized authority such as the state (Maybury-Lewis 1997, 8). Because such peoples (then and now) are considered to be alien and inferiors, indigenous or tribal peoples are among the world's most underprivileged minorities, facing constant threat of various forms of genocide (Maybury-Lewis 1997, 8).

Even though the Potawatomis did not experience extermination through physical genocide, the destruction of their way of life through cultural genocide, or as it is also referred to, "ethnocide," was advocated as necessary and appropriate for these "backward" people. As with other American Indian people across the United States, Europeans wrongly assumed that Potawatomi ways must be changed and their culture destroyed to enable them to coexist with others in the modern world. The totality of their ideas, attitudes, customs, and ways of living as members of a distinct society became threatened. Because the Potawatomis were so well-liked by the settlers moving into the area, it would not have been considered acceptable to massacre them. Instead, the government felt that the Potawatomis should be "helped" by forcing them to overcome what was perceived by the dominant society as "backwardness." The idea was that with their distinctive culture and traditional ways abandoned, the Potawatomis would simply assimilate into the population of the rest of the country and hence their lands could be quietly acquired by the dominant culture.

RECOLLECTIONS OF THE HISTORICAL DEVASTATION OF THE POTAWATOMI UNTIL 1840 IN KALAMAZOO

An examination of the forced removal of the Potawatomi from southwestern Michigan lends insight into the concept of the crime of cultural genocide. Before the first European settlers arrived in the lower third of what is now the state of Michigan, the Potawatomi, as well as the Ojibwa and Chippewa, existed without assistance. They freely hunted, fished, and practiced horticulture as they wished without being "civilized," having their "souls saved," or becoming assimilated into the dominant Euro-American culture. Even though factionalism existed among various bands living in the region, differences were settled without interference from an outside arbitrator with ulterior motives. Nativism among the Indians, as with patriotism among the whites, helped balance out the factionalism and disagreements to a certain degree. Were it not for factionalism that existed among tribes, perhaps they could have withstood the underlying motives of the settlers and held onto their homeland culture and ways of life for a longer period of time.

The French were the first to take advantage of the factionalism that existed among the various tribes. The Potawatomis remained in close contact with the French for 50 years and as a result, their world began to change. The enticement of French technology was a double-edged sword, both enriching and destroying traditional Potawatomi culture. They began to lose their self-sufficiency, becoming dependent upon French products.

When the British came along, they used thrift in their distribution of food and other provisions to the Potawatomis in an effort to secure their loyalty to be used as needed. The Potawatomis expected the British to be as generous as the French, but that did not happen. Because the French shared what little they had with the Potawatomis, many remained loyal to the French. As human nature would dictate, French and Spanish traders took advantage of this loyalty and used it to discourage any close Potawatomi–British ties (Edmunds 1978, 100). By discouraging British ties, the French and Spanish traders would be able to cut down on the competition to further their own monetary gains as well as to keep the Potawatomis on their side in case of future conflicts. The French and Spanish felt it would be to their distinct advantage if they could keep the Potawatomis dependent upon them; instilling their allegiance would be crucial to the French and Spanish in case of future conflicts.

Not wanting the French and Spanish to hold this advantage, the British decided to discard their old policy of thrift and distribute food and other goods with less restraint to the Potawatomi. However, Potawatomi dependency on the food and provisions provided by the French and Spanish, and later the British, did not come without high cost. The British used the bait of food and provisions to take advantage of their growing relationship with the Potawatomis, using them to attack American settlements along the Ohio River as part of a British offensive, eventually helping them gain the upper hand. And, with their relationship declining, the French left the Potawatomis dependent solely upon the British to supply them with what had become their necessities of life (Edmunds 1978, 100). The fate of the Potawatomi was now sealed: the paternalism that began early on in the relationship between the Potawatomi and the French and Spanish continued with the British. As with all such relationships, the one who is dependent is at the mercy of the provider. Eventually the Potawatomis would have to cede their lands in exchange for the services (economic extortion) upon which they had now become dependent, causing the loss of their homeland.

Time passed and eventually settlers occupied Potawatomi homelands.

White settlements began to intrude upon the Potawatomis, and the government decided to gain title to as much of their lands as possible. As settlers required more and more land, the government happily accommodated them by grabbing as much Potawatomi land as possible by whatever means were necessary. Bacteriological extermination through smallpox by the English commander, Lord Jeffrey Amherst, effectively eliminated much of the population of the Ottawas, Potawatomis, Wyandots, and Lenni Lenapes during the latter 1700s (Churchill 1997, 206). This and other methods such as cajoling, lying, exploiting, and cheating were used to gain the Potawatomi homelands. One way was to give the Potawatomis jobs and, for this opportunity, they would cede their lands to the providers of the jobs as payment for the privilege of working. In another example, three million acres taken from several Indian tribes by the treaty of Fort Wayne, which opened up most of Indiana below the Wabash River to white settlements (Edmunds 1978, 161–69).

Along with this land-grab came attempts at assimilation. The Quakers unsuccessfully sought to change the Potawatomis into Christian farmers in a misguided effort to help their "progression, civilization, and salvation" into mainstream society. Perhaps in an effort to ease the Christian conscience, trading millions of acres for the chance to progress and become part of what many thought was a superior race seemed like a fair and justifiable exchange.

After the war of 1812, a new sense of nationalism and pride sent thousands of land-hungry settlers into Potawatomi territory. Their slow acculturation of many old values of the French traders and feeble attempts at agriculture under the Quakers did not prepare the Potawatomis for the changes that would overwhelm them after 1815. White settlers moved in and began to farm their prairies. Protestant missionaries came to save and civilize their children. The Potawatomis opposed these actions but, because of their populations being decimated by disease, could no longer strike back as did warriors in the past. The new chiefs, now mostly of mixed-blood descent, dealt with the whites through diplomacy, not warfare (Edmunds 1978, 206).

Nationalism and pride led the whites to feel superior to the Potawatomis as well as all other American Indian tribes. Because Indian tribes previously tended to manage their own affairs without centralized authority of the state, the tendency was for them to become easily conquered by the state. Through this conquest, Indian people became considered alien, backward, and inferior. The capitalistic system of stratification developing during the early years of the United States, along with decades of oppression of the Indian peoples, placed Euro-Americans in the highest positions of power and control. Once in this position, those at the top of the pyramid will do whatever is necessary to fulfill their needs and maintain their position in the hierarchy. Greed flourished among the whites holding the most advantageous positions in society, and they did not need to justify taking what they needed to satisfy their goals of gain and progress.

With the fur trade now declining, the Potawatomis came to rely very heavily upon government annuities. They received none from 1813 to 1816 and hence continually needed more of the settlers' goods to sustain themselves (Edmunds 1978, 215). Without the annuities, purchasing necessary materials became increasingly difficult. The need for necessities created a new relationship with the British. After the war, the settlers believed rumors that another Indian conflict would soon begin and that the British were involved. To militarily deter any future Indian hostilities, the government built a series of new forts at Chicago, Green Bay, Prairie du Chein, and Rock Island.

These new posts contributed to the political fragmentation of the Potawatomis, as the post commanders conferred with different chiefs at their respective agencies. As a result, confusion over tribal leadership ensued (Edmunds 1978, 216). The concept of leadership of a tribe meant something different to white men than it did to the Indians. The Indians' flexible concept emphasized roles of different leaders at different times. Americans were not used to that sort of leadership, and their attempts to deal with different Indian leaders at the same time contributed to intratribal arguments.

Most of the bickering centered around annuities. This growing dependence upon annuities made the Potawatomis susceptible to the government's land-grabbing policies after the war. The Potawatomis were willing to give up their lands in order to secure the annuities necessary to obtain the food and provisions that had now become necessities. The immoral, unethical, and criminal practices of the government ensured a paternal relationship with the inevitable end results—the Potawatomis lost virtually everything.

In 1815, the United States resumed its land-grabbing tactics championed earlier by William Henry Harrison. The Treaty of 1816 at St. Louis marked the first time that the Potawatomis ceded any of their homelands (Edmunds 1978, 217–18). This treaty also marked the first attempt by the government to purchase lands and deliver annuities to specific bands within the tribe. The different villages of Potawatomis began to meet with the government separately, each claiming large areas of tribal homeland and each trying to gain the lion's share of the annuities. Separate negotiations caused factionalism and jealousy to flare up among the different tribes, and the American government seized this opportunity to further exploit the Potawatomis to its own greedy advantage. The Potawatomis bargained away their birthright, selling their lands piecemeal for the Americans' trade goods, money, and empty promises (Edmunds 1978, 220). Government officials knew they were victimizing a dependent people in a much less powerful position, but did so with no remorse.

To further the need for the American idea of progress in opening the Wabash valley to white settlers, the government unabashedly committed the criminal act of bribery by appropriating large sums of money for gifts to different tribal leaders. The Potawatomis "received nineteen hundred dollars in 'presents' plus an unknown additional share of six thousand dollars dispensed as bribes to individual chiefs" (Edmunds 1978, 220). Through this blatant criminal act of bribery, the U.S. government finally succeeded in cajoling leading chiefs from most of the villages in Michigan and Indiana out of 1,550 square miles of their land for a perpetual annuity of twenty-five hundred dollars in silver. So successful was the government in this, that officials decided to try to purchase all of the remaining Potawatomi lands in Michigan. Then on June 1, 1820, Secretary of War John C. Calhoun appointed Cass Sibley and Solomon Sibley of Michigan to serve as commissioners for the treaty. Although the proposed cession involved land in Michigan, Cass Sibley wanted to hold the treaty at Chicago, since the St. Joseph Potawatomis would be forced to leave their villages. If the Potawatomis could not see what they were losing, perhaps it would be easier to talk them into parting with their land. Once again, government funds were obtained to engage in the criminal act of bribing influential chiefs, while large quantities of food, whiskey, and trade goods were assembled at Chicago to ensure that the bribe would be effective.

About three thousand Potawatomis came to the meeting during August of 1821. Because the amount of land in the cession was so vast, Sibley had to use all his persuaion to convince the reluctant Potawatomis to cede such a large portion of their homelands. In the past they had willingly done so for small portions of land, but the size of this proposed cession came as a surprise. The chief complained that the whites were crowding onto Potawatomi land so quickly that "the plowshare is driven through our tents before we have time to carry out our goods and seek another habitation" (Edmunds 1978, 220).

Finally, Sibley used threats of withholding whiskey and other goods and giving these to other Potawatomis if the St. Joseph leaders continued to oppose the treaty. If the treaty was accepted, Sibley promised to give the Potawatomis "enough alcohol to make every man, woman and child in the nation drunk" (Edmunds 1978, 221). Metea, an influential tribal leader, opposed the treaty to the last, but other Ottawas, Chippewas, traders, and mixed-bloods urged acceptance. One old Potawatomi man finally grew impatient and pleaded with Sibley, "We care not for the land, the money, or the goods, it is the whiskey we want—give us the whiskey" (Edmunds 1978, 221). The dependency created in past dealings with the government ensured a paternalistic relationship, allowing disgraceful coercion and criminal extortion of the Potawatomi people. Hamiltonian methods of the ends justifying the means were used to play upon the weaknesses of the Potawatomis. These crimes perpetrated by the U.S. government exemplified its disdain toward the Potawatomis, which it obviously regarded as being inferior, backward, and alien withn their own land.

Being poor and in the position of needing to take care of their families the best way they knew how, the Potawatomis settled for the proposed treaty and ceded all their lands in southwestern Michigan "from the St. Joseph River east to the boundaries of the lands ceded in 1807 and 1817 and stretching as far north as the Grand River" (Edmunds 1978, 221). The treaty signed in 1821 had the greatest effect on the Potawatomis of Kalamazoo. The 1880 *History of Kalamazoo County* states that by the treaty of Chicago, the Potawatomis ceded all their lands with the exception of five small reservations. The Match-e-be-nash-e-wish Reserve, in Kalamazoo County, covered the ground now occupied by Kalamazoo village (Durant 1880, 76).

In the 1880 historical account, it is assumed that this land must have been in the hands of the government when the first entries of land were made in Kalamazoo, which were in November 1830, by Stephen H. Richardson and Titus Bronson. Richardson and Bronson purchased the southwest quarter of section 15, which is now in the heart of Kalamazoo village. The township was surveyed in 1827 by John Mullet, and the reservation in June 1829, by Orange Risdon. The fact of its being surveyed would indicate that it had recently come into possession of the government. From a chapter in the history of Hillsdale County, it appears that the Indians exchanged, in September 1827, all their reservations made at the Chicago treaty of 1821 for a consolidated reservation called Nottawa-Sepee, in St. Joseph and Kalamazoo Counties. The Match-e-be-nash-e-wish tract was probably given up at that time as well.

Early settlers around Kalamazoo had always been divided over the Potawatomis. According to Massie and Schmitt (1981, 32), the estimated number of Potawatomi people is 1,100 in southern Michigan at this time, although their numbers could have been much higher a century earlier. Some settlers held romantic notions about "nature's noblemen," while others remembered living all their lives among people with attitudes and customs much different from their own (Massie & Schmitt 1981, 32). Living in relative proximity to destitution was no different then than it is now. In order to move the destitution and poverty away from the good and civilized Christian settlers and to segregate those with drastically different customs and attitudes, Titus Bronson, the very eccentric founder of Kalamazoo, mapped out his village on the best land in the Match-e-be-nash-e-wish Indian Reserve without much thought or consideration.

This was only the tip of the iceberg. Pressure began mounting from everywhere to resolve the "Indian question." Sibley felt that the Potawatomis were "sojourners" on the land and should not be allowed to slow down the progress being made by the permanent settlers. Considering Sibley's attitude, which was encouraged by the mounting pressure from the settlers, removal would be the only possible option. Although claiming to be free from any animosity himself, Sibley encouraged the government to consider making military policy an excuse for removal, "since any concentration of former allies in Michigan might prove awkward if hostilities with the British should resume" (Massie & Schmidt 1981, 32). Extermination of one kind or another was in keeping with the concept of Manifest Destiny.

The large size of the Potawatomi tribe attracted the most legislative and administrative concern of any northern tribe in the process of removal. Such a large population of Indians occupying land more suitable for white settlers made removal a more immediate concern for the Potawatomi tribe than for other tribes of smaller size. The 17 treaties negotiated between 1832 and 1837 ensured that the "second-class" Potawatomis would not be allowed to remain on the most fertile land in the area. Only a short time after the arrival of white settlers, the Potawatomis gave up these lands—this tribe was the largest group ever to be removed from Michigan (Neumeyer 1968, 18). These treaties brought about the virtual destruction of the Potawatomi Indians in southwestern Michigan. This great nation of people virtually vanished from this area when its members moved westward across the plains as they were driven from their last stronghold (Donahue 1969). This stronghold, the Match-e-be-nash-e-wish Reserve, consisted of an area that now encompasses the city of Kalamazoo. Today, Western Michigan University is on the western border of the former Potawatomi village.

A SEARCH OF THE ARCHIVES

In the fall of 1946, Charles A. Weissert wrote a series of articles about the unconscionable con game that took place that allowed white settlers to pry the Potawatomis from their rich farmland (Weissert 1946). The articles describe the fertile lands bordering the Nottawa-Seepe reservation as being completely settled by 1831. According to the articles, the white settlers and Potawatomis lived together peacefully as neighbors until a few settlers began to supply the Indians with whiskey, resulting in much suffering for the entire tribe. Weissert describes the whiskey given to the Potawatomis as vile and being shared for the sole purpose of exploitation of the tribe. An intoxicated Potawatomi became an easy target to cheat and rob. Victimization by alcohol had a devastating effect on the Potawatomi people. Some of them traded guns, ponies, furs, and blankets for alcohol and neglected to hunt, fish, and trap. They became dependent upon the whiskey, and Potawatomi families suffered from cold and lack of food as a result.

To add insult to injury, the Potawatomis were hounded by government agents and settlers who wanted them to sell the reservation. Many wanted to sell, but no land transfer could be made without the consent of tribal chiefs who were scattered over nearly a five-hundred-mile area, and when the Black Hawk Indian War of 1832 broke out, the Potawatomi Indians refused to join forces with the renegade Indians. The fidelity of the Potawatomis was quickly forgotten, as a stronger determination emerged on the part of the settlers in the area to wrench the rich land away from the Indians. Then a final treaty, the Nottawa-Seepe Treaty of 1833, had to be dealt with by the tribes. The treaty was signed by a few self-appointed representatives of the Potawatomi Nation in Chicago, resulting in the final end of jurisdiction of properties and even occupational rights for the Potawatomis in the area.

Details of the transaction are unavailable, but it is known that Governor George Byron Porter was under public pressure to finalize this treaty. Porter met with Sau-an-quette, orator and politician of the Nottawa-Seepe Potawatomis, and "by blandishments in the way of gay clothing and military fixtures" (Weissert 1946) influenced him and others to sign the treaty, thus transferring their reservation to the United States. Referred to as the "Judas Iscariot of the Potawatomis," Sau-an-quette is described as being decked out for the signing of the treaty in the military apparel that had been given him as his 30 pieces of silver and as shouting, "I have sold the land and I will sell it again for two gallons of whiskey!" (Blair 1912, 297–98).

Although he was not their chief, Sau-an-quette and several of his followers attended the signing of the treaty. Probably by assumption, they were regarded as delegates from Nottawa-Seepe. When the Potawatomis learned that Sau-au-quette had sold their reservation for $10,000 in goods without consulting with the rest of the tribe, they were extremely upset. They held consultations, declared that Sau-an-quette had no authority to make the transaction, and decided not to accept the $10,000 payment that was to be made at the Marantette Trading Post (Weissert 1946). However, the Potawatomis depended upon the government for subsistence at this point, and the prospect of receiving $10,000 in goods became an irresistable temptation. Exploitation was simple, and the unethical, illegal means to achieve this land-grab were easily performed.

Victimization and Exploitation through Alcohol

What began as a peaceful relationship between the white settlers and the Potawatomis slowly eroded with the introduction of whiskey. The settlers exploited this relationship as the Potawatomis became dependent upon alcohol. They depended on white settlers to supply them with the whiskey to which they had become addicted and could be persuaded to give up their most prized possessions in order to receive a steady supply of it. This dependency further increased government paternalism and ensured its growth.

If grave injustices are committed by the leaders of a government, there tends to be a trickle-down effect, which appears to be the case here.

During this time, the U.S. government was in the business of land-grabbing through exploitation or any other means available to further its goals. If government officials knowingly conducted business in this manner, then it would seem to be acceptable for settlers in a small community to follow suit. Obtaining the rich farmland of the Potawatomis through the use of alcohol and other means of trickery was a commonplace occurrence. The desire for this land and the growing resentment by the settlers toward "second-class" Potawatomis left only one possible consequence—that of removal.

Land was not the only loss suffered by the Potawatomis. They began to lose their self-esteem, pride in themselves, their independent spirit, and respect for tribal customs as well as respect for the authority of tribal governance. After the fiasco brought about by Sau-an-quette, trustworthy leaders ceased to exist. By now it was too late, and the Potawatomis knew their removal was imminent. Small bands of them formed in an effort to fight for their right to remain in the area, but were driven off by a local militant organization in 1840 (Weissert 1946).

By this time, the Potawatomis were described more and more in a derogatory manner. In order to ease their conscience about the outright exploitation of such a peaceful people, blaming the victims for their own misfortune occurred. It became easy to depict the Potawatomis as shiftless savages prone to the evils of alcohol, and communities are well to be rid of people such as these (Weissert 1946). But a letter written on January 21, 1907 by the Reverend William Metzdorf of St. Francis, Wisconsin depicts the Potawatomis in a more favorable light. He wrote: "The idea that some people have of these Indians, that they are wild, cruel savages, or a race who cannot be civilized, is entirely wrong and false" (Durant 1880, 76). Reverend Metzdorf compassionately described the Potawatomis as peaceful people, having learned their bad habits from the whites. He attributes the unfriendliness on the part of the Potawatomis to the way in which they were treated by whites. Metzdorf ended his commentary with regret that the Indians were not given more sympathy and greater opportunities, and correctly concluded that the poor condition in which they found themselves would continue long into the future.

A Broken Relationship

In 1830, the Indians witnessed the arrival of the first permanent white settlers. The local Indians generally welcomed the settlers and for ten years they lived together peacefully. The settlers and Potawatomis hunted and fished on good terms with each other, obeying the unwritten laws of the woods. If the two were hunting together and game was taken, dividing it equally occurred, "except for the skin which went to the one who wounded the animal first" (Holmes 1964, 14).

When the settlers needed help, the Potawatomis, who had the expertise needed for survival in the area at that time, were there to lend a hand. Their expertise was worth everything to the early, struggling pioneers. Potawatomi expertise of the woods, hunting, and medicinal skills was invaluable for the survival of the settlers. A very well-known earlier settler, Basil Harrison, expressed his gratitude for the Potawatomis:

> We never could have got along without the Potawatomi in those days. He was a sort of leather stocking. They were our friends, and we were their friends. When we got out of provisions we were in a bad fix indeed; we had to hunt, and being poor hunters, we were sometimes in a condition where we would have starved if it had not been for the Potawatomis; they brought us game that they had killed, and they carried us through the hard places and preserved our lives. (Holmes 1964, 14)

The settlers and Potawatomis existed together in such harmony, according to these archival accounts, that it seems impossible for such deterioration to have occurred. Even though the Potawatomis were helpful, however,

> the mere presence of the Indian was quite undesirable for most whites. This was due mainly to the inevitable efforts of the red man to preserve his fast disappearing land rights. . . . The white's solution to the problems resulting from the contacts between the two people was to buy Indians' lands and then force the Indians to move west. (Holmes 1964, 14)

Removal

The most pressing issues facing Kalamazoo in 1840 consisted of attracting industry to the area and expanding markets. Issues regarding pioneering or living from the land were no longer of any consequence. Even the local newspaper, the *Kalamazoo Gazette*, was too concerned with national politics to even take notice and write about the Indian removal of 1840. The Potawatomis were not seen as individuals who were devastated at having to leave their ancestral homelands, but were treated as one mass of brown people to be herded out like so much cattle. Along with attracting industry and expanding the economic market, justification for suppression and removing the Potawatomi, as with other tribes throughout the country, was based on the idea of the "savage" and his usefulness to society. With the Potawatomi, early settlers remarked that the "white man could get more food by cultivating a square acre than the Indian could by hunting a square mile." Now that the notion of white superiority had been firmly established, settlers came to believe strongly that the conflict of the two cultures should and must result in "survival of the fittest." In the minds of the settlers of this growing community, the only solution was removal of the tribe.

The final relations of the Indians and whites centered around the great removal of 1840. In Kalamazoo County, Colonel Thomas A. H. Edwards gathered the Indians together for the long journey. The same whites who had been helped by the Potawatomis in this settlement now hunted them down for transport west of the Mississippi. Early settler Rebecca Holmes wrote: "[A]fter ten years of helping the settlers, they were rounded up and marched west at gunpoint" (Holmes 1964, 14). They were taken to Fort Leavenworth, where they remained for two years before finally being forced to move on at the instigation of the citizens of Missouri. Some years later, George Torrey, a young man in October 1840, wrote: "[W]hatever may be said as to the justice of the act, there is no doubt but their removal was devoutly wished for by the whites" (Holmes 1964, 14). Others were less certain and embarrassed by their own sentiment as many Potawatomis openly wept and all uncovered their heads as a gesture of respect when they passed the home of the prominent Judge Ransom (Holmes 1964, 14).

Many Potawatomis were reluctant to leave and were fearful that the land they were to be removed to would not sustain the only way of life they knew. They were confused as to why the removal had to occur, since many felt that they had a good relationship with the whites in the area. Some did manage to stay, but were assimilated into the dominant culture. In 1880, an archival document states that all those who stayed adopted the dress and customs, more or less, of the whites, and to a great extent gave up the chase. Documents reveal that portions of the tribe settled down to agricultural pursuits, and between 500 to 600 of their children attended public schools (Durant 1880, 78).

In 1927, an article appeared in the *Kalamazoo Gazette* regarding E. B. Simonds, an employee of the Edwards and Chamberlin firm, describing how the Potawatomis benefited by acquiescing to the dominant culture in the area. Simonds justified victimization of the Potawatomis by stating the futility of resisting progress and that the Indian should accept the conditions that have been forced on him and fit himself harmoniously into the new necessities of life (Massie & Schmitt 1981, 33).

However, many Potawatomis did continue to exist amidst the dominant, paternalistic culture that victimized, and now surrounded, them. On November 26, 1926 Jeanne Griffin wrote an article about Indians in the vicinity of Kalamazoo. Her facts were obtained from an interview with Chief Sam Mandoka of Athens Township, Calhoun County, Michigan. Griffin wrote that the Potawatomis from this region who did not wish to go west hid themselves in this area under fear of apprehension by the government. Some went up into northern Michigan but returned to live near Dowagiac and Hartford. According to her interview with Chief Mandoka, because of their fear of the government, the Indians who stayed complied with the dominant society and assimilated for the most part. Methodist worship replaced their old religion. Potawatomi culture virtually disappeared as native dress and dances became anachronistic. Agriculture and basket-making became the new method of subsistence, largely replacing the hunting and fishing that had sustained them so well in the past (Griffin 1926, 1–2).

The Past Few Decades

Mark Fritz, a *Kalamazoo Gazette* staff writer, in 1979 surmised that "the fall of the Potawatomi Nation parallels strongly the rise of civilization in Kalamazoo County, an area of critical importance to the Indians. For the three predominant Potawatomi bands, the Pokagon, Huron, and Notawasepi, integration into white society meant that the vitally important sense of community is lost" (Fritz 1979, 1).

For all the pain and tears caused, a few plaques commemorating the Potawatomis in obscure places around Kalamazoo have been placed. Most people in the city do not even know that these plaques exist. One of these commemorates a place called "Indian Fields" that once covered the area where the recently renamed Kalamazoo/Battle Creek International Airport now stands. An article from the *Kalamazoo Gazette* (1962) states that

> the only totem is the gleaming glass and steel airport control tower overlooking a four-mile tract which once contained garden beds and a tribal burial ground. The only winking eye in the darkness come not from wild animals but from aircraft landing and taking off from Kalamazoo Municipal Airport.

There is no mention in the article about whether the remains of the Indian people were taken to another place, or if they were simply disrespectfully paved over with runways to further industry and progress in the area. Perhaps those buried under the airport suffered the same disrespect of bones found in 1834 when excavations were made for a new hotel on the east side of town. During those excavations, a large number of Indian skeletons and loose bones were uncovered and simply thrown into the river (*Kalamazoo Gazette* 1925).

In 1961, another plaque took its place on the brick wall of the Kalamazoo train station. On remarking about this momentous occasion, the *Kalamazoo Gazette* presented this derogatory report:

> [O]n the day of departure, escorted by U.S. soldiers, the Indians presented a sorrowful sight as in single file, they set out on foot with their belongings on the backs of ponies, their dogs walking alongside. The sick and aged were carried on litters rigged between the ponies. Small children were carried in papoose boards on the backs of squaws. Though these children of the forest had a long and bloody history, the history books tell us that many an onlooker had tear-filled eyes. . . . This week's historical marker is located on the New York Central Railroad depot building in Kalamazoo.

CONCLUSIONS

Kalamazoo is quite a conservative town for the most part. As with most such towns, unpleasant occurrences such as these are considered momentarily, then put away and easily forgotten. History is always written from the point of view of the conqueror. The history books of young students growing up in this area begin with Columbus and totally ignore the rich and robust history of the people who lived here before the first settlers came—hence further victimizing the Indian people by fostering racist attitudes of white superiority.

The injustices inflicted upon the Potawatomi people of the area in southwestern Michigan are now so far in the past that they are not even mentioned as an important part in shaping the history of the region. For the most part, the only mention of the thriving Potawatomi community is that it did, in fact, exist. Perhaps covering up the past and not speaking of the criminally reprehensible injustices inflicted upon an entire nation of people is why one can live an entire lifetime in the area, go through the public school system grades K through 12, and never learn about the cultural genocide that occurred. More than 160 years have passed since the Potawatomis were victimized by removal from their homeland, and still they have not recovered from economic and cultural losses. Today, with opportunities for education and creative economic options, the future of the Potawatomis who remain in the region will most certainly be brighter than their past.

Today, the museum in Kalamazoo has undergone drastic changes and is housed in its own beautiful new building. When visiting, you will see a display depicting the beginning and growth of the Kalamazoo area. What you will *not* see are any references to the Potawatomi people living in the area during the early years of Kalamazoo. The only reference to any Indian people living in the area at the time is a small display of a few baskets. The information card gives a brief description of these beautiful pieces and the names of the donors. You will not find a display depicting the history of the Potawatomis and their contribution to the survival of the early settlers and the growth of their homeland known as Kalamazoo. School children taking field trips to the museum today receive less information about the Potawatomis than children who visited 40 years ago. The more things change, the more they stay the same.

However, lest we forget, today there stands a fountain in Bronson Park in Kalamazoo in the area where the Potawatomis lived, worked, and gave assistance to the settlers in need. With or without intention, this fountain stands as a silent reminder of the victimization and cultural genocide inflicted upon the Potawatomi people of southwest Michigan. If you look carefully, you can see that the sculptor fashioned one end of the fountain in the shape of an Indian bowing down to a white man.

References

Blair, E. H. (1912). *The Indian tribes of the Upper Mississippi Valley and region of the Great Lakes.* Cleveland: Arthur H. Clark.

Churchill, W. (1997). *A little matter of genocide: Holocaust and denial in the Americas, 1492 to the present.* San Francisco: City Lights Books.

Deloria, V., Jr. (1969). *Custer died for your sins: An Indian manifesto.* Norman: University of Oklahoma Press.

———. (1995). *Red earth, white lies: Native Americans and the myth of scientific fact.* New York: Scribners.

———. (1996). *Behind the trail of broken treaties: An American Indian declaration of independence.* Austin: University of Texas Press.

Diamond, J. (1992). *The third chimpanzee: The evolution and future of the human animal.* New York: HarperCollins.

Donahue, J. (1969). "Treaties of deception and degradation." *Kalamazoo Gazette* (September 28).

Durant, S. W. (1880). *History of Kalamazoo County.* Philadelphia: Everts and Abbott.

Edmunds, R. D. (1978). *The Potawatomis: Keepers of the fire.* Norman: University of Oklahoma Press.

Fixico, D. (1986). *Termination and relocation: Federal Indian policy, 1945–1960.* Albuquerque: University of New Mexico Press.

Fritz, M. (1979). "Potawatomi once thrived in Kalamazoo area." *Kalamazoo Gazette* (September 30):D1.

Gedicks, A. (1993). *The new resource wars: Native and environmental struggles against multinational corporations.* Boston: South End Press.

Griffin, J. (1926). "Indians in the vicinity of Kalamazoo: Facts gained from conversation with Chief Sam Mandoka, Athens Township, Calhoun County, Michigan." Unpublished paper.

Holmes, R. (1964). "The Kalamazoo Indians." *Kalamazoo Magazine* (February):14.

Hunter, J. (1987). "The Indians and the Michigan road." *Indiana Magazine of History 83* (September).

Hyde, G. E. (1962). *Indians of the woodlands.* Norman: University of Oklahoma Press.

Jaimes, M. A. (1992). *The state of Native America: Genocide, colonization, and resistance.* Boston: South End Press.

Jenness, D. (1932). *Indians of Canada.* Ottawa: University of Toronto Press.

Kalamazoo Gazette. (1925). "Burial grounds of Indians stood here" (October 18).

———. (1961). "Commemorate Indian fields" (August 2).

———. (1962). "Site of Indian village gives way to air age" (July 30).

Massie, L. B., and P. J. Schmitt. (1981). *Kalamazoo: The place behind the products.* Windsor Publications.

Maybury-Lewis, D. (1997). *Indigenous peoples, ethnic groups, and the state.* Needham Heights, MA: Allyn & Bacon.

Neumeyer, E. A. (1968). "Indian removal in Michigan, 1833–1855." Master's thesis, Central Michigan University, p. 18. Western Michigan University Archives.

Shaffer, C. (1929). "Dramatic Indian duel over treaty halted by Patrick Marantette, St. Joe trader" (October 13). Clipping, no page number.

Weissert, C. A. (1946). "Treaties of deception, degradation."

CHAPTER TWENTY

Victimization of Women

a theoretical perspective on dowry deaths in India

MANGAI NATARAJAN

MARRIAGES IN INDIA ARE USUALLY ARRANGED by parents and the wife becomes a member of the husband's family, in most cases moves in with them. Since most marriages are arranged with the assistance of third parties, the families generally do not know each other well. Nevertheless, the newly wedded bride is expected to switch her principal loyalty overnight to her husband's family. The husband's family may make little accommodation to the bride, but expect her to adjust to them. Since they are now supporting her, the husband's family believes that she must be considerate to their wishes. If they think she is not, they may feel justified in treating her harshly, even violently.

In the early stages of a marriage, a new bride who is being mistreated by her husband's family may not seek help from her own parents, because they will already have counseled her that a period of adjustment to her new situation may be needed. If she does complain, unless the abuse is repeated or extreme, most parents would probably be reluctant to intercede on her behalf with her in-laws or husband. This reflects the Hindu norm that once a girl is married, her parents have only limited rights to having a say in her new family's personal affairs. They might also hope that some mutual adjustment might occur between the bride and her new family so that there would be a reduction in harassment and ill-treatment. If the girl returns to her parents' house because of quarrels with her husband, this brings shame on her parents' family and prevents the marriage of any of her sisters. Moreover, she cannot take part in any religious ceremonies without her spouse. For all these reasons, an abused wife may not expect much support from her parents, and may only get their support in more extreme cases.

These marriage arrangements reflect the generally subordinate and powerless position of younger women, and patterns of domestic violence in India are indicative of this position. In particular, there are certain forms of victimization in India that would be unheard of in Western society: female infanticide, dowry deaths (bride burning), and *sati* (Ahuja 1987; Sood 1990). This last, *sati*, is different from the first two in that the widow "chooses" to commit suicide on the death of her husband.

This chapter is concerned particularly with dowry deaths; that is, murders and suicides of wives as a result of disputes over the dowry. In particular, it attempts to supplement sociocultural and personality explanations with some recent victimological and criminological theories that give greater weight to situational and decision factors.

The Dowry System

The dowry system is deeply rooted in Hindu culture and is the customary practice of giving gifts in cash and kind by the bride's family to that of the groom (Goody & Tambiah 1987). These gifts may be given before the marriage or at any time afterwards and include such things as appliances and furniture as well as cash and jewelry. The cost of the dowry may impose a significant additional burden on the bride's parents, who also have to pay for a customarily elaborate and expensive wedding. The amount of the dowry is determined by the groom's family status, his level of education, his occupation, and his income. Grooms who are physicians, engineers, lawyers, foreign-educated, or working abroad are often preferred and command the highest dowries.

The practice of dowry has its roots in the most common rite associated with a Hindu marriage (the majority of Indians are Hindus) "*Kanyadan*," the act of giving the bride to the groom. (The word literally means the "act of giving or donating a virgin to the groom on an auspicious day.") It is recommended in the *shastras* (certain rules prescribed in Hindu philosophy) that the bride be adorned with jewelry and then given away. According to the *shastras*, the ritual gift remains incomplete until the groom and his parents are given "*dakshana*," a token gift in their honor. This is supposed to be in recognition of the fact that the bridegroom and his kin deserve to be honored (and financially compensated) for accepting the girl into their fold.

Despite its religious origins, the dowry settlement has all the characteristics of a market transaction. Some scholars suggest that the practice of giving a dowry follows from a system of inheritance that excludes the female children and, by settling some of the family's wealth upon the daughters before the parents' death, to some extent compensates for the discriminatory effects of the system (Tambiah 1973). The nature and purpose of the dowry practice should therefore be considered within the context of property rights under a system of exclusively male inheritance (Harrel & Dickey 1985; Paul 1986; Upadhya 1990). However, D'Souza and Natarajan (1986) have argued that the spread of the dowry practice from upper-class Hindus to the middle and lower classes, as well as to other religious groups, is evidence of its real purpose in compensating for women's low economic value. This seems all the more true as the spread of the practice has been accompanied by a subtle change in the conditions of the dowry, which increasingly is seen as a gift made to the groom and his family rather than as an amount of capital belonging to the bride.

NATURE OF DOWRY DEATHS

When not satisfied with the dowry, the bridegroom and his parents may humiliate, harass, and physically abuse the bride. They may even murder her in order to arrange a second marriage. In some cases, also falling under the definition of *dowry deaths*, the bride might be driven to suicide. Although brides may be murdered in a variety of ways, dowry deaths are popularly known as "bride burning." In fact, many dowry deaths *are* by burning; one of the reasons is that such deaths can be easily concealed as accidents. In most Indian homes, kerosene is used as fuel for stoves and accidents are frequent. As the fire may destroy any evidence of violence, it can be difficult for the authorities to prove malicious intent (Garg 1990; Grover 1990).

Drowning is also a frequently used method of murdering the bride. Such deaths are facilitated by the wells that exist in many parts in India to provide drinking water. Since these are the sites of many accidental and suicidal deaths, murders are easily concealed. Likewise, because insecticides (organophosphorous compounds) and poisonous plants are widely available, there are high numbers of incidents of accidental and suicidal poisoning, which facilitate concealment of murder.

Essentially, the same three methods—burning, drowning, and poisoning—are used by brides driven to suicide (Rao 1983). This makes it difficult to compile accurate statistics about the proportion of dowry deaths due to homicide. In fact, most recorded dowry deaths are registered as "abetment to suicide" under section 306 of the Indian penal code (Kronholz 1986). A further complication lies in the fact that the rate of suicide among women is on the increase. Suicides by women are mainly due to family quarrels, especially problems with in-laws and spouses, and in many of these quarrels dissatisfaction with the dowry may play a part even if it is not the principal cause (Singh 1986).

National-level dowry-death statistics are not reported in India. Devi Prasad (1990) notes that there was a total of 1,649 dowry deaths reported in 18 of the 22 states in 1987, but these figures are of suspect reliability and likely to substantially understate the problem. For example, there is large, unexplained variation among states in rates of dowry deaths (the rate for

Assam was 0.15 deaths per million of the population, whereas for Delhi the rate was 13.9), and reported deaths for individual states show considerable annual fluctuations (in 1985, the figures for Bihar [3] and Andrapradesh [15] were very much lower than in 1987, which were respectively 120 and 98).

During recent decades there has been much greater recognition in Indian society that murder and suicide associated with disputes over dowries have become significant social problems. The Indian government has responded through legislation (Dowry Prohibition Act of 1961, amended in 1984) prohibiting dowry payments, but these laws are widely ignored, partly because the legal definition of dowry has a number of loopholes and also because the dowry system is seen to serve a valuable social purpose by many sections of society (Paul 1986; Kumari 1989).

Previous Literature

Studies of dowry deaths generally consist of an analysis of a few individual cases and hence the conclusions are based on limited data. However, a number of contributory factors have been consistently identified. One of the most important of these is that many families simply do not have the resources to make the large dowry payments that are expected and that they had promised (Khan & Ray 1984). This problem has become more acute as the practice of dowry, formerly confined to the upper classes, has increasingly been adopted by middle- and lower-middle-class families as a route to improved social status (Ahuja 1987).

A second important contributory factor is the joint family system (Ahuja 1987). As explained above, wives commonly move in with their husband's family. If the family also includes a number of the husband's siblings, the probability of conflict between the bride and these individuals is greatly increased. Quarrels often center upon accusations of insufficient dowry payments. In these arguments, husbands do not always support their wives and, when her parents live at a distance and cannot easily come to support her, she is even more isolated. In Khan and Ray's (1984) study, it was found that about 55 percent of dowry victims were living at quite some distance from their parents.

Problems may be exacerbated by the economic situation of the husband's family. Some families try to realize their debts by extracting a large cash dowry in exchange for their son's hand in marriage. Others try to realize their ambitions—for example, by obtaining education abroad for their sons or building an extension to their house (Ahuja 1987). In general, commentators believe that modernization and urbanization have resulted in a more materialistic society. Husbands and their families view the dowry as a way of satisfying their ambition to own electronic goods, scooters, and even cars.

The economic situation of the wife's family is also relevant. The bride's family more frequently has difficulty in paying when there is a large discrepancy between the educational backgrounds of the bride and groom and a large dowry has been demanded (Dasgupta et al. 1984). The bride's family may make unrealistic promises about its ability to pay a large dowry. This may be particularly likely to happen when it is anxious to marry one daughter off quickly because there are several other daughters waiting to be married. The only solution may be to pay the dowry in installments, which may make the groom's family dissatisfied and encourage them to pressure the girl to deliver the rest of what had been promised by her parents (Ghosh 1984; Ahuja 1987; Devi Prasa 1990). These economic discontentments may be aggravated by a variety of other factors such as incompatibility between spouses, unrealistic expectations of the wife, alcoholic family members, and the bride being young, lacking in education, and a stranger to her husband's family (Law Commission of India 1983; Ahuja 1987; Gautam & Trivedi 1987; Garg 1990).

Ahuja's Model of Violence against Women

The most complete attempt to date to explain dowry deaths in theoretical terms was made by Ahuja (1987), who developed a "social bond" theory of violence against women. This combines Hirschi's (1969) social-control theory with relative-deprivation theory to produce a theoretical framework that seeks to explain violence connected with the dowry principally in terms of variations among individual offenders in their social adjustment, values, and beliefs. His model emphasizes the social-structural conditions in which the perpetrators of violence suffer from feelings of insecurity and anxiety due to inappropriate upbringing, abnormal development in childhood, and unfortunate incidents in life. He also holds that certain women are seen as appropriate victims and that certain situations are suggestive of, or even opportune for, the use of violence.

Despite its comparatively sophisticated attempt to incorporate both psychological and sociological concepts, Ahuja's theory is open to a number of criticisms. In the first place, even accepting its general social-control premises, it could be argued that the offender's commitment, attachment, adjustments, and beliefs are not deficient, but simply that they are focused upon his parents rather than his wife. Second, the theory appears to over pathologize the problem of violence and pays too little attention to its instrumental value. Third, it is rather too general and has focused upon the common ingredients of violent crime at the expense of features that distinguish one crime from another; for example, bride burnings are very different from rape. Fourth, Ahuja's model is too offender-oriented and omits important factors such as the nature of the victim and her behavior and the roles of co-offenders. Fifth, as in the previous literature, too little attention has been paid in the model to the living situation after the marriage. For example, it appears that in many instances, neighbors ignore signs of distress in the marriage or may in fact be unaware that anything is wrong, which may be the result of either the family's physical or social isolation. Sixth, Ahuja ignores questions such as whether having a job protects the women from violence or whether sexual incompatibility or the wife's domestic incompetence or infertility increases the probability of violence. Finally, Ahuja largely ignores the family's decision-making processes in ridding themselves of the bride and thus fails to consider questions such as the following: How openly do the husband and his family plot between themselves to kill the bride or drive her into suicide? How justified do they feel in their actions? What assessment do they make of the risks of detection? To what extent do they consider the need to return any dowry paid? It makes one wonder how frequent the motive is for murder to free the groom to make another marriage with a better dowry? In cases where the wife commits suicide, little is known about her thought processes and why she chooses this course. In particular, it is unclear how far the wife's personality determines her choice and how far the particular circumstances of her current situation are the causal factor.

A Multifactor Model of Dowry Deaths

It will be clear from the description of the previous literature that two major groups of explanatory variables have not been properly addressed: the situational circumstances surrounding an act of dowry murder or suicide, and the thought processes of the parties involved. Two current criminological approaches address these topics—namely, *routine-activity theory* and the *rational-choice perspective.*

Routine-activity theory deals primarily with the situational variables and opportunities for direct-contact predatory violations. It specifies three minimal elements for predatory crime: a likely offender, a suitable target, and the absence of suitable guardians against crime (Cohen & Felson 1979). It seeks to explain how social changes can increase crime simply by increasing the vulnerability and attractiveness of targets and reducing the amount of guardianship.

The *rational-choice perspective* deals with the decision-making of the offender in committing the crime (Cornish & Clarke 1986). Under this approach, it is assumed that

> crime is purposive behavior designed to meet the offender's commonplace needs for such things as money, status, sex, and excitement, and that meeting these needs involves the making of decisions and choices, constrained as these are by limits of time and ability and the availability of relevant information. (Clarke & Felson 1993)

This approach treats the nature of the crime committed as central to an explanation of crime, since the decisions leading to one type of crime are different from those leading to another. It also emphasizes the distinction between criminal involvement and criminal events, since the influences on decision-making at these different stages will vary considerably.

In addition to concepts from the rational-choice and routine-activity perspectives, a more complete model of dowry deaths should incorporate two important concepts from the victimological literature (Fattah 1991).[1] The first is "vulnerability to victimization." Young wives in the type of marital arrangements described above are extremely vulnerable to victimization because they are isolated from their supportive social networks, they lack the ability to resist aggressive behavior, they have no means to earn their own living, and they are entirely dependent upon the husband's family for food and shelter.

The second victimological concept is that of "the culturally legitimate victim." From the description above of the ways that females are treated and marriages are arranged, it will be clear that Indian brides fit the model of the culturally legitimate victim. This culture provides the necessary justifications, rationalizations, and neutralizations that facilitate the killings (and suicides) that occur. It reduces the inhibitions and lowers the moral barriers that, in other cultures, would make such killings or suicides abhorrent. Finally, it supplies the economic incentives that promote this type of violence against women.

By integrating these various new concepts with existing theories as exemplified by that of Ahuja, a more complete model of dowry deaths results. This is described below, but first it should be noted that it is purely descriptive in nature and is meant to provide a framework for summarizing the various contributory factors identified in previous studies or suggested by a consideration of the new theoretical perspectives described above. In many cases, the relationships among these factors and victimization have not been empirically demonstrated. Likewise, the relationships among the various contributory factors have not been established. This means that the model may have little predictive power and its main value may lie in helping to shape research priorities.

The model falls into two parts, the first of which, influenced by sociocultural and victimological concepts, attempts to identify the kind of marriage arrangements that lead to a potential problem. These are groups of variables 1 through 9 as indicated in figure 20.1. The second part of the model is influenced by routine activity and rational-choice perspectives and attempts to deal with the more dynamic aspects of the phenomenon after marriage (groups 10–14). These groups are defines as follows.

Groups 1 and 2 cover the sociocultural factors (patriarchal traditional society; dowry system) that provide the context for the development of dowry problems. Dowry problems frequently arise within urban middle-class families with conservative outlooks.

Groups 3 through 6 concern the kinds of family and the needs of both the husband's and wife's families before the marriage. Economic needs are

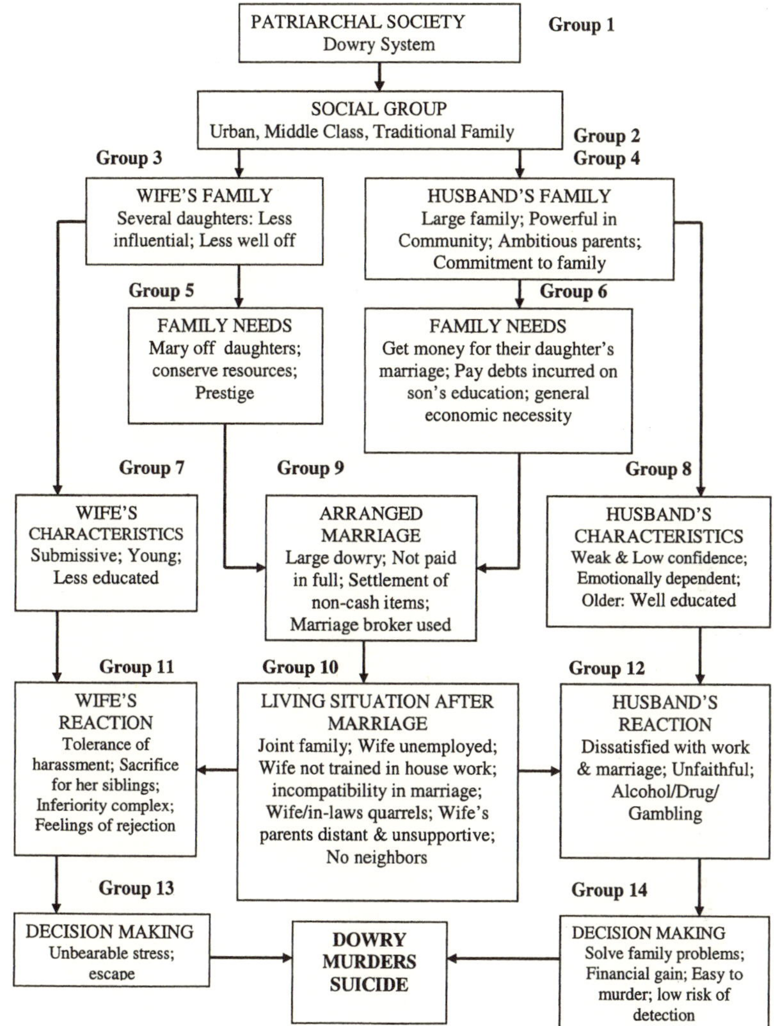

Figure 20.1 A model of dowry deaths.

important for both families. The husband's family may be trying to obtain resources through the dowry, by capitalizing on the husband's earning power. The wife's family may be trying to protect resources. The relative statues of the families are also relevant, with the husband's family generally being more influential.

Groups 7 and 8 deal with the personal characteristics of the wife and husband. Wives are more likely to be victimized if they are submissive, young, and less educated. Husbands are more likely to be aggressors, or to fall in with their parent's aggression, if they are weak and emotionally dependent. Husbands who are older and better educated than their wives are more likely to dominate their spouses and commit acts of violence against them.

The marriage contract (*Group 9*) attempts to reconcile the needs of the husband's and wife's families. The kind of arrangements that appear to lead to trouble include, for example, a large dowry not paid in full at the time of the marriage and dowries with noncash items over which disagreements arise about the quality of the goods supplied. Misunderstandings are likely to be greater if the families do not know each other well and have used a middleman to arrange the contract.

Group 10 deals with the living situation after marriage. In the joint family system, quarrels may center around the wife's insufficient dowry, especially when the wife is unemployed and not sufficiently trained in housework to satisfy the husband's family. As marriages are generally arranged, the chances of incompatibility between the husband and wife are high and the probability of disputes correspondingly great. The bride's parents will generally be unsupportive because of the prevailing belief that once a girl is married, her parents should not interfere in her new life, even if she comes to them for help. Even where they are supportive, they cannot come quickly to help her if they live at a distance away. The risk of physical abuse is increased when the husband's family lives in a quiet neighborhood or if there are no neighbors. That bride burning is basically an urban phenomenon may be partly due to the busy life in cities whereby neighbors tend to have little time to get involved in one another's affairs. The busy routines of urban dwellers thus leaves unguarded the defenseless young bride.

Groups 11 and 12 deal with the reactions of the husband and wife after marriage. The wife's personality will affect her reaction to her marital problems. She might tolerate the harassment and mistreatment so as not to bring any shame upon her parents. Since she is dependent upon her husband both emotionally and economically, she may completely lose confidence in herself. The fact that in many cases the husband has not chosen the wife may cause him much unhappiness, because he finds her unattractive or incompatible with his friends. These feelings of frustration may fuel his demands that the wife get more money from her parents.

Groups 13 and 14 deal with the husband's and wife's decision-making. If pressures upon the wife became intolerable, she may decide to take matters into her own hands and end her life. The husband, on the other hand, as a result of dissatisfaction at work and in his married life, may have affairs with other women, get involved in other activities such as gambling or alcohol or drugs. He may choose to deal with his difficulties and frustrations by plotting to kill his wife. This decision will be influenced by a perceived low risk of detection, the availability of an easy method of killing his wife, and the possibility of solving his problems by marrying some other woman with a better dowry settlement.

Conclusion

It has been argued above that the existing literature on dowry deaths has neglected the situational aspects of the crime as well as the decision-making of the offenders involved—theoretical components central to the routine-activity and rational-choice approaches. In particular, the living situation after marriage, the attitude of the husband, the behavior of the new bride, and the nature of the support provided to her by neighbors and her family have received insufficient attention. In the model presented above, these aspects have been incorporated, together with sociocultural variables of more traditional theoretical approaches and certain victimological concepts.

While the model seems to capture more fully the phenomenology of dowry deaths, it cannot claim to be a completely developed theory. First, certain perspectives on the phenomenon—from the feminist and Marxist literature, for example—are not fully represented in the present model. Second, because of the lack of research, the model contains numerous speculations about crucial causal factors. More needs to be learned, in particular, about the living conditions after marriage and the family dynamics and decision-making that lead to violence. Much more information is also needed about the victim's personality and her reactions, particularly when seeking to explain whether homicide or suicide is the outcome.

Apart from providing more complete or more satisfactory explanations of dowry deaths, however, the incorporation of rational-choice and routine-activity theory serves another and arguably more important purpose. This is to assist in thinking about preventive options—an urgent need, given the increasing prevalence of this serious and distressing form of violence against women. Most of the existing literature tends to discuss prevention in terms of reinforcing cultural values of nonviolence, educating women about their rights, and strengthening family ties. There is also general support in the literature for strengthening the government's efforts to prohibit the practice of dowry payments.

The routine-activity and rational-choice approaches would also direct attention to a variety of opportunity-reducing measures, such as creating neighborhood-watch programs, informant hotlines to report suspected violence against brides, and easier access to shelters for battered wives. In the longer term, a public-health approach to the problem of dowry deaths should consider possibilities for restricting access to lethal agents such as insecticides and open wells for water (Clarke & Lester 1989). Finally, brides' families need to be educated about signs of abuse, the dangers of using marriage-brokers, and the risks of sending their daughters away to distant families whom they barely know.

ACKNOWLEDGMENTS

I am grateful to Professors Ronald Clarke and Ezzat Fattah for their advice. This work was conducted in part while the author was a postdoctoral fellow in the Behavioral Sciences Training Program in the Drug Abuse Research Program sponsored by the Medical and Health Research Association of New York City, Inc., and the National Development and Research Institutes, Inc., with funding from the National Institute on Drug Abuse (5 T32 DA07233-09). Points of view expressed in this chapter do not necessarily represent the official views of these bodies.

NOTE

1. Fattah (1993) has noted that victimological concepts, such as those expressed in this chapter, are readily interpretable under the rational-choice/routine-activity framework developed to assist criminological explanation.

REFERENCES

Ahuja, R. (1987). *Crimes against women*. Jaipur, India: Rawat Publications.

Clarke, R. V., and M. Felson. (1993). *Routine activity and rational choice. Advances in criminological theory*, vol. 5. New Brunswick, NJ: Transaction Publishers.

Clarke, R. V., and D. Lester. (1989). *Suicide: Closing the exits*. New York: Springer-Verlag.

Cohen, E. L., and M. Felson. (1979). "Social change and crime rate trends: A routine activity approach." *American Sociological Review* 44:588–608.

Cornish, D. B., and R. V. Clarke (eds.). (1986). *The reasoning criminal: Rational-choice perspectives on offending*. New York: Springer-Verlag.

Dasgupta, S., M. Banerjee, et al. (1984). *A study of the dowry system in West Bengal*. Unpublished manuscript. Jaya Prakash Narayan Institute of Social Change, Calcutta.

Devi Prasad, B. (1990). "Dowry-related violence towards women: A sociological perspective," in *Violence against women*, ed. S. Sood (pp. 293–310). Jaipur, India: Arihant Publishers.

D'Souza, N., and R. Natarajan. (1986). "Women in India: The reality," in *Women in the world, 1975–1985: The women's decade*, ed. L. B. Iglitzin and R. Ross. Santa Barbara, CA: ABC-Clio Information Services.

Fattah, E. (1991). *Understanding criminal victimization*. Toronto, ON: Prentice Hall Canada.

———. (1993). "The rational-choice/opportunity perspective as a vehicle for integrating criminological and victimological theories," in *Routine activity and rational choice. Advances in criminological theory*, vol. 5, ed. R. Clarke and M. Felson. New Brunswick, NJ: Transaction Publishers.

Garg, S. A. (1990). *Bride burning*. Rohtak, India: Bright Law House.

Gautam, D. N., and B. V. Trivedi. (1987). *Unnatural deaths of married women with special reference to dowry deaths: A sample study of Delhi*. New Delhi: Police Research and Development.

Ghosh, S. K. (1984). *Women in a changing society.* New Delhi: Ashish Publishers.

Goody, J., and S. J. Tambiah. (1987). *Bridewealth and dowry.* London: Cambridge University Press.

Grover, K. (1990). *Burning flesh.* New Delhi: Vikas Publishing House.

Harrel, S., and S. A. Dickey. (1985). "Dowry systems in complex societies." *Ethnology 24*(1):105–20.

Hirschi, T. (1969). *Causes of delinquency.* Berkeley: University of California Press.

Khan, M. Z., and R. Ray. (1984). "Dowry death." *Indian Journal of Social Work 45* (3):303–15.

Kronholz, J. (1986). "Lingering cruelty: Bride burning seems on the rise in India." *Wall Street Journal* (August 21):15–17.

Kumari, R. (1989). *Brides are not for burning.* New Delhi: Radiant Publishers.

Law Commission of India. (1983). *91st report on dowry deaths and law reform: Amending the Hindu Marriage Act of 1955, the Indian Penal Code of 1896, and the Indian Evidence Act of 1872.* New Delhi: Government of India Press.

Paul, M. C. (1986). *Dowry and position of women in India.* New Delhi: Inter-India Publication.

Rao, V. (1983). "India," in *Suicide in Asia and the Near East,* ed. L. E. Headley (pp. 211–36). Berkeley: University of California Press.

Singh, H. (1986). *Forms of crisis intervention and types of immediate and structural measures to render assistance to women assaulted in the family.* United Nations Secretariat. Expert group meeting report on violence in the family, with special emphasis on its effects on women, Vienna, 8–12 August.

Sood, S. (ed.). (1990). *Violence against women.* Jaipur, India: Arihant Publishers.

Tambiah, S. J. (1973). "Dowry and bridewealth and the property rights of women," in *Bridewealth and dowry,* ed. J. Goody and S. J. Tambiah (pp. 59–169). London: Cambridge University Press.

Upadhya, C. B. (1990). "Dowry and women's property in coastal Andrapradesh." *Contributions to Indian Sociology, New Series 24*:29–59 (published in *International Review of Victimology 3*[4, 1995]:297–308).

CHAPTER TWENTY-ONE

Sexual Victimization by Airport Screeners, Post-9/11

terrorism, sexism, and capitalism at work

BONNIE BERRY

NOBODY NEEDS TO BE REMINDED of the occurrences of September 11, 2001. Besides the unspeakable grief surrounding the loss of life, the confusion of what it meant on a grand societal scale for the United States and all societies, and the disruption of ordinary ways of daily living, we are faced with the possibility of future attacks. The United States was not alone in searching for strategies to prevent future horrors, like the hijackings of 9/11 as well as not-yet-thought-of terrorist actions, from occurring again. Naturally, one place to focus preventive strategies is in the commercial airlines industry.

It quickly occurred to all who thought for a moment that, if the airlines could somehow have kept the hijackers off the ill-fated airplanes, 9/11 would not have happened. Since the event, a number of proposed remedies have been put into place, such as reinforced cockpit doors, additional training for the airline crews, the replacement of privately employed airport security with federally employed airport security, and (at least small-scale use of) bomb-detection devices.

The preventive reactions to terrorist activities (anthrax dissemination, the planting of bombs, attack on nuclear facilities, future hijackings, to name a few) were quickly subject to question, with public concern most notably surrounding the issue of effectiveness. That is, the public has expressed concern that the strategies devised by "homeland security" are not well-thought-out, are needlessly intrusive on civil rights, and, in essence, constitute too much window-dressing to prove helpful.

However, one security measure that seems unquestionably necessary is improved airport security. Immediately after the hijackings, the airlines and airports instituted what was assumed to be a helpful security measure: more strenuous and more intrusive screening of airline passengers and crews. Those boarding airplanes were subject to physical searches, along with more scrupulous baggage searches, under the stated belief that potential hijackers could be identified and thus prohibited from boarding. What was not taken into account was the lack of training and lack of incentives for the privately employed screeners, inappropriate targeting of airline employees, and the relationship between valid and legally condoned body searches and sexual exploitation of crews and passengers. As to the latter, one consequence of intensified airline passenger and crew searches had more to do with screeners taking sexual advantage of a captive, vulnerable audience than with airline safety.

While the purpose of airport screening is to screen passengers and luggage for any materials that could be used to impinge upon the safety of a commercial airliner, in fact, some airport screeners, in the wake of 9/11, intimidated and sexually victimized people who were absolutely no threat to the airlines, thus *increasing* real security risks. As will be shown, some of these privately employed security screeners used their mandate to scrutinize passengers and airline crews to commit sexual assault. They were implicitly supported in this behavior by their private employers, by National Guardsmen, and other airport law enforcement stationed at the airport, and indirectly by the airlines themselves.

This analysis will describe airport screeners' inappropriate treatment of flight crews (particularly flight attendants) and passengers, *without* an increase in security of the airlines, as documented by two data sources. Social-science literature on sexism, sexual harassment, and sexual exploitation support the interpretations. Finally, conclusions are provided on the larger picture of U.S. capitalism as a reason for failures in public safety, White House–led distractions via a focus on terrorism, and a resulting reduction in public rights to security.

Data Sources

Data for this study were supplied by the Association for Flight Attendants (AFA) and the Arizona Attorney General's office (AG). The AFA is the labor union representing 50,000 flight attendants at 26 airlines, with local councils nationwide. As one would expect, the AFA informs the flight-attendant population of ongoing labor issues and supports labor grievances to the appropriate organizations (the U.S. Department of Transportation, airline management, to name a few). The AFA maintains a Website posting notices and newsworthy items relevant to flight attendants, such as security breaches, new job procedures, and work-rule changes. Pertinent to this study, in the wake of 9/11, the Website encouraged flight attendants (or anyone else) who had been mistreated by airport security screeners to report the incident to AFA headquarters via email reports.

I became aware of the AFA's concern with security abuses from complaints registered to the Department of Transportation (DOT) by the AFA president, Patricia Friend, as reported in the *New York Times* (Sharkey 2001, 2002). I wrote to Ms. Friend and told her of my intentions to study the issue of security-screener assaults on flight attendants and was referred to Dawn Deeks, media spokesperson for the AFA, who turned over to me the complaints, as formally filed to the AFA. Ms. Deeks referred me to the Arizona AG, Janet Napolitano (now governor of Arizona), who has been integral in managing legal cases of passenger complaints about security-screener abuse. I contacted the AG and was referred to Lisa Glow, the chief counsel for the Office for Women, Arizona Attorney General's office. Ms. Glow provided me with the chronology of events regarding security-screener abuse of passengers, plus a record of the complaints themselves.

The AFA and the AG provided copies of letters to and from their offices (for example, correspondence between themselves and Norman Mineta, DOT secretary), memos, and other materials, all related to the need to gain relief from security-screener abuse. These correspondences juxtapose the requests from the AFA and the AG with the responses from the DOT and the Transportation Security Administration (TSA). Specific remedies were suggested by the AFA and the AG in these correspondences, including the need for same-sex screeners, screener identification badges, and training for the screeners, while the DOT and TSA replied with sympathy and often-nonspecific promises.

DESCRIPTIONS OF THE SCENARIOS

The AFA Reports

From November 2001 to January 2002, the AFA Website issued several notices of flight attendants being singled out and being groped by screeners. According to flight-attendant reports, passengers were not being subjected to the same intrusion as were flight attendants. Thus, we have two key issues: (a) unevenly administered searches, and (b) abusive behavior and illicit touching by screeners.

In November of 2001, a posting on the AFA Website described airport security screeners' "unprofessional and abusive behavior" toward flight attendants, including groping and fondling. This news was followed by a call from the AFA to have such screeners replaced with "real law-enforcement officers." That same month, the AFA president, Patricia Friend, wrote to Norman Mineta (secretary of the DOT), reporting that flight crews had "seemingly been targeted for extensive searches" with fondling and groping of female flight attendants by male screeners. She specifically recalled a report of a pregnant flight attendant being subjected to a body search, having her belly pressed against by the screeners, and being threatened with a strip search when she objected. Also described was the case of a female flight attendant who was

> repeatedly rubbed all over her body with a screening wand wielded by a male security guard. Although she asked him to stop touching her body, the guard continued to do so until she eventually stepped away from him. The guard got angry, then called for a female pat-down. The flight attendant was then frisked by a woman in latex gloves.

In another case, a female flight attendant was asked to put her food container through the scanner and, when the flight attendant pointed out that the food could spill and asked that it be hand-searched, the

> screener became irate and asked the flight attendant if she wanted a private room, without explaining why. The flight attendant indicated that she did not know why she would need a private room, at which time the screener had armed National Guardsmen surround the flight attendant and demanded she strip down.

Her fellow flight attendants went in search of the captain, but when the captain showed up and asked what was going on, he was told by the screeners that "there was nothing he could do, and they felt that [the flight attendant] was a security risk" (letter dated November 9, 2001 from Patricia Friend to Norman Mineta).

As to unfair targeting compared to passengers, Ms. Friend told Mr. Mineta that flight attendants were subject to "unevenly administered" security screening, such that passengers who set off metal detectors were allowed through while flight attendants who did not set off metal detectors were subject to a search. In closing, Ms. Friend reminded the DOT secretary that there are "mounds of evidence that . . . private contractors cannot properly administer critical security functions." Supervision, a bureaucratic response, said Ms. Friend, would not take care of the problem; the system's fatal flaw is the private contractors.

Receiving a sympathetic but noncommittal response from Mr. Mineta, Ms. Friend wrote again on February 7, 2002, recalling earlier complaints issued in November of 2001. Essentially, there was agreement from the DOT that the AFA concerns were valid, but no follow-up, and no indications of proposed or implemented remedies, were forthcoming from the DOT. Mr. Mineta stated the DOT position, strongly in support of the AFA, but the flight attendants were still having to issue numerous reports of continued abuse, "including illicit touching which rises to the level of sexual harassment."

To add insult to injury, the flight attendants were "afraid to provide their names and airline for fear of further reprisal from their carrier's management and the screening companies" (February 7, 2002 letter from Patricia Friend to Norman Mineta). Here we find that the victims were afraid to report their abuse for fear of reprisals from the screeners, screening companies, and their own employers. Among the recommendations Ms. Friend offered to Mr. Mineta at this point were: zero tolerance for the sexual harassment of crews and passengers by screeners, explicit statements that crews not be singled out for searches, and "clear procedures for crews and passengers to follow to interrupt an abusive search." Without such guidance, Ms. Friend wrote, "overzealous security screeners will continue to bully flight attendants and passengers into allowing illicit and illegal touching in the name of 'increased security.'" Early on, the AFA knew that the *manifest* function of screening was not the same as the *latent* (real) function of screening.

At the beginning of the year 2002, the AFA had posted on their Website advice for flight attendants who had been abused by screeners to report the incident online. Fifteen formal reports of screener assaults on flight attendants were filed with the AFA from September 11, 2001 to January 2002. More cases were *informally* presented to the AFA and local union-council leaders than were reported formally, but no exact figures were maintained by the AFA. According to the AFA media spokesperson, there had been about a hundred informal complaints reported to local councils (Deeks, personal communication, April 18, 2002). Ms. Deeks believes that all formal reports were filed by female flight attendants. However, male flight attendants have complained informally. (There is one report of this: a male flight attendant was frisked and made to open his pants in the boarding area while a passenger was allowed to board the same flight carrying long knitting needles. This was reported in a letter from Pat Friend to the DOT.) As to the gender of the assaultive screeners, they were both male and female.

All but three cases in the formal reports involved sexual exploitation. All the crew members reported being treated like "criminals" (in the case of luggage searches) or like "sex objects." In the case of sexual exploitation, the female crew members were routinely handled roughly in the breast and crotch regions. In their reports, they stated that they were singled out over passengers and, compared to pilots, were more often singled out for intrusive searches. Many were ignored when they asked for explanations. All had airline identification with them and most were in uniform. All faced the possibility of missing their flights, and some *did* miss their flights. Some were threatened with repercussions. Some were even threatened with drawn guns. As to the latter, a flight attendant requesting that her bags not be placed out of her sight (an FAA directive instructs that crew bags never be outside of the crew members' presence), resulted in the screener shouting, "I don't have to take this!" At this, another screener signaled a National Guardsman to come over, which he did, brandishing his weapon in a threatening manner.

In a not-atypical case, a flight attendant related in January 2002 that she reported for duty, in uniform. She was wanded by a female security screener, and the wand signaled over the flight attendant's watch and belt buckle but not over her bra (the flight attendant does not wear an underwire bra). The screener asked to touch the attendant's breasts, even though there was no indication of metal. The attendant replied that, no, the screener may not touch her breasts. The screener called a supervisor, who came over accompanied by a police officer with his hand hovering over his gun. The attendant explained again that she did not want to be touched. She was given two choices: either to be touched on the breasts or to undress behind a screened area. She chose the latter. She stepped behind the two-screened panel, which had one side fully exposed to a corridor, the corridor being situated between the luggage search table and a glass wall, near the National Guardsmen. Her identification tag was taken from her. She undressed while the screener watched. While undressed, the screener wanded her again, with the open side by the corridor left unattended and while her bags were hand-searched. She heard a male voice say, "There is always one." Soon after, a male airport employee walked by the unattended and open side of the "screened" area. She asked him for privacy as she was buttoning her shirt. The supervisor showed up and told her to wait there. The flight attendant waited and waited. Luckily, her flight was delayed because of weather; otherwise, she could have missed her flight and been charged by the airline. Besides the humiliation of the incident, she became worried that her name and identification information, which resided in security during the time of her ordeal, would incriminate her at some later point. The wand was not activated during the search of the breast area.

Flight attendants, so far as the AFA spokesperson knows, have not sought legal remedies; the reason being that they fear employer and other sanctions for doing so. Ms. Deeks refers to this as the "fear factor" and stated that the attendants did not "want to make any more noise than necessary." The attendants were upset, angry, and embarrassed by their treatment but seemed satisfied so long as the abuse stopped (Deeks, personal communication, May 13, 2002).

The complaint-filing subsite was removed from the AFA Website as of April 24, 2002. Also, as of that date, the AFA Website does not carry the story of groping incidences or a location point for flight-attendant assault reports.

When asked why the reports dropped off after January 2002, Ms. Deeks guessed that there may be two reasons: (a) publicity and awareness, and (b) the federal takeover of screeners' duties by the TSA. When the AFA began to ask for incident reports and newspapers began reporting screener assaults, screeners became wise to the fact that they could get into trouble for assaulting people. With the federal takeover, screeners became answerable to the federal government and were under federal oversight (Deeks, personal communication, April 18, 2002).

When asked why flight attendants would refrain from reporting abuse,

Ms. Deeks responded that the consequences to reporting are not insignificant. If a flight attendant complains, she can ask for the airport ground-security supervisor (GSS) to address the problem. If that person is unavailable, a National Guardsman could have been called upon, who would then arrive with guns drawn and ask the attendant what her problem was. Also, the GSS may be unable to take care of the problem right away and the flight attendant would then have to wait. Knowing that time is of the essence in flight schedules, the attendant often cannot afford to wait. If she misses her flight, it then becomes a disciplinary issue with the airline. She can, in other words, be molested by a screener, scared by a gun-toting guardsman, and punished by her employer (Deeks, personal communication, April 18, 2002).

I asked Ms. Deeks why screeners would specifically target flight attendants for abuse. She responded with several interpretations. One suggestion is that, when crews blamed the screeners for poor security prior to and after 9/11, the screeners took it as a personal attack on them. The crews did not mean to say that the screeners per se were doing a poor job, but rather that the problem was structural: private screeners were vastly underpaid, they were not trained, and the turnover rate was very high. But the screeners viewed crew complaints as an attack and, as a result, the screeners exercised a backlash against pilots and flight attendants, especially the latter. The screeners verbalized their resentment toward the crews in terms of the crews thinking that they are better than the screeners. A second and related notion is, as the screeners said, "this is what you asked for." Crews wanted more security, so the screeners responded with searching them even if the crew members did not set off alarms or cause any security concerns. A third interpretation is that screeners harassed flight attendants because they could. The screeners were suddenly granted the power to abuse them under the pretense of post-9/11 security, so they did. There were basically no constraints on the screeners. A fourth, overarching explanation is that there may have been pressure from higher up the security chain. That is, screeners were responding to orders, subtle or otherwise, to abuse crews. Perhaps this is part of the backlash picture; certainly the private contractors providing airport-screening services did not want to be threatened with losing their "gravy train" (Deeks, personal communication, May 2, 2002).

Flight attendants are singled out over pilots, who are more likely to be male, more likely to complain, and more likely to have their complaints taken seriously, with men and pilots obviously having more power than women and flight attendants. Anecdotally, it is known that female pilots were also molested by screeners but, as far as is known, there have been no formalized reports to that effect. Captain Peter Lara described to me conversations he had with two female first officers, both of whom reported that they had been "felt up" by screeners. As with the flight attendants, and not at all surprisingly, they found the incidents humiliating and embarrassing. Because they were molested in full view of passengers, these pilots felt that their credibility was nullified; hence the comment by one, "There goes my credibility" (Lara, personal communications, April 9–12, 2002).

Screeners may also believe, with some validity, that women in the employee role are less likely to complain than women and men with greater social power, thus explaining why flight attendants were more likely to be singled out than passengers. Passengers, being paying customers, may have been considered by the screeners to be more likely to complain and be taken seriously. Passengers were also more likely to have their complaints responded to positively; unlike the flight attendants, who could expect their employer to be unsupportive (Deeks, personal communication, May 2, 2002).

The Arizona Attorney General Reports

The chronology, as presented by the Arizona AG's office, shows roughly the same itinerary as that provided by the AFA. In January of 2002, Janet Napolitano (then attorney general for the state of Arizona) wrote to America West Airlines and the FAA about a passenger complaint, in which it was alleged that women were singled out for searches and pat-downs by male screeners. The letters continue to flow between the AFA, the AG, the DOT, the FAA, and the TSA. Overall, the DOT and FAA took a hands-off approach, although the TSA *did* try to set a useful policy for same-sex searches. In March of 2002, the TSA set standards for when to frisk and established a hotline and ombudsman to hear complaints. In April of 2002, the TSA set new security-screening procedures, complete with improved training, standardizing the search process, minimizing pat-down-abuses, and instituting same-gender searches (Arizona attorney general, Airline Pat-Down Searches Chronology).

Complaints of screener abuse, registered with the AG, were made available to me by Lisa Glow, the AG's chief counsel. The AG records show that 48 incidents of screener abuse were reported from September 2001 to September 2002 (one case was prior to 9/11). One case had two complainants; thus there are actually 49 complainants for the 48 cases. By gender, the victims were 88 percent female (n = 43) and 12 percent male (n = 6). There were at least 50 screeners involved in these cases; the confusion arises from records showing an unspecified number of male screeners involved in a few cases. Of those screeners, 34 percent (n = 17) are female and at least 54 percent (n = 27) are male, and 12 percent (n = 6) have the gender unspecified. The cases recorded by the AG resemble the flight-attendant complaints and, indeed, four of them are incidents of abuse of airline employees. Of the airline crews who issued complaints, one was a male airline captain, in uniform, who was inappropriately touched by a female screener.

Of the complaints themselves, 28 cases (58 percent) were about sexual assault, 19 cases (40 percent) were about luggage searches or mixed-gender searchers (but without sexual abuse), and one case (2 percent) has no specific complaint listed. The sexual-abuse complaints were quite stark. For example, in the case of one female passenger, she related that a male screener put his fingers down the back of her pants while male security onlookers made sexual remarks such as "you lucky man," "let me show you what to do with that wand," "do that real slow, especially over her butt," and "see if she has nice feet. You know what they say about women with nice feet." This complainant also had her breasts touched. In general, female passengers and crew members in the AG records were groped on the thighs, legs, breasts. When they complained, they were told that, if they did not submit, they would be disallowed boarding. In one case, a female passenger was told by a male security supervisor that she has no rights.

The outcomes of these cases of airline crew and passenger assaults are not yet entirely decided, but the routes for remedies are quite different. In the case of the flight-attendants' complaints to the AFA, as discussed above, no legal remedies were sought. In the case of the passengers' complaints, there is likely to be legal repercussions. In Lisa Glow's email of May 10, 2002, she mentioned, as illustrated by the charts she sent, that legal action is taking place, and that action seems to have been crucial to changing the screener-abuse picture. That is, the complaints reported by the passengers (and some airline crew members) to the Arizona attorney general had their cases attended to by the AG's Civil Rights Division, as well as by the police (such as local law enforcement, for sexual or simple assaults), airports authorities, airlines, the federal government, state government, and the complainants' lawyers. One of the reasons that the Arizona AG received complaints was that no one else was "acting on those complaints or taking them seriously. As the chief law-enforcement official of the state, people thought they should let the AG be aware of what was occurring" (Glow, personal communication, May 13, 2002).

I asked Ms. Glow the same question I asked Ms. Deeks: Why did this screener-abuse situation arise in the first place? The problem, as Ms. Glow sees it, "resulted in large part from putting people in positions of power and control without having proper safeguards, procedures, and training. Failing to take complaints seriously fed on the abuses" (Glow, personal communication, May 7, 2002). Also, because the complainants are largely women, the lack of concern was aggravated by their social powerlessness. From Ms. Glow's remarks, we might assume that private employment (read *profit-fed capitalism*, discussed below) and sexism are the keys to understanding this unfortunate phenomenon.

Summary

Both sets of victims—flight attendants and passengers—can be and have been threatened (told they couldn't board their flights if they didn't cooperate, told they didn't have rights, told they might get strip-searched, and so on). Both sets of victims felt singled-out, especially for being female. Both sets felt that the searches, or the nature of the searches, were unnecessary. The problem seems to have stemmed from placing people in power without proper training, knowledge of procedures, and accountability. Worse, the problem was aggravated by the complaints not being taken seriously by the DOT, the airlines, and certainly not by the private-security employers.

Screener Abuse and the Meaning of Sexual Exploitation

Sexism is at the very heart of the abusive behavior by screeners. Sexism is a primary explanation for the intrusive screener searches of flight attendants, just as it is for sexual exploitation and sexual harassment for other female populations. The gender ratio for flight-attendant victim cases and passenger-victim cases, with women heavily outranking men as victims, is startling yet not surprising. The Arizona AG data, the AFA reported cases, and the AFA spokesperson's comments clearly show this. What we have here is *institutionalized sexism,* which refers to discriminatory behavior, policy, or law as institutionalized, as indelibly linked to the organization (private airport security, for instance) and as systemically embedded in the organization without questioning the fairness of its practice. Institutionalized sexism does not necessarily *directly* prohibit one group's rights, such as women's rights to fair-and-equal treatment, but can do so more indirectly. As we see with Title VII of the 1964 Civil Rights Act, this legislation does not necessarily protect women employees from institutionalized sexism (Belknap 2001, 368).

To place the assaults on flight attendants and passengers within the broader context of sexual exploitation (assaults, rapes) of other, nonairline-boarding populations, we might consider sex-as-a-tool-for-power phenomena. Besides "assaults" to describe screener sexual abuse, better, if not more cumbersome, terms include *sexual exploitation* and *sexual victimization,* with sexual exploitation (including abuse of power) as exercised by the offender over the victim, whether that abuse of power is economic, physical, and/or status in nature and whether that abuse takes the form of rape, sexual assault, or sexual harassment (Russell 1996), and sexual victimization referring to "any forced or coerced sexual intimacy," including "rape, molestation, sexual harassment, attempted rape, and sexual assault with foreign objects" like security wands (Belknap 2001, 228).

As we have seen in the above case scenarios, among the corollaries common to sexual assaults against flight attendants and against other women are the justifications ("she was asking for it") and responses (an absence of punishment for the assaulters and multiple punishments for the victims). An aged interpretation of sexual victimization has been that the victims "ask for it," and thus we have the erroneous concept of "invited abuse." Richard Gelles (1979) writes that sexual-abuse victims as well as battered women are often accused of having provoked the abusive behavior. Indeed, sexual-assault victims and battered wives are often accused of "asking for," "deserving," or "enjoying" their victimization (Gelles 1979, 121; see also Wolfgang [1958] on "victim-precipitated" violence). Strangely, this notion of invited abuse fits with what is known about screener abuse of flight attendants: the security screeners felt "invited" to abuse the flight attendants, since the flight attendants "invited" the increased security measures.

Additionally, underreporting, common to all sexual assaults, applies to the cases of abuse by screeners against flight attendants, and might be assumed from a comparison of formal-to-informal complaints, had such a comparison been documented. Battering and sexual victimization are the criminal offenses least commonly reported to the police (Young 1992), and when victims *do* tell of the offenses, they ordinarily keep the incident "private" (Stanko 1992). The underreporting of sexual and physical exploitation to police and researchers is directly situated in the victims' feelings that the events were too personal to discuss, in the victims' embarrassment and shame, and in their fear of reprisal by the abuser (Smith 1994), which, as we have seen, is precisely the case for assaulted flight attendants. According to Dawn Deeks, the AFA media coordinator, informal reports to her and to the local councils were more common than formal reports of flight-attendant assaults. And, as we have seen, the flight attendants *did* have reason to fear reprisals from their employers (the airlines), from the screeners, and from airport security personnel (such as the National Guard).

Belknap (2001) has argued that gender-power disparity and female victimization reinforce each other. Indeed, the purpose of sexual exploitation is to put women in their place, to make it unmistakably clear that they possess less social power than men. With sexual victimization, the victimization is an act of power, of domination, of forced submission: "it is a way for a victim to experience that she does not have control over her own body . . ." (Belknap 2001, 213). Domination is the objective, and sex is the tool by which dominance is achieved.

This power differential is not restricted to physical power but is also, perhaps more significantly, pervasive in economic- and social-power differentials. Verbal abuse, like physical abuse, violates "a woman's sense of dignity and self-worth" and often this is where sexual harassment comes into play (Schechter 1982, 17). Thus we see that sexual victimization ranges from sheer force to coercion (a psychological means to gain power, as in the use of threats). Using coercion, the abusive security screener issued threats, enforced by physical and sexual power, to achieve control; an example would be threatening the flight attendants or passengers that they would miss their flights (and thus be punished by the airline, in the case of flight attendants) if they were not cooperative.

Sexual harassment may be closer to the mark in explaining security-screener assaults on flight attendants, if for no other reason than this gender-laden, abusive conduct occurs in the workplace. Flight attendants have an unfortunate and long history of sexual and other harassment as enacted by passengers and fellow crew members. This phenomenon is almost entirely due to the flight attendants' (traditionally female) gender and their relative powerlessness (compared to paying customers and pilots). Recently, sexual harassment of flight attendants has been alleviated somewhat by (a) a change in attitude and behavior on the part of flight attendants to one of enhanced power and awareness, (b) a change in gender composition to include more male flight attendants in the flight-attendant population, thus granting the flight-attendant population more social power, since men have more power, and (c) sensitivity training and recent policy to disallow sexual harassment perpetrated by crew members onto other crew members (Lara, personal communication, June 9, 2002).

Sexual harassment has been defined as unwanted sexual attention occurring in work conditions, including unwanted touching, verbal (sexual teasing, jokes, comments, or questions) or visual behavior (leering), and unwanted pressure for sexual favors with implied threats of retaliation for noncooperation (Stanko 1985, 60). Sexual harassment was not a labeled behavior until 1975 (Evans 1978) and litigation of sexual-harassment cases did not come about until the mid-1970s, when Title VII of the Civil Rights Act of 1964 included protection against sexual harassment in the workplace. Title VII, as written in 1964, did not link sexual harassment to gender discrimination (Rifkind & Harper 1993), but Catherine MacKinnon (1979) proposed that sexual harassment *is* a form of gender discrimination (Erickson & Simon 1998).

Of course, both genders are subject to sexual harassment, but women are far more likely to be the victims (Antecol & Cobb-Clark 2001; Kalof, Eby, Matheson, & Korska 2001). Specifically regarding the sexual harassment of men, Lee (2000) concludes that the male experience of workplace sexual harassment has the unique undercurrents of what constitutes "acceptable" masculinity, as when men operate in traditionally women's work roles, such as would be the case for flight attendants. The male flight attendant described above in the AFA informal reports may have been viewed as inhabiting a stereotypically woman's occupational role and thus placed in the role of (less powerful) women vis-à-vis the screener's abuse.

As to the gender ratios in sexual exploitation, the National Crime Victimization Survey studied workplace violence between 1992 and 1996 in the United States and found that the vast majority of perpetrators of violence in the workplace (83 percent) are men and that one-third of the victims are women (Warchol 1998). In support of this, in a study of violence against college women, Belknap, Fisher, and Cullen (1999) found that women comprise about one-third of violent victimizations. The gender ratios of sexual victimization and workplace violence are not dissimilar to what the Arizona AG's office found in their examination of security-screener assaults on passengers, with the victims mostly being female (88 percent) and the abusers mostly male (at least 54 percent). Airlines, like criminal-justice agencies, have traditionally been male-dominated; specifically, males dominated the better, power-laden, high-paying jobs (as pilots, management officials, and so on). So, it is not surprising that female employees are more likely to be sexually harassed in male-dominated workplaces (Pogrebin & Poole 1997; Stohr, May, Beck, & Kelley 1998).

In light of legal remedies to sexual harassment and making the leap from security screeners to police officers and placing both in work contexts, compare Vaughn's (1999) analysis of law (specifically, civil liability under state tort law), sexual harassment, and police sexual violence to the Arizona AG's response to screener assaults. Vaughn described vicarious liability under the doctrine of *respondent superior* and discusses police sexual-violence cases litigated pursuant to intentional and negligence torts, concluding that there is insufficient data collection on the problem, perhaps as a consequence of the absence of criminal-justice agencies' monitoring of their employees' misconduct. Recall that the chief counsel for the AG's office, Lisa Glow, has suggested that *because* the complainants resorted to legal remedies, these cases face successful resolution.

And finally, regarding the social construction of sexual harassment, Black and Allen (2001) address media-generated constructions, and Wilson (2000) explores, more broadly, social constructions. Black and Allen (2001) point out that, by anecdotal accounts, we know that Anita Hill's testimony against Clarence Thomas and the outcome of those hearings had an important impact on the politics of sexual harassment. Wilson (2002), exploring the social perception of sexual assault and sexual harassment in education, argues that understanding the harassment phenomena necessitates analysis of the victims' experience *along with* the complex thinking and behavior surrounding the phenomenon, as would be the case in understanding the structural supports for such sexual exploitation. According to the AFA and AG's spokespersons, one reason that screener abuse of flight attendants ceased was because of the publicity surrounding the issue; that is, it has been helpful for the public to gain an understanding of security-screeners' sexually intrusive behavior in an institutionalized context. Sexual exploitation, under the guise of "increased security," is, in truth, an offense that has nothing to do with increased airline safety.

SCREENER ABUSE, CAPITALISM, AND OTHER POWER ISSUES

Besides sexism, there are other, related power differentials that require attention in this phenomenon of screener abuse of airline crews and passengers. As far as is known, flight attendants were more commonly abused by screeners than were pilots; flight attendants obviously have less social and economic power than pilots and are more likely to be women. Comparing flight attendants to passengers, flight attendants claim that they were more likely to be targeted than passengers and to have less recourse to resolving the issues of abuse (Sharkey 2001; Deeks, personal communication, 2002; AFA Website). Flight attendants, compared to passengers, had or felt they had less leeway to complain about screener abuse; and the airlines were much more responsive to passengers than they were to their own employees. Passengers *pay* to fly and the airlines certainly do not want to alienate them.

Another crucial factor contributing to screener abuse is the profit-orientation on the part of private screening companies and the airlines. It can be effectively argued that the problem of screener abuse came about because of the airlines' resistance to contract with better-trained, better-qualified, and better-compensated screeners. Until recently, all airport screeners were privately employed, with the onus being on the private employers to select and train their employees. But they did not; they employed those who cost the least. Private-security employment agencies, such as Argenbright, hired those with few employment options (the uneducated, those unable to speak and understand English, many with prison records), and the privately employed screeners were almost totally untrained in proper screening procedures. Even after the tragedy of 9/11, when the question arose whether to rid commercial air travel of privately employed screeners, a hue-and-cry erupted from those who financially benefit the most from keeping the security system unchanged, notably the private security employers. The private security organizations, obviously, did not want to lose their contracts with the airlines; but neither did the airlines want to employ better-qualified and better-compensated screeners to the extent that it would jeopardize their profit margins. With the creation of the Transportation Security Administration (TSA), U.S. airports came under pressure to rid the screener population of privately employed screeners and to install, instead, federally employed screeners, under the reasoning that federal oversight will guarantee accountability.

Summary: Terrorism, Sexism, Capitalism, and the Unmet Need for Secure Airlines

The backdrop to this analysis has been, appropriately, sexism and sexual exploitation. Against common sense, post-9/11 flight attendants and passengers were sexually molested by airport screeners under the guise of increased security. Terrorism served as the excuse for bodily and other intrusions by screeners against airline crews and passengers.

As of May 2002, Argenbright remained in full force at Chicago and other airports despite its poor history and despite the supposed implementation of the TSA guidelines. As Frank Rich (2002, A27) put it:

> Remember Argenbright, the rent-a-guard company that was found to have employed convicts and illegal aliens to enforce airport security? It's still manning the fort in five major airports, from Orlando to O'Hare, where it no doubt continues to do a crack job of strip-searching little old ladies. This week *USA Today* reported that the new Transportation Security Administration has failed to fix the known security flaws that could allow the easy planting of bombs in the virtually unscreened cargo on passenger jets; the paper also found evidence that the same agency is cutting back on marksmanship training for the federal air marshals it is hiring to do the shooting. . . . As for the airport bomb-detecting machines mandated by Congress, the *Wall Street Journal* finds 190 in place, with a mere 1,100 still to go.

By November 2002, all screeners were TSA employees, but baggage screening is far from complete.

Overall, the public is not any safer than they were before 9/11. Flight attendants remain concerned about the "back door to airport terrorism: ground-crew security" (Morrison 2002). Thousands of airport mechanics, caterers, and ramp workers continue to have access to airplanes and runways without passing through metal detectors or undergoing regular searches; this access continues in spite of provisions in the new Aviation and Transportation Security Act that require tighter measures. This lack of security has caused enough concern among flight attendants that the Southwest Airlines flight-attendants' union has filed a grievance with their airline and has caused AFA President Friend to state that we are only creating the "illusion of security" for public view, and meanwhile there is nothing being done to truly increase security (cited in Morrison 2002).

As further depressing evidence that little is being done to increase security, the *New York Times* editors refer to the National Strategy for Homeland Security, unveiled on July 16, 2002, as "almost perfunctory" (2002a). The editors point out that the strategy has taken "more than eight months to prepare, a glacial pace given the severity of the threat" (p. A22) and that the proposal was put forward by the White House only after intense pressure from Congress. Other than the central proposal to create a Department of Homeland Security, the Bush "administration has been slow in developing a coherent domestic security strategy," leaving the public at risk and to wonder why we continue to be at risk (p. A22). The *Times* editors added, on July 22, in their discussion of the Terrorism Information and Prevention System (a system that encourages informing on fellow Americans of any activity thought to be relevant to terrorism), that such a suggestion is likely to be ineffective in fighting terrorism and is, additionally, un-American. They write: "The Bush administration's post-Sept. 11 anti-terrorism tactics—secret detentions of suspects, denial of the right to trial and now citizen spying—have in common a lack of faith in democratic institutions and a free society" (2002b, A18).

The Homeland Security Bill was signed on November 25, 2002 and it leaves much to be desired. The bill, besides not guaranteeing security, is replete with special-interest provisions that are helpful to Republican Congressional members, to the White House, and to the corporations that support them. For example, the Homeland Security Department is permitted to contract with companies that leave the United States to avoid taxes, and the makers of vaccine ingredients as well as airline security-screening companies are guaranteed immunity from lawsuits (Firestone 2002).

All this is by way of saying that, as a nation, we are as likely to be at risk as we were before 9/11. We hear repeated warning by the Bush administration that we can expect any number of new attacks, while little is being done to prevent them, presumably leaving us as vulnerable as we were before "homeland security" was put into place. Moreover, I am hardly the first to suggest that, given the current administration's agendas (to increase the wealth of the already-wealthiest, to reduce women's rights, to rid the nation of social security and living wages, to destroy the environment, and so on), terrorism serves well as an excellent distraction. More tragedies may be exactly what are needed to maintain a high level of public fear and, thus, divert attention from our diminishing civil liberties and human rights.

In summary, airline security was not improved by abusive searches; indeed, the security of the airlines was further jeopardized by inappropriate screener intrusion. It is anybody's guess as to whether the TSA would have replaced and trained screeners had it not been for the AFA and the Arizona AG's complaints of assault problems. We can, however, safely assume that the assaults on flight attendants and passengers are only one example of many that our safety is *not* a high priority among the pro-business Bush administration. The current governmental structure is heavily reliant upon and ideologically inseparable from profit-driven corporations. It is difficult to avoid the conclusion that *systemic* failure is operating—fueled by sexism, greed, and a lack of interest in public safety—located distinctly in the current White House and in corporate structures with a stake in inadequate and labor-unfriendly security.

We reserve our guaranteed rights to be safe in our persons and our property. We all have the right to be free from abuse—from terrorists and from formally sanctioned corporate and governmental structures.

REFERENCES

Antecol, Heather, and Deborah Cobb-Clark. (2001). "Men, women, and sexual harassment in the U.S. military." *Gender Issues 19*:3–18.

Arizona Attorney General's Office. (2002). "Airline pat-down searches chronology."

Belknap, Joanne. (2001). *The invisible woman: Gender, crime, and justice*, 2nd ed. Belmont, CA: Wadsworth Publishing.

Belknap, Joanne, Bonnie Fisher, and Francis Cullen. (1999). "The development of a comprehensive measure of the sexual victimization of college women." *Violence Against Women 5*:185–214.

Black, Amy E., and Jamie L. Allen. (2001). "Tracing the legacy of Anita Hill: The Thomas/Hill hearings and media coverage of sexual harassment." *Gender Issues 19*:33–52.

Deeks, Dawn (AFA media coordinator). (2002). Personal communication (April 18).

———. (2002). Personal communication (May 2).

———. (2002). Personal communication (May 13).

Erickson, Rosemary J., and Rita J. Simon. (1998). *The use of social science data in Supreme Court decisions*. Urbana: University of Illinois Press.

Evans, Laura J. (1978). "Sexual harassment: Women's hidden occupational hazard," in *The victimization of women*, ed. J. Roberts-Chapman and M. Gates (pp. 202–23). Beverly Hills, CA: Sage Publications.

Firestone, David. (2002). "Domestic security bill riles 9/11 families." *New York Times* (November 26):A17.

Gelles, Richard J. (1979). *Family violence*. Beverly Hills, CA: Sage Publications.

Glow, Lisa (chief counsel, Office for Women, Arizona Attorney General's Office). (2002). Personal communication (May 7).

———. (2002). Personal communication (May 10).

———. (2002). Personal communication (May 13).

Kalof, Linda, Kimberly K. Eby, Jennifer L. Matheson, and Rob J. Korska. (2001). "The influence of race and gender on student self-reports of sexual harassment by college professors." *Gender and Society 15*:282–302.

Lara, Peter (captain, United Airlines). (2002). Personal communications (April 9–12).

———. (2002). Personal communication (June 9).

Lee, Deborah. (2000). "Hegemonic masculinity and male feminisation: The sexual harassment of men at work." *Journal of Gender Studies 9*:141–55.

MacKinnon, Catherine A. (1979). *Sexual harassment of working women*. New Haven, CT: Yale University Press.

Morrison, Blake. (2002). "Attendants question ground security." *USA Today* (April 30). Available at <http://www.usatoday.com>.

New York Times. (2002a). "A master plan for homeland security" (July 17):A22.

———. (2002b). "Informant fever" (July 22):A18.

Pogrebin, Mark R., and Eric D. Poole. (1997). "The sexualized work environment: A look at women jail officers." *Prison Journal 77*:41–57.

Rich, Frank. (2002). "Thanks for the heads-up." *New York Times* (May 25):A27.

Rifkind, Lawrence J., and Loretta F. Harper. (1993). *Sexual harassment in the workplace: Women and men in labor*. Dubuque, IA: Kendall-Hunt.

Russell, Diane E. H. (1996). *Sexual exploitation: Rape, child sexual abuse, and workplace harassment*, 2nd ed. Beverly Hills, CA: Sage Publications.

Schechter, Susan. (1982). *Women and male violence*. Boston: South End Press.

Sharkey, Joe. (2001). "Some female flight attendants are complaining of being 'fondled and groped' by security guards." *New York Times* (December 5):C6.

———. (2002). "Despite a long-standing policy of same-sex screenings, charges of airport groping continue." *New York Times* (March 20):C11.

Smith, Michael D. (1994). "Enhancing the quality of survey data on violence against women: A feminist approach." *Gender and Society 8*:109–27.

Stanko, Elizabeth A. (1985). *Intimate intrusions: Women's experience of male violence*. London: Routledge/Kegan Paul.

———. (1992). "The case of fearful women: Gender, personal safety and fear." *Women and Criminal Justice 4*:117–35.

Stohr, Mary K., G. Larry Mays, Ann C. Beck, and Tammy Kelley. (1998). "Sexual harassment in women's jails." *Journal of Contemporary Criminal Justice 14*: 135–55.

Vaughn, Michael S. (1999). "Police sexual violence: Civil liability under state tort law." *Crime and Delinquency 45*:334–57.

Warchol, Greg. (1998). "Workplace violence, 1992–1996." Bureau of Justice Statistics, U.S. Department of Justice (July 8).

Wilson, Fiona. (2000). "The social construction of sexual harassment and assault of university students." *Journal of Gender Studies 9*:171–87.

Wolfgang, Marvin. (1958). *Patterns in criminal homicide*. Philadelphia: University of Pennsylvania Press.

Young, Vernetta D. (1992). "Fear of victimization and victimization rates among women." *Justice Quarterly 9*:419–42.

Websites

Airline Pilots Association: <http://www.alpa.org>.

Association of Flight Attendants: <http://www.afanet.org>.

Department of Transportation, Aviation Consumer Protection Division: <http://www.dot.gov/airconsumer/problems.htm>.

Federal Aviation Association: <http://www.faa.gov>.

Transportation Security Administration: <http://www.tsa.gov>.

PART FOUR

The Differentially Vulnerable

CHAPTER TWENTY-TWO

Social Distance and Vulnerability

the case of sexual orientation

JAMES GAROFALO
JANE BRYANT

NEARLY HALF A CENTURY AGO, Gresham Sykes and David Matza offered a framework for understanding juvenile delinquency that questioned the notion of a separate delinquent subculture comprised of norms and values in opposition to the dominant culture. They argued that delinquents were imbued with the norms and values of the dominant culture and that, in order for delinquent acts to be committed, various mechanisms—techniques of neutralization—were necessary to counteract the constraints of those norms and values (Sykes & Matza 1957).

In recent years, the popular image of the young offender has departed substantially from the image contained in the Sykes and Matza framework. At the close of the twentieth century, the image of the "superpredator" was dominant: the young male who robs, maims, and kills without hesitation or remorse, who is completely outside the moral constraints of society (see, for example, Elikann [1999]). This image implies that the offenders don't make distinctions among potential victims, and that the risk of victimization is almost completely dependent upon exposure and proximity to the offenders. But we know that, in some types of crimes, offenders consciously select victims on the basis of the victims' characteristics. The clearest example of this is *hate-crime victimization*, in which by definition, some perceived characteristic of the victim is a primary factor in the offender's motivation.

The foundation of this chapter is the argument that an understanding of hate-crime offending can benefit from incorporating a perspective similar to the one offered by Sykes and Matza (for an example, see Byers,

Crider, and Biggers 1999). Economic factors, peer-group influences, and other variables may well affect the motivation to commit hate-crime offenses. However, we maintain that an important element influencing which segments of the population are vulnerable to hate-crime victimization is the extent to which members of those segments are viewed as undeserving "others" rather than "one of us." The deeper and more widespread the attitudes of "otherness" are, the more vulnerable the disvalued group is to hate-crime victimization because the constraints against victimizing members of the group are diminished. This position appears especially tenable in light of the evidence suggesting that, on average, hate-crime offenders are young males without extensive criminal records who act spontaneously in groups—not criminal sociopaths or even active members of organized hate groups (Garofalo 1997; Levin 2002).

In this chapter, we explore the notion of "otherness" through the concept of *social distance.* Operationally, we define *social distance* as the degree to which a person wants to avoid contact with a member of some specified group. While social distance, so conceived, is not synonymous with prejudice, it is a reasonable indicator of the degree to which a person does or does not feel a sense of social connectedness with members of particular groups. And the logic followed here is that the less social connectedness one feels with others, the more one feels free to behave in negative ways toward them.

Our specific focus is on social distance in regards to sexual orientation, because the existing literature leads us to believe that negative attitudes toward gays and lesbians are, in some ways, different than negative attitudes toward other groups. This is not meant to imply that the attitudes are worse, just that they stem at least partly from somewhat different sources and are structured differently (see, for example, the discussion of various forms of hate in Perry 2001).

Social distance is examined using questionnaire responses, and attitudes toward gays and lesbians are further illustrated with responses to an open-ended question posed to a different set of subjects. The linkage between social distance and the willingness to act in a prejudicial manner toward gays and lesbians is tested using questionnaire responses to hypothetical scenarios.

DATA

A questionnaire was completed by the 151 students who attended a specific class on a single day in February 2000 at Southern Illinois University, Carbondale. The course—"Crime, Justice, and Social Diversity"—is a lower-division, undergraduate course and part of the university's core curriculum; thus, enrollment consists of students from virtually every major on the campus. The 151 students who completed the questionnaire were primarily freshmen (53 percent) and sophomores (25 percent); thus, the respondents constituted a group that was younger (mean age of 20) than the total undergraduate student population of the university (mean age of 23.5). In comparison to the total undergraduate population, the sample contained slight underrepresentations of females (35 percent versus 43 percent in the population) and African Americans (11 percent versus 15 percent in the population).

The questionnaire collected information about common respondent characteristics (age, gender, race, and so on) and asked respondents to assess their felt social distance with respect to 19 specific groups. After an explanation of how to make the ratings, the 19 groups were listed. Next to the name of each group was a ten-centimeter line, along which the respondent was to rate personally felt social distance from the group, with a higher score indicating greater social distance. Additional questionnaire items dealt with the amount of contact respondents had had with various groups during their high school years, and opinions on a series of controversial issues relating to diversity, the sources of influences on respondents' thoughts, and beliefs about the world. Finally, respondents were asked to indicate their levels of agreement with four hypotheticals, two of which related to gays and lesbians: "If I were on a jury, *I would not* vote to convict a man who punched a gay male after the gay male made a pass at him," and "If I were a family court judge, I *would* remove a young child from a household in which the child's mother resided with her lesbian mate." The full questionnaire appears in Bryant (2000). Additional, qualitative data were collected from students in prior offerings of the same course. These data consist of open-ended, written responses that students gave to a news feature about same-sex marriages.

Findings: Social Distance

Table 22.1 displays the means and standard deviations of the social distance scores from the 151 questionnaire respondents. Marks made by the respondents on the ten-centimeter lines assessing social distance were scored by rounding to the nearest half-centimeter, then multiplying the values by ten; thus, possible scores range from 0 to 100 in five-point intervals.

As table 22.1 shows, all of the mean social-distance scores are less than 50 (the midpoint score on the scales), suggesting that respondents had a general unwillingness to express extreme feelings of social distance. However, it is clear that great variability in felt social distance exists across the 19 groups rated. The second highest amount of social distance was expressed toward gay males—a mean score of 41, exceeded only by the mean score of 45 for people who had served time in prison. The social-distance score for gay males is substantially higher than the score for lesbians—a mean score of 26, which is about the same as the score for high school dropouts.

At the other end of the social-distance continuum, ten groups received

Table 22.1

Means and Standard Deviations of Social-Distance Scale Scores

Reference group	*Mean score*	*Standard deviation*
Served time in prison	45.17	32.35
Gay male	41.13	38.26
Alcoholic	38.15	28.78
Arrested for drunk driving	28.94	30.67
Attempted suicide	27.91	27.86
High school dropout	26.46	29.74
Lesbian	25.86	32.41
Cigarette smoker	19.24	24.10
Juvenile arrested for shoplifting	18.00	23.88
Deaf	14.54	22.71
Blind	14.50	22.43
Confined to a wheelchair	12.75	20.34
African American	12.28	20.95
Overweight	12.12	18.31
Rape victim	10.96	21.52
Jewish	9.20*	15.71
Hispanic	8.81	15.93
Polish	6.48	14.30
Italian	5.96	13.07

Notes: *n = 150. For all other scores, n = 151.

mean social-distance ratings of less than 15. It is telling that eight of those groups are defined by race, ethnicity, religion, or physical disability. These are all characteristics for which there are clear legal prohibitions against discrimination in many realms of life.

Intercorrelations among the social-distance scores suggest that there is some degree of independence among the degrees of social distance felt toward categories of characteristics. For example, a nine-variable correlation matrix that includes the four race/ethnicity designations (African American, Hispanic, Italian, Polish), the three disability designations (confined to a wheelchair, blind, deaf), and the two sexual-orientation designations (gay man, lesbian) shows distinct clustering of correlations within those three categories, and generally weaker correlations across the categories. However, it is also apparent that social-distance ratings for some of the characteristics have a degree of uniqueness and are less likely to reflect general, underlying negative feelings about "otherness." When the social-distance correlations of each characteristic with the other eight characteristics are summed, social-distance ratings with respect to African

Table 22.2

Mean Sexual-Orientation Social-Distance Scale Scores by Selected Predictor Variables

Predictor variable	SOCIAL-DISTANCE REFERENT *Gay males*	*Lesbians*
Gender		
males	57.74	28.40
females	14.04	21.67
Religiosity		
religion very important	47.50	36.15
religion not very important	40.04	23.87
Class background		
working-class family	39.64	18.97
nonworking-class family	41.82	27.48
Type-of-place background		
rural/farm area	49.84	37.66
nonrural/farm area	39.70	23.06
Past acquaintances		
no gay male acquaintances	50.46	29.34
gay male acquaintances	23.04	19.61
no lesbian acquaintances	47.37	28.11
lesbian acquaintances	29.33	22.12

Americans, gay men, and lesbians stand out as having the least interconnection with the other social-distance ratings. The sums for these three are 1.6, 2.1, and 2.3, respectively, while the other six sums range from 2.9 to 3.5.

Correlates of Expressed Social Distance from Gays and Lesbians

Table 22.2 displays mean social-distance scores with respect to gay males and lesbians, broken down by some key respondent characteristics: gender, religiosity (how important religion is in the respondent's daily life), class background (self-characterization of family's economic status when respondent was between ages 6 and 18), community type (type of area in which respondent lived from ages 6 to 18), and interpersonal contact with gays and lesbians (acquaintanceships during high school). Responses to the religiosity, class background, community type, and interpersonal contacts items have been reduced to dichotomies in order to highlight respondent characteristics thought to be associated with higher levels of prejudice toward gays and lesbians: religion being very important in the person's life, working-class background, rural background, and absence of acquaintances who were gay or lesbian.

Class background made relatively little difference in the degree of social distance felt from gays and lesbians—especially social distance from gay males—and the difference that does occur is the opposite of what was predicted; respondents who self-identified their backgrounds as working class showed slightly lower social-distance scores than did other respondents. The differences according to religiosity and community background are in the directions expected, and (as was the case with class background) the differences were more pronounced for social distances felt from lesbians than from gay males. The interpersonal-contacts variables also showed differences in the expected direction, but with these variables, the differences were more pronounced for social distances felt from gay males than from lesbians. Interestingly, having or not having had lesbian acquaintances during high school made hardly any difference in the amount of social distance felt from lesbians. In contrast, substantially lower levels of the social distance felt toward gay males are associated with having had gay male acquaintances during high school *and* with having had lesbian acquaintances during high school.

The largest difference found in table 22.2 is between male and female respondents in their felt social distance from gay males—a mean of 57.7 for males versus 14.0 for females. This gender difference is not reproduced in expressions of social distance from lesbians—a mean of 28.4 for males and 21.7 for females. This finding is consistent with other research showing that males and females do not differ much from each other in their attitudes toward lesbians, but that males' attitudes toward gay males are much more negative than both their own attitudes toward lesbians and the attitudes of females toward gay males (Bernstein & Kostelac 2002; Kite & Whitley 1998).

The overwhelming influence of gender in the social distance felt toward gay males is further confirmed by multiple-regression analysis using gender, religiosity, class background, area background, and gay and lesbian acquaintances during high school as independent variables. As can be seen from table 22.3, gender was the only independent variable in the regression that had a significant effect on the social-distance ratings (although having had gay male acquaintances in high school did come close to reaching significance), and the effect of gender was substantial, accounting for a 40-point difference on a 100-point scale in the social-distance ratings, even when the effects of the other variables are taken into account.

When the same independent variables were included in a multiple regression with social distance from lesbians as the dependent variable, neither gender nor having lesbian or gay acquaintances in high school had significant effects. Although the effects of religiosity, class background, and area background on social distance from lesbians were significant in the regression model, the sizes of those effects were relatively small, and the overall R^2 for the model was only 0.11.

Table 22.3

Multiple Regression of Social Distance from Gay Males with Six Predictor Variables (*n* = 144)

Predictor variable	B	*Standard error*	*Beta*	*t value*	*Signifi-cance*
Gender	40.463	5.493	.512	7.367	.000
Religiosity	7.754	6.774	.078	1.145	.254
Class background	–7.486	6.811	–.077	–1.099	.274
Type-of-place background	6.818	6.522	.073	1.045	.298
Gay male acquaintances	–12.601	6.700	–.156	–1.881	.062
Lesbian acquaintances	–8.949	6.376	–.111	–1.403	.163

Note: All predictors are dichotomies: male = 1, religion important = 1, working-class background = 1, rural/farm background = 1, had gay male acquaintances in past = 1, had lesbian acquaintances in past = 1.

Social Distance and Willingness to Take Adverse Actions

Showing that our respondents felt substantial social distance from gay males and lesbians—especially the very large amount of social distance from gay males expressed by male respondents—does not, in itself, demonstrate special vulnerability to victimization among gay males and lesbians. However, our data also show that the degree of social distance felt from lesbians and gay males is related to the respondents' expressed willingness to act in manners that can be considered prejudicial toward those groups. As noted earlier, the survey included some relevant hypotheticals to which respondents were asked to react: "If I were on a jury, *I would not* vote to convict a man who punched a gay male after the gay male made a pass at him," and "If I were a family court judge, I *would* remove a young child from a household in which the child's mother resided with her lesbian mate."

Table 22.4 shows the mean social-distance scores of respondents who reacted affirmatively and negatively to those items. The questionnaire allowed for responses of "completely agree," "generally agree," "generally disagree," and "completely disagree"; the responses have been dichotomized for presentation within the table.

The data in table 22.4 show clear differences in social-distance attitudes between respondents who would and would not choose to remove a child from a lesbian household, and between respondents who would and would not vote as jurors to convict a defendant who had punched a gay male after the gay male made a pass at him. The largest difference is in the social-distance ratings of lesbians between respondents who would (mean scale score = 76) and those who would not (22) remove a child

Table 22.4

Mean Social-Distance Scores by Responses to Two Hypothetical Scenarios

	MEAN SOCIAL DISTANCE FROM:	
Hypothetical	*Gay males*	*Lesbians*
Would remove child from a lesbian household		
yes	65.56	76.11
no	39.57	22.48
Would vote to convict a man who punched a gay man		
no	59.66	39.66
yes	36.69	22.36

from a lesbian household. The issue of children in households with lesbian caretakers seems particularly salient to the respondents; the second largest difference in table 22.4 occurs for this same issue, with those preferring to remove the child showing higher social distance from gay males (mean = 66) than those who would not remove the child (40).

Qualitative Analysis of Antigay/Lesbian Attitudes

The survey data we have reviewed indicate that our college-student respondents feel a substantial social distance from gays and lesbians—especially from gay males—and that the degree of social distance is associated with expressed willingness to act in a discriminatory manner toward gays and lesbians. What are the feelings and beliefs that generate this sense of social distance? We can get some clues from the open-ended responses that other students in the same course gave to an in-class writing and discussion assignment.

The undergraduate course from which the respondents were drawn consists of twice-a-week lectures and once-a-week small-group discussion sections. During the fall 1998 and spring 1999 semesters, one of the assignments in the discussion sections required the students to read and react to an article by a *Chicago Tribune* columnist that had appeared in the local newspaper (Zorn 1996). The article began with a series of "quotes" condemning same-sex marriages as unnatural, immoral, and otherwise detrimental to society. Then, the author revealed that the quotes, dating from 1823 to 1964, had actually referred to interracial marriages. He had simply changed the referent to demonstrate the similarity of "the strangled rage, fear and righteous indignation" underlying past feelings about interracial marriages and current feelings about same-sex marriages.

The contents of the written reactions from 74 students in three discussion sections during the spring semester 1999 were analyzed for insights about the bases of negative attitudes toward gays and lesbians. About half of the students were opposed to, or at least indifferent about, legal prohibitions of same-sex marriages. But many of those students made a distinction between their personal views—opposed to same-sex marriages—and their views about the law, which they did not believe should be intruding into intimate relationships between adults. Among the students who supported legal prohibitions of same-sex marriages, about half expressed some degree of tolerance for same-sex relationships, but believed those relationships should not be sanctified as legal marriages; the rest condemned both the relationships and the possibility of same-sex marriages. Of interest here, however, is not the distribution of opinions about whether same-sex marriages should be legal, but rather the rationales used by the students who expressed opposition to same-sex relationships and/or marriages. Within these rationales, three basic themes were prominent: religion and unnatural and personal disgust.

Religious beliefs were often cited as reasons for opposing not only same-sex marriages, but also gay and lesbian orientations generally. One male student wrote: "I feel that they [homosexuals] should abstain from sexual acts because God did not intend for them to take place." A female student, who expressed opposition to both same-sex and interracial relationships, wrote: "I believe we should live by the Bible and allow church and state to become one again." Recall that the results of our survey data showed that, in multiple-regression analyses, religiosity was not significantly related to the social-distance felt toward gay males, and only modestly related to the social-distance felt toward lesbians. We suspect that the indicator of religiosity used in the survey (*How important is religion in your daily life?*) is too broad to differentiate among types of religious beliefs—for example, a strong adherence to religious beliefs that stress "love thy neighbor" versus a strong adherence to religious beliefs that stress "fire and brimstone."

Religious objections tended to overlap with the view that homosexuality is unnatural. A female student wrote: "There is nothing normal about a homosexual relationship" and added "it's a sin." Similarly, a male student wrote: "This is wrong. This is not the nature God gave to us"; his solution: "I hope for the good of the world that lesbians and gays will disappear." Another male student used the rationale of unnaturalness to support the following line of reasoning: "Although it [legal prohibition of same-sex marriage] may look discriminatory, I do not consider it discriminatory of us against them, but them discriminating against us because they are the ones against nature."

A strong element of personal disgust and revulsion was evident in some of the responses, particularly among male students. One male student wrote: "I myself think that it [homosexuality] is disgusting." Another wrote: "All I know is that I do not want any part of it [homosexuality], and it makes me sick." Another was slightly more tolerant, but still repulsed: "If that's what they [homosexuals] want, who cares, as long as I don't have to be around it." A similar notion seems to underlie the following statement from another male student: "People who are gay should keep it in the privacy of their own home, and not bring it out in public." Sentiments such as these illustrate what Nava and Dawidoff (1994) have called "the ick factor," which plays a major role in shaping negative attitudes about homosexuals, particularly the very negative attitudes about gay males that are prevalent among men.

DIFFERENTIAL VULNERABILITY

We have discussed our findings about the feeling of social distance from gays and lesbians, the correlates of those feelings, the association of those feelings with expressed willingness to act in adverse manners, and some of the themes that appear to underlie negative attitudes toward gays and lesbians. At this point, we return to the argument presented at the beginning of the chapter—that the willingness to view gays and lesbians as "others" acts as a "technique of neutralization," which weakens the constraints against victimizing gays and lesbians, thus making them particularly vulnerable to victimization, especially hate-crime victimization.

Our data do not establish a direct link between feelings of social distance and the actual commission of victimization against a particular group. However, the findings reported in this chapter are consistent with our contention that a high degree of social distance—viewing people in a given group as "others"—contributes to a willingness to commit victimizations against people in the disfavored group. For example, hate crimes in the United States are committed overwhelmingly by males, and among hate crimes motivated by the perceived sexual orientation of the victim, the crimes are primarily antigay male rather than antilesbian (Levin 2002; Perry 2001; Garofalo 1997). Consistent with these patterns, the respondents in our survey expressed substantially greater social distance from gay males than from lesbians, and male respondents showed particularly high levels of social distance from gay males. In the qualitative data that we discussed, there was a strong element of personal revulsion expressed against gays and lesbians, and this element was strongest among male respondents in reaction to gay males. It seems reasonable to assume that a sense of personal revulsion toward a category of people contributes to a sense that harming the people in that category does not constitute "real" victimization, because the people in that category are less worthy of respect.

In the midst of this discussion, there is one caveat we should introduce. When we refer to "hate crimes" in this chapter, we are, more specifically, referring to the hate crimes that come to the attention of the criminal-justice system. In that set of hate crimes, when the incidents are motivated by the victims' perceived sexual orientation, the offenders are overwhelmingly male and strangers to their victims, and the great majority of the victims are gay males rather than lesbians. However, a substantial proportion of the victimizations suffered by gays and lesbians are committed by family members—particularly parents and siblings—and the distribution of gay males and lesbians in those victimizations is more equal than the distribution among hate crimes known to the police (for examples, see discussions in Herek and Berrill [1992]). It is also likely that the motivating mechanisms at work in these family-related victimizations differ from the motivating mechanisms we are discussing here.

Our survey data *do* show associations between the degree of social distance from gays and lesbians and the expressed willingness to act in ways that can be considered discriminatory. In the hypothetical scenarios, respondents with higher social-distance scores were more likely to say that they would act—as judges or jurors—against the interests of gays and lesbians, voting to not convict a man who had assaulted a gay male after the gay male had made a sexual advance, and deciding to remove a child from a home headed by a lesbian couple. In both instances, one can infer that a feeling of greater social distance is associated with a feeling that gays and lesbians are less entitled to the protection of the law.

There is another sense in which the "outsider" status of gays and lesbians in the minds of many people can contribute to heightened vulnerability to hate-crime victimization. Unlike the targets in other categories of hate crimes, many gays and lesbians do not want their sexual orientation known, and therefore may be reluctant to report their victimizations to the police. There are indications of negative attitudes toward gays and lesbians among rank-and-file police officers, and members of gay and lesbian communities often feel distrustful of the police (Bernstein & Kostelac 2002; Berrill & Herek 1992). This combination of factors could stimulate a sense of impunity among potential offenders in hate crimes directed against gays and lesbians. In essence, the potential offenders may feel that there is a reduced likelihood that they will experience sanctions because the victims are unlikely to report the crimes to the authorities. Harry (1982, 546) has referred to this scenario as "derivative deviance": "the victimization of stigmatized persons because of their inability to avail themselves of the protections of civil society without threat of discrediting."

Conclusion

Any group that is disfavored, that is the target of animosity from a substantial segment of the population, should be considered as especially, if not uniquely, vulnerable to criminal victimization. Research accumulated over the past 30 years informs us that there are a variety of factors—such as the proximity to potential offenders, target attractiveness, and so forth—related to the risk of victimization throughout the population. People in disfavored groups share in the risk associated with those factors, but they have an additional, special risk—the risk of being victims of hate crimes, derived from the negative attributions directed at them.

In this chapter, we have used a measure of social distance as an indicator of the extent to which gays and lesbians are considered to be "others"—that is, members of groups for which large segments of the population do not feel a sense of shared social identity. This sense of "otherness" is particularly pronounced in the feelings of males toward gay males. The findings we have discussed are consistent with the conclusion that this pronounced sense of social distance burdens gays and lesbians—but especially gay males—with a special vulnerability to criminal victimization, because their status as members of a common community is devalued in the minds of potential offenders.

References

Bernstein, Mary, and Constance Kostelac. (2002). "Lavender and blue: Attitudes about homosexuality and behavior toward lesbians and gay men among police officers." *Journal of Contemporary Criminal Justice 18*:302–28.

Berrill, Kevin T., and Gregory M. Herek. (1992) "Primary and secondary victimization in antigay hate crimes: Official response and public policy," in *Hate crimes: Confronting violence against lesbians and gay men*, ed. G. M. Herek and K. T. Berrill (pp. 289–305). Newbury Park, CA: Sage Publications.

Bryant, Jane Marie. (2000). *Perceptions and prejudice: A study of social distance and sexual orientation.* M.A. thesis, Center for the Study of Crime, Delinquency, and Corrections, Southern Illinois University, Carbondale.

Byers, Bryan, Benjamin W. Crider, and Gregory K. Biggers. (1999). "Bias crime motivation: A study of hate crime and offender neutralization techniques used against the Amish." *Journal of Contemporary Criminal Justice 15*:78–96.

Elikann, Peter. (1999). *Superpredators: The demonization of our children by the law.* New York: Plenum.

Garofalo, James. (1997). "Hate crime victimization in the United States," in *Victims of crime*, 2nd ed., ed. Robert C. Davis, Arthur J. Lurigio, and Wesley G. Skogan (pp. 134–45). Thousand Oaks, CA: Sage Publications.

Harry, Joseph. (1982). "Derivative deviance: The cases of extortion, fag-bashing, and shakedown of gay men." *Criminology 19*:546–64.

Herek, Gregory M., and Kevin T. Berrill (eds.). (1992). *Hate crimes: Confronting violence against lesbians and gay men.* Newbury Park, CA: Sage Publications.

Kite, Mary E., and Bernard E. Whitley, Jr. (1998). "Do heterosexual women and men differ in their attitudes toward homosexuality? A conceptual and methodological analysis," in *Stigma and sexual orientation: Understanding prejudice against lesbians, gay men, and bisexuals*, ed. Gregory M. Herek (pp. 39–61). Thousand Oaks, CA: Sage Publications.

Levin, Brian. (2002). "The characteristics of hate-crime victimizations in the United States," in *Victims and victimization*, ed. David Schichor and Stephen G. Tibbetts (pp. 225–48). Prospect Heights, IL: Waveland.

Levin, Jack. (2002). *The violence of hate.* Boston: Allyn & Bacon.

Nava, Michael, and Robert Dawidoff. (1994). *Created equal: Why gay rights matter to America.* New York: St. Martin's Press.

Perry, Barbara. (2001). *In the name of hate: Understanding hate crimes.* New York: Routledge.

Sykes, Gresham M., and David Matza. (1957). "Techniques of neutralization: A theory of delinquency." *American Sociological Review 22*:664–70.

Zorn, Eric. (1996). "Same-sex marriage: An issue as clear as black and white." *Southern Illinoisan* (May 27).

CHAPTER TWENTY-THREE

The Perilous Existence of Children as Freaks in Circuses, Carnivals, and Freak Shows

AMIT R. PATEL

"HURRY, HURRY! STEP RIGHT UP! Get a glimpse of the Dog-Faced Boy and the Six-Legged Twins—see the freaks of nature—right this way!" This may be a statement heard from a circus announcer, but it intuitively fits the deep, dark secret of circus freak shows and the exploitation of children with physical deformities. Fascination with human oddities is as old as the creation of the circus. Children performing in circuses or as a part of freak shows are especially vulnerable, and their victimization experiences in these institutions have been severely disregarded by society. This chapter chronologically examines the history of circuses in relation to the inclusion of children in circuses, their vulnerabilities, and their victimization experiences in the underground "carny" culture.

HISTORICAL PERSPECTIVES

Prehistoric man had displayed behavior in cave drawings depicting the sacrificial killing of malformed children as forms of bizarre rituals. Other societies, including the ancient Egyptians, Greeks, and Romans, have also kept children with malformations in the everyday household to serve as questionable forms of entertainment and as symbols of curiosity or astonishment (Fiedler 1978). In these ancient societies, these unique children served as frequent reminders to the whole culture of their status and class, thus gawking and poking fun at these particular individuals served as a reaffirming symbol of superiority. Children were especially vulnerable during this time due to the lack of legislation that made no distinctions between adults and children. This particular vulnerability left children performing the roles of adults such as entertainers and laborers. These unfortunate careers seem to epitomize the peculiar vulnerabilities and victimization experiences that children with deformities have suffered in this particular era and yet that is still evident today.

Children with odd deformities or physical handicaps were first introduced into the world of circuses, particularly being displayed in freak shows. According to Bogdan (1988), P. T. Barnum, the famous circus creator, had introduced freak shows during the 1840s. "P. T. Barnum became the proprietor of an organization in New York City, the American Museum, the looms large in the history of the American Freak Show." The ability of adults to dictate the roles of these vulnerable children served two purposes: as a form of entertainment, and, more likely, as an economical value or profit for the owner. Consequently, these children were serving roles as child laborers, sexual gratifiers, and most unfortunately as human prodigies for human eyes to awe at. By the early twentieth century, circuses became a formally recognized institution in society. This very early form of public entertainment had exploited children in a number of ways, including the enthrallment that viewers felt seeing innocent, vulnerable, and helpless children on stage and who pay money just to satisfy some dark desire of their primitive psyches. Continually, in the modern world today, circuses that travel in rural and remote parts of the United States are known to still harbor innocent children with genetic defects for profit. Literature has introduced and referred to such children as "freaks": children with anomalies, deformities, genetic disorders, malformations, prodigies, abnormalities, mental retardation, monstrous formalities, and so forth as especially noted by Bogdan (1988).

The historical roots of freak shows combine fascination with human oddities and medical science. Since scientists were interested in examining human anomalies early in medical history, this particular curiousness had sparked the interest in exhibiting such individuals. During the early nineteenth century, Bogdan (1988) finds that freak shows were termed "Raree Shows" and "Halls of Human Curiosities," whereas the names "Sideshow," "Ten in One," "Kid Show," and "Human Wonders" were catchphrases coined in the twentieth century. These terminologies describe the exhibition of sometimes very ordinary individuals with extraordinary physical characteristics. This was especially the case for children who were coerced in the circus lifestyle. For example, Bogdan (1988) writes about the unfortunate case of "the Jones twins who were born as Siamese and displayed in freak shows. To the demise of the medical world, the twins died while on tour with a carnival show" (Bogdan 1988). These twins desperately required medical attention due to severe malformation; however, they succumbed to the will of their parents in having grown up in the circus world. In such saddening situations, if medical help was sought, these twins may have lived. Ethical infringement of privacy of those who were physically or mentally handicapped was a commonality and an ill-fated reputation of early medical practices: "The etiology of monstrosities is as vague as ever, and medical pride bows in abject submission when confronted with the task of averting the misfortune, or even comforting the pangs of sorrow and distress incident upon a monstrous conception" (Jones & Martensen 1997). Children diagnosed with rare genetic disorders were untreated and left to the circus owner's discretions to direct their most unfortunate fates.

CHILDREN AS DIFFERENTIALLY VULNERABLE

Circus children are almost uniformly being denied a formal education. One of the first written examinations of children's denial of formal education in circuses has been documented in Australia. "Children brought up in circus families had to concentrate upon the development of their performing skills, often to the exclusion or detriment of a formal education" (St. Leon 2000). This fact contributes to the speculation that children may be subjected to brainwashing and being denied to make their own choices—especially under the assumption that children with deformities may not have the mental capacity or rights to a formal education. "These children, abandoned, illegitimate, and/or of Aboriginal extraction, were usually acquired by a circus under the most prurient circumstances and in inverse proportion to the number of natural children of the proprietor" (St. Leon 2000). Those children who were deemed anomalies by race were also denied formal education in Australian circuses. "For some circus children, attendance at a town school posed a special problem in that the experience served to emphasize their coloration" (St. Leon 2000).

Universally, school children in the United States find it amusing and humorous to poke fun at disfigured and handicapped classmates. The creation of separate institutions for disfigured children or children with mental handicaps has added to marginalizing these populations further by keeping them separated from the rest. The realization here is that schools in the twenty-first century are not adequately prepared for the special needs of children with deformities or handicaps. Studies have shown that individuals with deformities are looked at adversely. Individuals "with abnormal facial features were rated as significantly less employable, attractive, intelligent, honest, trustworthy, and capable" (Newswire Association 2001). Thus, we realize that in some countries, such children are given up to be employable in circuses where they would be a source of economic gain, both for the parents and circus-owner:

> Freak shows of the nineteenth century brought together a hybrid cast of performers that included the physically or mentally disabled, natives from non-Western countries, and persons with unusual talents . . . the nation's

> grand civilizing institutions unwittingly engaged with the sensational, profit-driven mode of the freak show. (Adams 2001)

To this effect, children are victimized by affluent circus-owners and circus-watchers in very many facets, where their denial of basic human rights in society continually allows and catalyzes a breeding ground for these unique victimization experiences.

Victimization Experiences

Do children in the circuses, performing in freak shows or who are forced to work in them, have detrimental experiences? Unfortunately, most accounts of child victimization in circuses have been for the most part undocumented. This may be a result of either a lack of concern, or a true realization that children in circuses are kept hidden in the grim and oppressed world of child labor. Children in circuses have been victimized through various facets; however, most notable is their sexual exploitation. The focus of freak shows were to portray "the exotic, which cast the exhibit as a strange creature from a little-known part of the world; and the aggrandized, which endowed freaks with status-enhancing characteristics" according to Bogdan (1988). As a result of these stigmas, the demand for freaks grew and their level of victimization increased. These freaks were not only being viewed, but would perform sexual acts to fulfill adult pleasures. The idealization in the innocence portrayed by children with anomalies in freak shows is completely lost. These children are

> perceived to one degree or another as erotic. Indeed, abnormalities arouses in some "normal" beholders a temptation to go beyond looking to knowing in the full carnal sense the ultimate other, sexual contact not withstanding. The desire [having sexual contact with children] is itself freaky . . . a dream of breaching the last taboo against miscegenation. (Thompson 1996)

For boys, it is believed by myth that African males "are all credited with being monstrously hung." "Some African-American males with extraordinarily long penises" have been displayed in freak shows (Fielder 1978, 139). These men and boys are used for the sexual gratification of adults who crave curiosities of both experiencing sex outside their race, and having sexual contact with children. Girls who have physical deformities on their vaginas have also performed in circuses. These girls would display their physical impairments such as a double clitoris or an extraordinarily small vaginal opening for viewers to see (Fielder 1978, 139). Not only were these children subject to gawking and stares, but also to expectations of fulfilling sexual desires of these gawkers in the name of gaining profit for the circus-owner.

Besides the United States, countries such as Africa and India have also joined in this unfortunate realm of victimizing children by incorporating them into circuses. Third World countries such as these, plagued by uncontrollable population upsurges and the sheer disarray of political advocacy for children's rights allow circus-owners to maintain the public's demand for performing children. More often, these facts are known and remain unchanged, in part because the United Nations and other international organizations cannot fully enforce child-exploitations laws. However, one such organization that attempts to initiate positive change is the Makawanpur Women's Development, a recent advocacy group for human rights in India that helps to enforce exploitation laws: "Taking of many underage children, especially girls, to the different Indian cities to play in circuses has become another form of human trafficking." This form of exploitation occurs at the will of the parents: "The agents go to the villages and often convince the family that they would earn more money" if their child would work for the circus. Oftentimes, the child is worked all day, unfed, receives no salary, and is exploited physically, mentally, and emotionally.

The Makawanpur Women's Development advocates human rights and plays a key role in policy development in India. Most often, such acts of disregard and utter shamelessness have yet to be challenged, in the eyes of most human rights activists around the world. Those who advocate freak shows and displaying human oddities assert that "it has constituted a legitimate performance, and that it has been based on uncoerced consent of those displayed, who have found value and status in their roles as human exhibits" (Gerber 1993). Such statements question the legitimacy of children having the full ability to consent to debasing roles in freak shows. Circus children have undoubtedly experienced and continue to experience this type of victimization throughout the world.

THE PSYCHOLOGICAL EFFECTS

The question remains of whether these children who grew up in the so-called freak shows and circuses have long-term psychological effects, "especially in the light of the extent to which people with physical anomalies have experienced broad and abiding social oppression and marginalization" (Gerber 1993). Individuals with facial deformities or disfigurements "live life at a significant disadvantage, particularly in the work force" (Newswire Association 2001). Continual and repeated social rebuke of these individuals has had a psychological effect to the extent in which it manifests a likelihood of any number of disorders such as severe bipolar disorder, multiple-personality disorder, antisocial personality disorder, or anxiety disorder, to name a few. One study conducted in the United States (in Boston) links early abuse and emotional trauma to personality disorders such as schizophrenia and manic-depressive disorder (Mishra 2000). Young girls subjected to child abuse, especially repeated sexual abuse, developed smaller corpus callosums in the brain, which causes psychological abnormalities such as anxiety and depression in adulthood (Mishra 2000). Other studies done according to the American Psychiatric Association have concluded that children with facial deformities are likely to have a major depressive disorder, suicidal thoughts and attempts, and dysthymic disorders (Stoddard & Stroud 1992). In the case of children, "for the boy it would cause self-pity and, for the girl, it would make getting a boyfriend more difficult . . . it would attract staring and teasing" (Demellweek 1997, 471).

The ramifications of such sobering studies, even in the twenty-first century, conclude the digression and deterioration of our society as a morally and ethically sound institution for children with physical abnormalities. The exploitation of children in circuses, carnivals, and freak shows has fostered the notion that people with deformities do not receive equal treatment in society: "The stigma of disfigurement poses considerable challenges in maintaining self-esteem, building self-confidence, and coping effectively with the intrusive (often negative) reactions of others" (Kish & Lansdown 2000). Given this oppressive outlook for individuals with disfigurements, they may resort to other means of obtaining a living, such that it includes working at a freak show (as a last resort) or other illegal means of obtaining money. The need to modify laws prohibiting children from participating in circus sideshows or freak shows must be institutionalized worldwide in order to protect these innocent victims against an intentionally adjective society.

Legal Statutes and Policy

Child labor is an issue that plagues the world's workforce. Almost every country has witnessed and harbored child labor to the extent in which it warrants attention. Child labor comes in many forms and thus worldwide statutes, laws, and regulations have been recently established to help clarify the meaning and conditions of child labor and to punish those who use child labor. For example, in the twentieth century, the formation of the International Child Labor Enforcement task group was created to help reduce the cases of child labor around the world. This group has advocated the abolishment of child slave labor and the effects it has on those children—physical, emotional, and mental: "The employment of children in conditions which, taken together and viewed in the context of the social and economic background of the region, are likely to be harmful to their mental, physical or moral growth and eventually to the development of their potential" (Sawyer 1988).

Under the U.S. Customs regulations, section 307, child slave labor is minimally defined as: "When a child is a virtual prisoner and is not free to choose to leave the work site and the employment . . . employment in hazardous industries or under extreme conditions, [and] the denial of generally available educational opportunities" (U.S. Customs, section 307).

These conditions, if determined that they exist, have punishable penal and/or civil consequences for those parties in violation. The penalties for violating these regulations are costly, which may hopefully deter future incidences of child exploitation. The causes of child labor and types of exploitation are numerous: "children are an easily renewable resource. Either they produce by working . . . or be hired out or sold for whatever payment" (Sawyer 1988). The socioeconomic condition of the parents highly dictates what may happen to the children. Such is the case in India, where parents are selling their children to the circus in hopes of making money and obtaining better social conditions. This not only allows the parents to make money, but also shifts the burden of raising that child to another.

Attention must be given to the development of future policy concerning child labor and exploitation. Policies should involve combating society's problems, such as poverty, education, and health care. Poverty and the lack of adequate health care and education are all major problems of Third World countries. The lack of formal institutions to oversee health care and the basic quality of life in these countries may be the problem at its root. This is where child labor is a commonplace in the workforce. To combat these problems, future policy may be directed at the creation of a universal health-care policy for all peoples, regardless of class, race, or socioeconomic status. Second, future policy should consider properly educating all members of a society to the extent in which it reduces the chances of a child being exploited for reasons of helping to maintain the household income. Third, future policy must consider targeting and combating child labor where it is most concentrated—Third World countries and rural areas. These recommendations are the ideal; the enactment and enforcement of such policies are at the present moment in their infancy.

The victimization and exploitation of children in circuses, carnivals, and especially children displayed and working in freak shows have been for the most part overlooked or disregarded. Acknowledging such marginalized populations throughout the world that exploit children in the name of profit and amusement is a start towards helping to remedy the problem. These acts of employing children in circuses have been at great cost to innocent children who suffer the further torment of having been sexually, mentally, and emotionally debilitated. The absence of an intervening or powerful moral, ethical, or lawful force is likely to continue this ill-fated world of oddity exhibitionism—and especially of those children who are the victims of this dark form of entertainment. Further research and policies must include the need for more powerful and intervening human-rights activists who seek to dispel, combat, and abolish the grim world of displaying children for profit-gain and entertainment. The need for more medical intervention in cases where the parents cannot afford health-care benefits to their children will also help reduce the number of children being sold and exported to circuses. Furthermore, sending adequate amounts of nutrition and food supplies to poor countries can also help to better stabilize the social conditions of families across the world. The need to "normalize" children with disfigurements in society may help to reduce incidences of victimization and also help to spread the awareness that child exploitation, no matter what its form, is a crime against not only the individual but society as a whole.

REFERENCES

Adams, Bluford. (1997). *E Pluribus Barnum: The great showman and the making of U.S. popular culture.* Minneapolis: University of Minnesota Press.

Adams, Rachel. (2001). *Side show U.S.A.: Freaks and the American cultural imagination.* Chicago: University of Chicago Press.

Albrecht, Ernest. (1995). *The new American circus.* Gainsville: University Press of Florida.

Bogdan, Robert. (1988). *Freak show: Presenting human oddities for amusement and profit.* Chicago: University of Chicago Press.

Bouissac, Paul. (1976). *Circus and culture: A semiotic approach.* Bloomington: Indiana University Press.

Brown, James, Colin Demellweek, Gerry Humphries, et al. (1997). "Children's perceptions of, attitudes towards, unfamiliar peers with facial port-wine stains." *Journal of Pediatric Psychology 22*(4):471–85.

Fiedler, Leslie. (1978). *Freaks: Myths and images of the secret self.* New York: Simon & Schuster.

Gamson, Joshua. (1992). *Freaks talk back: Tabloid talk shows and sexual nonconformity.* Chicago: University of Chicago Press.

Gerber, David A. (1993). "Volition and valorization in the analysis of the 'careers' of people exhibited in freak shows." *Disability, Handicap & Society 7*(1):53–69.

Grootaert, Christiaan, and Harry Patrinos. (1999). *The policy analysis of child labor: A comparative study.* New York: St. Martin's Press.

Jones, David S., and Robert L. Martensen. (1997). "Medicine, morality, and congenital anomalies." *Journal of the American Medical Association 278*(24): 2191.

Kish, Veronica, and Richard Lansdown. (2000). "Meeting the psychological impact of facial disfigurement: Developing a clinical service for children and families." *Clinical Child Psychology and Psychiatry 5*(4):497–512.

Murray, Marian. (1956). *Circus!* New York: Appleton-Century-Crofts.

Newswire Association. (2001). "Facial deformities impact employability, perceptions of honesty and intelligence, American Society of Plastic Surgeons study finds." Orlando: PR Newswire Association, p. 1197.

Sawyer, Roger. (1988). *Children enslaved.* New York: Routledge.

Schlemmer, Bernard. (2000). *The exploited child.* New York: Zed Books.

St. Leon, Mark. (2000). "Educational practice in Australian circus, 1847–1930." *International Journal of Educational Research 3*:285–95.

Stoddart, Helen. (2000). *Rings of desire: Circus history and representation.* Manchester, UK: Manchester University Press.

Thompson, Rosemarie G. (1996). *Freakery: Cultural spectacles of the extraordinary body.* New York: New York University Press.

Wilkins, Charles. (1998). *The circus at the edge of the earth.* Toronto: McClelland & Stewart.

CHAPTER TWENTY-FOUR

Discredited Victims of Childhood Violence

HAROLD PEPINSKY

I SHARE HERE WHAT I HAVE BEEN LEARNING from ten years of rather intense listening to ongoing victims and survivors of childhood violence, who time and again are and have been discredited. I have come to suspect that if I know any adult well enough for that adult to open up to me about childhood trauma, that having been discredited by adult caretakers has been the most deeply shaping of what makes him or her feel vulnerable here and now. Some time ago, my mother, who taught me to question authority, told me how she had written a short story in primary school that she particularly wanted to show to her beloved teacher. The teacher failed my mother because the teacher believed that my mother had "copied" from a book, what we now typically call "plagiarism." The teacher did not believe my mother's protests, and how could my mother prove her innocence? In some public school systems today in the United States where I live, I can imagine that on an occasion like my mother's, a child might be expelled, under a policy of "zero tolerance" for violation of school rules.

If the day ever comes where we get past oppressing people for their gender or sexual orientation or for the color of their skin or blaming people for their own poverty, I expect that adults will still be given the benefit of the doubt when their versions of events differ from children's.

INCEST

In 1992, I began meeting children who were complaining that trusted adult caretakers were molesting them, principally while they visited fathers separated or divorced from their mothers. Often, children's stories were corroborated by physical evidence of sexual assault. I have been asked, from long distance, to comfort a hysterical child by her mother on the telephone. Reportedly, the children were invariably resistant to visits, and upset and hurting they returned. Parents who try to present this evidence to modify custody or visitation arrangements are known as "protective" parents.

I had been teaching a seminar on "feminist justice" since 1987. I asked several local protective parents (including a father who eventually lost all parental rights) and a grandparent to help me teach the seminar, beginning in the fall of 1993, with "children's rights and safety" as a special topic. Among them, Debbie Dugan and her mother Mary Cunningham had been among four private telephone numbers given out nationwide in such cases by 1-800-4-A-CHILD. Debbie and Mary, and fellow activist Sandy Bell, had accumulated a massive set of files documenting evidence sent to them from protective parents across the country. On the telephone and at rallies, they had met numerous other protective parents. We made up a reader for the seminar containing a selection of this material, and had a wide selection of protective parents and professionals to invite to share their experiences and insights in the seminar. For a couple of years, I myself became active in rallies and protests, and met many other concerned people in this way as well.

I offered to testify at no charge in some of the custody and visitation disputes when protective parents around the country began to call me, too. In several cases, I qualified as an expert witness on "peacemaking" (as defined in Pepinsky and Quinney [1991], and Pepinsky [2001]). I qualified as someone who would testify to the best interests of the children involved, with the objective of helping them to love both parents safely, at their own pace. I recommended that a therapist the children "liked" be invited by the court to testify as to changes in conditions in which children were prepared to be with either parent. Just once, a judge accepted my recommendation.

In these disputes, I presented peacemaking as the art and science of enabling children in custody disputes to grow up to love both parents. I argued that this interest of the children would best be met by judges following ongoing advice from counselors or therapists the children saw and liked as to what kind of contact with either parent would allow the children to feel safe. For the moment, it would be safest for the court to suspend or restrict visitation with parents whom children resisted being with. I came to regard the U.S. constitutional guarantee of freedom of association as being as sacred for children as for adults, such as parents who purported to own their children.

In one case, the judge actually ordered as I proposed. I heard of one case nationally where after years, a mother was allowed to move away from a father alleged to have molested their daughter. Otherwise, in scores of cases where I have at least reviewed documentation if not met the parties involved, the result is as Leora Rosen and Michelle Etlin (1996) report in all but four of the more than 200 cases they review: the parent who asks the court to protect a child receives at most a temporary order that visitation with alleged assailants (typically parents and grandparents) be supervised. At some point, if not immediately, the court orders unsupervised overnight visitation with suspected perpetrators. Every time the protective parent resists, the judge holds the protective parent in contempt and punishes her or, occasionally, him too. Sooner or later, the noncompliant protective parent loses all contact with the child. Sometimes, protective parents try to disappear with their children before that happens. They are chased relentlessly by the F.B.I. and others. When you see a picture of a missing child as on a milk carton, I have learned that that child might want desperately *not* to be found (Carpenter & Dietrich 1997; Dietrich 1998).

All in all, it appears that there are some 2,000 such custody disputes each year in the United States (Rosen & Etlin 1996). It appears to me that this is considerable progress toward bringing a problem of incest and other sexual violence against children to public light. Just over 40 years ago, Denver pediatrician Henry Kempe was the senior author of a landmark article titled "The Battered-Child Syndrome" (Kempe et al. 1962). Kempe and colleagues wrote that the common wisdom at the time was that only one child in the United States in a million was ever a victim of a serious physical assault by an adult of any kind. That would work out to fewer than a hundred cases of child abuse a year. Kempe and colleagues proposed that as they examined broken bones and contusions more carefully, it was obvious that they resulted from intentional, rather than accidental, blows. By now, there are several thousand substantiated complaints of sexual assault each year alone in my home state of Indiana.

I cannot cite figures, but from those who work for the protection of children, I hear that prototypically, boyfriends of welfare mothers are identified and punished as child molesters. What makes child molestation so hard to "prove" to judges in custody cases, it appears, is that complaints are generally against biological fathers—fathers with enough economic means to pay premium legal and evaluation fees to sue to take the children away from their mothers. If it has taken 30 years of secret legal settlements to buy-off parishioners when they accuse Catholic priests of sexual assault, we are all the more resistant to recognizing that middle-class or wealthy fathers without criminal records could possibly do anything as horrible as molesting their own children. Sometimes, as I have listened to judges explaining their decisions in these cases, it almost feels as though they are taking all the more pains to make children spend time with their fathers to compensate for the harm that the allegations of sexual violence, especially if at all true, cause to the sacred and all-important father–child bond.

It is common for evaluators hired by fathers to report a finding to courts that mothers have put stories of abuse into their children's heads. I have seen this repeatedly, even where the only evidence at hand was that children had first disclosed sexual abuse to people other than their mothers. For instance, in the case where the judge followed my peacemaking recommendation, the first-grader had first spoken out to her teacher during a session on good touch/bad touch. Child-protective-services workers threatened to take the mother's child from her on grounds of neglect unless she filed a complaint with them. The clinician hired by the father nonetheless reported and testified her belief that the mother had put the bad-touch story into the child's head. Fortunately for this child, the judge noticed the inconsistency.

Unfortunately for other children, judges generally end up blaming mothers or counselors. I have had the sad experience of hearing a judge order unsupervised, overnight weekend visits with an alleged abuser, and simultaneously to order a young pair of sisters to stop seeing a counselor they liked, warning the mother that if anything more about abuse came from the children, the judge would call the mother to account.

In another case (in which the judge did not allow me to testify), a child returned from a visit. His mother took him to an emergency room where the child was diagnosed as having cigarette burns on his arm. The judge refused to accept the doctor's report as evidence without the doctor himself being present to testify. Shortly thereafter, again on grounds that the mother was putting stories into the child's head, the mother suddenly lost custody and contact with her son. One of the first mothers in such a case during the early 1970s, Faye Yager (who later founded Children of the Underground; see Carpenter and Dietrich [1997] and Dietrich [1998]), lost custody even after her child was diagnosed with running gonorrhea to a father who a decade later was caught as the first child molester on the F.B.I.'s "ten most wanted" list, serving a prison term in Florida for molesting neighborhood children. Time and again, judges simply never get around to hearing witnesses such as counselors, doctors, or child-protection workers who believe the children, meanwhile punishing mothers for any resistance to court orders that the children be delivered up to their alleged abusers.

As a rule in these cases, mothers have left abusive husbands. I surmise that these cases have arisen because women now have more support for escaping domestic violence and obtaining divorces. Once living apart from violent fathers, children get to feeling safe enough to disclose that they, too, have been violated. For their part, mothers are less likely to deny that their children's fathers could be doing sexual violence to their children. Adults I know who report having survived incest in childhood, such as Daly (1998) and including some of my own students as we study incest, report that while adult relationships last, bystanders such as mothers refuse to see or believe that loved ones like fathers could be sexually abusing their own children. I surmise that the taboo against saying bad things about one's parents, or being believed in the process, is stronger than the incest taboo itself. Globally, over the past several decades, we have just begun to recognize that women could be criminally battered, let alone raped, by their husbands. Recognition that children can be fondled, let alone sodomized, let alone raped by biological parents who are otherwise people of high social standing follows slowly—more slowly by far than recognition that priests and scout leaders can sexually assault children in their care.

RITUAL SADISM

During the first offering of the seminar on children's rights and safety in the fall of 1993, someone asked about "ritual abuse," where groups of people allegedly torture, rape, and occasionally kill or "sacrifice" and eat people as well as animals. For some time, this practice has been known as "SRA" or "satanic ritual abuse," although those of us who believe the practice to be real and widespread generally recognize that there are a number of liturgies of various pagan and religious types in otherwise similar rituals. I think "abuse" is a pretty mild word for the violence that is described, and so I am calling the practice "ritual sadism."

In that class in 1993 when ritual abuse was asked about, I had read that virtually all such reports were fictitious. The book by Richardson, Best, and Bromley (1991) is probably the most widely cited work arguing that reports of ritual abuse and multiple personalities are mostly false. When someone asked about ritual abuse, I said that it hardly ever occurred if it occurred at all. Mary Cunningham suggested I read a book by De Camp (1996), and Sandy Bell suggested I meet someone, Rick Doninger (Stop Mind Control and Ritual Abuse Today [SMART] 1996), who with his wife Pam had collected evidence that children were being taken out of school by school workers to sadistic rituals. Rick visited the seminar. I read the book, which I continue to regard as the most complete documentation of a single case published under one cover. Despite my not wanting to believe what I was hearing, seeing, and reading, my skepticism rapidly gave way to horrified belief that such rituals are commonplace across Europe, Canada, and the United States.

In the spring of 1994, Rick Doninger brought a survivor of ritual sadism to the seminar. Debbie and Mary brought another survivor, Jeanette Westbrook. Jeanette is among the few survivors willing to speak publicly about her victimization. She is as far as I know unique in having persuaded a prosecutor (the Kentucky attorney general) to charge her own father on several felony counts. Since she and the police officers who spent several years preparing her case thought that the worst of what she had undergone would sound too bizarre for a jury to believe, Jeanette's father was charged with three counts of simple rape. He was at the time (1992) the director-general of the National Board of Boiler Pressure Vessel Inspectors, whose job it is to inspect nuclear power plants for leaks. Her father had just returned from a state visit to Eastern Europe, when the Kentucky attorney general issued an extradition request to Ohio authorities. Jeanette's father thereupon died suddenly at home. There was no autopsy and the personal physician merely listed the death as of "natural causes." You can read Jeanette's story at (Westbrook 1997). You can read numerous survivor accounts and find related literature at two Web sites (Advocacy Committee for Human Experimentation Survivors and Mind Control [ACHES-MC] updated; Stop Mind Control and Ritual Abuse Today [SMART], both updated).

While I encourage people to meet survivors and hear their stories, I long ago accepted advice against trying to prove to anyone that ritual sadism is as widespread as I believe it to be (namely, that I would think any community in the United States that does not have at least one active sadistic cult that includes occult intergenerational homicidal sadists of high public standing to be a rarity). My point here rather is that the more serious the violence people allege having suffered as children, and the more serious the trauma of betrayal by parents and other trusted caretakers (Freyd [1996], whose parents founded the False Memory Syndrome Foundation in 1992; as earlier corroboration, see Herman [1992]), the less likely people who allege childhood violence will be believed regardless of how much corroborative evidence there is.

For well over 30 years, I have been paid full-time by state taxpayers to be a student and teacher of criminology and criminal justice. No one among my colleagues and students would vilify anyone more than a father who led a group of pedophilic, organized serial murderers who among other things raped and otherwise tortured his own "favored" son or daughter. Rick Doninger has asked my students, semester after semester, "can you imagine anything more horrible [okay, he says "evil" but so does President Bush] than doing this to your own child?"

I have a personal saying, that my commitment to making peace in the face of violence, rather than making war on personal enemies (batterers?) and enemies of state, rests on my conviction that the social world is much worse than war-makers would ever allow themselves to consider. As in Jeanette and deJoly's cases, paradoxically, I see people who have survived and freed themselves from the clutches of organized sadism, and who against the weight of public denial of realms where it was presumed that "father knows best," formed enduring partnerships of trust and mutual support—strong and enduring marriages. Those strong enough to gain independence, to recover and corroborate their own memories, and to tell their stories to strangers are all extraordinarily "together" people. At the same time, invariably, they report having at some earlier point relied crucially on validation that something wrong had been done, in moments of personal friendship, to grow to define themselves as "survivors" who know they had been wronged, rather than as "victims" who fear that they had asked for or wanted to be hurt and terrified. I have Jeanette, deJoly, and many other ritual sadism survivors in mind as I hear victims of rape and other personal violence say, "I am not a victim!" From them, as from others including my sheltered self, I seek information as to how we leave physically and emotionally battering relations as we choose new "family" members who accept us for what we are, and believe and attend to our tales of betrayal trauma. I have seen and heard scarring stories far beyond my prior imagination or media exposure. In the process, I find myself distilling what works to help any of us survive victimization.

What's at Stake?

These days, "PC" commonly means "politically correct" and "personal computer." I am writing this chapter on a PC. In place of political correctness, I use "PC" as "politically convenient." It is politically convenient—PC to me—to label our children as our most ignorant, misguided, socially disorganized part of something we call "society," a vision of social order. We scapegoat children for our domestic social problems (Males 1996, 1999). As I have seen in my child-advocacy work for ten years, we discredit our foremost messengers of the depth and breadth of our personal violence here at home. That is convenient for our politicians, who play on our fears and name our enemies for us. Among survivors of childhood sexual abuse and child victims, I am led to adopt Walt Kelly's "Pogo" comic-strip phrase: "We have met the enemy and the enemy is us." It is politically inconvenient (non-PC) to suppose that evidence that children and adult survivors offer of class-, race-, and nationality-blind violence against them, by fathers (including priests and presidents), by teachers, by youth-group leaders, pervades our lives far more than the threat of politically identified enemies such as "terrorists."

Here, to me, are the stakes. We all have choices to make in everyday life. We can be driven by "politically correct" fear—that we will suffer for identifying with and having compassion for public enemies. We can choose at any moment instead to be driven by empathy, by compassion, by a recognition that our offenders are too close to home to "nail" and thus make us safe. The United States, with about 4 percent of the world's population, now incarcerates one-fourth of all the world's adult prisoners. (There is no world count of youth detention; we only know about adults.) The only path I have found, especially in the classroom, to resisting this maxed-out punitiveness in what is currently the world's military-industrial center—in the midst of an explosion in the crime-control industry (Christie 2000)—is to invite people to break the taboo and criticize their own parental victimization. Whether we as children have been illegally violated, we have universally suffered, like my mother, being told to shut down our feelings and beliefs, our truths, for the sake of our adult caretakers, for "your own good" (Miller 1990). We have all been told to swallow our childhood grievances, count our blessings, and move on to a world constructed by our adult owners. I find that when I break through the taboo against criticizing parental figures, and likewise when my students and others are free to share their own grievances, that compassion replaces punitiveness toward offenders.

This is my faith. My continuing determination to bring what I consider credible stories of childhood rape and torture to my students and colleagues in professional meetings rests on my experience that once we experience childhood victimization to be legitimate and inclusive, we free ourselves from the war-on-crime-and-terrorism politics of fear. To paraphrase President Franklin Roosevelt, "The only thing we have to fear is being driven by fear itself." Let us not be afraid to listen to what we as children suffer at the hands of our nearest and dearest. Children's testimony should carry no less weight because the witnesses are small; let us be honest about trying to explain how and why their adults can hurt them with virtual impunity.

References

Advocacy Committee for Human Experimentation Survivors and Mind Control (ACHES-MC). (Updated). Available at <http://www.aches-mc.org>.

Carpenter, M., and A. Dietrich. (1997). "Children of the underground." *Pittsburgh Post-Gazette* (December 14–18, five-part series).

Christie, N. (2000). *Crime control as industry: Towards gulags, Western style*, 3rd ed. London: Routledge.

Daly, B. (1998). *Authoring a life: A woman's survival in and through literary studies*. Albany: State University of New York Press.

De Camp, J. W. (1996). *The Franklin cover-up: Child abuse, satanism, and murder in Nebraska*, 2nd ed. Lincoln, NB: AWT.

Dietrich, A. (1998). "Children of the underground." Available at <http://www.msnbc.com/modules/ps/underground/launch.asp>.

False Memory Syndrome Foundation. (1992). Available at <http://www.fmsf.org>.

Freyd, J. J. (1996). *Betrayal trauma: The logic of forgetting childhood abuse*. Cambridge, MA: Harvard University Press.

Herman, J. L. (1992). *Trauma and recovery: The aftermath of violence—from domestic abuse to political terror*. New York: Basic Books.

Kempe, C. H., F. Silverman, B. Steele, W. Groegemuller, and H. Silver. (1962). "The battered-child syndrome." *Journal of the American Medical Association 181*: 107–12.

Males, M. A. (1996). *The scapegoat generation: America's war on adolescence*. Monroe, ME: Common Courage Press.

———. (1999). *Framing youth: Ten myths about the next generation*. Monroe, ME: Common Courage Press.

Miller, A. (1990). *For your own good: Hidden cruelty in child rearing and the roots of violence*. New York: Noonday Press.

Pepinsky, H. (2001). *A criminologist's quest for peace*. Available at <http://www.critcrim.org/critpapers/pepinsky-book.htm>.

Pepinsky, H., and R. Quinney. (1991). *Criminology as peacemaking*. Bloomington: Indiana University Press.

Richardson, J. T., J. Best, and D. G. Bromley (eds.). (1991). *The satanism scare*. New York: A. de Gruyter.

Rosen, L., and M. Etlin. (1996). *The hostage child: Sex abuse allegations in custody disputes*. Bloomington: Indiana University Press.

Stop Mind Control and Ritual Abuse Today (SMART). (Updated). Available at <http://members.aol.com/SMARTNEWS/index2.html>.

———. (1996). "Rick Doninger: The blue house case." Available at <http://members.aol.com/SMARTNEWS/Sample-Issue-08.htm>.

Westbrook, J. (1997). "CKLN-FM Mind Control Series—Part 12: Jeanette Westbrook, MSW, presentation and interview." Available at <http://www.mindcontrolforums.com/radio/ckln12.htm>.

CHAPTER TWENTY-FIVE

Anti-Abortion Stalkers

CHARLOTTE A. DUDLEY

HARASSMENT, PUBLIC PROTESTS, arson, blockades, vandalism, death threats, anthrax, bomb threats, and even murder. All of these measures are those undertaken by anti-abortion stalkers, thinking in most cases that they have been ordained by their God to kill these medical professionals they deem "baby killers from hell." From 1977 to September 2000, there were 420 reported cases of the stalking of abortion providers, abortion clinic staff, and/or patients (Baird-Windle & Bader 2001). In 2001, Clayton Lee Waagner, declaring himself an anti-abortion "warrior" called by his fundamentalist God, posted an Internet message on the Army of God Web page threatening to stalk and kill abortion providers and anyone else who worked at an abortion clinic. Although he admitted to stalking several abortion providers, after authorities found his abandoned truck filled with ammunition and a list of abortion clinics and their addresses, he claimed that he was unable to bring himself to kill those abortion providers he had stalked. This chapter will focus on stalking legislation, problems associated with such legislation, and the unique and largely ignored stalking victimization of abortion providers, their staff, and their patients. In addition, policy implications will be provided, offering logical changes that will work to better protect this vulnerable group from potential stalking victimization.

Despite the legality of abortion in the United States and the anti-stalking legislation enacted in the aftermath of the murder of actress Rebecca Schaffer in 1989, one can see that there should be public concern for this phenomenon that has placed abortion doctors and their staff in constant fear of losing their lives, as well as distracting women from their civil right to choose to terminate a pregnancy. Why are pro-lifer's sometimes so driven by their God to take life away? It seems to be a great irony and phenomenon that demands political attention and psychological evaluation, as well as a clearly defined public policy to stop this stalking behavior that can lead to a blockage of civil rights, constant fear, and even death for those individuals who provide this service for women across America.

The problem with stalking legislation is that stalking is a relatively new "crime" in America, and these relatively new laws against it can be easily interpreted as being too loosely defined. What is a stalker exactly? And how do we know who these people are? And once we know who they are, how can we stop them before they physically harm anyone? And lastly, how do we determine if a "threat" is a real threat or merely a paranoid delusion, a preconceived notion of the one being supposedly "stalked"? And concerning the sometimes violent anti-abortion stalkers, where do we draw the line between the First Amendment right to free speech and public protest and the legally defined "stalking" behavior? These are all problems with the stalking legislation that need to be dealt with on a political and social level in order to protect everyone's civil rights as American citizens, and ultimately to save people's lives from this sometimes deadly and fear-invoking crime.

The power of anti-abortion stalkers is that they believe so fervently in their cause. They are willing to kill, die, and go to jail for their cause, believing that they are enforcing a more moral and religious code than the law-makers. Believing themselves to be morally superior agents of God, stalking behaviors and murder are justified. Unfortunately, the anti-abortion stalker's power also lies within the rights outlined in the First Amendment. Most abortion stalkers, despite displaying behavior that matches the legally defined description of what constitutes stalking in America, do not believe that they are indeed "stalking" abortion providers. Picketing at all hours in front of abortion providers' homes, sending life-threatening letters, making life-threatening telephone calls, following doctors and their families, finding women who have or are about to have an abortion and harassing them in a public sphere, are not constituted in their minds as stalking; in their view, it is their constitutional right to freely speak and protest against what they believe is morally wrong. These people answer to a higher authority than U.S. law enforcement—they believe that they answer to a God whom they believe endorses and encourages their deadly and harassing behavior to anyone engaging in pro-choice activity. So how do we stop them? Abortion to these people is murder and should be illegal. It is in fact so wrong, that their God has justified them in killing these "killers"—an irony and hypocrisy that the majority of rational citizens do not understand.

Stalking is illegal. Sending death threats and invoking so much fear into a person, or people, where they sincerely think their life and life of their family is in danger, is illegal in all 50 states in America. Regardless of your political or religious views, abortion is an American right . . . as much as free speech. The crime of stalking, though, is a difficult "crime" to prevent and discontinue because it involves a series of actions, instead of one, clearly defined criminal act. Many have argued that the language in stalking statutes is either too vague or too broad—so broad that everyone was getting convicted, or so narrow so that it is nearly impossible to convict anyone. Laws against this behavior have been criticized as not being clearly stated so that a reasonable person could understand what behaviors are criminal, and as acting to outlaw constitutionally protected behaviors such as picketing and free speech, as well as being criticized for redundancy, in that there are already sufficient laws that forbid stalking behavior.

Unfortunately, it seems as if the conservative law-makers, of whom the majority are pro-life, are reluctant to enact and uphold legislation that protects the abortion providers in America from this deadly stalking behavior. In fact, despite the shootings, the terrorism, and the deaths that have resulted from this form of stalking, it seems as if this is the least of the conservatives' priorities—a concern that does not seem to concern them at all.

Legislation

Stalking is not a new behavior by any means, nor is it a rare behavior exclusive to infringing upon the lives of celebrities. "Stalking" is merely a new word to describe the predatory, fear-invoking, and harassing behavior of an individual toward another that occurs on a continuum, over a period of time. It was not until the 1989 murder of actress Rebecca Schaffer and the four subsequent ex-intimate "stalking" murders that took place in Orange County, California, that the word "stalking" made it into the criminologists' and law-makers' vocabulary. In 1990, California was the first state to enact anti-stalking legislation, and since then all 50 states, the District of Columbia, and federal legislation has followed suit, using California's law as a model and passing similar laws (Harmon 1999). California, the American trend-setter in stalking legislation, defined the crime of "stalking" as "any person who willfully, maliciously, and repeatedly follows or harasses another person and who makes a credible threat with the intent to place that person in reasonable fear of death or great bodily harm" (California Penal Code 646.9 [A]).

Harmon (1999) looks at the effectiveness of anti-stalking legislation as well as some of the problems the statute has encountered as an effective means in combating stalking. She notes that most of the problems with early legislation was the Constitutional basis of whether the wording of the law was guilty of either vagueness or overbreadth. The vagueness aspect is deficient in that the definition of the illegal behavior was not clearly stated and too ambiguous for "reasonable people" to understand just what behavior was being prohibited. The overbreadth problem "occurs when legislation written to control stalking also has the effect of prohibiting constitutionally protected behavior (e.g., picketing, free speech, lawful assembly)" (Harmon 1999, 21). Most current stalking legislation, Harmon contends, is modeled after the California law but has been slightly modified to overcome these Constitutionality problems. Most legislation today reads:

> . . . the act of willfully and repeatedly following or harassing another individual or that individual's immediate family, and a stalker is one who makes a credible threat, or intentionally or knowingly engages in a pattern or continuing course of conduct that would cause any reasonable person to suffer emotional distress or fear of death or great bodily harm. (p. 21)

California defines harassment as "a knowing and willful course of conduct directed at a specific person that seriously alarms, annoys, torments, or terrorizes the person, and that serves no legitimate purpose," implying that the behavior is deliberate and "has taken place on more than one occasion" (Harmon 1999, 22). But several of the terms in the legislation are loosely defined and misinterpreted by courts as well as law-enforcers and have been debated as to whether the terminology is effective in apprehending stalkers before the behavior escalates to violence. These include the phrases "intentionally," "course of conduct," "repeatedly," "emotional distress," "reasonable person," and "credible threat." "Repeatedly," the most easily defined, refers to a behavior occurring "more than twice," or, as defined in some states, "more than once." But the other terms constitute differing degrees of legitimacy across state and federal legislations. It can be easily argued that the stalking behavior was not necessarily "intentional" nor did it cause any real "emotional stress." These words and phrases, though, depend on how the victim, the stalker, the police, and the courts define and attribute these words in a specific context. Should a criminal legislation be so open as to how one happens to define a behavior in a given situation? This language defining stalking, and what the anti-stalking legislation consists of, Harmon contends, works to protect the victim of a stalker from further "harassment" and the "possibility of injury," as well as to protect the American right as outlined in the First Amendment—the right to free speech and assembly.

McCandless (1999) argues that the current anti-stalking legislation is not effective, in that the language used in these statutes is guilty of both being too vague and too broad. McCandless asserts that it might not be fair to "assume that an individual who is exercising her or his right to speech is also guilty of stalking" just because "another person defines that speech to be harassing" (p. 27). In fact, she asserts that stalking laws are merely redundant, in that trespassing, invasion of privacy, harassment, and inflictions of emotional distress laws are sufficient enough to impede the stalking behavior. She also ascertains that in order to criminally prosecute the stalker, the victim is in fact the one laden with the burdens of proving their victimization, first to law enforcement, then before a court of law. The victim, she feels, is also unjustly responsible for not only having to engage in "avoidance behavior," but to uphold the task of documenting every instance of contact with the stalker in order to prove that the stalking actually took place. Another problem she notices is that stalking crimes seem not to be the "district attorney's highest priority" (McCandless 1999, 29), never mind that law-enforcement agents are sometimes not even aware of the complexities of these new laws. In addition, "stalking is most often classified as a misdemeanor" (p. 29), which means light jail sentences and fines—albeit offering no justice or real protection for the stalked victim from the potentially dangerous stalker.

Research

Forrest and Henshaw conducted a study in 1985 on the harassment of U.S. abortion providers, and although stalking was not part of the lawmakers', law-enforcers', or criminologists' vocabulary at the time, it is interesting to note that the extent of the harassment these providers and patients endured could, by today's legislation, be deemed as "stalking." They found that "47 percent of abortion providers experienced anti-abortion harassment," and that during 1984, 73 percent "of the facilities were the target of at least one illegal activity" (Forrest & Henshaw 1987, 9). This hostile harassment consisted of such activities as picketing outside clinics, picketing outside staff members' homes, picketers blocking entry to clinics, making physical contact with patients and providers, tracing the identity and license-plate numbers of patients, jamming telephone lines, distributing of anti-abortion literature inside clinics, mass scheduling of no-show appointments, vandalizing and destroying facilities, as well as death threats, bomb threats, actual bombings, and arson.

According to this study, Forrest and Henshaw (1987) found that "anti-abortion harassment was seldom limited to one type of activity. Only 6 percent of all respondents were subjected only to picketing, while 82 percent experienced multiple forms of harassment." Sixteen percent of the providers reported that "patients had been harassed with phone calls or visits at home after anti-abortion activists had traced their license plates to ascertain the women's identities" (p. 10). "Most instances of anti-abortion harassment are not single, isolated occurrences, but rather part of a pattern of continuing pressure" (p. 11). Is this behavior "stalking behavior," occurring on a continuum, or just the constitutionally protected First Amendment right of the American people? The harassment of abortion providers, their staff, and patients seems to profoundly constitute the "act of willfully and repeatedly following or harassing another individual or that individual's immediate family," and these anti-abortion demonstrators seem clearly to be making a "credible threat" and "intentionally" engaging "in a pattern or continuing course of conduct that would cause any reasonable person to suffer emotional distress or fear of death or great bodily harm." Although stalking was not a crime in 1985 when this study was conducted, one can plainly see that the harassing and life-threatening behavior of stalking is not a new behavior employed by the anti-abortion movement, done in an attempt to undermine and terminate abortion rights in America.

Pathe and Mullen (1997, 12) describe stalking as "behaviors in which one individual inflicts on another repeated unwanted intrusions and communications," which can involve specific or implied threats to the victim: following, surveillance, making physical approaches, letters, telephone calls/messages, email, graffiti, vandalism of property, as well as threatening the family or friends of the victim. All of these behaviors describe acts of the anti-abortion radical. The impact of this stalking behavior, they found, "had a deleterious impact" on all of the victims' "psychological, interpersonal, and/or occupational functioning" (Pathe & Mullen 1997, 14) such as anxiety, sleep disturbance, weight fluctuations, headaches, and nightmares. "Eighty-two percent had modified their usual activities as a direct consequence of their harassment" (p. 14), and some even lost or were forced to change jobs in order to avoid the harassing stalker. The abortion provider is no different as a stalked victim than the ex-intimate partner. Many providers, and even clinical staff, have reported that they have decided to change locations or professions due to the harassment of anti-abortion activists, the continuity of the anti-abortion stalker's purpose, the fear invoked upon them, and the definite threat felt to their lives, their well-being, and their families.

Snow (1998, 90) examines the phenomena of the anti-abortion stalker and deems the behavior "cause stalking." The "cause" here is "life" as well as the desire to abolish the American right to terminate a pregnancy—abortion. Although otherwise normal, law-abiding people, "when involved in a cause they truly believe in, [they] feel morally correct in resorting to what could be considered criminal activities to support and further their cause." Snow declares that these types of stalkers, although not wholly delusional, believe that sometimes the killing of an abortion provider is considered to be a "justifiable homicide." Through harassment and invoking fear on those who perform and have abortions, the anti-abortion stalker is hoping to curb and/or eliminate this form of behavior that they (the majority being radical Christian Fundamentalists) deem a murderous "evil."

These repeated behaviors, deemed illegal under current anti-stalking legislation, are the same behaviors committed by the pro-life activist. Most of these activists hide, however, behind the mask of the First Amendment and do not constitute their own behavior as "stalking"—never mind as being illegal behavior. In the courts, this issue of the right to free speech and assembly on behalf of the anti-abortion stalker/activist has been nearly exhausted and not led to an accurate protection of the abortion providers' rights as outlined under the current anti-stalking legislation. Snow (1998) has found, however, that a "number of anti-abortion activists *have* [italics added] been convicted of stalking" (p. 87), although in 1997 the Supreme Court "held that 'in your face' protesting, such as that done by anti-abortion activists . . . is protected speech under the First Amendment" (p. 93). But the death threats, the bombings, and these "in your face" protests, at clinics and at providers' homes, have caused so much fear that a lot of abortion doctors will not show up to work without bulletproof vests! Although "in your face" protesting is no longer legal after a Supreme Court ruling in 2000, instilling an eight-foot "bubble zone" between protesters and abortion clinic staff (Baird-Windle & Bader 2001), it seems as if there is a "reasonable threat" to their lives despite this "bubble zone," never mind the emotional distress caused by the fear of injury or death. This behavior clearly constitutes stalking. So, should not the anti-stalking legislation described above prevent the violence against abortion providers before it occurs, despite First Amendment rights?

Implications and Policy Suggestions

Most stalking behavior exists between intimate or ex-intimate partners, where an overwhelming number of the victims are females and the perpetrators male. It is reported that the majority of women killed per year in the United States were stalked by an ex-intimate prior to their murders. In addition, violence is most likely to stem from stalking behavior if an intimate relationship was shared prior to the stalking (Mullen, Pathe, & Purcell 2000), so it is no wonder that anti-stalking legislation is more than necessary.

It seems as if these threatening, fear-invoking, and harassing behaviors directed toward abortion providers, clinic staff, and patients, as described by Forrest and Henshaw (1987) constitutes stalking. Although stalking was not necessarily illegal in 1985, we can see that radical Christian Fundamentalists are employing overt stalking behaviors to further the anti-abortion movement. So why are these stalking laws not applied more rigidly to the pro-life fanatic? If two or more of these "harassing" behaviors and "credible threats" occur, does that not constitute stalking? Or have our conservative, pro-life law-makers allowed the protection of these activists under the First Amendment because it protects their own interests as well? Why is this behavior, which in many instances has ended in bloodshed and death (never mind the fear so that a bulletproof vest has become a normal part of the abortion physician's garb), not been recognized as stalking, and apprehended, before death and mayhem result?

Several organizations are impacted by this criminal form of "cause," or anti-abortion, stalking. The American Coalition of Life Activists, one of the most militant anti-abortion groups, deems it their civil and American right to protest and express freely their views on the abortion debate. This organization created and still maintains the controversial Web site known as the Nuremberg Files, which can be found at <www.christiangallery.com/atrocity/>, initially posted in 1997 (Baird-Windle & Bader 2001). This site still, despite the Ninth Circuit of Appeals decision in early 2002 deeming the material to be "threatening," denounces abortion providers as murderers, and gives the names, addresses, home telephone numbers, and sometimes Social Security and license-plate numbers of abortion doctors. The Wild West–style "wanted" posters, however, have been removed since the court's decision. These posters displayed the faces of abortion doctors, with those already killed by anti-abortion radicals marked in black, indicating that they were no longer wanted (obviously suggesting to pro-choice advocates that those abortion providers displayed on the Web site were to be the radicals' next target). However, still posted on the Nuremberg Files Web site are the names of those abortion providers who have been murdered, with honorable credit given to the person or people who carried out the "abortion of the abortionist." John Leo (2002, 43) reports that the Nuremberg Files Web site never called for any sort of violence, only that the doctors ought to be "brought under surveillance and 'brought to justice' in Nuremberg-like trials for crimes against humanity." Being "under surveillance," though, sounds like stalking, and giving names, numbers, and addresses of abortion providers easily supplies the information necessary for the would-be anti-abortion stalker to easily find his or her victim.

Conversely, the organization at odds with these pro-life militants is the Planned Parenthood Federation of America, a medical organization that provides the majority of abortions for women. Planned Parenthood, the Feminist Majority Foundation, and the National Abortion Federation all, after the initial court decision that the information posted on the Nuremberg Files Web site was in fact protected under the First Amendment (although not protected anymore), called on Attorney General John Ashcroft to speak out against the increasing threats and violence targeting abortion providers and their clinics. Ashcroft complied, saying that despite his conservative views on the moral issue of abortion, he would uphold former President Clinton's 1994 law (Freedom of Access to Clinic Entrance Act [FACE]) that made violence at abortion clinics a federal crime (Charatan 2001). Planned Parenthood, however, won the civil suit against the anti-abortionists' form of inadvertent harassment (and inversely stalking, though not legally defined as such) in the 6-to-5 Ninth Circuit of Appeals ruling against the American Coalition of Life Activists. This overturned the former ruling, "saying in effect that the 'wanted' posters acted as true death threats, even without explicitly threatening language" (Charatan 2001, 126). This definition of "threat," some believe, is a very narrow and dated definition and leaves us with the need to come up with a more realistic, tight, and effective definition of "threat"—the very same problem that has plagued the anti-stalking legislation since its initial enactment in 1990.

There are several pro-life (anti-choice) organizations that overtly call for, and practice, the violent harassment of abortion providers, their staff, and patients, though not all anti-abortion organizations endorse and encourage violence in their moral protests. The Planned Parenthood Federation of America profiled 14 of the leading anti-choice organizations in America, six of which overtly declared that they engaged in the tactic of harassing and intimidating abortion-clinic doctors, staff, and patients. The American Life League, a predominantly Catholic organization, challenged FACE, enacted in 1994, on First Amendment grounds, but lost. Human Life International endorses clinic blockades and "sidewalk counseling," which involves harassing the women who are entering clinics in order to obtain abortions. Life Dynamics Incorporated employed the tactic of espionage, utilizing 4,000 "spies for life" to research abortion clinics and physicians. Missionaries to the Preborn, a more radical anti-abortion organization, whose leader Reverend Matthew Trewhella (a protester convicted of arson, trespassing, and disorderly conduct) overtly declares that the killing of abortion doctors and their staff is "justifiable homicide." They engage in tactics such as clinic blockades, and even went so far as to trap an abortion physician in his home, against his will, and then went to picket his son's soccer game. Operation Save America, formerly Operation Rescue, is a Christian anti-abortion organization that overtly encourages and engages in such activism as picketing at clinics and homes of clinic employees, as well as engaging in the "sidewalk counseling" of patients. In April 1999, Operation Rescue went to Buffalo, New York to stage a protest in front of an abortion clinic where a week earlier an abortion physician, Dr. Barnett Slepian, was shot to death by a fanatical anti-abortion militant (Stein 1999). The Pro-Life Action League, despite its nonviolent mission statement, is run by Joseph Scheidler, a man who has been arrested 16 times for 21 acts of intimidation, including physical violence outside abortion clinics. This organization has, through clinic blockades, succeeded in the closing of a hundred abortion clinics across the country; it employs the radical tactic of picketing at clinics and homes of employees and engages in espionage in order to "steal" information from pro-choice organizations and abortion clinics.

The National Women's Health Organization (NWHO), a big player in the fight against the harassment, intimidation, and stalking of abortion providers, believes that it is a woman's American right to obtain an abortion in a medically safe atmosphere, and an American right for doctors to provide this much-needed and -demanded service without being in constant fear of danger. In 1986, NWHO filed suit against Joseph Scheidler, leader of the Pro-Life Action League, for conspiring and racketeering against their clinics across the United States (Baird-Windle & Bader 2001). The president of NWHO stated in 1993 that despite all the arrests made of those who terrorized, stalked, and harassed abortion providers and their facilities, the majority of charges were soon dropped, no jail time resulted, and/or minimal fines ended up being the "punishment" (*Lancet* 1993). The American College of Obstetricians and Gynecologists, the Planned Parenthood Federation of America, the National Abortion Federation, and the American Civil Liberties Union are some of a few other pro-choice organizations that generally agree.

Thus it is obvious that Congress, and the federal government at large, has become increasingly involved in this harassing form of deadly behavior directed at abortion providers, in that they have the power to enact specific laws in order to outlaw stalking behaviors in general, as well as placing limits on how far the First Amendment will protect those engaging in violence, and threats of violence, against abortion providers as well as stopping those who stalk before they kill. Despite the 1973 *Roe v. Wade* Supreme Court decision, which ruled that state laws prohibiting abortion are illegal and a violation of the due-process clause of the Fourteenth Amendment, three years later, in 1976, Congress passed the Hyde Amendment that cut off Medicaid funding for women who could not afford abortions (which was again upheld in 1980). In 1988, the U.S. Department of Health and Human Services prohibited federal funding for clinics—money that was utilized by clinics to aid financially deprived women in obtaining abortion counseling (Baird-Windle & Bader 2001). From these examples, it is clear that Congress has power and motive to harness the pro-choice movement, as well as the motive and power to be less stringent on the anti-abortion radicals who stalk, harass, threaten, and kill abortion providers.

Several agents/actors are impacted through this form of stalking, in addition to the impact felt by those who must make laws to protect all American citizens from this criminal and sometimes deadly behavior. Political conservatives argue that imposing penalties on those who harass and/or stalk abortion providers will "hamper legitimate anti-abortion freedom of speech protected by the First Amendment," while civil libertarians believe that these penalties are a necessary way to provide "supportable relief for victims of criminal behavior that pose no threat to free expression" (*Lancet* 1993, 940).

But the "law enforcers" (the police, prosecutors, judges, and courts) are also big actors in the effectiveness of combating this deadly and criminal form of anti-abortion stalking. Stalking, in general, is a difficult crime to prove, and therefore police are hesitant to make arrests before an actual and visible form of violence occurs, believing that there is no way to distinguish between a *perceived* and *real* threat. Court systems have a hard time prosecuting stalkers with no "substantial" or hard evidence—how do you prove a "credible threat" or the "emotional distress" that is a result of this fear? In addition, in a court of law, it ends up being one person's word (the victim) against another's (the accused stalker). But as far as anti-abortion stalking goes, it seems as if there may be more personal agendas involved when it comes to arresting and prosecuting these potentially violent protesters and stalkers. If the police and courts, not to mention the law-makers, believe that abortion is a "moral wrong" and religious sin, than perhaps these actors end up being that much more hesitant to make arrests and to prosecute, hence leaving the anti-abortion radical unpunished and free to promote their cause, not to mention remaining unaffected by the anti-stalking legislation. "Despite 136 arrests this year [1993], stalking of doctors and patients by the radicals continues to make a misery of their lives" (*Lancet* 1993, 939). Access to abortion clinics in America is declining and in consequence, the safety of women in obtaining this much-demanded procedure is in jeopardy.

These systems and actors are involved in creating the policy agenda for and against this form of stalking. In 1993, FACE was passed, imposing penalties on those who destroy or damage a facility or who use force, or the threat of force, to intimidate, injure, or obstruct those who conduct or obtain abortion services. But in George W. Bush's inauguration speech in January 2001, he claimed, in so many words, that he would begin his term by "blocking aid to international family-planning agencies and by nominating anti-abortion fanatics to run the Justice Department" (Shapiro 2001, 6).

There are quite a few limits surrounding the creation, implementation, review, and reformulation of the policy regarding anti-abortion stalkers. The first and foremost is the constitutionally protected right to free speech, as outlined in the First Amendment of the U.S. Constitution. The second is the protection of all American citizens of their civil right, protected under law since the 1973 *Roe v. Wade* decision, to freely obtain an abortion. Unfortunately, this latter aspect does not permit, under law, the right to obtain an abortion without the "threat" and/or "harassment" of anti-abortion activists. As far as policy-making goes though, in enforcing and criminalizing this pro-life stalking behavior, it seems as if the conservative agenda, the majority of whom are pro-life, does not feel all that inclined to protect those abortion providers and those women who engage in a practice and procedure that they themselves do not advocate, support, or believe in at all, despite what the current legislation dictates concerning abortion rights. Especially now, with an extremely conservative, pro-life president, cabinet, and Congress in power, it seems as if providing a clear and tough policy to prevent this deadly stalking behavior against abortion providers, their staff, and patients and severely punish those for engaging in this stalking before death results might not be the first priority in their conservative agenda, although it seems obvious that a clearly outlined policy is needed to protect the civil rights of the pro-choice providers in America.

Recommendations and Conclusions

It seems obvious that many changes need to be made in the criminal-justice policy regarding these radical and sometimes violent anti-abortion stalkers. The purpose of first enacting anti-stalking legislation in 1990 was to better empower law enforcement to criminalize stalking behavior and stop it before it escalated into violence. Unfortunately, stalking cases are very hard to enforce and police tend to be hesitant in arresting accused stalkers, believing that false claims may be made and that the victim may be merely overreacting to innocuous behavior. If and when arrests are made, stalking is then very hard to prove in a court of law, when the language defining what behavior consists of the crime of stalking is guilty of being potentially ambiguous.

Regarding anti-abortion stalking, it seems as if in addition to these very real limitations in the anti-stalking legislation, we are faced with the moral problem and issue of whether abortion is murder and an illegal act under a Christian God's law, or an American civil right for women to freely engage in as they see fit, in our supposedly free and democratic society. If the law-makers, the law-enforcers, and the criminal-justice system at large believe more fervently in the former view, than there are serious issues that need to be dealt with. In the U.S. Constitution we all have the right to freely practice and believe in whatever religion and God we see fit and we do not have the right to kill people, regardless of whether others are engaging in a practice we believe our God does not approve of. It could easily be argued that these law-makers, enforcers, and the criminal-justice system at large are not doing everything in their power to protect abortion providers, their clinics, and patients from victimization in general, including stalking victimization. The policy-makers are letting their beliefs, opinions, and own agendas get in the way of the American right to abortion and the American right to be equally protected from victimization under anti-stalking legislation. Why is the act of stalking, threatening, harassing, and even murdering abortion providers not quite as criminal as a lone man stalking, threatening, and harassing a former lover?

As far as goes the policy implications regarding this sometimes deadly crime of stalking abortion providers, it is recommended first that the Nuremberg Files Web site be shut down completely, and that the posting or disclosure of anyone's personal information (addresses, telephone numbers, license-plate numbers, Social Security numbers, or names of family members), whether it be posted on the Internet or given out by motor-vehicle agencies, be illegal under federal legislation, unless permission is given in writing to whomever is disclosing or providing this information. Stalking by proxy (stalking made easier due to another's discoveries or publicized personal information) would be eliminated, at least partially (Mullen, Pathe, & Purcell 2000). This posting of personal information on the Internet is one of the principal contributors of victimization by anti-abortion stalkers and anti-abortion violence of abortion providers, their practices, and their patients.

Second, the right of protesters to protest at any individual's home address should be outlawed, especially if there are young children residing at the home. Stiff federal penalties for staging protests in residential areas should be enacted. By outlawing only this aspect of free speech and protest I think would protect the pro-life's First Amendment right to free speech and protect the life and safety of abortion providers, as well as reduce the paranoid climate of fear invoked upon them and their families when these personally invading protests take place.

Policy that would require that the proper authorities be notified at least a week in advance when any anti-abortion group or organization wishes to stage a protest in front of an abortion clinic with its hundred-foot "bubble zone" (legislation introduced and required for all anti-abortion protests) is a third suggestion. On June 28, 2000, the Supreme Court ruled that an eight-foot "bubble zone" separating clinic staff and patients from protesters was not an unreasonable violation of the free speech protected under the First Amendment (Baird-Windle & Bader 2001). But an eight-foot buffer is not nearly sufficient enough to reduce the fear in clinic staff and patients from being recognized and hence possibly targeted for present and/or future harassment. Under an increased "bubble zone" distance, physicians, the clinic's staff, and their patients would be notified that a protest would be taking place, and all would be able to take the necessary precautions to avoid conflict with the protesting crowd. Police and security officials should be required to be present, at the state government's cost, to control the crowd to ensure that all of the protesters have no weapons on their person or in their vehicles while protesting, and also to prevent protesters from harassing or offering "sidewalk counseling" to patients and from "following" patients or staff home. This measure, again, would not restrict the pro-lifer's right to free speech but restrict its place and manner, thereby allowing physicians to practice, and women to obtain, these procedures in safety, free from the fear of harassment and potential stalking behavior.

Fourth, anti-stalking legislation should be revised to explicitly include the anti-abortion stalker. Sending death threats (whether the threats are verbal or chemical), making life-threatening telephone calls, and/or setting up surveillance against anyone, regardless of their profession, should be included in the language in such anti-stalking statutes. Law enforcers as well need to be educated more vigorously on the existing stalking legislation and informed about taking all threats seriously, especially when these threats are made against abortion providers, regardless of law enforcers' personal, political, or moral beliefs on the abortion issue. Judges and prosecutors also need to be more informed on the legality of these statutes, while realizing that their personal and moral beliefs need to be "checked at the door" when investigating and convicting such cases.

Fifth, it should be mandatory for the mental-health professionals to evaluate those accused of stalking before final adjudication on their cases. Despite the moral opposition to abortion, there are several pro-life organizations that demand and practice peaceful protesting and lament the violence and assassinations of abortion providers. Perhaps there is some mental or emotional deficiency that pushes the anti-abortion protester into this predatory stalking behavior. It should be mandatory in all states to perform a mental-health evaluation of all accused stalkers in hopes of better understanding the psychological aspects of this crime, and hence better prevent its occurring in the future.

Political and religious forces both contribute to the debate surrounding the policy process regarding anti-abortion stalking and violence. Republicans, in general, do not support abortion, and in fact denounce the morality of it in every sense of the word. George W. Bush himself knocked down federal funding for stem-cell research—research that would potentially cure hundreds, if not thousands, of diseases and illnesses plaguing the Western world today—believing that it would promote and endorse abortion. The Republican majority in power at present seems to be much less sympathetic to the abortion providers who live their professional and personal lives in constant fear of being harassed and/or murdered by the fanatical anti-abortion stalker, and more sympathetic toward those protesters and stalkers and their First Amendment right to free speech, their right to protest, and their right to stalk, murder, and harass. This does not seem fair, logical, or democratic at all. Opinions and ideologies are clouding the laws and negatively affecting the criminal-justice policy and process, in that justice seems to extend *only* upon those deemed criminal by those in power—not the anti-abortion stalker, but the stalker who victimizes celebrities and ex-intimates.

There are religious forces that contribute to this debate by denouncing abortion as a moral wrong and sin that God will not forgive. However, these denominations do not necessarily encourage or endorse violence as a necessary response to the "sin" of an American woman's right to terminate a pregnancy if she so chooses. It seems as if some of the Christian Fundamentalists are so opposed to abortion that they will go to any length—be it stalking, harassment, death threats, or murder—to stop what they deem to be morally wrong. But there is a *separation* of church and state, so whom are they to say that stalking and murder are justified behaviors in the face of abortion? Just because they do not agree with the law does not give them the right to stalk, harass, or kill abortion providers, their staff, and their patients. The pro-life view about the lack of morality involved in abortion should not hold weight in the debate of whether a person should be arrested, tried, and prosecuted for stalking behavior before it escalates into violence and death, which was the initial purpose in enacting anti-stalking legislation—to stop potentially violent behavior *before* death or violence results, not after. Religious beliefs do not justify homicide under any circumstances. The right to believe in any god and to practice any religion in America does not justify homicide, nor does it justify stalking behavior. Stalking, however defined, is an illegal criminal act—abortion is not.

Stalking of abortion providers is a problem that has been largely ignored. Although not all anti-abortion stalkers are, or will be, moved to kill, their harassment and threat is real enough to cause a "reasonable person" to live in a constant, and psychologically tormenting, prison of fear. We need to enact and uphold a policy or policies that will stop and deter the fanatical and radical anti-abortion advocate before stalking and harassing behavior turns into violence, as it has so many times in the past. The National Abortion Federation collected statistics on all acts of anti-abortion violence from 1977 to September 2000 and found that there have been a total of seven murders, 17 attempted murders, 115 incidents of assault and battery, 332 death threats, 8,246 harassing calls or hate mail, and 420 reported incidents of stalking (Baird-Windle & Bader 2001).

If most anti-stalking legislation today indicates that it is a crime to "willfully and repeatedly" follow or harass "another individual or that individual's immediate family," and in producing a "credible threat," the stalker "intentionally or knowingly engages in a pattern or continuing course of conduct that would cause any reasonable person to suffer emotional distress or fear of death or great bodily harm," is it not feasible for radical anti-abortion protesters to be guilty of the crime of stalking when following, videotaping, harassing, and threatening abortion providers and their patients? The threat here is entirely credible, considering the violent statistics listed above. The harassment is "willful" and seems to occur "repeatedly" against providers and their clinics. In addition, is this harassing behavior not committed intentionally and knowingly to cause "emotional distress" and the "fear of death or great bodily harm" upon these abortion providers? Is this not the motive behind violent anti-abortion organizations? And most important, physicians are considered to be "reasonable" people. Should the "threat" not be taken seriously if physicians and abortion-clinic staff feel as if they have to wear bulletproof vests everyday to work?

If these radical anti-abortionists are waging a religious war against the pro-choice movement and abortion providers in general and are employing tactics such as stalking to intimidate their moral enemy into defeat, then anti-stalking legislation needs to come to the abortion providers rescue, and policy dealing with this issue needs to be revised. Women's civil rights are at stake. Practicing physician's lives and psychological well-beings are at stake. Abortion is not the enemy. The stalking, homicidal anti-abortionist is the enemy of an American right to freely choose.

REFERENCES

Baird-Windle, P., and E. J. Bader. (2001). *Targets of hatred: Anti-abortion terrorism.* New York: Palgrave.

Charatan, F. (2001). "U.S. abortion clinics afraid of new violence." *British Medical Journal 323*:126.

Forrest, J. D., and S. K. Henshaw. (1987). "The harassment of U.S. abortion providers." *Family Planning Perspectives 19*:9–13.

Harmon, R. (1999). "Are stalking laws effective?" in *Controversial issues in criminology,* ed. John R. Fuller and Eric W. Hickey (pp. 18–24). Needham Heights, MA: Allyn & Bacon.

Lancet. (1993). "This is a deadly game." *Lancet 342*:939–40.

Leo, J. (2002, June 10). "An unspoken threat." *U.S. News and World Report 132*: 43.

McCandless, N. J. (1999). "Are stalking laws effective?" in *Controversial issues in criminology*, ed. John R. Fuller and Eric W. Hickey (pp. 26–32). Needham Heights, MA: Allyn & Bacon.

Mullen, P. E., M. Pathe, and R. Purcell. (2000). *Stalkers and their victims*. Cambridge: Cambridge University Press.

Pathe, M., and P. E. Mullen. (1997). "The impact of stalkers on their victims." *British Journal of Psychiatry 170*:12–17.

Planned Parenthood Federation of America. (n.d.). *Profiles of 14 leading anti-choice organizations*. Available at <http://www.plannedparenthood.org/library/facts/14anti-choiceFS.html>.

Shapiro, B. (2001). "The doctor killers." *Nation 272*:6–7.

Snow, R. L. (1998). *Stopping a stalker: A cop's guide to making the system work for you*. New York: Plenum.

Stein, J. (1999). "Has violence killed the anti-abortion movement?" Available at <http://salon.com/news/feature/1999/04/28/abortion/>.

index

about the editor and contributors

JOANNE ARDOVINI-BROOKER earned her Ph.D. from Western Michigan University in 1997. She joined the Department of Sociology at Sam Houston State University in 1998. Prior to that she was a research associate at the Institute for Leadership Transformation, Office of the Vice President for Research, at Western Michigan University. Dr. Ardovini-Brooker specializes in feminist theory, methodology, and pedagogy, as well as social problems, deviance, victimization, race and ethnic relations, and criminology.

DIANE C. BATES earned her Ph.D. from Rutgers University in 2000. She joined the College of New Jersey in 2003. Her research to date has focused on social, economic, and sustainable development, with an emphasis in Latin America. After extended field research in Ecuador's Amazonian region, she has published research on deforestation and conservation in the tropics, population displacement, and environmental inequality. Her current research involves community transformations that result from environmental change.

BONNIE BERRY directs the Social Problems Research Group in Gig Harbor, Washington. Her Ph.D. is in sociology from Ohio State University, and her areas of specialization include social movements, the study of crime and deviance, and social problems. She is presently examining the animal-rights movement, the fat-acceptance movement, and all manner of social inequalities.

ROBERT L. BING III is an associate professor and chair of the Department of Criminology and Criminal Justice at the University of Texas at Arlington. He earned a Ph.D. in criminology from Florida State University. His research interests include corrections, plea-bargaining, sentencing, criminal-justice education, and organizational politics in the courtroom. Dr. Bing has written over 20 articles in criminology and criminal-justice journals and has co-authored the book *Race and Crime.*

ANITA NEUBERGER BLOWERS earned her Ph.D. from the State University of New York at Albany. She is currently an associate professor in the Department of Criminal Justice at the University of North Carolina at Charlotte, where she also participates in the university's gerontology program. Her areas of specialization include court processing, domestic violence, criminal-justice policy, and elder abuse.

PAULINE K. BRENNAN earned her doctorate degree from the State University of New York at Albany. She is an assistant professor at the University of North Carolina at Charlotte, where her research and teaching activities focus on legislatures, public opinion, women in the criminal-justice system, and corrections. Her most recent book, *Women Who Receive Jail Sentences in New York City*, predicts sentence severity among this little-studied population.

JANE BRYANT received her Master's degree in administration of justice in 2000 from Southern Illinois University–Carbondale, where she is currently working toward her Ph.D. in political science. She has been employed in the public administration of housing programs for nearly 20 years. Additionally, she teaches sociology and political science courses at John A. Logan College, Carterville, Illinois, on a part-time basis.

CHARISSE T. M. COSTON earned her Ph.D. in criminal justice in 1988 from the School of Criminal Justice at Rutgers University. Her Master's and doctoral theses focused on lifestyle characteristics, victimization experiences, and the fear of crime among homeless women in New York City. Currently, she is an associate professor and graduate coordinator in the Department of Criminal Justice at the University of North Carolina at Charlotte. Her current research interests include victimology and the fear of crime within and between especially vulnerable populations, serial murder, deviance, and critical theory in gender studies.

MARTHA R. CROWTHER earned her Ph.D. from Duke University in 1998. She is an assistant professor of clinical psychology and coordinator of the PhD/MPH program at the University of Alabama. Her primary research and clinical interests are in geropsychology. She examines the nature, impact, and consequences of custodial grandparenting as well as designing effective interventions to reduce stress in the population. Additionally, she has explored the relationship among spirituality, mental health, and well-being across the lifespan. She has published journal articles and book chapters on sexuality and aging, psychology and aging, and cultural diversity in research training.

CHARLOTTE A. DUDLEY earned her Master's degree at the University of North Carolina at Charlotte. She presently serves as the deputy editor of the *Journal of Forensic Psychology Practice*. Her Bachelor's degrees are in English and sociology from the University of Vermont in Burlington.

JAMES O. FINCKENAUER is a professor at the Rutgers University School of Criminal Justice. From 1998 to 2002, while on academic leave, he was director of the International Center at the National Institute of Justice in Washington, D.C. His research and teaching interests include international and comparative criminal justice and transnational organized crime. He is the author or co-author of six books, including *Russian Mafia in America*, as well as numerous articles and reports. Dr. Finckenauer is editor of *Trends in Organized Crime* and is second vice-president of the Academy of Criminal Justice Sciences.

LAURA T. FISHMAN is an associate professor of sociology in the Department of Sociology at the University of Vermont. She holds an M.A. in sociology from the University of Chicago, and a Ph.D. in sociology from McGill University. Her research interests include AIDS, drugs, crime and prisons; families of prisoners; and images of crime, race, and gender. Her book *Women at the Wall: A Study of Prisoners' Wives Doing Time on the Outside* was published in 1990.

JAMES GAROFALO is a professor and director of the Center for the Study of Crime, Delinquency, and Corrections at Southern Illinois University–Carbondale. He has been involved in research and writing on victimization for more than 25 years. During the past ten years, hate crime and hate victimization have become primary areas of his research interest.

JOHN J. GIBBS earned his Ph.D. from the State University of New York at Albany and is a professor of criminology at Indiana University of Pennsylvania. His areas of research interest include measurement, theory testing, and pedagogy.

KATE HANRAHAN earned her Ph.D. from Rutgers University and is a professor of criminology at Indiana University of Pennsylvania. Her research interests include the fear of crime, corrections, and pedagogy.

ADEL A. HELAL is a coordinator at the Naif Arab Academy for Security Sciences in Riyadh, Saudi Arabia, which is an affiliated group of the United Nations. Additionally, he coordinates research with other institutes, universities, and research centers around the world.

CATHERINE A. JENKS is an adjunct lecturer at California State University, Los Angeles. She earned her Master's degree from Florida State University and is currently completing her dissertation on public opinion regarding civil liberties. Her background includes teaching and research in the areas of courts and juvenile justice, and she has planned an active research agenda.

DAVID A. JENKS is an assistant professor at California State University, Los Angeles. His earned his Ph.D. from Florida State University. He is currently working with the Los Angeles Sheriff's Department and Los Angeles

Police Department. His current research and teaching interests include policing, international and comparative criminal-justice systems, the Hispanic population in Los Angeles, and criminal-justice education.

MANGAI NATARAJAN is an associate professor at John Jay College of Criminal Justice, City University of New York. She has been conducting comparative research on women policing for more than a decade and has published widely on the topic. Her major research interests include, developing and testing theoretical models for cross-cultural research on issues relating to women and children including domestic violence, crime prevention, drug trafficking, drug abuse, and health issues. Her doctorate is in criminal justice and was earned at Rutgers University.

AMIT R. PATEL received his Master's degree from the Department of Criminal Justice at the University of North Carolina at Charlotte. His areas of expertise in research and publication include race relations, especially-vulnerable populations, and child murderers.

HAROLD PEPINSKY teaches criminal justice at Indiana University in Bloomington. His most recent book, *A Criminologist's Quest for Peace* (2001), is available for free use at <http://www.critcrim.org/critpapers/pepinsky-book.htm>.

COURTNEY C. PETERSEN earned her Master's degree in criminal justice from John Jay College of Criminal Justice, and currently is a Ph.D. candidate in criminal justice at the Graduate School and University Center at City University of New York. She is a graduate teaching fellow in the sociology department at John Jay College. Her research interests revolve around the areas of juvenile justice, restorative justice, substance abuse, and race and gender issues.

LEON E. PETTIWAY is a professor of criminal justice at Indiana University in Bloomington. His research has centered on crime in an urban context by integrating principles from urban and social geography. He is the author of *Honey, Honey, Miss Thang: Being Black, Gay, and on the Street* as well as *Workin' It: Women Living Through Drugs and Crime.* His chapter in this volume is a result of his growing interest in the construction of knowledge and the application of Eastern philosophy to issues of crime and justice.

BABETTE M. PROTZ is completing her Master's degree in special education at the University of North Carolina at Charlotte, with a concentration on students with behavioral and emotional disabilities. Her studies continue to explore these populations. She presently teaches emotionally troubled youth exclusively in the county's public school system.

PAULA K. RECTOR recently earned her Master's degree in criminal justice from Northern Arizona University, and is currently an instructor in the department there. Her work has focused on the intersections of race, class, and gender identities. Her most recent work concentrates on the criminal-justice response to pregnant drug-users and how identity intersections influence the outcome of pregnant drug-users in the system.

LINDA ROBYN is from the Anishinabe (Chippewa) nation. She received her Ph.D. from Western Michigan University, Kalamazoo in 1998. Her current research and interests include American Indians and the justice system, environmental justice, and state/corporate crime.

LEE E. ROSS is an associate professor of criminal justice at the University of Wisconsin–Parkside, where he serves as chair of the criminal-justice department. A graduate of Rutgers University, his research interests span a variety of areas, from his seminal work on religion and social-control theory to more recent publications on African-American interests in law enforcement. As editor of *African-American Criminologists, 1970–1996: An Annotated Bibliography*, his scholarship can be found in a variety of academic journals.

DOROTHY S. RUIZ earned her Ph.D. in sociology from Michigan State University. She is currently an associate professor in both the Departments of African-American and African Studies and Sociology at the University of North Carolina at Charlotte. Her research interests focus on the sociology of aging.

NANCY A. WONDERS is a sociologist and professor of criminal justice at Northern Arizona University. Her research focuses on inequality, law, and justice. Her published work has appeared in journals as well as in a variety of edited collections. Dr. Wonders has addressed such topics as the impact of globalization on women, global sex tourism, the contributions of feminist theory to criminology, difference and the administration of justice, the role of the state in law and policy formation, and violence against women as a form of political crime.

CAROLYN WEI ZHU is a senior research associate at the Robert Graduate School of Management and Urban Policy at the New School University in New York. She received her Ph.D. in economics from Duke University in the subfields of econometrics and health economics. She has served as a N.I.H. postdoctoral fellow at the Center for the Study of Aging and Human Development at Duke University. Her research interests include the health and consequences and costs of providing informal care to chronically ill elderly, patterns of home health-care utilization, and end-of-life issues.